PENGUIN BOOKS

THE BIG BOOK OF
American Irish Culture

Bob Callahan is a book columnist for the *San Francisco Examiner* and the executive director of the Turtle Island Foundation. His short-lived *Callahan's Irish Quarterly* is widely considered the finest Irish magazine ever published in the United States. He was assisted in this "labor of love" by a team of Bay Area writers, designers, historians and folklorists.

THE BIG BOOK OF

American

Irish

Culture

EDITED BY

Bob Callahan

Art Direction by
Dennis Gallagher

PENGUIN BOOKS

Editor: Bob Callahan

Associate Editors: Tom Clark and Dan O'Neill

Research Editors: Bill Blackbeard, Donna deCesare
and Rhona Klein

Copy and Line Editors: Karen Fisher and Judith Dunham

Grip: David Callahan

Art Direction: Dennis Gallagher

Design: Lucy Nielsen, Cathleen O'Brien, Madeleine Corson,
Stuart Cuttriss, Matthew Foster, Ruth Hagopian, with
special thanks to John Sullivan

Photo retouching: John Boring

Typesetting: Jan Tolman/ConText

PENGUIN BOOKS
Published by the Penguin Group
Viking Penguin Inc., 40 West 23rd Street,
New York, New York 10010, U.S.A.
Penguin Books Ltd, 27 Wrights Lane,
London W8 5TZ, England
Penguin Books Australia Ltd, Ringwood,
Victoria, Australia
Penguin Books Canada Ltd, 2801 John Street,
Markham, Ontario, Canada L3R 1B4
Penguin Books (N.Z.) Ltd, 182–190 Wairau Road,
Auckland 10, New Zealand

Penguin Books Ltd, Registered Offices:
Harmondsworth, Middlesex, England

First published in the United States of America by
Viking Penguin Inc. 1987
Published in Penguin Books 1989

10 9 8 7 6 5 4 3 2 1

LIBRARY OF CONGRESS CATALOGING IN PUBLICATION DATA
The big book of American Irish culture/edited by Bob Callahan; art
direction by Dennis Gallagher.
p.   cm.
Originally published: New York, N.Y.: Viking, 1987.
Bibliography: p.
ISBN 0 14 01.0326 0
1. Irish Americans.   I. Callahan, Bob.   II. Title: American Irish
culture.
E184.I6B54   1989
973'.049162—dc19   88–25132

Printed in the United States of America
Set in Galliard

Contents

"It's been a long jig, my boy, and I am only now beginning to see the pathos in it."

Dion Boucicault
(19th century playwright, on his deathbed)

"Cast your bread upon the waters, and a carp will beat you to it."

Hugh E. Keogh
(early 20th century Chicago sportswriter)

The Long Jig

BY
BOB CALLAHAN

Although I had been thinking about some of the characters in this book for years, the idea for an actual collection of American Irish cultural lore first occurred to me while reading William Kennedy's novel, *Legs*. In the opening chapter to that wonderful book, Kennedy's narrator remarks: "I had come to see Jack [Diamond] as not merely the dude of all gangsters, the most active brain in the New York underworld, but also as one of the truly new American Irishmen of his day. Horatio Alger out of Finn McCool and Jesse James, shaping the dream that you could shoot your way to glory and riches. I've said it again and again to my friends who question the ethics of this somewhat unorthodox memoir: 'If you like Carnegie and Custer, you'll love Diamond.' "

Kennedy's book was filled with a number of fascinating suggestions. "Horatio Alger out of Finn McCool and Jesse James"? "Truly new American Irishmen"? I didn't realize it at the time, but, my appetite sufficiently whetted, I was about to begin to collect together what just might be the very first book of American Irish folklore and folk legend ever assembled.

It is a very strange thing, I believe, that the Irish in this country have waited this long to begin to think in detail about something as basic as an indigenous folk culture. Afro-American Culture, sure. Jewish-American Folklore, of course. But the Irish? It has taken a very long time, I believe, for the Irish themselves to fully appreciate the wacko sense of humor, the rich feeling for new American street language, the remorseless social engineering and the amazing flights of fancy, horror, imagination and joy that have all gone into the adven-

ture of the people we have become right here in the New World.

Here, I think, the arithmetic of immigration has more or less held sway. The first few generations of Irish immigrants held onto their Irish identity very, very tightly. In fact, they often used it as a shield. Men who would not even talk to each other on the streets of Dublin soon became fast Saturday afternoon saloon companeros on Flatbush Avenue. The next few generations ran screaming however out of some of these very same immigrant ghettos—indeed, you can hear some of those screams in the pages of this volume. For the next couple of generations, being "ethnic" amounted—in some foolish, but oh so very American way—to the same thing as being second-class. The entire history of ethnic America, we now know, is also the history of a terrible psychic scar, a terribly painful, open psychic wound. It took the old "coffin ships" weeks—sometimes months—to reach the harbors of Boston and

New York. It has taken most American immigrants—and certainly the Irish—more than one hundred years to finally get over that terrible voyage wound.

As far as I can tell, we are by no means over it yet.

Chapter by chapter, *The Big Book of American Irish Culture* offers the reader a representative cross section of Irish achievement in certain unique areas of American popular culture. The Irish made their mark in these particular areas because, as far as it can be known, no one actually offered any of these new "peasants" the position of bank president on the day their boat finally reached the docks. I, for example, am quite sure most of my own ancestors would have taken the job had it actually been offered. It really can get weary being "just another romantic rebel able to tap-dance up a storm." If the truth be told, we have never actually needed a folksinger to sing us a song about that.

The Irish in the New World had before them only two fundamental cultural choices: they could hold on tightly to the traditional Celtic heritage they possessed —the marvelous fiddle music, the mad, uncanny pre-Devo hip-hop dances, the ancient, haunting, nearly unpronounceable language—and I do respect those who did—or they could get about the business of inventing huge chunks of what has now become known as the American Experience.

With all due respect to the fiddlers and the dancers, this book is for those who came up with something new. This book is for the inventors (who, of course, often can be great dancers and great fiddlers as well).

The Big Book of American Irish Culture is certainly not another social history. We already have a number of those books, and some of them are quite useful. From the point of view of this collection, you are free however to inhale all the American Irish social history you need simply by examining the records of the last dozen graduating classes at the Federal Bureau of Investigation; or, should you have the time, by conducting a poll of the last two or three hundred thousand duffers to have putted their way through the Westchester Country Club.

This book is not about social history.

This particular book is about culture—or "kulchur" as both Krazy Kat and Ezra Pound would have us spell it. In addition to their contributions to politics, labor, law and various other forms of hardball, the Irish in the New World helped to shape the development of American popular music, dance, cartoon and comic strip illustration, pulp fiction, vaudeville, television, musical comedy and the American movie. Since these arts are precisely the arts that the rest of the world considers indigenous to America, America's original contribution to world culture, this is—I was almost going to say—"no small potatoes."

In the end, it has been almost solely our sense of humor that has allowed us to travel all these miles.

In conclusion, I need certainly acknowledge and thank some of the key players whose play has gone into the building of this book. The first thanks is to the writers and illustrators past whose work has served as an inspiration to all of the contemporaries who contributed to this project. I need thank, in particular, Dennis Gallagher for his always elegant art direction; my associate editors and friends, Tom Clark and Dan O'Neill; my agent, Barbara Lowenstein, for drawing out of me a detailed proposal for this book in the first place; my editor, Gerald Howard, for his enthusiastic support and for reintroducing me to the writings of Jimmy Cannon; my research editors, Bill Blackbeard, Donna deCesare and Rhona Klein, for helping to uncover a couple of mountains of rich material; my copy and line editors, Karen Fisher and Judith Dunham, for taking this material through form after form, time and time again; and, finally, my spiritual accomplices and late-night "consultation" experts—William Kennedy, Robert Kelly, Ishmael Reed, Maureen Owen, Warren Hinckle and Pete Hamill—who, piece by piece, have introduced me to some of the more important aspects of this world in conversations that have taken place, often in rather strange environments, over a period of many, many years. I am, of course, ultimately responsible for those boneheaded errors which hopefully do not occur in this book with all that much frequency. This book is dedicated to John Maher. Try not to let the door hit you on the way in. ❧

The Hoofer's Club

▶

*With Uncle Sam
(Walter Huston) providing
the appropriate salute,
George M. Cohan (James
Cagney) hoofs his way
through* Yankee Doodle
Dandy, *a 1942 Warners
production.*

THE LEADER OF OUR CLAN

By Bob Callahan

It must have seemed particularly bizarre from the point of view of Kerry. The cousins had slipped through the Great Famine Door, and those who actually made the Atlantic crossing seemed to have been swallowed whole by the American Civil War. Thereafter, and for a long while, there was only silence. Suddenly word broke through those legendary northern mists that, yes, Paddy was alive and well on something called the American vaudeville stage. Families by the name of Keohane, and Rooney, and Foy seemed to be dancing into a brand-new possibility and a brand-new century. Yes, Paddy was alive and well. In a brand-new world, he had once again started kicking.

This is a song about George M. Cohan. Co-HAN, not co-EN. And yet, when I was growing up in a factory town in Connecticut, I always thought he must have been this older Jewish guy. Jimmy Cagney called him "the greatest song and dance man of all time." "George M. Cohan," Cagney said, "is the real leader of our clan." This is also a song about the history we have let slip through our hands.

Cohan was born in Providence, Rhode Island, on July 3, 1878. Or perhaps his baptismal certificate was wrong, and he was born on July 4, 1878—just as he always claimed. He was most certainly the grandson of Michael Keohane and Jane Scott of County Cork who came out of Famine Ireland back in 1848.

Cohan's father, Jerry Cohan, was widely known as one of the best traditional Irish dancers in all of New England. According to the Cohan biographer, John McCabe, Jerry Cohan's specialty was working New World variations on standard Irish jigs and reels. It appears to have been a great age for traditional Irish dancers. On Coney Island, a man by the name of Monahan had earned something like an international reputation for dancing a "very expressive" Irish jig, while balancing a full glass of beer on his head.

George M. Cohan grew up on the Irish-American musical stage. As a member of the "Four Cohans," he traveled almost from birth with his father, mother and sister "Josie" in something called a "Hibernicon," an Irish-American early vaudeville show complete with dances, musical instrumentation and a yard full of bad ethnic jokes. By the time he was sixteen George could moo with the best of the old moo cows, and still bring Bridget home before midnight fell on Tara Hall.

The "Four Cohans" hit Broadway in 1901. Within the year, George had written, composed the lyrics and the songs for, directed, produced and played the lead in his very first Broadway play. Although his family would stay on and play supporting roles in future productions, by 1901 George M. pretty much ran his own show.

Indeed, by 1904—although critics hated to admit it—George pretty much owned Broadway. In 1904 he opened *Little Johnny Jones* —the show that introduced

12

two brand new Cohan tunes, "Give My Regards to Broadway" and "Yankee Doodle Boy." In 1906, he opened *George Washington, Jr.*—the show that gave us "You're a Grand Old Flag" (a song that George had originally wanted to title "You're a Grand Old Rag"). And, in 1908, Cohan opened *Fifty Miles From Boston*—the show that gave us "Harrigan." George, as they say, had become a smash.

Quite frankly, the critics had no idea what to make of a typical Cohan production. "The show goes by so fast," one newspaper commented," that it almost bewilders, leaving the impression of a great machine shooting out characters, chorus, songs, and dances with rapid fire quickness and precision."

Well, the average Cohan production was a "great shooting machine." Cohan may have been the only playwright in all of American history whose mind invariably thought "Roman candle" when the critics began to speak of questions of form.

In point of fact, Cohan never began any of his plays with a written book. An idea would get stuck in the back of his head, and George would call together his family and cast, and the entire ensemble would then begin to roll out the next production.

As the crowds for these new plays grew and grew, the critics increased their attacks. The *New York Times* called him a "vulgar, cheap, blatant, ill-mannered, flashily-dressed, insolent Smart Aleck" — which, no doubt, he also was. He was also a jingoist, and a union-buster to boot. Most importantly, however, George M. Cohan had become nothing more or less than the very spirit of turn-of-the-century America itself, with the throttle pushed all the way to the floor.

George's critics were still thinking in terms of the leisurely, highbrow European comic-opera tradition of the nineteenth century. For better, and for worse, Cohan was already living in the century of the motor car.

It would take some of these critics years before they finally caught up with him. The occasion came with the 1923 production of *The Song and Dance Man* —by far, Cohan's most respected play. *The Song and Dance Man* tells the story of "Hap" Farrell, a second-rate variety actor—an early Willie Loman figure—who lives with the illusion that he is perhaps the best actor at his craft in the world. As William Shannon has written, Cohan—who probably was the best song and dance man America ever produced—made Hap "the embodiment of the tradition of the Irish actor as comic entertainer up until that time."

And, by that time, what a long and strange tradition it had already become.

When Cohan first put on his dancing shoes, audiences were still allowed to sit on the stage with the entertainers, eat brown-bag lunches and chat among themselves during the more boring numbers. Although the age of the great "Black Irish" minstrels had already passed, in those days the Irish-American theater still meant the broad-stroke ethnic portraits of a Harrigan and Hart, and the interesting Irish melodramas of a Dion Boucicault. When George finally got off this train, the tradition had been enlarged to include the new sophisticated comedies of a Preston Sturges, the elegant warmth and mannerisms of a Spencer Tracy and the arrival from Pittsburgh of a kid named Kelly—a new song and dance man who had gotten a break in a film based on a John O'Hara short story, "Pal Joey."

And, of course, the tradition had also come to mean the dark, Freudian Catholicisms of Mr. Eugene O'Neill.

O'Neill and Cohan worked together just once. O'Neill hired Cohan to play the role of Nat Miller in the play, *Ah! Wilderness*. "Cohan was just perfection in that play," J.D. Salinger would later say.

A remarkable Edward Steichen photograph survives from that collaboration. The portrait is all spook lighting and shadows. Cohan is sitting in the foreground, on a stool, his hands raised, outstretched as if he were backing someone away. He is, in fact, gliding. It is almost as if Cohan had also finally mastered the art of how to dance, sitting down.

In direct counterdistinction, O'Neill is standing behind George, dressed in a very smart, very fashionable formal suit. Something dangerously approaching a demonic smile is threatening to spread across the rest of O'Neill's very young, mustached and darkly handsome face.

There is also something odd about the relative size of the two men in this photograph. Cohan is slightly larger than life whereas O'Neill is portrayed in normal proportion. The photographer has perhaps superimposed the image of the one man over that of the other.

Click. The photograph has been taken.

The yin and yang of an entire people are in this portrait. It is an altogether haunting piece of work.

Ah! Wilderness would prove to be Cohan's last hurrah. In 1940 Jack Warner approached him about making a movie out of his life. Yes, Cohan would allow such a movie, if the script was right. No, he was far too old to star in it himself. How about this younger guy, Cagney, some of his people asked?

And so Jimmy Cagney became George M. Cohan in more ways than one. Cagney even learned how to dance up the side of certain walls—just the way George used to dance—in his Academy Award-winning role in the 1942 production of *Yankee Doodle Dandy*.

Cohan would be dead from cancer within ten months of the studio's first sending of the final cut of *Yankee Doodle Dandy* for Cohan's private screening. His own son, George, sat with him as he watched the film without comment. When the final credits began to roll, young George asked, "Well, how did you like it, Dad?"

"That Cagney," Cohan snapped back with real wonder in his voice. "What an act to have to follow!"

When he died ten months later, a Solemn Requiem Mass was held for Cohan at St. Patrick's Cathedral. A number of people in the city of New York still remember the moment during the final funeral procession when the Cardinal turned the other way, and the organist struck up the chorus to "Over There." The ancient sound that had always been contained within that march filled the entire church. Cohan was gone, but yet, of course, he wasn't. The great George M. possessed your basic, aboriginal Irish, truly firecracker heart. He will certainly remain the best thing the Irish ever gave America—just for the Fourth of July. 🐾

IN THE TRADITION

By Jack Donahue

Directly ancestral to American tap, the Irish jig is an ancient step dance in which the dancer's chief occupation is with intricate leg movement and footwork. The tapping is done with both toes and heels, while the dancer holds his or her arms close to the sides, always keeping the upper half of the body erect and nearly motionless. The dancing is incredibly fast and involved, with a skillful dancer able to execute as many as fifteen separate taps per second. In Ireland long ago, dance master Jerry Ames will claim, the human body was transformed into a musical instrument, creating a rhythmic kind of "shoe music" which became an essential element in the historical evolution of American popular dance.

▼

George Primrose and William H. West, costars of the 1890's Primrose and West Minstrel troupe.

In Boston, in my youth, boys simply did not worry about what they were going to do when they grew up: you were going to be either a dancer or a fighter. A snappy left jab under my heart made my decision easy. I have been hoofing every since. People today complain about the sound of construction in the streets of New York, but New York has all the peace and quiet of a church compared to a Boston street corner of my youth—at least when all the young tap dancers leaped into action.

The old Howard Athenaeum used to have a slogan: "Always something going on from one until eleven." We could get a seat in the gallery for a dime, and if the dime wasn't forthcoming, we could use trading stamps —thirty being good for one admission. If the good housewife missed these little tributes to her buying powers, the chances are she was unknowingly helping a son or even husband to pass a few pleasant hours in congenial company. Intimacy was the keynote of the gallery, benches taking the place of the more formal seats that graced the balcony and orchestra. On the main floor they charged a quarter. Here the tired businessman came to get his second wind at close range, but we who had reached the heights, by climbing three flights of stairs, cared little for the dancing women or the weak warbling of the singers; we tolerated the comedians and saved all of our love for the hoofers, if they were good. And they had to be good; we wouldn't be fooled. A stolen routine or a missed tap was quickly detected, and the offender would find that species of the entire bird kingdom were perched in the rafters. Though boasting of their entertainment as family burlesque, as constant a visitor as myself can only recall seeing two women in the audience. Both wore heavy black veils and left immediately after Princess Secude's specialty. They used to bill her as the girl "who sings with her hips." Today, with the product certainly not improved any, more women than men are in attendance. Perhaps they find it an ideal place to slip off and smoke a cigar and have a few good laughs. After a real hot number they would lower the drop and a specialty man or team would come out and work in one. We used to call them cool-offs. Unless he or she was a dancer, they were very apt to find the audience hard to reach. Only the very big stars—the Howard played one big name every night—could hold such a difficult spot, for, barring myself and a few other dance-lovers, I'm afraid that most of the congregation had come to worship at the shrine of Venus. But whatever you came for, you certainly got a run for your money. For the lads who aspired to the rings, there were such attractions as John L. Sullivan, Jim Corbett, Bob Fitzsimons, while young Matty Baldwin and Georgie Byers, sitting on the bench with me, up on the shelf, would watch and dream their youthful dreams of fistic glory. Incidentally, both of these boys were to have their share of fame before they hung up their gloves.

But for me, the big moment would not arrive till George Primrose would step out on the stage, the orchestra would strike up "Swanee River" and the old master would go into one of those beautiful soft-shoe routines. He belonged to the old school of tap dancers. He covered the whole stage with his graceful stepping, done to you four-time. But things were beginning to speed up. The four-four dance was being replaced by the two-four buck dancer. The buck dancers got in more taps and they didn't use so much stage. In fact, one Paddy Shea worked in the barrooms around Boston, doing a fast buck dance with a glass of beer on his head, and without spilling a drop.

Milt Wood was one of my early favorites; a man weighing close to two hundred pounds. He was the first winner of the Richard K. Fox Trophy, in a contest held at Tammany Hall, New York. He did a dance around the rungs and on top of a kitchen chair. I broke three chairs at home before I finally gave the trick up as impractical.

The first man to do a buck dance up and down a flight of stairs was Al Leach, who worked with the Three Rosebuds; others who used the stairs were Eddie Mack, of Mack, Goldie and Burns, and Dan Burke, a clog dancer. The difference between buck and clog dancing lies in the greater use of the heels in the latter; hence the old Irish expression: "He's a handy man with his heels."

The eccentric-dancing craze was started by Doc Quigley; the type of dancing he did is known today as legomania dancing. Tom Smith was doing one of the best comedy single acts in vaudeville until the aviation bug hit him a couple years ago. His daughter, Eleanor, at seventeen has held the world's endurance-flight records for women flyers. George M. Cohan was an eccentric dancer, featuring semi-Russian or floor steps. His best-known trick was to run up to the proscenium, throw one foot against it and jump over it with the other foot while still in the air. His work was characterized by the snapping back of the head and arms in cakewalk fashion.

Montgomery and Stone are said to be the originators of stop-time dancing. One step generally taking eight

bars of music, they would step after the first note of the seventh bar and dance without music until the last two notes of the eighth bar. McIntyre and Heath began their careers as hoofers, and they will offer proof that they were the first to do buck-and-wing dancing. A wing is done by taking the weight off one foot and describing an arc with it in the air while the foot on the floor continues to tap. When the wings are done with both feet, one after the other, the effect is given of a bird in flight; hence the name. Ryan and White were two boy buck-and-wing specialists. George White of that team is still a hoofer at heart, though his scandals take up a lot of his time these days.

Then there were the novelty dancers: Ames and Corbett, who danced on kettledrums; the Innes Brothers, who did their famous West Point drill dance; Moon and Morris, the back-to-back dancers; Louis Stone, the upside-down dancer; and—my favorite of all—the Irish Purcell Brothers, who danced chained to each other, dressed up in the most fashionable, contemporary prison garb.

It was a great tradition; and an education that would stay with me for the rest of my professional life.

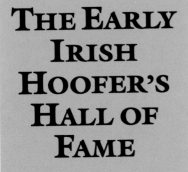

THE EARLY IRISH HOOFER'S HALL OF FAME

John Durang of Philadelphia is credited with being the earliest known Irish-American dance master (1789) to perform the Lancashire clog, along with assorted Irish jigs, reels and hornpipes, in a decidedly "Negro" manner.

Marrying an old Scots-Irish fiddle tune to an Afro-American shuffle dance, **Thomas Dartmouth "Daddy" Rice** is credited with "inventing" the first truly popular minstrel dance, the "Jump Jim Crow."

Daniel Decatur Emmett is credited with writing "The Blue Tail Fly (Jim Crack Corn)," based in part on an old Irish hornpipe and which became a staple in many early minstrel routines.

Wedding a number of different Afro-American dance steps to the music of various old Irish jigs and reels, banjo player **Billy Whitlock** is credited with establishing a body of dance routines for the original Christy Minstrels.

Known primarily for his waltz clog, **Pat Rooney, Sr.** is credited with the popularity of at least two of the most famous turn-of-the-century tap steps. In "Off to Buffalo," Rooney's hands would pump up and down, and one foot would kick high as he perfected the classic exit dance step. In "Falling Off a Log," Rooney spun one foot in front of the other to create a controlled, rolling appearance, hence the step, "Falling Off a Log."

Eddie Horan is said to be the first hoofer to dance the walking waltz clog with a cane, a routine that soon became mandatory in song and dance acts everywhere.

Kitty O'Neill, the first great Irish-American woman hoofer, is credited with introducing a noisy, hard-soled soft shoe to create her own, inimitable sand dance.

It is **Barney Fagan**, the Irish clog dancer—not Bill Robinson—who is credited with the first toe-to-heel, syncopated version of the Irish jig.

Harry Kelly and **John T. Kennedy** are credited with the introduction of the very first, truly fast tap steps (an innovation soon perfected by the lightning-fast Condos Brothers).

Although George M. Cohan is credited with "The Lively Bootblack," a fast-tempo parody of the old buck-and-wing, Cohan's "Russian Step" —the routine in which he ran up the side of one stage wall, then kicked out—was actually invented by **Harry Pilsner**, who may, or may not, have been Russian, although, as Groucho Marx would probably say, wiggling his cigar and flashing his eyebrows, "he probably was in a hurry."

—Tapper Malloy

SHOWGIRL

Joseph Patrick McEvoy had an eye and an ear for the razzmatazz and sisboombah of the Jazz Era; during the 1920s—and a good part of the letdown decade that followed—McEvoy produced national hits in many fields, writing such letter-and-postcard novels as *Show Girl*, illustrated newspaper serials like "The Potters," Broadway shows such as the Ziegfeld production of *The Comic Supplement* (which he cowrote with W. C. Fields), and a comic strip that spanned four decades, called "Dixie Dugan."

The comic strip was a heartbreaker. Based on McEvoy's best-selling three-novel series of the 1920s (*Show Girl, Show Girl in Society*, and *Show Girl in Hollywood*), the strip that was later to be known as "Dixie Dugan" began as—what else—"Show Girl," and was launched nationally on the brink of the Wall Street Crash in October 1929. Drawn by the skillful John H Steibel, who had illustrated "The Potters" as a published play and serial, the "Show Girl" comic strip began as a lively and exhilarating portrayal of the raucus, gin-soaked, speakeasy world of the Broadway hoofing life during the Roaring Twenties, easily the best thing of its kind in the comics (and a real eyebrow-raiser in the sticks). But the public, swiftly disillusioned by the bursting of the economic bubble that had given dash and flash to this now expiring decade, wanted no more of the hip-flask naughtiness it had relished only short months before, and McEvoy was forced to make prompt and drastic alterations in his strip and its heroine, dropping the "Show Girl" title and replacing it with plain "Dixie Dugan." Poor Dixie now became a diligent office girl, living at home (properly) with Ma and Pa, and fending off nice hometown boys on dates, rather than the stage-door wildmen whom she had had to wrestle with before.

The laundered "Dixie Dugan" became a national comic page institution through the 1950s—well-drawn but always dull and predictable. McEvoy's direct connection with the strip's authorship was highly questionable after the early 1930s.

—*Bill Blackbeard*

THE SONG AND DANCE MAN

By Clive Hirschhorn

The consummate song and dance man, Gene Kelly received his first big break when he was chosen by John O'Hara, himself, to play the lead in the Broadway musical version of Pal Joey, *a play based on a series of short stories O'Hara wrote concerning the adventures of an amoral, small-time, old-fashioned Irish-American song and dance man. In later years, Kelly paired his own classical training with the comic dance style of vaudeville veteran Donald O'Connor to realize a collaborative summary of Irish-American dance history up to that time, suggestive of the new world just then opening to all hoofers with the arrival of the magic of film.*

Early in 1940, George Abbott and Rodgers and Hart were planning to stage a musical adaptation of John O'Hara's *New Yorker* short stories, "Pal Joey." Bob Alton, fresh from his stint on *Panama Hattie,* was engaged as dance director, O'Hara himself agreed to do the book, and Vivienne Segal was chosen to play Vera Simpson, the society lady who befriends Joey Evans, the owner of a sleazy nightclub.

The question around Broadway was—who was going to play Joey?

One morning, Johnny Darrow, who was in California, received a phone call from Richard Rodgers who wanted to know "whether that guy Kelly," whom he had seen in *The Time of Your Life,* could sing as well as dance. Sure, Darrow said, and asked Rodgers what he had in mind. "Something," said Rodgers and volunteered no more information. "Give me a ring in three weeks' time and we'll talk about it."

Immediately Darrow called Gene and told him about his conversation with Rodgers. Obviously, Darrow said, Rodgers had Gene in mind for *Pal Joey,* and suggested

▲

Gene Kelly touches the sky in the 1966 CBS television documentary "Gene Kelly in New York, New York."

◀

Gene Kelly and friend from the 1933 M.G.M. production of *Thousands Cheer.*

that he was ready. Gene cleared his throat and began with one of Rodgers' own compositions—a ballad called "I Didn't Know What Time It Was."

"I thought," said Gene, "that if I sang one of his own songs, it would impress him, little knowing that there's an unwritten law that says never sing a song back to a composer at an audition, unless of course he specifically asks you to do so. But there I was, singing one of Rodgers' most beautiful—and difficult—numbers, and not singing it very well because I couldn't sing then—and I still can't. Well he didn't bat an eyelid. Though years later, when I was directing *Flower Drum Song* on Broadway, if any of the kids came to an audition and sang one of his numbers, he'd blandly tell them that flattery would get them no place at all. On this occasion, though, he said nothing, and when the song came to an end, there was no reaction at all. I was convinced I'd blown it. All he did was ask me to sing something else—a bit faster. So I went straight into a lively ditty I used to do in the 'cloops' called 'It's the Irish In Me,' which had a lot of pep and dash to it, and which I knew how to put across.

"After I was through, O'Hara, who hadn't said a word throughout the audition, called out from the back of the theatre: 'That's it. Take him.'"

The show opened at the Ethel Barrymore Theatre in New York on Christmas Eve, 1940. It wasn't until December 26, however, that the reviews finally appeared. Gene and the cast were at Lorenz Hart's apartment when, just after midnight, they received Burns Mantle's notice in the *New York Daily News*. It was an enthusiastic review which praised everything and everyone, not least of all Gene, of whom Mantle generously wrote: "Mr. Kelly is able to give the part personal attractions that justify the O'Hara picture. He is likeable as an individual and gifted as a dancer." "Technically his range," Mr. Mantle went on, "is wide without including any impulse toward the eccentric, which makes for an agreeable artistic balance. It was a fortunate day for him, and for us I think, when Mr. O'Hara and Mr. Abbott picked him out of the group that helped to make *The Time of Your Life* a prize-winning play."

"*Pal Joey*," he concluded, "adds definitely to the cur-

to Gene that he find himself a singing coach as soon as possible, and learn as much as he could about how to project a song.

Three weeks later, Darrow returned to New York and called Rodgers, who told him he'd like to hear Gene sing. They arranged to meet the following Saturday morning at the Century Theatre at ten o'clock.

The atmosphere at the Century Theatre was polite but formal. Gene was introduced to the creative team, all of whom, except for Alton of course, were strangers to him. Then he and his singing teacher—a middle-aged woman whom he had asked to play the piano for him that morning—positioned themselves on stage. Abbott took a seat halfway down the stalls and signaled rent competition in musical entertainment, and this is cheering."

Next came Richard Watts Junior's rave review in the *Herald Tribune*. "The quality that has made Mr. O'Hara's writing so robust, salty and realistic has been captured with fine gusto, and combined with one of Richard Rodgers' most winning scores, some of Lorenz Hart's finest lyrics, the brilliant staging of dances that Robert Alton always provides, an utterly satisfying cast and George Abbott's most expert manipulation; the result is a delight. Put *Pal Joey* down as an outstanding triumph of a suddenly awakened theatrical season."

And of Gene he said: "It was a happy stroke of casting that placed Mr. Kelly in the title-role. This young man is genuinely life-saving to *Pal Joey* for, if the chief part were not properly cast, the new musical show might have been too merciless for comfort. Mr. Kelly does nothing obvious about softening his characterization, but he does manage to combine a certain amount of straightforward personal charm with the realism of his portrait, so that Joey actually achieves the feat of being at once a heel and a hero. *Pal Joey* is a hard-boiled delight." ❧

◀ **Donald O'Connor's greatest struggle from the 1947 Universal production of *Something in the Wind*.**

THE ORIGIN OF THE O'CONNOR

The greatest Irish comic dancer of the past four decades—and a true descendant of Ned Harrigan, George M. Cohan and James Barton—Donald O'Connor was born in Chicago on August 28, 1925. In his life in film, O'Connor has enjoyed a rather varied career. He was first known as a childhood star in such late 1930's teenage comedies as *Sing You Sinners* and *Patrick the Great*; he was next featured in a series of brilliant dance films with Gene Kelly, including the incomparable *Singing in the Rain*; he then entered his goats and chickens phase with the *Francis, the Talking Mule* movie series. In more recent years, he has had the honor of playing the role of Buster Keaton in *The Buster Keaton Story*.

Like Keaton, Donald O'Connor remains first and foremost a child of the American vaudeville stage. As James Robert Parish and Leonard Carl have written, "Donald O'Connor's father—John Edward 'Chuck' O'Connor of County Cork—was an agile acrobat featured with Ringling Brothers-Barnum and Bailey Circus as a 'leaper'—a performer who would run up a ramp and then hurl himself over four large elephants.

'Chuck' O'Connor also did a trampoline turn, some trapeze flying, and moonlighted as a boxer with the sideshows to earn extra money for his growing family. While working a show in Washington, Pennsylvania, the elder O'Connor met a fourteen-year-old circus bareback rider and dancer, Effie Irene Crane. They married three days later, formed their own vaudeville act and over the years became the parents of seven children."

In one form or another, the O'Connor family act survived the great Depression. In 1937, with vaudeville more or less in a state of collapse, the O'Connors were playing on the West Coast when the opportunity arose for Donald, and his brothers Jack and Billy, to play bit parts in a long forgotten Warner musical, *Melody for Two*. Donald O'Connor soon proved to be a natural in this medium as well. The next year he was featured in four new Paramount musicals. His national film and stage career—which continues to this day—was well underway.

—Bob Callahan

THE GREAT JAMES BARTON

By Marshall and Jean Stearns

James Barton and George Primrose provided the link between the old minstrel stage and the new age of "hoofers on film" opened, most masterfully, by the great achievements of Gene Kelly and Donald O'Connor. Barton was perhaps the greatest of all Irish-American hoofers—and a figure certainly worthy of full biographical study. Primrose was in fact one of the last of the old "cork-faced" strutters and the inventor of the elegant soft-shoe dance style. The achievements of these two men reflect the final integration of elements from both Afro-American and Irish-American dance traditions. When such integration is achieved, the hyphen can be allowed to dangle, and the art that results can be seen as truly "American" in both spirit and form.

With his father a performer in the Primrose and West Minstrel show, and his mother a ballet dancer, James Barton got off to a very fast start. He was born in Gloucester, New Jersey, in 1890. "My Uncle John taught me my first step when I was two years old," Barton has said. "I was part of the family act by the time I was four. I starred in *The Boy Comedian* at the age of seven."

Because of his rare ability to dance any step he saw and make it his own, Barton developed rapidly without any attempt to copy anyone. Yet he does remember what a deep impression both Bert Williams and George Walker once made upon him. He appeared on the same bill with both of these master dancers at the old Howard Theatre in Boston when he was just eight years old. "Walker did a great strut," Barton recalls, "and Bert Williams brought down the house with a terrific grind—a kind of shuffle which combined rubber legs with rotating hips."

From 1898 to 1902 Barton traveled in a "knockabout" vaudeville act. From 1907 to 1915 he took just about any work he could get—with side excursions into ice-skating, bicycle racing and semiprofessional baseball. From 1915 to 1919 Barton worked the Columbia burlesque chain as a dancing comedian in a show called *Twentieth Century Maids*. "That was before the strippers came in, and killed burlesque," Barton has recently said.

By the time he was thirty, Barton had played the Morris, Fox, Lubin, Sun, Orpheum, Loew's, Pantages, Columbia and Keith circuits in everything from "Uncle Tom" shows—he was cast in all the roles except Little Eva—to repertory theater.

Although burlesque and vaudeville reached a large, nationwide audience at the time, the critics tended to ignore these shows. Barton received little attention until he arrived on Broadway. At that, his discovery was largely an accident. During an Equity strike, while Barton was rehearsing a small part in *The Passing Show of 1919*, a benefit was staged at the Lexington Opera House with Ed Wynn and Ethel Barrymore

James Barton, master hoofer and major character actor.

23

final beauty, and so 'genius' will have to be our word.

"Barton manages to be sublime and grotesque at the same time. We are even tempted to say that he promotes good manners, good taste, and good morals. At any rate he proves that the body can be made absolutely subservient to the human will. The job is anatomically thorough. Once Barton swings into the music no part of him draws a bye. Nor is any emotion neglected. Broad strokes and infinitely subtle ones are combined in this complete interpretation of the cosmos, step by step."

"We felt the curse of Adam slipping from our shoulders," Broun concluded, "as we watched James Barton move."

After his triumph in *Dew Drop Inn,* James Barton continued to be sought after by Broadway producers. Unfortunately for dance, his broadly explicit and satirical pantomime ultimately obscured the perfection of his footwork. Producers concluded that Barton should be an actor—not a dancer—and he would be in and out of Broadway shows—as well as a select list of Hollywood movies—for the rest of his career.

From 1934 to 1939 Barton starred in *Tobacco Road* on Broadway. Dan Healy is convinced that Barton could have become a first-rate Shakespearean actor. Like Charlie Chaplin—to whom he was compared by critic Alexander Woollcott—Barton was also a master of pantomime. Indeed, when Chaplin himself attended a Barton performance at the Palace, "The Little Tramp" was on his feet after the show, applauding vigorously and stamping his cane. Barton was delighted. "Chaplin," Barton would later say, "was one of the few performers I have ever impersonated."

James Barton died in 1962 at the age of seventy-one. His obituary in *Variety* made one critical point. Identifying Barton simply with *Tobacco Road,* the obituary stated, was a little like trying to make Bill Robinson famous for the simple fact that he could run backwards. Barton was—first and foremost—a dancer.

The *Variety* obituary went on to note that Barton had also played the leading role of Hickey in O'Neill's *The Iceman Cometh.* In 1961, he had also made a brief appearance in a barroom scene with Marilyn Monroe and Clark Gable in *The Misfits.*

In his day James Barton was actually preferred by the critics to Jolson, Cantor, Bojangles, Astaire and Bolger—or, as *Variety* said, "to whoever anybody was inclined to mention as a master." A few movie shorts such as *After Seben* and *The Whole Show* survive, and just dimly document Barton's superb dancing style.

James Barton was an original who, aided by an Irish background of jigs and reels, absorbed the rhythms and movements of Negro dancers early in his career, and ultimately added his own earthy, uninhibited genius for satirical pantomime.

(performing a bit from *Camille*). Barton was backstage when Ed Wynn was mildly injured. As Alexander Woollcott would later write: "It was then announced that Ed Wynn would be unable to appear. A Mr. Barton had kindly volunteered to take his place. No one then knew Mr. Barton. There were silent groans throughout the house from a number of Ed Wynn's fans. And then Mr. Barton ambled on stage, and danced a few steps, and owned that audience to a man."

The pattern of Barton's subsequent popularity is clear. Whenever he was allowed to dance, and improvise his own steps, the impact was tremendous, the recognition immediate. Again and again, alone and unassisted, he literally stopped any show in which he appeared. Barton reached the peak of his early critical acclaim in a 1913 musical, *Dew Drop Inn.* Taking over the role which had been written for Bert Williams—who had died the month before the show reached Broadway—and donning blackface, Barton became a smash hit.

Reviewing the musical for the *New York World* on May 17, 1923, Heywood Broun forever cast Barton's legend into stone.

"James Barton does a number of things well, and one thing better than anyone else in musical comedy," Broun began. "When Barton starts to dance even a cautious reviewer should begin to consider using the word genius. In his medium he creates a superb and

THE MASTER OF THE OLD SOFT SHOE

George Primrose is generally credited with the development of the soft-shoe dancing style. Because his career extended past the turn of the century, Primrose was seen and admired by many young dancers. Primrose is supposed to have been Bill Robinson's idol. "Every motion of George Primrose," soft-shoe master Willie Covan has said, "created a beautiful picture."

An Irishman whose real name was Delaney, George Primrose was born in Canada in 1852. At the age of fifteen, he joined the minstrels. Primrose toured in a number of shows, eventually forming a partnership with William H. West which lasted almost thirty years.

After the "Primrose and West Minstrels" broke up, Primrose joined Lew Dockstader for a few years. Primrose died in San Diego in 1919.

"Prim was the greatest stylist of them all—not necessarily the greatest technician—with the finest Soft Shoe I ever saw in my life. When he died, he took it with him," dance-master Harland Dixon has commented. Dixon joined the "Primrose Minstrels" in 1906, and at once adopted Primrose as his lifetime model. "Primrose was of medium height, weighed a little over a hundred and ten, and could wear clothes like Fred Astaire," Dixon recalls. "He smoked cigars, but he didn't drink. I never heard him raise his voice, or swear. I never saw him practice a step, and I never saw him perspire—even during the minstrel street parades on the hottest summer day. He wore a high, stiff collar, and looked up over the audience as he danced. He had a flat stomach, dancer's legs, and incredibly mobile hips and shoulders. Just the way he walked was poetry."
—*Marshall and Jean Stearns*

Easy Street

▶

*Along with a few
charming-looking friends,
Diamond Jim Brady
(Edward Sutherland) waits
for a table for dinner in the
1935 Universal production of*
Diamond Jim, *written
by Preston Sturges.*

HELLO, SUCKER

By Paul Sann

T exas Guinan never lost patience with the "revenooer" posses that rode her down for selling "likker" on the Glittery Gulch called Broadway. Quite the contrary, she tried to make them feel at home; sometimes she had the band strike up "The Prisoner's Song" when the federal men arrived to haul her before the bar of justice. She kept the customers in high spirits too. Once she came back to her nightclub from court and sang this ditty:

Judge Thomas said: "Tex, do you sell booze?"
I said, "Please don't be silly.
I swear to you my cellar's filled
With chocolate and vanilly."

Texas also insisted that she didn't have to sell the hard stuff because she got as much for sparkling water as people paid for Scotch before Prohibition. She said the customers brought their own whiskey on their hips, and what could she do except provide setups. Of course, you could buy a booster in her joints if you knew the headwaiter, or if you looked as if you knew him, or if you knew somebody who was pretty sure he knew him, or maybe if you were just thirsty and didn't have the seedy look of a Dry agent.

Miss Guinan, a garish blonde with a brassy voice that could penetrate even the din of her own clubs, had a name for the customer—"Hello, Sucker" —and a slogan to go with it. "Never give a sucker an even break," she used to say. Hayseed or Wall Street broker, she flattered them all with the same high prices: $25 for a fifth of Scotch or $2 for a pitcher of water if you brought your own, $25 for champagne, $20 for rye. The "couvert" charge—an invention of the Lawless Decade—might run anywhere from $5 to $25 per head, depending on what that traffic would bear at a given time. Everybody paid with a smile. Well, nearly everybody; there were bouncers on hand to deal with the penny-pinchers.

Mary Louise Cecilia Guinan came off a ranch in Waco, Texas. Her parents hoped for a musical career for her but she went off and rode bronco in a circus instead. Then she drifted into vaudeville and found her way to Hollywood, where there was a demand for girls

The one profession the Irish became most closely associated with during their first decades in this country was the gentle art of saloon keeping. Usually relegated to the lower part of town, or the other side of the tracks, the Irish became bar owners, then nightclub proprietors, and finally the dollar behind so many of our modern resort hotels, gambling casinos and various professional sports franchises.
In those early years, America enjoyed the Irish as entertainers, and nobody ever put on a better show than Mary Louise Cecilia "Tex" Guinan, the New World's first, authentic, two-gun, western female movie star and the coproprietor—with her bootlegger friend, Larry Fey—of the famous El Fey Club in New York City. Mae West's entire act, it sometimes seems, was lifted more or less intact from the real-life antics of this Irish cowgirl from Waco, Texas.

▶

"Tex" Guinan at her El Fey Club in Manhattan, 1927.

who could handle a horse and lariat. For a while she did well enough in Westerns to be called "the female Bill Hart," and she certainly was one of the more authentic lady gunslingers on the celluloid prairie. In those days she had a mop of black hair menacing enough to scare off the villain even without a six-shooter. But the movies were then mute, and Miss Guinan definitely wanted to be heard.

Texas Guinan came east for a Broadway musical early in the 1920s, discovered the nightclubs and got herself hired as mistress of ceremonies at the Beaux Arts. There her wisecracks and lung power caught the attention of Larry Fey, sometime entrepreneur, sometime racketeer, and he set her up at the El Fey Club. That was the beginning of a profitable partnership.

Miss Guinan went from El Fey to the Rendezvous, the 300 Club, the Argonaut, the Century, the Salon Royal, the Club Intime and any number of Texas Guinan Clubs, depending on how often the Prohibition people shut her down. Opening new joints after raids, Tex wore a necklace strung with gold padlocks just to show the federals there were no hard feelings. One of her diamond bracelets featured a little gold police whistle.

The Guinan traps—and seventy or eighty other Manhattan spots of the time—were the forerunners of the sardine-packed nightclubs that came in with Repeal. Her floors were so jammed that the dancing girls had to exhibit their high-kicks and other charms right in the customers' faces. The "big butter-and-egg men," to quote a phrase from Tad Dorgan, didn't seem to mind.

Miss Guinan's celebrated closing line for the chorus, "Give the little girls a big hand," was only topped once. A gentleman in the audience arose and said, "Give the little girl a great big handcuff." It was another pinch, but the hostess laughed with the crowd: she owed her fame to her brushes with the Eighteenth Amendment. She would have been known to nothing more than a select group of free-spenders in the Big Town except for the fact that someone was always trying to put her in the pokey.

The frolicsome hostess didn't complain. She made a pretty good living out of her troubles—up to $4,000 a week. Where it went, no one ever knew. When the thrice-married Prohibition queen died in 1933, at forty-nine, there was $28,173 in her estate. ❧

THE QUEEN OF THE QUIP

Known as the "Queen of Nightclubs," Texas Guinan had the rare gift of epigram. Never disconcerted by any mishap or trouble, this quick-witted woman always had some wisecrack on her lips. Here are only a few of those famous remarks drawn from the greater gallery of eternal Guinanisms.

🦋 When her nearly-nude show was forbidden in Waltham, Massachusetts, famous for its clocks and watches, she exclaimed:

"The Mayor of the Watch City is giving me the Works."

🦋 A few minutes later, when the reporters called to ask her comment on the closing of her show, which was called "Too Hot for Paris," she remarked:

"Some people are so narrow-minded that their ears touch in back."

🦋 Her constant entanglements with the police never seemed to faze her. After one of her numerous arrests, she smiled at the police, and said:

"I'm nature's gift to the padlock makers, and the federal court is my alma mammy."

🦋 When she was playing a vaudeville engagement, a rival performer started to kid her.

"Listen here," said Texas, "I think your act is rotten—and that's only a hint."

🦋 One night in Hollywood, Tex was cornered by a pest who said: "I am going to tell you a story without a point to it."

"Say," interrupted Miss Guinan, "you should be back making motion pictures."

Mary Louise Cecilia "Tex" Guinan, 1932.

🦋 On her return from France, she was asked if she had shown French officials her birth certificate.

"Of course I did," she replied. "Did you think I was won in a dice game?"

🦋 Just before Texas went on the federal court witness stand in her own defense after the raid on her Club Royale, she was handed a glass of water.

"This is great stuff," she said, "for going under bridges."

🦋 Miss Guinan had a caustic brand of wit reserved for certain people to whom she took an instant dislike. Speaking about one popular Broadway actress, she remarked: "Her brain is good as new."

🦋 When the queen of the nightclub hostesses was going on a diet she told a friend she wanted to become as thin "as my first husband's promises."

🦋 Once during a discourse on the high percentage of divorces around Broadway, Tex remarked:

"It's having the same man around the house all the time that ruins matrimony."

🦋 When the Club Argonaut was finally reopened, Texas Guinan explained how she had pulled the whole thing off: "Dante got his whiskers singed in an imaginary inferno, and then he wrote a book. My draperies caught fire, and the insurance boys came by and wrote me a check."

🦋 After being arrested so many times for her nightclub irregularities in New York, she and her troupers went to the Pacific Coast. As she waved goodbye somebody in the crowd asked her what her new address would be.

"Oh, any courthouse in California," she replied.

—*Margaret Brennan*

An Evening at Jay Gatsby's

By F. Scott Fitzgerald

Jay Gatsby is F. Scott Fitzgerald's greatest Irish hero precisely because he is a bootlegger and a fraud. He is an alien being even at his own most miraculous parties: in the end, most of his newfound friends will desert him. The critics say that James T. Farrell is our greatest class critic; yet even Farrell never framed the proposition quite as neatly as "rich girls don't marry poor boys, Jay." Now that's putting the whole business right out there where the goats and chickens can get at it. As John Corry documents, the "legitimate" Irish eventually did make it to Long Island. And yet this ultimate "lace curtain" set carried with it a kind of random eccentricity that marked them as distinctly Irish nonetheless, and thus still "outside the pale" no matter how high they might build their mountains of newly earned, cold hard cash.

There was music from my neighbour's house through the summer nights. In his blue gardens men and girls came and went like moths among the whisperings and the champagne and the stars. At high tide in the afternoon I watched his guests diving from the tower of his raft, or taking the sun on the hot sand of his beach while his two motorboats slit the waters of the Sound, drawing aquaplanes over cataracts of foam. On weekends his Rolls-Royce became an omnibus, bearing parties to and from the city between nine in the morning and long past midnight, while his station wagon scampered like a brisk yellow bug to meet all trains. And on Mondays eight servants, including an extra gardener, toiled all day with mops and scrubbing brushes and hammers and garden shears, repairing the ravages of the night before.

Every Friday five crates of oranges and lemons arrived from a fruiterer in New York—every Monday these same oranges and lemons left his back door in a pyramid of pulpless halves. There was a machine in the kitchen which could extract the juice of two hundred oranges in half an hour if a little button was pressed two hundred times by a butler's thumb.

At least once a fortnight a corps of caterers came down with several hundred feet of canvas and enough coloured lights to make a Christmas tree of Gatsby's enormous garden. On buffet tables, garnished with glistening hors d'oeuvre, spiced baked hams crowded against salads of harlequin designs and pastry pigs and turkeys bewitched to a dark gold. In the main hall a bar with a real brass rail was set up, and stocked with gins and liquors and with cordials so long forgotten that most of his female guests were too young to know one from another.

By seven o'clock the orchestra has arrived, no thin five-piece affair, but a whole pitful of oboes and trombones and saxophones and violas and cornets and piccolos, and low and high drums. The last swimmers have come in from the beach now and are dressing upstairs; the cars from New York are parked five deep in the drive, and already the halls and salons and verandas are gaudy with primary colours, and hair bobbed in strange new ways, and shawls beyond the dreams of

Castile. The bar is in full swing, and floating rounds of cocktails permeate the garden outside, until the air is alive with chatter and laughter, and casual innuendo and introductions forgotten on the spot, and enthusiastic meetings between women who never knew each other's names.

The lights grow brighter as the earth lurches away from the sun, and now the orchestra is playing yellow cocktail music, and the opera of voices pitches a key higher. Laughter is easier minute by minute, spilled with prodigality, tipped out at a cheerful word. The groups change more swiftly, swell with new arrivals, dissolve and form in the same breath; already there are wanderers, confident girls who weave here and there among the stouter and more stable, become for a sharp, joyous moment the centre of a group, and then, excited with triumph, glide on through the sea change of faces and voices and colour under the constantly changing light.

Suddenly one of these gypsies, in trembling opal, seizes a cocktail out of the air, dumps it down for courage and, moving her hands like Frisco, dances out alone on the canvas platform. A momentary hush; the orchestra leader varies his rhythm obligingly for her, and there is a burst of chatter as the erroneous news goes around that she is Gilda Gray's understudy from the Follies. The party has begun.

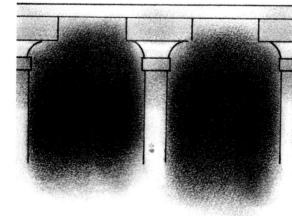

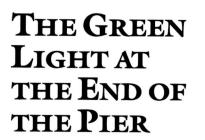

THE GREEN LIGHT AT THE END OF THE PIER

The precise moment when the Irish Catholics passed truly into society is unclear, but it is almost certain that the place where it happened was Southampton. True, there were Irish living in the marbled sepulchers of Newport, but Newport was full of the gaudy rich, meat packers, steel barons, and oil men, who looked for something they could not find in Cleveland, say, or Detroit, and who went to Newport to be snubbed and to indulge themselves in the innocent vulgarity that only the seriously rich can afford. Southampton was right for the Irish. Southampton, said one of its great ladies, was a "backwater of God," which is an imprecise description, but at least suggestive of the the kind of thing that was good about the place.

Jack Murray's place was called Lighthouse Farm and it had behind it a stable, a garage, laundry, chicken coop, caretaker's house, and cottage for the groom. There was a field for growing

32

vegetables, too. Tom Murray's house was bigger than Jack's and it had even more buildings scattered about it. The McDonnells had only their cottage, without other buildings, but in the cottage were ten bedrooms, a music room, library, living room, dining room, breakfast room, poolroom, and two kitchens, all of which, except the kitchens, were done up graciously in chintz and deep rugs by the McMillen decorators in New York. The McDonnell cottage also had rooms for the help, but apparently no one ever thought to count them. Driven by some insatiable lust, perhaps their only one, the McDonnells and Tom Murrays kept adding terraces, rooms, and whole wings to their houses, and whenever they did a priest would come in and bless each one. The priest would pray, make the Sign of the Cross, and then sprinkle holy water. The family, meanwhile, would be following the priest about, and soon he would turn and bless them, too. The terrace, or the room, or the wing would now be open.

The Jack Murrays had seven children, the Tom Murrays had eleven, and the McDonnells had fourteen. "I'm afraid to dive in," Al Smith, a frequent visitor to the pool, would say. "I might swallow a baby." —*John Corry*

33

BRINGING UP FATHER

Despite the catcalls of the cynical, the America of the last half of the nineteenth century proved a genuine Land of Opportunity for many of the dirt-poor immigrants who came from Ireland and elsewhere. Many such Irish were self-lifted by bootstraps of talent and determination into wealth and careers; others fell into money and position largely through luck and good connections.

Jiggs was universally symbolic of the accomplished Irish businessman of the early twentieth century—still rooted in the proletarian world of his immediate past (and so endlessly longing for the companionship of old drinking cronies not so fortunate as himself) while being urged in the direction of sophistication in the arts and society by his social-climbing wife, Maggie, and his wealth-acclimated daughter, Nora, themselves symbols of widely familiar family types in the socially civilizing process engendered by new money.

The day-to-day focus of "Bringing Up Father" as a comic strip was—understandably—on the friction and fracas between Jiggs and Maggie in the domestic arena (whether Jiggs was going to get away with the boys for a night or get hauled off to the opera etc.).

From time to time, however, George McManus would dwell on Jiggs' usually casual contacts with the business world, resulting from boredom, an occasional sense of opportunism, or simply Maggie's badgering him "to do something useful" (as if accumulating the wealth that gave Maggie and himself the leisure about such options had not in itself been "useful" enough for both their lifetimes). At one point, Jiggs even tried owning and managing a Hollywood studio. Little ever came of these latter-day business ventures, but they were clearly moves toward the upwardly mobile proprieties on Jiggs' part, each turn in such a direction an acknowledgment of the hard work or good fortune that brought him into bucks and—however unconsciously—into his position as ongoing victim for Maggie's and Nora's more civilizing works.

—*Bill Blackbeard*

If the truth be told, a number of important Irish families became hideously wealthy only a generation or so out of the old country. Many of these families were of good solid Northern Irish Protestant stock, but a significant number had roots in poor, peasant Catholic Ireland as well. Marcus Daly made a huge fortune at Anaconda; both the Buckleys and the Cullanans made the big dollar through oil. Cyrus McCormack invented the reaper, *as all schoolchildren know, and his family founded a newspaper empire with his wealth. Yet, the most legendary of all of these "Irish" businessmen was Henry Ford. Of County Cork descent, Ford became a mythical character even in his own lifetime. John Dos Passos has captured something of the man, and the myth, in his prose poem "Tin Lizzie"—a phrase, incidentally, coined by the great Tad Dorgan.*

TIN LIZZIE

By John Dos Passos

"Mr. Ford the automobileer," the featurewriter wrote in 1900.

"Mr. Ford the automobileer began by giving his steed three or four sharp jerks with the lever at the righthand side of the seat; that is, he pulled the lever up and down sharply in order, as he said, to mix air with gasoline and drive the charge into the exploding cylinder.... Mr. Ford slipped a small electric switch handle and there followed a puff, puff, puff.... The puffing of the machine assumed a higher key.... She was flying along about eight miles an hour. The ruts in the road were deep, but the machine certainly went with a dreamlike smoothness. There was none of the bumping common even to a steamer.... By this time the boulevard had been reached, and the automobileer, letting a lever fall a little, let her out. Whiz! She picked up speed with infinite rapidity. As she ran on there was a clattering behind, the new noise of the automobile."

For twenty years or more,

ever since he'd left his father's farm when he was sixteen to get a job in a Detroit machineshop, Henry Ford had been nuts about machinery. First it was watches, then he designed a steamtractor, then he built a horseless carriage with an engine adapted from the Otto gas-engine he'd read about in *The World of Science*, then a mechanical buggy with a onecylinder fourcycle motor, that would run forward but not back;

at last, in ninetyeight, he felt he was far enough along to risk throwing up his job with the Detroit Edison Company, where he'd worked his way up from night fireman to chief engineer, to put all his time into working on a new gasoline engine,

(in the late eighties he'd met Edison at a meeting of electriclight employees in Atlantic City. He'd gone up to Edison after Edison had delivered an address and asked him if he thought gasoline was practical as a motor fuel. Edison had said yes. If Edison said it, it was true. Edison was the great admiration of Henry Ford's life);

and in driving his mechanical buggy, sitting there at the lever jauntily dressed in a tightbuttoned jacket and a high collar and a derby hat, back and forth over the level illpaved streets of Detroit,

scaring the big brewery horses and the skinny trotting horses and the sleekrumped pacers with the motor's loud explosions,

looking for men scatterbrained enough to invest money in a factory for building automobiles.

He was the eldest son of an Irish immigrant who during the Civil War had married the daughter of a prosperous Pennsylvania Dutch farmer and settled down to farming near Dearborn in Wayne County, Michigan;

like plenty of other Americans, young Henry grew up hating the endless sogging through the mud about the chores, the hauling and pitching manure, the kerosene lamps to clean, the irk and sweat and solitude of the farm.

He was a slender, active youngster, a good skater, clever with his hands; what he liked was to tend the machinery and let the others do the heavy work. His mother had told him not to drink, smoke, gamble, or go into debt, and he never did.

When he was in his early twenties his father tried to get him back from Detroit, where he was working as mechanic and repairman for the Drydock Engine Company that built engines for steamboats, by giving him forty acres of land.

Young Henry built himself an uptodate square white dwellinghouse with a false mansard roof and married and settled down on the farm.

but he let the hired men do the farming;

he bought himself a buzzsaw and rented a stationary engine and cut the timber off the woodlots.

He was a thrifty young man who never drank or smoked or gambled or coveted his neighbor's wife, but

he couldn't stand living on the farm.

He moved to Detroit, and in the brick barn behind his house tinkered for years in his spare time with a mechanical buggy that would be light enough to run over the clayey wagonroads of Wayne County, Michigan.

By 1900 he had a practicable car to promote.

He was forty years old before the Ford Motor Company was started and production began to move.

Speed was the first thing the early automobile manufacturers went after. Races advertised the makes of cars.

Henry Ford himself hung up several records at the track at Grosse Pointe and on the ice on Lake St. Clair. In his .999 he did the mile in thirtynine and fourfifths seconds.

But it had always been his custom to hire others to do the heavy work. The speed he was busy with was speed in production, the records, records in efficient output. He hired Barney Oldfield, a stunt bicyclerider from Salt Lake City, to do the racing for him.

Henry Ford had ideas about other things than the designing of motors, carburetors, magnetos, jigs and fixtures, punches and dies; he had ideas about sales;

that the big money was in economical quantity production, quick turnover, cheap interchangeable easilyreplaced standardized parts;

it wasn't until 1909, after years of arguing with his partners, that Ford put out the first Model T.

Henry Ford was right.

That season he sold more than ten thousand tin lizzies, ten years later he was selling almost a million a year.

In these years the Taylor Plan was stirring up plantmanagers and manufacturers all over the country. Efficiency was the word. The same ingenuity that went into improving the performance of a machine could go into improving the performance of the workmen producing the machine.

In 1913 they established the assemblyline at Ford's. That season the profits were something like twentyfive million dollars, but they had trouble keeping the men on the job, machinists didn't seem to like it at Ford's.

Henry Ford had ideas about other things than production.

He was the largest automobile manufacturer in the world; he paid high wages; maybe if the steady workers thought they were getting a cut (a very small cut) in the profits, it would give trained men an inducement to stick to their jobs,

wellpaid workers might save enough money to buy a tin lizzie; the first day Ford's announced that cleancut properlymarried American workers who wanted jobs had a chance to make five bucks a day (of course it turned out that there were strings to it)

such an enormous crowd waited outside the Highland Park plant

all through the zero January night

that there was a riot when the gates were opened; cops broke heads, jobhunters threw bricks; property, Henry Ford's own property, was destroyed. The company dicks had to turn on the firehose to beat back the crowd.

The American Plan; automotive prosperity seeping down from above; it turned out there were strings to it.

But that five dollars a day

paid good, clean American workmen

who didn't drink or smoke cigarettes or read or think,

and who didn't commit adultery

and whose wives didn't take in boarders,

made America once more the Yukon of the sweated workers of the world;

made all the tin lizzies and the automotive age, and incidentally,

made Henry Ford the automobileer, the admirer of Edison, the birdlover,

the great American of his time.

But Henry Ford had ideas about other things besides assemblylines and the livinghabits of his employees. He was full of ideas. Instead of going to the city to make his fortune, here was a country boy who'd made his fortune by bringing the city out to the farm. The precepts he'd learned out of McGuffey's Reader, his mother's prejudices and preconceptions, he had preserved clean and unworn as freshprinted bills in the safe in a bank.

He wanted people to know about his ideas, so he bought the *Dearborn Independent* and started a campaign against cigarettesmoking.

When war broke out in Europe, he had ideas about that too. (Suspicion of armymen and soldiering were part of the Mid-West farm tradition, like thrift, stickativeness, temperance, and sharp practice in money matters.) Any intelligent American mechanic could see that if the Europeans hadn't been a lot of ignorant underpaid foreigners who drank, smoked, were loose about women, and wasteful in their methods of production, the war would never have happened.

When Rosika Schwimmer broke through the stockade of secretaries and servicemen who surrounded Henry Ford and suggested to him that he could stop the war,

he said sure they'd hire a ship and go over and get the boys out of the trenches by Christmas.

He hired a steamboat, the *Oscar II*, and filled it up with pacifists and socialworkers,

to go over to explain to the princelings of Europe that what they were doing was vicious and silly.

It wasn't his fault that Poor Richard's commonsense no longer rules the world and that most of the pacifists were nuts,

goofy with headlines.

When William Jennings Bryan went over to Hoboken to see him off, somebody handed William Jennings Bryan a squirrel in a cage; William Jennings Bryan made a speech with the squirrel under his arm. Henry Ford threw American Beauty roses to the crowd. The band played "I Didn't Raise My Boy to Be a Soldier." Practical jokers let loose more squirrels. An eloping couple was married by a platoon of ministers in the saloon, and Mr. Zero, the flophouse humanitarian, who reached the dock too late to sail,

dove into the North River and swam after the boat.

The *Oscar II* was described as a floating Chautauqua; Henry Ford said it felt like a Middle-Western village, but by the time they reached Christiansand in Norway, the reporters had kidded him so that he had gotten cold feet and gone to bed. The world was too crazy outside of Wayne County, Michigan. Mrs. Ford and the management sent an Episcopal dean after him who brought him home under wraps,

and the pacifists had to speechify without him.

Two years later Ford's was manufacturing munitions, Eagle boats; Henry Ford was planning oneman tanks, and oneman submarines like the one tried out in the Revolutionary War. He announced to the press that he'd turn over his war profits to the government,

but there's no record that he ever did.

One thing he brought back from his trip was the Protocols of the Elders of Zion.

He started a campaign to enlighten the world in the *Dearborn Independent*; the Jews were why the world wasn't like Wayne County, Michigan, in the old horse-and-buggy days;

the Jews had started the war, Bolshevism, Darwinism, Marxism, Nietzsche, short skirts and lipstick. They were behind Wall Street and the international bankers, and the whiteslave traffic and the movies and the Supreme Court and ragtime and the illegal liquor business.

Henry Ford denounced the Jews and ran for Senator and sued the *Chicago Tribune* for libel,

and was the laughingstock of the kept metropolitan press;

but when the metropolitan bankers tried to horn in on his business

he thoroughly outsmarted them.

In 1918 he had borrowed on notes to buy out his minority stockholders for the picayune sum of seventyfive million dollars.

In February, 1920, he needed cash to pay off some of these notes that were coming due. A banker is supposed to have called on him and offered him every facility if the bankers' representative could be made a member of the board of directors. Henry Ford handed the banker his hat,

and went about raising the money in his own way:

he shipped every car and part he had in his plant to his dealers and demanded immediate cash payment. Let the other fellow do the borrowing had always been a cardinal principle. He shut down production and canceled all orders from the supplyfirms. Many dealers were ruined, many supplyfirms failed, but when he reopened his plant,

he owned it absolutely,

the way a man owns an unmortgaged farm with the taxes paid up.

In 1922 there started the Ford boom for President (high wages, waterpower, industry scattered to the small towns) that was skillfully pricked behind the scenes

by another crackerbarrel philosopher,

Calvin Coolidge;

but in 1922 Henry Ford sold one million three hundred and thirtytwo thousand two hundred and nine tin lizzies; he was the richest man in the world.

Good roads had followed the narrow ruts made in the mud by the Model T. The great automotive boom was on. At Ford's production was improving all the time; less waste, more spotters, strawbosses, stoolpigeons (fifteen minutes for lunch, three minutes to go to the toilet, the Taylorized speedup everywhere, reachunder, adjustwasher, screwdown bolt, shove in cotterpin, reachunder, adjustwasher, screwdown bolt, reachunderadjust screwdownreachunderadjust, until every ounce of life was sucked off into production and at night the workmen went home gray shaking husks).

Ford owned every detail of the process from the ore in the hills until the car rolled off the end of the assemblyline under its own power; the plants were rationalized to the last tenthousandth of an inch as measured by the Johansen scale;

in 1926 the production cycle was reduced to eightyone hours from the ore in the mine to the finished salable car proceeding under its own power,

but the Model T was obsolete.

New Era prosperity and the American Plan

(there were strings to it, always there were strings to it)

had killed Tin Lizzie.

Ford's was just one of many automobile plants.

When the stockmarket bubble burst,

Mr. Ford the crackerbarrel philosopher said jubilantly,

"I told you so.

Serves you right for gambling and getting in debt.

The country is sound."

But when the country on cracked shoes, in frayed trousers, belts tightening over hollowed bellies,

idle hands cracked and chapped with the cold of that coldest March day of 1932,

started marching from Detroit to Dearborn, asking for work and the American Plan, all they could think of at Ford's was machineguns.

The country was sound, but they mowed the marchers down.

They shot four of them dead.

Henry Ford as an old man

is a passionate antiquarian

(lives besieged on his father's farm embedded in an estate of thousands of millionaire acres, protected by an army of servicemen, secretaries, secret agents, dicks under orders of an English exprizefighter,

always afraid of the feet in broken shoes on the roads, afraid the gangs will kidnap his grandchildren,

that a crank will shoot him,

that Change and the idle hands out of work will break through the gates and the high fences;

protected by a private army against

the new America of starved children and hollow bellies and cracked shoes stamping on souplines,

that has swallowed up the old thrifty farmlands of Wayne County, Michigan,

as if they had never been).

Henry Ford as an old man

is a passionate antiquarian.

He rebuilt his father's farmhouse and put it back exactly in the state he remembered it in as a boy. He built a village of museums for buggies, sleighs, coaches, old plows, waterwheels, obsolete models of motorcars. He scoured the country for fiddlers to play oldfashioned squaredances.

Even old taverns he bought and put back into their original shape, as well as Thomas Edison's early laboratories.

When he bought the Wayside Inn near Sudbury, Massachusetts, he had the new highway where the newmodel cars roared and slithered and hissed oilily past (*the new noise of the automobile*)

moved away from the door,

put back the old bad road,

so that everything might be

the way it used to be,

in the days of horses and buggies.

While real industry, and a precious lack of fantasy, was responsible for most of the great fortunes acquired by a small but significant number of Irish immigrant families, the Irish imagination was captured by the near outrageous behavior of a character like Diamond Jim Brady. An early Irish "Jaba the Hutt" type character, Brady flaunted his newfound wealth in a near imaginary world of wealthy restaurants, fabulous-looking dinner companions and a country mile of glittering—seemingly throwaway—possessions. Brady was the great dream being of early Irish immigrant consciousness. By day the typical Paddy and Bridget swept streets and scrubbed mansion floors. At night, however, with the tales of the Big Man's latest exploits featured in all the evening newspapers, they could only fantasize about what a night on the town might be like with the fantastic James Buchanan Brady. He seemed to have Yankee America by the tail.

DIAMOND JIM BRADY

By Lucius Beebe

James Buchanan Brady was a product of railroading when it was by far the most powerful American industry and the construction and operation of carriers the major preoccupation of the American people. Born into a typical Irish working-class family on New York's lower West Side when it was predominantly an Irish community, young Jim had his first job, as station agent and baggageman, at the New York Central's suburban station at Spuyten Duyvil on the far shore of Harlem River at the northern tip of Manhattan Island.

Something about the boy, perhaps his determination to learn telegraphy as a stepping-stone to better things, brought him to the attention of John Toucey, the celebrated and all-powerful general manager for the Vanderbilt family's immensely important New York Central & Hudson River Railroad. He became Toucey's chief clerk, a highly responsible position of confidential trust and delegated authority and one which, with his office in Grand Central Terminal, brought him into contact with such worldly men as Chauncey M. Depew, the railroad's urbane and affable president. Brady admired Depew as one of the town's best-dressed executives and a large part of his salary went to patronizing the same tailors, haberdashers, and hatters that enjoyed Depew's more consequential patronage. As a result the general manager's chief clerk soon acquired a reputation for sartorial splendor. His silk hats were the glossiest, his frock coats the most conservatively cut of any Central employee. His thirst for knowledge about the railroad business was as insatiable as his passion for clothes and soon he was able to supply, accurately and without hesitation, detailed figures and statistics essential to his

41

employer: costs of engine repairs, the performance of brake rigging, the reliability of electrical equipment under given weather conditions.

Brady's commissions were soon fantastic. He perfected the newly emergent technique of expense-account entertaining. He took his out-of-town customers to mammoth dinners at the best restaurants: Sherry's, Delmonico's, the Waldorf, but most especially at Charles Rector's, on Broadway between Forty-third and Forty-fourth Streets. Rector's was a favorite with highfliers from the West, railroad presidents, copper kings, masters of men, mills, and mines wherever huge fortunes were coming into being. Stuffed with lobster Newburg and White Seal champagne and fetched by their host's lordly ways with stage favorites and headwaiters, railroad nabobs from Kansas City and Omaha placed equally opulent orders with Brady for brake rigging and draft gear, patent couplings and switch stands.

Brady basked in affluence and ordered his suits by the dozen. He also began to collect diamonds. In an age when the size of a man's diamond ring was an explicit statement of his credit rating, diamonds were nothing to be embarrassed about. Desk clerks in fashionable hotels and maitres d'hotel at luxury restaurants appraised a potential customer on the degree in which he glittered. After six when they changed into evening dress, men of circumstance became dazzling. "Them as has 'em wears 'em," said Brady. Although he never touched liquor himself, Brady blossomed into the most expansive wine buyer on Broadway, a provenance he gradually widened to include Manhattan Beach and Saratoga. In time he became celebrated for the fantastic consumption of orange juice which accompanied his formidable meals, and modern medicine would be quick to see a cause-and-effect relationship between the deluge of citrus juice and the later ailments which were to beset him.

Brady's diamond collection became so large that its owner was hard put to wear even a fraction of it at a given time. The better to display his assets, he had diamonds mounted in what was to become his most famous visual asset, the transportation set. This comprised large-size stones embedded in platinum in the shape of bicycles, automobiles, and locomotives, for shirt studs, Pullman-car vest studs, tank-car cuff links, and an airplane lapel button. Altogether the set contained 2,637 diamonds and 21 rubies. It was valued at $87,315.

Brady's possessions increased in what seemed to spectators to be geometric progression and multiplied so fast he was hard put to keep track of them. They included a racing stable, a fleet of primeval automobiles, a magnificent town house in upper Manhattan, suites at the Gilsey House for entertaining out-of-town buyers, suits by the hundreds, and, of course, the celebrated gold-plated bicycles on which he took the air in Central Park and which he bestowed on favorite companions male and female.

Medical appraisal of a later generation would list Brady as a compulsive eater. He was a gourmand rather than a gourmet, but so heroic were his skirmishes with the roasts, entrees, and *pièces montés* as to elevate them to an actually epic dimension. Brady not only ate the full twelve-course dinner which was the conventional evening snack of the early decades of this century, he usually consumed three or four helpings of the more substantial dishes, beginning his repast with a gallon of chilled orange juice and finishing with the greater part of a five-pound box of the richest available chocolates. In between he might well consume six dozen Lynnhaven oysters, a saddle of mutton, half a dozen venison chops, a roasting chicken with caper sauce, a brace or so of mallard or canvasback ducks, partridge, or pheasant, and a twelve-egg souffle. During this interlude of ingestion he drank no wine or liquor of any sort. It was a spectacle that unnerved some spectators while others gathered around the Brady table at Bustanboy's, Jack Dunstan's, or the Cafe Martin to cheer him on his progress through the cutlets and make side bets on whether or not he'd fall dead before dessert.

Brady's abstinence from liquor in no way inhibited his friends and guests who might well number a dozen of the prettiest girls from the Ziegfeld chorus line and the president of the Santa Fe Railroad. For them a bucket brigade of wine waiters was in attendance opening Mumm's, White Seal, and Irroy at such frequent intervals that their corks sounded like drumfire. At the end of the evening the management showed the host the corks as evidence of bona fide consumption. Brady was happiest when they had to be brought to him in a laundry basket.

THE TURKEY TROT

By 1910, Broadway had gone wild about the turkey trot. Here was something it could understand. Here was something which interpreted its emotions with absolute accuracy. And in the vanguard of the dance's most fanatic devotees was Diamond Jim Brady. The delirious surgings of the music, the almost marital intimacies of the dance steps, were the very thing to appeal to a man who was trying to cram as much living as possible into the years remaining to him. He took the turkey trot and the tango unto his massive bosom and practiced their steps until the dances became things peculiarly his own.

Night after night Diamond Jim turkey-trotted and tangoed in the cabarets and midnight roof gardens, moving slowly uptown to each club in turn as the moon sank lower in the morning sky. With his hands and shirtfront almost covered with jewels it was often said that he carried his own illumination with him. He was more famous than any of the dancing idols of the day, Castle, Maurice, or beautiful Joan Sawyer.

He spent thousands of dollars on lessons from the Castles and Maurice, but Diamond Jim always danced in the same grave way. Once the music started he made for the exact center of the room and stayed there, taking short slow steps, his lips pursed in a whistle and his enormous left hand with its glittering diamond rings moving rhythmically up and down his partner's back with gentle pats.

With his usual passion for doing things in the grand manner, Jim soon evolved the ingenious scheme of maintaining a stable of dancing partners. When Diamond Jim Brady strolled into Churchill's or Rector's on an evening, surrounded by his chattering entourage, he looked for all the world like a dancing sultan with some of his harem out for an airing.

The newspapers loved all these doings. Scarcely a Sunday passed without a feature story on Diamond Jim and his doings.

—Parker Morrell

The Liar's Club

▶

*Spencer Tracy and Pat
O'Brien contemplate the
verdict in the 1951 M.G.M.
production of* The People
against O'Hara.

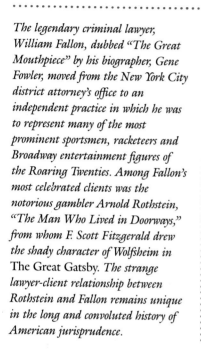

The legendary criminal lawyer, William Fallon, dubbed "The Great Mouthpiece" by his biographer, Gene Fowler, moved from the New York City district attorney's office to an independent practice in which he was to represent many of the most prominent sportsmen, racketeers and Broadway entertainment figures of the Roaring Twenties. Among Fallon's most celebrated clients was the notorious gambler Arnold Rothstein, "The Man Who Lived in Doorways," from whom F. Scott Fitzgerald drew the shady character of Wolfsheim in The Great Gatsby. The strange lawyer-client relationship between Rothstein and Fallon remains unique in the long and convoluted history of American jurisprudence.

▶
William Fallon, Broadway lawyer.

THE GREAT MOUTHPIECE

By Gene Fowler

Fallon became acquainted with Arnold Rothstein, the most publicized of underworld financiers, in January 1919. Off and on thereafter, Fallon was Rothstein's mouthpiece, and represented various Rothstein serfs.

Mr. Rothstein was bulleted not many months ago. He died in Polyclinic Hospital, refusing to name his executioner. Whether his passing was a loss to mankind or a gain to either branch of the Hereafter is a problem too weighty to handle in hot weather and hard times.

The man appeared constantly in newspaper banners and bodytype as "The Master-Mind of the Criminal Empire." The fixing of the Black Sox baseball scandal was attributed to him. He was said to have engineered sinister racetrack coups. Mysterious and far-reaching dope plots were laid at his door. His critics presumed him to be at the bottom of the strikes, goldbrick schemes, fake prizefights, and to be a fence for gem and bond thieves. The press posed Mr. Rothstein as the "brains" of nearly all the skullduggery brewed by the sonny-boys of modern crime.

Somehow, I gag at the portrait of Arnold Rothstein as Master-Mind. I tried to swallow it, but was forced to regurgitate, and eventually to expel.

Mr. Rothstein, weighted down with lethal lead and clipping-bureau offal proclaiming him a Master-Mind, died an exalted pawnbroker. His pocketbook was the skull; his bankroll the brains. He was an excellent executive, as we Americans judge such things.

A.R. was a tremendous gambler, with a joss-house pallor and an arterial system that, instead of blood, held a solution of arsenic in ice water. He would write you a bail piece of $50,000 on the cuff—but if you owed him a $10 premium on a similar bond, Mr. Rothstein would hound you to death to get it. Few men have been so scrupulous as he in collecting debts, or so lax about meeting obligations. Indeed, the metal suppositories that goosed him into the grave were etched with IOUs.

Mr. Rothstein did have a hold on the underworld. But that hold and his grip on the popular imagination were two entirely different things. His usurer's soul and the availability of his bankroll placed him automatically in the king-row of the criminal checkerboard.

Aside from money matters, and a vanity that would have cracked a Versailles mirror, Mr. Rothstein was a pleasant enough companion. He didn't eat with his knife, and his conversation was not half as dull as that heard at author's teas (which accounts for his not having been shot sooner). He detested liquor, and usually refused to traffic with anyone that drank to excess. He contributed to charities, lent his limousine to gentlemen of the cloth, and made self-conscious gestures in the directions of art. He fancied himself a connoisseur of Oriental rugs and of certain achievements in oil.

The Rothstein mask failed from the first to awe Fallon. He played smart-aleck jokes on Rothstein, defied him and quarreled with him frequently concerning drink. Rothstein strove with a curious, childlike zest to outdistance Fallon intellectually. Repeated defeats seemed to teach the gambler no lesson. It cannot be said that either man loved the other. Yet they worked efficiently together.

Both were overflowing with little vanities. Each was aware of the other's pet conceits. It was a great blow to Rothstein when he heard that Fallon had said:

"A.R. has mouse's eyes."

Rothstein retaliated by spreading the report that Fallon not only cut his own hair, but touched it up with henna. In these childish battles, Fallon won because he could laugh. Rothstein lost because he could not laugh.

When Fallon heard of the Rothstein charge concerning dyed hair, he said:

"Did you ever see a mouse that had false teeth?"

This was a crusher. Mr. Rothstein had shopped painstakingly for his set of false teeth. The Rothstein gumware was so excellent that few of his acquaintances along Broadway knew that the teeth were from the hand of the potter.

Mr. Fallon sensed that Rothstein had an almost neurotic fear of ill health. He called one day at Rothstein's insurance offices. During the conversation, Fallon leaned forward suddenly. "Good Lord! A.R." He then sat back as though he had spoken out of turn.

"What's wrong?"

Fallon manufactured a guilty look. "I was just thinking out loud."

"Thinking what?"

Fallon fumbled. "Are you feeling well?"

"Certainly. Why not?"

Rothstein looked steadily at Fallon. "What are you getting at?"

"Don't you think you should go to Atlantic City?"

"I never felt better in my life."

"That just goes to show how appearances can deceive. Are you sure your stomach isn't upset?"

"I know it isn't."

"Then it must be your gallbladder."

"There's nothing wrong with me."

"Is that what the doctor told you?"

"Hell no!" said Rothstein. "I haven't been to the doctor. There's nothing wrong."

"I hope you're right," said Fallon, rising to leave.

"What's your hurry?"

"No hurry, only I'm not going to tax the strength of a sick man."

Rothstein was mad. "Who says I'm sick?"

After Fallon left, Rothstein went immediately to a doctor's office. The doctor found nothing wrong. Rothstein went to another doctor, and still another. Finally, and after a fourth going-over, he was convinced that nothing was seriously the matter with him. When he heard how Fallon was broadcasting the joke, the Great Pawnbroker was furious. With all his press-built reputation as a Master-Mind, and his pose as the inscrutable czar of the underworld, we find Rothstein asking this question of Fallon's partner:

"Between us, do you think Fallon is smarter than I am?"

Mr. Rothstein often stood in Broadway doorways, looking at passersby, and conferring in whispers with mysterious persons. Mr. Fallon said of him:

"Rothstein is a man who dwells in doorways. A mouse standing in a doorway, waiting for his cheese."

&

FALLON'S BROADWAY

There are three Broadways within the memory of men. There was the street of Frank Gerety, a prewar promenade for all the world. The war created a second Broadway that had a cycle of some ten years—a dizzy, sensual, pointless Broadway. A third Broadway—the Broadway of now—had its inception at approximately the time when the talking picture began to squawk like a lad whose voice is changing. This last Broadway was a merger of Los Angeles and Coney Island, retaining the worst features of both.

Mr. Fallon came to Broadway on the heels of the old order. The grand Broadway tradition was crumbling, but all was not entirely lost. His career was concurrent with the second, war-whelped Broadway, in a decade of national deterioration.

Each of the three Broadways had its corresponding underworld. The first had its gangs, cliques, and rings of plug-uglies. These were muscled pioneers, the forebears of modern mobsters. They were the servants of politicians; not yet the masters. Mr. Fallon arrived during the intermediate period that bridged two milieus of crime. He found the underworld in flux. Crime was ceasing to be mere enterprise. It was becoming an industry.

With an entire nation gibbering over easy money, the Fallon Broadway became a wild and vulgar spending-ground. Fallon's fees were the first tremendous ones paid by captains of modern crime-syndicates for legal advice. He became, in fact, a corporation counsel for the underworld. He did not seek this condition; it was thrust upon him. After a few successes, Fallon was deeply involved, and his services were virtually commanded by men powerful in politics and in criminal circles.

—Gene Fowler

THE FUNERAL OF JAMES MARTIN MACINNIS

By Warren Hinckle

Poolhouse Johnson, a waiter enjoying the dimensions of a wrestler, crawled out of a taxicab at 9:45 A.M. yesterday in front of St. Ignatius Church, the Jesuit house of God, a stop to which he is not accustomed.

The meter read $3.80. Poolhouse dipped into the trench of his pocket and pierced out the tariff, plus six bits tip. Then he remembered the where and why he was there. He put back the cabbage and gave the cabbie a fiver with a buck float. "Keep the change," said Poolhouse.

Various lawyers of substance were standing on the sidewalk wearing hound dog faces and pallbearers' cloth. "Look what I almost did," said Poolhouse, a man known to many and currently the maitre d' at Amelio's. "Here I am going to the funeral of the biggest tipper in town and I almost fuss around with six bits for the hack. Today I have tipped in the manner of the deceased."

The deceased who so inspired Poolhouse was James Martin MacInnis, a face card of this town, the greatest mouthpiece of San Francisco, a city known for its talkers, a singular man whose career hangs as a full moon in the long night of the law.

A Mass of Christian burial was celebrated for MacInnis, yesterday at St. Ignatius. Christian was the adjective appropriate. MacInnis graduated from University of San Francisco in the 1930s and went on to defend purported Communists and other freethinkers outside the loyal herd. MacInnis' religious heritage is perhaps summarized by a stack of four Bibles in the bookshelves of his home—on top of the Bibles is a book titled *Deceptions & Myths of the Bible.*

After some initial soul-searching, the Jesuits decided to let bygones be and bury their boy and his bride on the turf whence he came. They did it up well. Even Sally Stanford, the famous Sausalito madam, received Communion. There was not a whiff of sulfur within the cold blue-gray walls of the Jesuit cathedral. As the duo coffins wheeled down the aisle, grown judges cried.

Outside the church the fog had blessed in to smother the heat. It would have been untoward for a man as immensely civilized as Jim MacInnis to be buried in unseasonable heat.

Jim MacInnis was one of the most famous lawyers in the world and a class act back when San Francisco had class to export. If he had a janitor on the witness stand he treated him as if he were royalty.

MacInnis was generous and extravagant and kind to friends and enemies to a fault, if that be blamable. Money to him—and he made as much as any criminal lawyer of his time—was merely a medium of exchange. He charged his cash clients and carried the cashless. His sense of humor and fatalism left him unflappable in the tempests of life and he carried with him the class and polish of an Irish gentleman's club.

The papers said Jim MacInnis died at sixty-eight, but that was wrong. He would have been sixty-six this January 3, when a group of his admirers and friends will gather at the North Beach Restaurant to tell tales of the master's life. "Jim wouldn't mind the mis-

take," said William A. Newsom, a state court of appeals judge and a former law partner and close friend to MacInnis. "He always preferred that people thought he was older but looked younger."

The collected stories of MacInnis' life would make a new, improved edition of human nature. Wednesday night before the Rosary at St. Ignatius, Newsom was sitting at the Sugar Plum in Laurel Village, recounting MacInnis-ania. This was the closest bar we could find near the twin spires of St. Ignatius.

Newsom told a story another judge had told him. MacInnis was representing one of the many exwives of a well-known auto dealer, in a divorce action. The master had had the auto man on stand all afternoon and had inflicted many cuts on the man. At 4:30 P.M., when the court prepared to recess, only MacInnis, the witness, the judge, a court reporter and a bailiff were in the room. The auto dealer got up off the stand and, as he passed MacInnis, he said in a low voice that nonetheless resounded throughout the courtroom, "You p—-k," using a vulgar word for the male organ.

MacInnis was putting his papers into his briefcase. He stopped and asked his accuser, in the mock solemnity for which he was famous, "Sir, was it to me that you addressed that expletive?"

The auto dealer muttered something about, "I didn't say anything to you." MacInnis immediately spun about and addressed the bench, and said in tones of sincere regret: "It is with the greatest of regret I must inform your honor that it was your honor that the witness called a p—-k."

In another court, at another time, MacInnis was battling Harry Neubarth, then a deputy San Francisco D.A., before an Irish judge known for his propensity to doze in the afternoon from the midday's wine. MacInnis was vainly trying to direct the judge's attention to what he considered the unfair tactics of the opposing counsel.

MacInnis got down on his knees, and then lay prone on his back on the floor. At this the judge finally looked over the bench and asked if anything was wrong. "I'm just trying to see if I can get as low as Mr. Neubarth, Your Honor," MacInnis said.

MacInnis had a heart bigger than South of Market. After Russ Wolden, the former San Francisco assessor, one of the few clients MacInnis failed to keep out of jail (on bribery charges), got out of the big house, MacInnis set Wolden up in an office in his law offices at the then Stanford Court Apartments. "He knew Russ didn't have anything to do and he wanted him to have somewhere to go every morning," Newsom said.

Wednesday night, at the Rosary, a fiddler stood on the marble altar under the Eucharist-red arched roof of St. Ignatius and played

MacInnis in Court

Back in the days before every home had a television set, the most gripping dramas in San Francisco ran daily in the courtrooms at the Hall of Justice and City Hall.

There was no admission charge, but the audience often had to show up early to be assured of a seat.

Generations of young attorneys packed the courtrooms when a spectacular trial was in session.

There were superstars of the bar, lawyers whose every appearance caused a buzz in the hallways and brought reporters and hangers-on rushing to courtrooms. Attorneys waiting for their own cases to be heard joined the rapt audiences.

Some of the great names have been forgotten by all but veteran lawyers, but there were indeed giants of the profession whose techniques, once observed, were never forgotten.

Many lawyers and judges and reporters, too, considered James Martin MacInnis the best in the business.

"He had a baby face and a great vocabulary," Marvin Lewis said of MacInnis. "He had more words than Webster. He was a great trial lawyer."

James Brosnahan, an outstanding attorney, called MacInnis "the dean of the criminal bar in San Francisco. He was the absolute top."

MacInnis was a master at eliciting information from witnesses, particularly witnesses presented by the other side.

Lincoln Mintz, a distinguished trial lawyer in his own right, said MacInnis' use of language was the envy of every attorney who heard him.

"When he spoke, it was like music," Mintz said. "He spoke as most of us wish we could write on the third draft. Mr. MacInnis was a classic gentleman of the old school. I never heard him say a bad word about anyone."

—Harry Jupiter

"Danny Boy." There were plenty of tears. Hal Lipset, sitting in a front pew, stood up. "I swear to God," he said, "I just saw Jim's coffin open and a hand slip the fiddler a C-note." There are others, who know Jim MacInnis well, who believe that happened.

WILLIE SUTTON
IN IRISHTOWN

By Willie Sutton with Edward Linn

I was born on June 30, 1901, on the corner of Nassau and Gold in a section along the Brooklyn docks known as Irishtown. Irishtown was wedged in between the East River on the north, the Navy Yard on the east, and the Washington Street entrance approach to the Brooklyn Bridge off to the west. The Manhattan Bridge was built while I was nine or ten and we kids used to drive everybody crazy by clambering up the structural ironwork which was going up a block away from my home.

My father, William Francis Sutton, Sr.—I'm William Francis Sutton, Jr.—was a hard-working blacksmith who earned fifteen dollars a week, which was not a bad salary in those days. My mother's father, who was totally blind, also lived with us. He had gone blind from working over the coffee roasters for the A & P stores. He had a pension. We were the first family in the neighborhood to have a Victrola, a brand-new Victor in which the music was produced from round cylinders and projected through a cone-shaped horn.

In our household, the final arbiter of all disputes was my grandfather, James Bowles. He had followed my mother to America after she had immigrated from Ireland. Blind as he was, he was an autocratic figure. As a very young boy I was given the job of taking him wherever he wanted to go. He had friends from the old country living on the East Side of Manhattan, and I would sometimes take him over the Brooklyn Bridge on the horse-drawn trolley cars. Usually, though, he would be wanting to go to Carney's saloon, a few blocks away, to have a beer or two with his cronies. I would sit at the table behind them, sipping a soft drink, and sooner or later the talk would always get back to the troubles in Ireland. My grandfather dominated every discussion, and his voice would turn thunderous as he damned the English. When we were alone, he would fill me with stories of Ireland's fight for independence, telling me about the martyrs who were being shot down in the streets like dogs.

Irishtown was a tough neighborhood, but it was a toughness without any strut or swagger. There was constant warfare for control of the docks, because to control the docks meant that you controlled the gam-bling, the loan-sharking, the pilfering, and the kickbacks. Plus the loading racket, which was the sweetest racket of all. Two rackets, really. A flat rate, otherwise known as extortion, was levied against the importer, and then another charge was levied against the truckers for every crate they loaded. Lead pipes and brass knuckles were standard equipment. Murder was commonplace. No one was ever convicted. A code of silence was observed in Irishtown more faithfully than *omerta* is observed by the Mafia. Nobody ever talked in Irishtown.

Sands Street, the sailor's honky-tonk, ran just parallel to High Street, and directly into the Navy Yard three blocks away. A three-block carnival. Three blocks of whorehouses and street-hookers, free-flowing liquor and noisy revelry. It was a street of happily blended sounds. The music pouring from the dance hall, the sea chanteys arching over the swinging doors of the saloons, the ricky-ticky piano telling of great happenings at the nickelodeon, and the high-pitched laughter from the throats of waist-holding couples as they paused for a moment to look in the store windows. I was about ten when I began to hang around Sands Street with my school chums Charlie McCarthy and Eddie Lynch. They were just as fascinated by the street as I was, and we eagerly absorbed the exciting tales being told by the lush rollers, the burglars, the gamblers, and the gangsters. They became my first heroes. They wore good clothes, their shoes were always shined, and they looked as if they belonged in them, not awkward and uncomfortable like the working men of Irishtown in their Sunday go-to-church suits.

The East River was our real playground and our lifeline. We swam through the raw untreated garbage which was dumped regularly into the river. Everything came up river by barge, including the livestock that was headed for the Tillary Street Slaughterhouse. A cattle drive through the narrow cobblestone streets of Irishtown? I saw it often. The barges, carrying cattle or sheep, would dock a couple of blocks from St. Ann's, the first school I attended. The cattle would be driven down Hudson Avenue, past the tenement houses and the neighborhood stores, to the slaughterhouse, which was actually on Hudson Avenue, a little east of Tillary.

The sheep didn't have to be driven. They would

follow the Judas Sheep, which, at this slaughterhouse anyway, was literally a black sheep. Two big iron doors would swing open and the sheep, baaing piteously, would be crowded into the building. The slaughtering was done in open view on what could be compared to the loading platform of a factory. It was slaughter on the assembly line. One of the workers would simply run a long knife through the animal's throat. I had nothing against the workers. They were German immigrants, most of them, with thick accents. But that Judas Sheep, I came to hate it. I swear that he knew what he was doing. There was an expression of exaggerated innocence on its face that no other sheep had. I hated

it so much that I got all of my friends together and planned to drown it when the next load of sheep arrived. After the gangplank of the barge had been lowered we came running forward, swinging sticks and throwing rocks, and drove the black sheep right into the river. It never occurred to any of us that the other sheep were going to follow it straight into the river. What a mess!

I have never forgotten the Judas Sheep. Or ever stopped hating it. How could I? I kept seeing the same expression of exaggerated innocence in the faces of the hired killers, the woman stranglers, and the sex fiends I later ran across in prison. ❧

SPIVLO V. MAHONEY

By Vincent Hallinan

When I was about nine years old, my career in life was set. I was to become a lawyer. While this decision was my father's, he was impelled to it by a certain entity or personage whose very identity was then, and continues to be, an unfathomable mystery. The title of this deus ex machina was repeated a thousand times in our home; scarcely a visitor departed without having heard the significant part he had played in our family history. Yet he was but a disembodied spirit, a vibration in the ether, a name that was recited.

That name was Spivlo V. Mahoney.

But if only a name, it was indeed a name to be conjured with. And conjured with it was, to a glorious purpose.

This is the role it played in the small drama of our family troubles. We were poor. My parents were Irish immigrants. My father worked as a conductor on the California Street cable cars in San Francisco twelve hours a day, and got one day off a month. His salary was $70. On this he supported his family, which then contained seven children.

He was singularly honest and honorable. His head was scarred from policemen's clubs wielded in bitter strikes to raise the wages and shorten the hours of the company's platform men. If his principles amounted to bigotry and his loyalties to fanaticism, at least they were not for sale. He would burn at the stake before he would betray a cause or a friend.

When the great earthquake and fire of 1906 devastated San Francisco, we were living in a four-room cottage in its Western Addition. The rent was about $12 a month. The house had a basement which ran its full length and width. When the fire was over, this basement became desirable storage space for people who had managed to remove their furniture from their homes before the flames reached them. Our landlord proposed to capitalize on this windfall. As it was impossible that we could pay more than our present rent, he served us with a thirty-day notice to vacate the premises. The eviction of our family, with its numerous small children, was catastrophic. There was no place to go.

In those days, before the automobile, streetcars were the general means of conveyance. Prominent persons were regular passengers on my father's car, and he was friendly with many of them. Among the more cordial was Charles Heggerty, attorney for the Southern Pacific Railroad Company. My father hastened to this giant of the bar with our sorry problem. The magnanimous Heggerty gave it his full attention. Having read the notice, he perused a section of the code and said:

"I'm pretty sure this notice is legally defective. When the thirty days are up, they'll file an unlawful-detainer action. Try to avoid being served for as long as possible. Meanwhile, I'll look up the authorities on this and we'll see if we can't kick the case around for a while."

As the ominous day approached, my father proceeded to follow the lawyer's instructions. He never answered the doorbell in person or left the house without inspecting its environs from behind the curtains. The older children, as well as all the immediate neighbors, were alerted for anyone who looked like a process server. If a suspicious character was observed

What with the early experiences of the Irish in America, a thirst for social justice might even be considered synonymous with the very term: Irish-American. Sadly, however, the Irish have not always lived up to their highest ideals. Vincent Hallinan of San Francisco and Paul O'Dwyer of New York remain exceptional in this regard. At ninety, Vincent Hallinan is still an active figure in the Bay Area peace movement. Paul O'Dwyer, at eighty, has never forgotten where the lads thought to store all the picket signs. Courage and stamina. Even today it would take a foolish man to challenge either of these great sages to a bicycle race around Central Park.

in the vicinity when my father was due home from work, one of us met him around the corner to warn him. He then detoured into the rear entrance of the house behind ours, climbed the back fence, and thus avoided danger.

The cable company's platform men were enlisted in this campaign of evasion. If a stranger boarded a car, inquiring for Pat Hallinan, each played his part. The conductor—it might be my father himself—called out to the motorman, "What car is that fellow Hallinan on?"

The reply usually was: "That one that just passed us. Hop off and run after it. He'll stop at the next corner."

A wave to the conductor of the other car ensured that it wouldn't stop. After a chase of two or three blocks the process server gave up. To prevent being brought up within the jurisdiction of the court while turning in his car at night, my father had another stratagem. The conductor preceding him met him a block from the carbarn, took over his position, and turned in his vehicle also.

After some four months of this the plaintiff's lawyers enlisted the aid of the company officials. My father was called to the superintendent's office where a deputy sheriff was waiting to serve him.

Then Heggerty really began kicking the case around. The courts were in a chaotic condition, and it was not difficult to procure delays, even in an unlawful-detainer action, which had precedence. A demurrer or two were sustained, and it was another three months before the plaintiff finally got his case to trial. It was then that our good genius emerged to confound him.

Spivlo V. Mahoney!

As my father told it a thousand times: "When they had finished their case, Charley Heggerty says, 'Your Honor, I move for a nonsuit.' 'On what grounds, Mr. Heggerty?'

says Judge Van Nostrand. 'On the grounds,' says Charley Heggerty, 'that the notice to vacate is fatally defective.' 'Have you any authority for that?' says Judge Van Nostrand. 'I have, Your Honor,' says Charley Heggerty, 'it's *Spivlo v. Mahoney.*'"

"And," my father would continue in his most impressive tones, "do you know that Judge Van Nostrand had never heard of Spivlo V. Mahoney?"

Over the many years that I heard this saga repeated I never lost my wonder and concern at the monumental ignorance of Judge Van Nostrand in never having heard of *Spivlo v. Mahoney*. It wasn't until I was a lawyer myself and saw the thousands of books and recognized that there were numberless decisions in them that I realized the wonder would have been if Judge Van Nostrand had heard of *Spivlo v. Mahoney*.

At any rate, it must have been of convincing authority, for the nonsuit was granted and the plaintiff had to start all over again. Altogether it took him eighteen months to get us out of that cottage. Even then, with his back to the wall, Heggerty was able to bluff a settlement under which we agreed to move out and the landlord waived all the back rent. This, then, was the incident that determined my career. 🍂

THE IRGUN CONNECTION

Paul O'Dwyer, 1985.

I first learned of the Irgun Zvai Le'umi through an advertisement in the *New York Times* in 1945 that outlined the Irgun's objectives and pointed the way for Americans to participate. I soon joined a support committee. Because I was a non-Jew, I was used quite frequently as a fund-raiser in New York, Philadelphia, Hartford, and other New England cities. Our purpose was to get arms and ammunition and skilled manpower to Israel so that the Irgun could conduct the fight against Britain.

Early in 1948 I was sent to Ireland to call on Mayor Robert Briscoe, the Jewish mayor of Dublin. Because he had been an I.R.A. man in 1919, I knew he would sympathize with the Irgun. For a variety of reasons Briscoe agreed to arrange for all the Irgun printing—literature and documents—to be done in Ireland. He had already arranged for volunteers.

I was often criticized for my association with this organization; yet, when pressed, I responded to one critic as follows: "The Irgun did a very intelligent job of chasing the British out of Israel. If Israel had had to wait for freedom to come from the conference table, we would all be getting Social Security before the matter even came up for a second reading. To ask me to turn my back on the Irgun would be like asking me to denounce the Irish Republican Army. I have not been merely a name on an Irgun ad, I have been working actively to help them and support them for a number of years."

After independence, I withdrew from further involvement. The battle had been won, and much as I admired the courage of the Irgun, and many of their leaders, I did not share their political philosophy. My interest was in freedom for Israel, and not in a particular political party.

—By Paul O'Dwyer

ON FRANK MURPHY

By William V. Shannon

It was Franklin Delano Roosevelt who first brought a battery of bright young Irish lawyers, politicians and intellectuals to national prominence. Tom Walsh of Montana became Roosevelt's first attorney general. John McCormack of Massachusetts became Roosevelt's number one congressional "quarterback." Joseph P. Kennedy became Roosevelt's ambassador to Great Britain. And Frank Murphy of Michigan became one of Roosevelt's most fascinating appointments to the Supreme Court of the United States. Murphy's the one. It is Frank Murphy who deserves our lingering attention.

O f all the personalities who came to the center of the national stage during the New Deal, the most romantically and flamboyantly Irish was Frank Murphy. While others were shaped by the interplay between their Irish heritage and American life, Murphy was someone Ireland could have produced unaided. He stepped, as it were, directly out of the pages of James Joyce or a play of Sean O'Casey; one can visualize him mourning Parnell in the committee room on Ivy Day, or standing with Padhraic Pearse and defying the British during the Easter Week Rising, or fasting to death with Terence MacSwiney in his prison cell. Rebel, ascetic, romantic, priest manqué, and orator, Frank Murphy brought the spirit of the Irish revolutionary tradition to the stirring adventures of the New Deal. "Crisis," he liked to say of his own career, "has become a banality." His very Irish sense of histrionics thrived on it.

His grandfather was hanged by the British in Ireland; his father emigrated to America as a youngster, joined the Fenian movement, and at sixteen was briefly jailed in Canada for his part in the picaresque Fenian attempt to liberate Ireland by conquering Canada. His father then settled down as a country lawyer in Harbor Beach, Michigan, where he was known as the town radical, an ardent Bryan Democrat, and dedicated Anglophobe.

Murphy had never been outside his hometown before he journeyed at the age of sixteen to Ann Arbor to attend the University of Michigan in 1909. After a notable record in World War I in which he became a captain at twenty-five, Murphy studied briefly at Lincoln's Inn, London, and at Trinity College in Dublin. Ireland in 1919 was in the midst of the revolutionary upheavals that finally culminated in independence. Murphy became friendly with Sinn Feiners, was shadowed by British police, and was sorely tempted to join the fray, but family obligations drew him back to Michigan.

Since he had early formed his private motto—"All clients are bastards" —Murphy sought public employment and found it as an assistant federal district attorney. During the next three years he achieved extensive newspaper publicity through his convictions of grafters and bootleggers. Securely launched on a political career, he was never out of public office until his death.

When Murphy ran for mayor in 1930, he said in his initial campaign speech, "What Detroit needs is the dawn of a new day, the dew and sunshine of a new morning." He was promptly labeled in the newspapers the "Dew and Sunshine candidate." Since Detroit has nonpartisan elections and the two parties were not at that time effectively organized as citywide machines, Murphy was free to run in the style he liked best: as a lone wolf. He won by a substantial majority. As mayor, he conducted an administration that was an unorthodox combination of financial reform, rigid economy, social welfarism, and radicial rhetoric. He professed to disdain all professional politicians, insisted righteously that he never made appointments on any basis except merit, and skillfully dramatized his appointments of Republicans, Rhodes scholars, and nonpolitical experts. He asserted that it was the city's duty to feed the unemployed, and he strained the city treasury's resources to do so, but he also busily cut padded payrolls and skimped on normal expenses to hold overall expenditures close to pre-Depression levels.

In 1933 Roosevelt appointed Murphy as governor-general of the Philippines. He stayed three years, returned home, and was elected governor of Michigan.

Two days before Murphy took office as governor of Michigan, a sit-down strike was called at General Motors. Most of his two years as governor were taken with strike mediations. He resolutely refused to use troops to clear the factories of strikers; by patience in marathon negotiating sessions, he achieved peaceful settlements in a half-dozen major strikes. In retrospect, his course of action seems only elementary common sense; a show of force that led to bloodshed would have been irresponsible. But those shortsighted conservatives who mistook the sit-down strikes as dress rehearsals for another French Revolution were tireless in their attacks upon Murphy for his refusal to "get tough" and "take a stand for law and order."

Murphy's conception of public issues enabled him to see the industrial strife of 1937-1938 from an angle of vision different from the usual liberal or conservative cliches of class warfare. The sit-down strikes, he said, were a "reassertion of the personality—the dignity of the offended human reasserting itself after the frightening experience of the Depression." He was defeated for reelection as governor in 1938, but a week after leaving office, he became attorney general in the Roosevelt cabinet.

Frank Murphy served an exciting year as attorney general. As an Irish moralist, he most enjoyed the part of his work that involved tracking down wrongdoers. By aggressive enforcement of the criminal laws, he stayed on the front pages of the nation's newspapers almost every day. Joseph Alsop and Robert Kintner in their syndicated column quoted President Roosevelt as telling a visitor that before Murphy was done, he would make the achievements of Tom Dewey, then Manhattan's Republican district attorney, look like "small potatoes." They speculated on a 1940 Democratic "dream ticket," Roosevelt and Murphy.

In January 1940, Roosevelt unexpectedly appointed Murphy to the Supreme Court on the death of Justice Pierce Butler, the court's only Catholic member. Although he protested vehemently that he would prefer to stay in the cabinet, Murphy finally accepted. Most lawyers would not consider a place on the Supreme Court an unhappy ending to their career. But for Murphy it was. He was simply not suited by temperament or intellectual interest for the politically detached and impersonal style of life required of a judge. Murphy was a politician to his fingertips. Like Fiorello La Guardia or Al Smith, he was an egotist and an actor who desperately, almost physiologically, needed an audience and a place in the center of the stage. Murphy spent nine years on the court before his death in 1949. The sheltered world of the court with its slow pace and stately routines was no place for an Irish rebel in search of a cause.

JUSTICE BRENNAN

Justice William J. Brennan, Jr., the son of a labor leader, has had his say in over twenty-five percent of the cases before the Supreme Court in this century.

He has written more opinions than any other justice in United States history, with the exception of William O. Douglas.

Not bad for a kid who started his career delivering milk and making change for trolley riders to aid the family income.

Brennan has always recognized his debt to his "Da," who emigrated from County Roscommon, Ireland, in 1893, and settled in Newark, New Jersey. "Everything I am," Brennan has said, "I am because of my father."

Justice Brennan has long been considered the warmest member of the Supremes, famed for his charm and sly wit.

He would be the first to understand George Bernard Shaw's fine line on the nature of the Celt: "Put an Irishman on the spit," Shaw said, "and you can always get another Irishman to turn him."

Although many Americans of Irish descent had recently adopted a decided conservative bent, Brennan has been one the great liberals of American jurisprudence.

His deep friendship with Chief Justice Earl Warren led to many of the landmark decisions that changed the face of modern America.

When asked what made Warren such a great chief justice, Brennan answered: "He had everything. He was hardworking, he knew how to work with people. He was marvelous with people. He would take approaches that would often escape my eye.

"He was just extraordinary."

The same could be said for Justice Brennan.

—J.P. O'Shea

The Stage Door

▶

John Barrymore and Lewis Stone listen attentively as Lionel Barrymore tells his tale in the 1932 M.G.M. production of The Grand Hotel.

JOHN BARRYMORE PLAYS HAMLET

By Gene Fowler

Irish culture on both sides of the Atlantic exploded into world significance during the Roaring Twenties. On the Dublin stage, the critics began to rave about the genius of the Abbey Theatre and the new social realism of the brilliant Sean O'Casey. In America, the theater now belonged to the Barrymores and the Byzantine psychological depth of angry, young Eugene O'Neill. Reading the daily newspapers from that era, you can actually feel the electricity. The Barrymores had become the first family of the American theater. And the Irish prince in that particular clan was undoubtedly wild man Jack. John Barrymore, the critics said, was at his best when playing the part of the Dane.

The wearing of tights had been one of Barrymore's chief antipathies. This seems a curious aversion when we consider his superb physique.

"When I first got into these skin-fitting jollities," Barrymore said of his tights, "I felt as if I had put on the intimate wear of Peg Woffington. Good God! What an ass a grown male can become on occasion! I think I wore these dainties for the first time in *Pantaloon*. I am not sure. No one is ever sure of anything in respect to tights."

He snorted like St. George's monstrous adversary, then continued: "When I had to play the Jest in these counterfeits of nudity, I decided to conquer or be conquered. I spent at least three hours before a pier glass. True, I had to take a few drinks to brace myself. Then I began to stare at the asinine fellow in the mirror. I sneered at him, I reviled him, I questioned his authenticity in matters of romance. I walked, I turned this way and that, never taking my eyes from the fellow in the quicksilver. Finally I grew sick from the idiot-vision. Fortunately I hadn't taken enough alcohol to see two miserable, mincing scoundrels, else I should have died. Finally I got so tired of surveying myself, so sick, so damned fed up with tights that I no longer gave a damn how they looked, on me or on anyone else. I had 'em licked."

Jack borrowed a pair of underdrawers from Lionel to wear beneath the Hamlet tights. Not only did he regard his brother's shorts as a good-luck charm, but the garment was adroitly tailored so as not to form awkward creases on the thighs. When, toward the fiftieth performance of *Hamlet*, Barrymore's valet discreetly suggested a change of underpants, Jack bellowed: "Damn it, no! I opened in these drawers, and by God! I'll close in them!"

What Jack did not know until long afterward was that the underwear originally had belonged to Kid McCoy. Lionel, one day at the gymnasium, had borrowed the apparel from the jaunty expugilist to wear under the tights of *Macbeth*. By the time these drawers had done double duty in *Macbeth* and *Hamlet*, even a ragman would have refused to collect them for his heap.

"Do you believe," I asked Lionel one day, his own

◀

A legend is born, John Barrymore's Hamlet, New York City, 1922.

fiftieth anniversary on the stage, "do you really believe that Jack was on the level when he said that *Hamlet* was the easiest role he ever played?"

"Of course he was," replied the half-centuried stalwart. "You must take into account that when the Bard wrote *Hamlet* he had Jack in mind."

It was not always apparent whether Jack was elaborating or joking. His claim that Hamlet was an "easy" role brought a challenge, yet perhaps the reply was not wholly a jest.

"To begin with," he said, "not only does every actor play Hamlet, provided he live long enough, but every member of the audience plays it, each in his own unyielding fashion. That's why we have so many thousands of essays, dissertations, comments, and multitudinous opinions, all of them sharply, yes, fiercely diverse, as to how the greatest character in all literature should be portrayed, and who did it best. The same is true of the simple, sane, charitable preachments and life of Our Lord. Yet a thousand religions and a hundred thousand sects have been squabbling over matters that probably never were contained in the Messiah's texts."

One thing that enchanted Jack with the *Hamlet* play was the physical leeway it permitted an actor. "You can play it standing, sitting, lying down, or, if you insist, kneeling. You can have a hangover. You can be cold-sober. You can be hungry, overfed, or have just fought with your wife. It makes no difference as regards your stance or your mood. There are, within the precincts of this great role, a thousand Hamlets, any one of which will keep in step with your whim of the evening. Why, one night in London, after I had been overserved with Scotch at the home of—never mind her name—I got halfway through my 'To Be' soliloquy when it became expedient to heave-ho, and quickly. I sidled off to the nearest folds of the stage draperies and played storm-at-sea. I then resumed the soliloquy. After the performance one of the fine gentlemen who had sponsored me for membership in the Garick Club confided: 'I say, Barrymore, that was the most daring and perhaps the most effective innovation ever offered. I refer to your deliberate pausing in the midst of the soliloquy to retire, almost, from the scene. May I congratulate you upon such imaginative business? You seemed quite distraught. But it was effective!' To which I replied: 'Yes, I felt slightly overcome myself.'"

Asked why, in the play, he alone of many notable Hamlets seemed so calm, almost joyously serene, upon seeing his father's ghost, Barrymore replied:

"The ghost, if I may be so impertinent as to have a personal opinion, is actually the God-damnedest bore since the ancient time when Job began to recite his catechism of clinical woes. Talks his head off. I am sure that Shakespeare modeled him after some unbearable bore back in Stratford, some town pest who got on everyone's nerves; the sort of stupid bastard whose wife was bound to cheat on him out of sheer ennui. But in the play, Hamlet is fond of the old boy who was once

his father, no matter what dull company he might be at Billy LaHiff's Tavern. So I, as Hamlet, also must be fond of him. The play, you know, rather depends on this bond of sympathy to promote the revenge. Ergo, when the ghost of the father appears, I am a bit startled, and for the moment confused, yet I actually am glad to be with him once again. So I don't rant or scream. I listen attentively to the old man, hear his gossip, then engineer the appropriate murders. After the play I go at once to LaHiff's or Dinty Moore's, where, as a civilian, I devoutly thank God that the confounded old bore of a wraith cannot, in all likelihood, reappear at my elbow to cadge a drink."

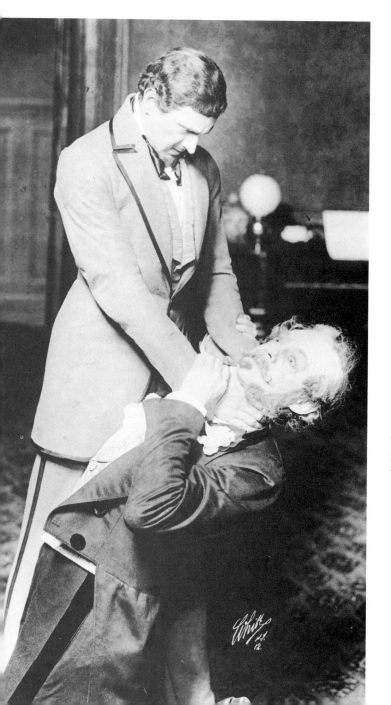

THE RELUCTANT ROMANTICIST

Barrymore's playing of the glittering *Peter Ibbetson* role in 1914 established him as an enduring romanticist. Love letters and sentimental gifts came in with the tide. Yet he was so lacking in conceit that he could not regard himself as a ladies' man. He maintained that the label had been pasted on him when he was not looking.

He attributed the growing legend of his love life to circumstances other than publicity.

"I was working so assiduously," he said, "that a succession of heart flip-flops began to annoy me. Whenever I became excited, one of these harmless yet startling cardiac beats would make me jump, or call out like a moose. One evening, when enjoying the company of a lady, and with romance at its meridian, the heart went 'zoom.' I reacted with sudden bounds and cries. The lady mistook this for sheer ardor. She confided in some other lovely creature, and so help me God I had a similar experience with that one. The results of word-of-mouth advertising were incredible. Likewise the series of heart flutters. It got so that I was being exploited all over town like a patent medicine. Never could shake the reputation, even after the heart had returned to its former monastic serenity."
—*Gene Fowler*

John Barrymore chokes his brother Lionel in the 1917 stage production of *Peter Ibbetson*.

DION BOUCICAULT

By Albert Johnson

Substantive Irish drama began, not in Ireland, but in America. The first major Irish dramatist was Dion Boucicault, a Dubliner of Huguenot descent. Boucicault wrote his first authentic "Irish" plays for the New York stage. And, yes, they were often corny. In Boucicault's plays, however, the stage-Irish character of countless previous English light comedies learned for the first time how to bite back. As Boucicault wrote him, Paddy now became an authentic "trickster" figure—to use the modern anthropological vernacular. While New York immigrant audiences cheered, Boucicault's Paddy began to outwit his various English colonial lords.

Although he is now almost forgotten, Dion Boucicault was for almost a half century one of the most celebrated, versatile and successful men of the theatre, both in America and in England. His accomplishments were extraordinary. He was a playwright, play doctor and adapter, actor, director, stage technician, manager, teacher and magazine writer. In the first six categories he was an acknowledged master during the last half of the nineteenth century.

Boucicault is supposed to be responsible for starting the matinee. He introduced the principle of a director as opposed to the then usual procedure of a prompter or stage manager. He created the first elaborate box set complete with authentic properties, furniture and stage carpets. He inaugurated the first road company and the first percentage arrangement for a dramatist, instead of the traditional small outright payment.

A Dublin, Ireland-born foreigner who entered actively, and wholeheartedly, into the life and theatre of America, Boucicault fought for and secured the first author's copyright in 1856. In a more colorful vein, he is said to have originated the open-front shirt, and was one of the first in New York to have a tiled bathroom.

▶ **Shaun-the-Post escapes from his castle cell, from Boucicault's *Arrah-na-Pouge*.**

▲

Myles-na-Coppaleen saves a drowning Eily O'Connor, from Boucicault's *The Colleen Bawn*.

The walls of his apartment at the caterer Pinard's were of Minton china, and all of his bathroom fixtures were made of sterling silver.

Dion Boucicault is also considered the "father" of Irish drama. Though there had been a number of earlier, sporadic plays that were so-called Irish, or that contained so-called Irish characters, Boucicault's *The Colleen Bawn* was the true beginning of an Irish drama that deserves the name Irish. As Boucicault himself said in a speech that even his enemies might credit for its good taste and modesty: "I have written an Irish drama for the first time in my life. The field of Irish history is so rich in dramatic suggestion that I am surprised that the mine has never been regularly opened before. I had long thought of writing a play from material gathered from my native country, but this is the first time I ever tried it. I hope that this play will lead other, greater men, of finer genius and talent than I possess, to create more Irish plays."

The Shaughraun is generally considered Boucicault's finest Irish play. The play is of special interest because it was written and produced more than thirty years after Boucicault's still widely popular *London Assurance*—at a time when it was rumored that perhaps the master had lost his magic touch. Yet Lester Wallack—with Augustin Daly, one of the two leading American managers of the day—offered Boucicault a quarter of a million dollars for the play, and the author's services as an actor for the next five years. Boucicault wisely refused —and made a small fortune on this play alone. His acting as "Con" —the devil-may-care Irish vagrant— was instantly acclaimed; it is generally considered his finest role. Although founded on an incident that occurred in County Sligon during the Fenian insurrection of 1866, *The Shaughraun* is one of the few completely

original plays that Boucicault ever wrote. A smash hit in America, and then in England, it was soon translated into both French and German as well.

The critic Allardyce Nicoll has indicated George Bernard Shaw's debt to his contemporary, and countryman, by calling attention to the close similarity of the scene in which the Devil's Disciple is questioned by Swindon and Burgoyne to the scene in which Con, the Shaughraun, is questioned by the authorities. Clearly Shaw remains in Boucicault's debt.

Sean O'Casey has written affectionately of Boucicault's Irish plays, which he relished in his boyhood, particularly *The Shaughraun*, in which as a teenager he played, on a few hours' notice, the role of Father Dolan with an amateur company at the Mechanics' Theatre on Abbey Street. "Dion Boucicault was really quite as great a choice as Shakespeare," O'Casey later said. "Shakespeare's good in bits; but for colour and stir, give me Boucicault!"

Throughout his life Dion Boucicault was a man of, and for, the theatre. He intimately knew, wrote for, directed and acted with most of the top-notch theatre people of his age. Nobody really knows how many plays, originals or in adaption, finally came from his pen. Estimates still vary from more than a hundred to more than four hundred—the latter being the playwright's own estimate. As Barrett H. Clark has written, there are in one private collection alone fifty plays by Boucicault which remain to this day unpublished.

That Dion Boucicault himself was conscious of the irony of the theatre after his half century of labor in it, despite the fortune that he had made, and spent, is manifest in a deathbed letter he wrote to one critic. "It has been a long jig, my boy," he said, "and I am just now beginning to see the pathos in it." ❧

BARRYMORE AND BOUCICAULT

In 1875, Maurice Barrymore—father to the clan—was asked to appear in the Boston Theatre's production of *The Shaughraun*, which Dion Boucicault, author and star of the play, was to direct for its first Boston presentation. Barry accepted the offer. It was a chance to work with the celebrated Boucicault, whose play, *London Assurance*, had introduced him to acting. Besides, Barry did not wish to leave the city and friends who had taken him so quickly to heart.

The Boston Theatre company dreaded the arrival of Dion Boucicault. His value as a stage director was unassailable, but he was a fabled martinet. He had a way of completely changing his ideas at each rehearsal, a practice somewhat perplexing to actors, and delighted in confusing actresses to the point of tears. During the first walk-through of *The Shaughraun* on a bare stage, he shrieked at Mrs. Thomas Barry, "Are you going to walk over that table?" The startled actress, the first lady of the Boston stage, stepped aside quickly. "Here, here," Boucicault jabbed, "don't run about like a chicken with its head cut off!" Imaginary or not, a table was a table to Mr. Boucicault.

He was a curious fellow to look upon, this Boucicault, glittering eyes, scrubby mustache, bald dome fringed with hair dyed very black. Cold and bilious, he could also be a seductive conversationalist. Sharp and sarcastic, he was the most prolific playwright of his time. At the age of fifty-three, he had already authored, translated or adapted one hundred and fifty plays. Theater people tended to overlook his social limitations.

"Young man," reprimanded the author, "the business you are performing is worthy of a schoolboy."

"Mr. Boucicault," Barry answered, somewhere between admiration and contempt, "I have written the directions as you gave them to me yesterday and performed them accordingly."

"Ah!" replied Boucicault in his sweetest Dublin brogue, "yesterday, certainly, my boy, I told you to do it that way, but the world is just twenty-four hours older, and we have advanced that much; so do it this way today."

Before rehearsals had finished, animosity turned to interest, finally to friendship. The author and his romantic lead became boon companions. For the rest of the engagement, on most nights they could be found drinking at Atwood's Chop House or wenching in Ann Street.

—*James Kotsilibas-Davis*

Maurice Barrymore as Marquis de Montauran from *The Choirans* (1887).

Dion Boucicault as The Shaughraun, ca. 1875.

THE BARRYMORES: A FAMILY PORTRAIT

"When ten Barrymores (including in-laws) gathered in Ethel's Hollywood garden in 1932," James Kotsilibas-Davis writes, "everything was reduced to a polite purr. Ethel was gracious toward Irene Fenwick Barrymore, Irene gracious toward Dolores Costello Barrymore, and the brothers simply charming to everyone. (Dolores did not discover until her husband Jack's death that he had shared a youthful affair with Irene.) The only temperament evinced at the gathering was the refusal of the children to smile for the camera."

The Barrymore Clan gathers in Hollywood in 1932, just prior to the shooting of Rasputin.

Standing: John Drew Colt, John Barrymore, Samuel Colt.

Seated, left to right: Irene Fenwick Barrymore holding John Blyth Barrymore, Jr., Lionel Barrymore, Ethel Barrymore, Dolores Costello holding Dolores Ethel Mae Barrymore, Ethel Barrymore Colt.

KISS ME AGAIN, VICTOR HERBERT

By Allen Churchill

Dion Boucicault may have been the playwright with the big message, but turn-of-the-century Broadway audiences flocked instead to the comedies and light operas of Boucicault's fellow Dubliner, Victor Herbert. Herbert was born in Ireland on February 1, 1859. His mother, Fanny Lover, was the daughter of the nineteenth-century Irish novelist, Samuel Lover. Herbert came by his sweet waltz sound naturally enough. At the age of twenty-three, he became first cellist in the legendary German orchestra of Johann Strauss. Active in Irish affairs throughout his life, Herbert was the president of the mildly seditious "Sons of Irish Freedom" on March 26, 1924, the day he died.

In the years before 1910 nearly one quarter of the Broadway productions were musicals, an art form in which the Great White Way always excelled. Among them were *The Ham Tree* (McIntyre and Heath, juggler W. C. Fields), *Easy Dawson* (Raymond Hitchcock, John Bunny), *The Earl and the Girl* (Eddie Foy), *The Mayor of Tokio* (Richard Carle), *The Vanderbilt Cup* (Elsie Janis), *The Rich Mr. Hoggenheimer* (Sam Bernard), *A Yankee Tourist* (Raymond Hitchcock, Wallace Beery), *The Dairymaids* (Julia Sanderson), *Miss Innocence* (Anna Held), *The Boys and Betty* (Marie Cahill).

Much of the flavor of musical Broadway was contributed by a genial man born in Ireland. His name was Victor Herbert and from his head came melodies of distilled, light-opera perfection. Victor Herbert had played the cello in the orchestra of the Metropolitan Opera House. His urge to compose first led him to write *The Wizard of the Nile*. Songs from this did not sweep the country, but the show's catchword "Am I a wiz?" did. Later, in *The Fortune Teller*, another Herbert operetta provided another national twister. This was a bit of nonsense verse:

I had a little bird and its name was Enza
I opened the cage and in-flu-enza.

In 1900 Victor Herbert wrote the music for *The Singing Girl*; in 1903, *Babes in Toyland*; in 1904, *It Happened in Nordland*. Then in 1905 he crashed through to success. His show that year was *Mlle. Modiste*, and it was a rousing hit. Starring was Fritzi Scheff, a girl with a grand-opera voice and an operetta spirit. Fritzi wore backless gowns and sang "Kiss Me Again" with such sweet fervor that every stylish woman in America dreamed of changing places with her. On Broadway itself another Victor Herbert song ranked in popularity with "Kiss Me Again." On late nights at Rector's big Wil-

▼
Victor Herbert as the Leader of Gilmore's Band.

"DO WRITE A SONG FOR US MR HERBERT!"

liam Pruette, who sang "I Know What I Want When I Want It" in the show, rose grandly to his feet and rumbled out the song while the supper throng joined in, accenting every "Want" with a bang of fist or glass on the Belfast-linen tablecloths.

When not composing lightsome music, Victor Herbert was a compulsive spender of easily made money, a titanic consumer of pilsener beer, and a fanatical bettor on horses (horseplayer is a word too ordinary for this gifted man). His gay operettas brought him fame and money, yet he disparaged his talents, living out life in the belief that his melodies would not last beyond him. "Don't kid me," he said, when complimented on his work. "I'm a good tunesmith. Six months after I'm dead no one will remember my name." He tormented himself in other ways. He was a man cheerful and seemingly carefree, but he always moved like lightning, as if driven by a frenzy to get things done at top speed. "He was feverishly industrious," recalls the lyri-

cist Harry B. Smith, who collaborated on fourteen operettas with Victor Herbert, "and always seemed to work at high pressure when there was no need for it. He would dash across a room merely to get another piece of paper, across a street simply to get on the other side."

Herbert astonished his friends by an ability to play the piano with full orchestra effects. His heart, despite inner tensions, seemed as big as his body. He particularly hated to hurt anyone. Over the years an actor friend had dedicated himself to the composition of a musical masterpiece called *Grand Mass in F*. Finally, it was done, and Herbert agreed to render an opinion. *Grand Mass in F* proved a succession of wild dissonances about which Herbert could find nothing good to say. Still, he bent down to peer hard at the sheet music. Straightening, he clapped the composer heartily on the shoulder. "By Jove, it is in F," he roared enthusiastically.

THE SWAN OF ERIN

The Hayeses were scamp Irish. There are the careful, thrifty Irish and there are the other kind. We were the other kind. But Mother, even as a child, dreamed of something else. She tried to find it in the rotogravure section of the Sunday pages, where she lapped up every bit of information she could concerning the cream of society. Life was a drawing-room comedy to my mother, and she felt she had been relegated to the kitchen.

It is true that my grandfather was the nephew of Catherine Hayes—the Swan of Erin, as she was known. Catherine was a singer beloved throughout the Emerald Isle, and the toast of London when she appeared at the Albert Hall. She became a great favorite of the forty-niners in California when she toured America, no doubt to find her own gold in the streets. Surely she did achieve celebrity, and I actually have a picture of her on some sheet music which she made popular. The song was "John Anderson My Jo" with words by Bobbie Burns. Mother never quite recovered from the blow when she heard that Catherine had wanted to adopt her nephew at the height of her fame. Mother was sure that her father would thus have become world renowned at something or other, thereby opening the portals of international society to

her. She never quite forgave the family, who wouldn't allow it because the Swan was a renegade and a Protestant, and giving the child over to her would certainly have sealed his eternal doom.

I was still under five years old when Mother found me in our four-legged tub with a towel draped around my head and waving one of those rattan fans with the painted pictures that we used in Washington, D.C., in those hot, pre-airconditioned summers.

"And who do you think you are, Darling?" Mother asked, picking up the Fairy soap.

Now all children love to pretend, and any number of them might have responded as I did. I had seen a painting in a gallery and had asked who the naked lady was, surrounded by so many adoring friends.

"I'm Clee O'Patrick in her bath!" I answered grandly. The significance mother attached to this bit of pretense was wholly disproportionate to the fact. The family was soon informed that a new Bernhardt was in the works, though not quite dry behind the ears.

With Catherine Hayes lurking in my past, and Mother now seeing to my future, my destiny seemed completely assured.

—*Helen Hayes*

THE BLACK IRISHMAN

By Croswell Bowen

The theatre was in his bones: his father was the celebrated James O'Neill, an actor of the old uninhibited school who played the lead in *The Count of Monte Cristo* some six thousand times, and a substantial part of Eugene O'Neill's childhood was spent in theatre wings.

Dramatic conflict was part of his earliest life: his mother, born Ella Quinlan, was a devout Catholic who, Eugene remembers, never approved of her husband's profession but, because she was an old-fashioned wife, followed him wherever he went. In addition, that part of Eugene's boyhood that was spent away from the theatre centered around the waterfront in New London, Connecticut, where he could absorb the romance of the sea and sense the dry rot of provincial New England.

But most important of all was the disposition through which Eugene has always viewed the world. Recently in New London, "Captain" Thomas Francis Dorsey, an intimate friend of James O'Neill and something of a fabulous Irishman himself, was cussing Eugene, whom he had known well as a boy.

"Always the gloomy one." the Captain said, "always the tragedian, always thinkin'. My God, when he looked at you he seemed to be lookin' right through you, right into your soul. He never said much and then spoke softly when he did speak. Brilliant he was, too, always readin' books. We're all Irish around here and knew the type. He was a Black Irishman."

A Black Irishman, the Captain went on to explain, is an Irishman who has lost his Faith and who spends his life searching for the meaning of life, for a philosophy in which he can believe again as fervently as he once believed in the simple answers of the Catholic catechism. A Black Irishman is a brooding, solitary man—and often a drinking man too—with wild words on the tip of his tongue.

American letters are the richer for Black Irishmen. And of the lot of them, and the list includes F. Scott Fitzgerald, James T. Farrell, and John O'Hara, among others, O'Neill is the blackest one of all.

O'Neill himself gives full weight to his Irish heritage. Talking to his son, Eugene, Jr., a bearded professor of Greek, he said not long ago, "One thing that explains more than anything about me is the fact that I'm Irish. And, strangely enough, it is something that all the writers who have attempted to explain me and my work have overlooked."

It is no accident that O'Neill's newest play, *The Iceman Cometh*, certainly the biggest event of this season, is about "pipe dreams" —which may be a Black Irishman's name for Faith. It is no accident that its characters are lost men to whom the world and its ways are an eternally insoluble enigma. It is no accident that Larry Slade, the one character who at the end is left utterly without illusions, is a tired anarchist and an Irishman.

It has been said by a number of reviewers that, when the curtain falls, nothing is left for Larry but to die. One observer has thought of an alternative. "Larry," he said, "could write plays."

During the rehearsals of *The Iceman*, O'Neill sat most of the time next to Eddie Dowling, the director. Dowling tended to have the actors overplay some parts. O'Neill was for more subtle touches.

At one rehearsal a puzzled actress asked, "Was Hickey, the salesman, a good man?"

"Raw emotion," O'Neill said, "produces

With the passing of Boucicault and Herbert, one Irishman alone dominated the American theater during the next decade. "One thing that explains more than anything else about me," Eugene O'Neill told critic Croswell Bowen, "is the fact that I am Irish. And, strangely enough, it is something that all the writers who have attempted to explain me and my work have overlooked." O'Neill was one kind of Irishman, to be sure, certainly not the whole shop. Yet, in the Irish mind he was of the kind who remains the most haunting, the most ancient and the most spooky of all.

73

the best and worst in people. Remember, goodness can surmount anything. The people in that saloon were the best friends I've ever known. Their weakness was not an evil. It is a weakness found in all men.

"Revenge is the subconscious motive for the individual's behavior with the rest of society. Revulsion drives man to tell others of his sins.... It is the furies within us that seek to destroy us. In all my plays sin is punished and redemption takes place.

"Vice and virtue cannot live side by side. It's the humiliation of a loving kiss that destroys evil."

An eager, aggressive young actor stood up and asked O'Neill where he stood on "the movement." Two of the characters in the play are disillusioned radicals.

"I am a philosophical anarchist," O'Neill said, smiling faintly, "which means, 'Go to it, but leave me out of it.'"

O'Neill gives people the impression sometimes when he is talking to them that he is a cross between a Bowery bum and a Victorian gentleman. During a large press interview in September, a girl reporter came in late. "I've heard," the girl said, "that the cast of *The Iceman* consists of fourteen men and four tarts."

"Fourteen men and four—ladies," O'Neill replied.

A reporter asked him what he was going to do on the opening night. "If I weren't in temperance," O'Neill said with a twinkle in his eye, "I'd get stinko."

My longest talk with Eugene O'Neill took place on the darkened stage of the Martin Beck Theatre where *The Iceman* was about to open. Around us were the sets by Robert Edmond Jones, O'Neill's old friend from the Provincetown days. We sat on a bench backstage, for a while, talking about his early life. He seemed old and sick, but I did not agree with *Time* that "his paralysis agitans involved his whole emaciated body in one miserable stammer."

He looked sharply at me as he talked and his face was still a face difficult to put out of your mind. He was well-groomed and expensively and quietly dressed in a double-breasted blue suit, but he gave the impression of a down-and-out man who had been completely outfitted the day before by some well-meaning friend.

He was still handsome. His hair was only slightly graying, a distinguished iron gray. He was thin and slightly bent over. His eyes were deep-set and sad and occasionally he cocked his head as he eyed me. His jaw was lean and and forceful.

After talking awhile, O'Neill got up and walked over to one end of a stage bar. He pulled up a stool, sat at the bar, and motioned for me to join him. He seemed to straighten up and come alive.

"Of course," he said, "America is due for a retribution. There ought to be a page in the history books of the United States of America of all the unprovoked, criminal, unjust crimes committed and sanctioned by our government since the beginning of our history—and before that, too. There is hardly one thing that our government has done that isn't some treachery—against the Indians, against the people of the Northwest, against the small farmers."

As he talked, he seemed in the tradition of all the great half-drunken Irishmen who sound off in bars all over the world. Their talk is always the same, extravagant, rambling, full of madness and violence, but studded with enough essential truth and insight to force you to listen with troubled fascination.

"This American Dream stuff gives me a pain," he went on. "Telling the world about our American Dream! I don't know what they mean. If it exists, as we tell the whole world, why don't we make it work in one small hamlet in the United States?

"If it's the Constitution that they mean, ugh, then it's a lot of words. If we taught history and told the truth, we'd teach school children that the United States has followed the same greedy rut as every other country. We would tell who's guilty. The list of the guilty ones responsible would include some of our great national heroes. Their portraits should be taken out and burned." He fondled a prop whiskey glass and a prop bottle with water and caramel syrup in it.

As his words took on more and more vigor, I got the feeling that O'Neill was, in a sense, the conscience of America asserting itself. I realized that one could say of him even today what his boss on the *New London Telegraph* had said of him in 1912: "He was the most stubborn and irreconcilable social rebel that I had ever met." He wrote about oppressed workers (*The Hairy Ape*) and about the tragedy of color discrimination (*All*

God's Children Got Wings) long before they were fashionable subjects. I got the feeling that O'Neill's social views spring from the very pit of his soul, from a deep abiding love of humanity, from a deeply cherished dream of what the world could be.

"The great battle in American history," he went on, "was the Battle of Little Big Horn. The Indians wiped out the white men, scalped them. That was a victory in American history. It should be featured in all our school books as the greatest victory in American history."

O'Neill brought his fist down on the top of the bar. "The big business leaders in this country! Why do we produce such stupendous, colossal egomaniacs? They go on doing the most monstrous things, always using the excuse that if we don't the other person will. It's impossible to satirize them, if you wanted to."

The actors and stagehands began drifting back onto the stage. Two grips came to move the bar. We moved to the side. The conversation shifted to religion. Had he, I asked, returned to Catholicism, as one biography had implied he might?

A great look of sadness came into O'Neill's eyes. "Unfortunately, no," he said.

"*The Iceman* is a denial of any other experience of faith in my plays. In writing, I felt I had locked myself in with my memories."

When he said that, I thought of another remark he'd made: "Those people in the saloon were the best friends I ever had." ❧

THE FOG PEOPLE

Long Day's Journey Into Night is not only a great play about one family; it is also the great play about the American Irish. The five characters in the play are distinctive individuals and also archetypes of Irish-American character. The father is the immigrant of remarkable talents whose gifts have been marred by the ordeal of immigration; he has borne the terrible psychic strains of inventing himself as a new character in a new society. The mother is the conventional, "lace-curtain" Irishwoman who yearns for the safety and respectability of an ordinary, middle-class existence. The elder son has, in O'Neill's words, "the remnant of a humorous, romantic, irresponsible Irish charm—that of the beguiling ne'er-do-well, with a strain of the sentimentally poetic, attractive to women and popular with men." The younger son is the brooding "dark Irishman." Cathleen, the maid, appears as the ignorant greenhorn recently arrived from Ireland, while offstage, Bridget, the cook, grumbles about the work and boasts about her relatives.

In *The Iceman Cometh* and *Long Day's Journey Into Night*, O'Neill returned to subjects he knew intimately, and treated them in a straightforward, realistic manner. He abandoned the masks, the soliloquies, and the long asides with which he had experimented in the 1920s. He made no use of flashbacks or any other juggling with the time sequence. There was no striving for mythic overtones from Greek tragedy. His only technical device was the use in *Long Day's Journey* of the repeated boom of the foghorn, a device reminiscent of those which he used in two of his early great plays, the steamer whistles in *Anna Christie* and the jungle drum in *The Emperor Jones*. For all else, he depended solely upon his conception of his characters and their use of language.

He beautifully summed up the style of these final plays in a speech of Edmund in *Long Day's Journey*. Congratulated by his father for having "the makings of a poet," Edmund says: "The makings of a poet. No, I'm afraid I'm like the guy who is always panhandling for a smoke. He hasn't even got the makings. He's only got the habit. I couldn't touch what I tried to tell you just now. I just stammered. That's the best I'll ever do. I mean if I live. Well, it will be faithful realism, at least. Stammering is the native eloquence of us fog people."

—*William V. Shannon*

The original 1956 cast of *Long Day's Journey Into Night*— Florence Eldridge and Fredric March (seated), with Bradford Dillman and Jason Robards, Jr.

The City Desk

▶

*Pat O'Brien and Adolphe
Menjou stop the presses in the
1931 Howard Hughes
production of*
The Front Page.

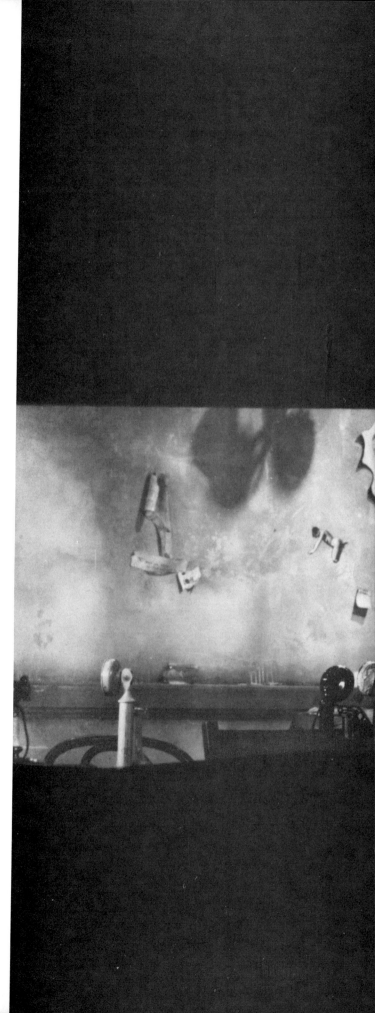

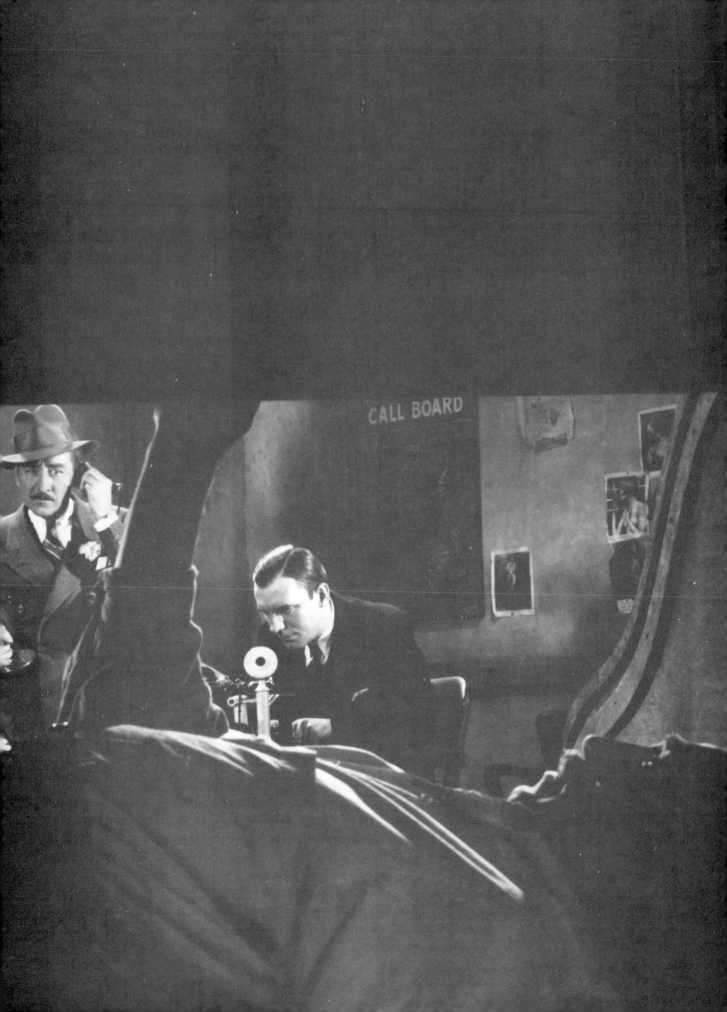

MR. DOOLEY

By Franklin P. Adams

Finley Peter Dunne was an artist. I use the word jealously. He revered the art of saying things perfectly; he hated slovenliness of thought and expression. That, perhaps, is why he had so acute an appreciation of Ring Lardner, an artist comparable to Dunne. And both were cursed, or blessed, with such lofty ideals of writing that almost never were they satisfied with their product; yet I know of no prose writers who could boast—though neither ever did—of so negligible a percentage of second-rateness.

The Dooley articles began in Chicago in 1893. That was the Chicago of the World's Fair; and Dunne was a newspaperman twenty-six years of age, already a veteran reporter of eight years' standing. He became a reporter for the *Tribune*; then he went to the *Evening Post*, where the first "Mr. Dooley" piece appeared in August 1893; in 1897 he became editor of the *Journal*, wherein the "Dooley" pieces were printed until 1900, when he decided to come east.

And still for four or five years "Mr. Dooley" continued to appear weekly, syndicated in the newspapers by R. H. Russell. *Collier's Weekly* then published him with illustrations by C. D. Gibson. I met Dunne in the fall of 1907, when he, as one of the editors of the *American Magazine*, was writing a monthly department, "In the Interpreter's House." It was an editorial article on current matters. It was not written in dialect. Though like most writers he hated work of any kind, the medium of plain English was a relief to him after years of the dialect grind.

It may be that the interest in Irish dialect had waned. For in the 1890s of "Mr. Dooley's" wide popularity, the country was full of first- and second-generation Irish; the fathers of the boys I played with, John Finerty, Harry McCormick and John Tait, were born in Ireland. And the stage was full of Irishmen; every vaudeville house had one or two Irish acts on its bill; the Russell brothers, John W. Kelly, Bobby Gaylor, Johnny Ray, Ferguson and Mack, Maggie Cline and Johnny Carroll; there were still echoes of Harrigan and Hart, and the tenor voices of Chauncey Olcott and Andrew Mack, in Irish plays written for them, were heard in the land. Every burlesque show had its Irish comedian.

About the time the "Dooley" sketches first appeared in the *Evening Post*, the *Chicago Record* printed a daily column called "Stories of the Streets and of the Town." This was the work of George Ade, and in that column he wrote his first "Fable in Slang." Let Mr. Ade remember Dunne:

When I arrived in Chicago in 1890, Peter Dunne, although still quite young, was a star reporter on the *Herald*. Even his newspaper stories showed a careful and precise use of words, and his witticisms were crystal clear and models of brevity. When I first met him I was properly awed, because he gave the impression of being informed, wise, vested with authority, superior, cynical and controversial. Early in the nineties the Whitechapel Club was organized, which is still remembered as a collection of harum-scarum irresponsibilities who scorned the conventions and shared an abiding enthusiasm for alcoholic liquors. It was more than that. It was really a roundup of interesting intellectuals whose opinions and doctrinal beliefs were

By the age of Martin Dooley, the Irish had already been active in American journalism for more than forty years. The first nationally popular Irish-American columnist was Private Miles O'Reilly, who commented on the course of the Civil War in the pages of the old New York Herald. *Like Finley Peter Dunne's "Mr. Dooley," Private Miles O'Reilly was also a fiction created by Charles Graham Halpine, an Irish-born, Trinity College graduate. Halpine was in fact a brigadier-general in the 69th Regiment and later became a successful anti-Tammany Hall reform politician. In those days, to be Irish and successful in America, it was always a good idea to show up in public wearing a mask.*

F Opper

far in advance of the Chicago environment of that time, although they have since come into favor and received governmental endorsement. Not all of what they stood for will ever be approved by popular vote, because they were irreligious and probably might have been classified as agnostics. They had such scathing contempt for the self-seeking political bosses and the stuffed shirts of the millionaire aristocracy of their own town, and such a hatred for the tyranny of wealth, that they probably might have been socialists, with a leaning toward outright anarchy. Certainly they believed that many of the so-called anarchists, convicted for encouraging the Haymarket massacre, had been framed by the courts and prosecutors who had been urged to extreme severity by the panicky millionaires. Many of them had been behind the scenes and their radical opinions were fortified by the unpublished stories which they knew so well but never had been permitted to write.

The "Dooley" sketches were caustic and witty editorials written in the Irish dialect. I don't think Pete ever took them very seriously or agreed with the public that they were more deserving of attention than his chaste and correct editorials done in dignified English. He was like me in that popularity was thrust upon him, and he was marked for all time as a specialist in the production of a certain freak sort of "humor." I am sure that none of us ever regarded his output as "humor," but merely truth concealed in sugar-coated idiom and dialect. Pete was a positive character with a most engaging personality. He had a smile that was positively radiant. He was a remarkable person, with a vast understanding and an x-ray intelligence, and our friendship will always be one of my prized memories.

The expression of that social consciousness, as articulated in the "Dooley" sketches, would never have been printed unless they had been written in dialect. For editors, fearful of calling names, feel that the advertisers and the politicians and the social leaders—money, politics and social ambition being the Achilles' heels of editors and publishers—are journalism's sacred cows. But if pretense and hypocrisy are attacked by the office clown, especially in dialect, the crooks and the shammers think that it is All in Fun. And when the Dunnes and the Lardners die, the papers print editorials saying that there was no malice in their writing and no bitterness in their humor. Few popular writers ever wrote more maliciously and bitterly than Lardner and Dunne. They resented injustice, they loathed sham and they hated the selfish stupidity that went with them. 🍂

▲
Portrait of Finley Peter Dunne.

MR. DOOLEY GOES TO THE OLYMPICS

I wint out to give a few raw rahs fr me fellow colleejens, who was attimptin' to dimonsthrate their supeeryority over th' effete scholars iv England at what I see be th' pa-pers is called th' Olympian games. Ye get to th' Olympian games be suffocation in a tunnel. Whin ye come to, ye pay four shillin's or a dollar in our degraded currency, an' stand in th' sun an' look at th' Prince iv Wales. Th' Prince iv Wales looks at ye, too, but he don't see ye.

Me frind, th' American ambassadure was there, an' manny iv th' seats iv larnin' in th' gran' stand was occupied be th' flower iv our thought conservatories. I r-read it in th' pa-apers. At th' time I come in they was recitin' a pome fr'm th' Greek, to a thoughtful-lookin' young profissor, "all together." "Rickety, co-ex, co-ex, hullabaloo, bozoo, bozoo, Harvard," says th' lads. I was that proud iv me belovid counthry that I wanted to take off me hat there an' thin an' give th' colledge yell iv th' Ar-rchey road reform school.

I was resthrained be a frind iv mine that I met comin' over. He was fr'm Matsachoosetts, an' says he: "Don't make a disturbance," he says. "We've got to create a fav'rable impression here," he says. "Th' English," he says, "niver shows enthusyasm. 'Tis regarded as unpolite." "Let us show thim," he says, "that we're gintlemen, be it iver so painful."

I resthrained mesilf be puttin' me fist in me mouth.

They was an Englishman standin' behind me, Hinnissy, an' he was a model iv behaviour. Ye cudden't get this la-ad war-rmed up if ye built a fire undher him. He had an eye-glass pinned to his face an' he niver even smiled whin a young gintleman fr'm Harvard threw a sledge hammer wan mile, two inches. A fine la-ad, that Harvard man, but if throwin' th' hammer's spoort, thin th' rowlin' mills is th' athletic cintre iv our belovid counthry.

—*Finley Peter Dunne*

THE AMAZING NELLIE BLY

By Ishbel Ross

Journalism provided one of the few career opportunities open to Irish-American women at the turn of the century. Nellie Bly (Elizabeth Cochrane) was a true pioneer in this field, though she was hardly alone in taking full advantage of the opportunities awaiting any Paddy's daughter with a gift for language and the stamina required to work a good, solid eighteen-hour day. In time the role of Irish-American women journalists became so substantial as to inspire one interesting comic strip, "Dixie Dugan," one Academy Award-winning movie, Kitty Foyle, *and eventually one Emmy Award-winning television series, "The Mary Tyler Moore Show." It is a vital tradition—today more relevant than ever.*

It was Nellie Bly who first made America conscious of the woman reporter. She burst like a comet on New York, a dynamic figure, five feet three, with mournful gray eyes and persistent manners. She dramatized herself in a new form of journalism, going down in a diving bell and up in a balloon, posing as a lunatic, a beggar, a factory hand, a shop girl and a Salvation Army lass.

But Nellie's great coup, which neither she nor any other newspaper woman equaled again, was her trip around the world in 72 days, 6 hours, 11 minutes, outdoing the dream of Jules Verne's Phileas Fogg and creating no end of an international stir.

She sailed from New York on November 14, 1889, and came home in triumph on January 25, 1890, the *World* bringing her across the country from San Francisco by special train and greeting her with the smash headline leading the paper, "Father Time Outdone!"

With two small satchels, two frocks, a toothbrush, some flannel underwear, a bank book, a ghillie cap and sturdy plaid ulster, Nellie galloped and ran, roasted and froze, sped from ship to train, to burro, to rickshaw, to sampan, to barouche, until she reached the terrific climax of outdoing Father Time for Joseph Pulitzer. It was exhilarating journalism, good for the *World*, superb for Nellie, entertaining for the public, and it did no one any harm.

One had only to follow her career from its beginnings in Cochrane Mills, Pennsylvania, to know that Nellie was destined for front-page notice. She was born on May 5, 1867, in the small town founded by her father, who was a judge. Her name was Elizabeth Cochrane. She had enterprising blood in her veins. Her grand-uncle, Thomas Kennedy, went around the world before she was born but it took him three years and he came back with wrecked health

Nellie started her newspaper

▼
America's first leading woman journalist, Nellie Bly.

83

career with an original idea. She went through factories and workshops in Pittsburgh, her crusading spirit already in full flower. Her articles spat their indignation. They all had personal quality which gave her a steady and constant following in later years. At first she made $5 a week. Eventually she was to make $25,000 from her writings in a single year.

Everything by Nellie was written in the first person. Her style had many airs and graces, comments and interpolations. Yet it was clear, readable and somewhat cunningly devised, although the sentiment often seemed forced and her desire to right the wrongs of the world was overpowering. She thought up nearly all of her own stories, although her paper backed the crusades.

What Nellie's own opinions were no one ever knew, for she had stock sentiments which she trotted out to suit any occasion. She was strongly moralistic. Her stories evoked much money for charity, particularly her ten-column account in 1893 of the work of the Salvation Army after she had dressed as a Salvation Army lass and worked at the Front Street headquarters.

She interviewed murderers, passed a night in a haunted house hoping to meet a ghost and described her own sensations in great detail. She wrote a biting piece about society women whom she discovered in poolrooms betting on the races. She exposed a famous woman mind reader and described the misery of starving tenement dwellers. Little went on in the social order, in fact, that did not call for one of Nellie's smug sermons. The evildoer had reason to draw the blinds when she was about. This was all good for the *World*, which was then riding high as an instrument of reform.

On January 28, 1922, the *World* ran a half column on an inside page announcing the death of Nellie Bly, the most successful star the paper ever had. She had died of pneumonia on the previous day in St. Mark's Hospital at the age of fifty-six. Funeral Services were held for her at The Little Church Around the Corner.

&.

HER FATHER'S DAUGHTER: THE DOROTHY KILGALLEN STORY

It was all in the carriage. From her prim and protected College of New Rochelle schoolgirl days to the age of her great celebrityhood as a regular panelist on the popular television show, "What's My Line," Dorothy Mae Kilgallen played the role of ultimate Ms. Goody Two Shoes to the adoration of millions of upwardly mobile Irish Catholic families throughout this country. She was every father's favorite elder daughter and every Irish Catholic mother's best image of herself; and she used this image—indeed she may have invented it in the first place—as a tool to help her disarm many an unsuspecting elder judge, and many a hard-boiled courtroom attorney, on her road to becoming one of the most powerful crime reporters in the history of American journalism.

Dorothy Mae first went to work for William Randolph Hearst's *New York Evening Journal* on her college break in the summer of 1931. Perhaps as a joke at first, always somewhat prissy Ms. Kilgallen was assigned to the crime desk of this increasingly scandal-oriented, famous New York newspaper. Dorothy among the Dope Fiends. Dorothy among the Ax Murderers. Kilgallen thrived on it. When autumn arrived, she was hooked. She abandoned college for the life of a high-crime beat reporter.

Her crime prose was immaculate— as neat and precise as her dress code, it sometimes seemed—and she was able to serve up this prose by the yard. She once wrote, and the *Journal* published, more than 250,000 words—the equivalent of about five average-sized novels—during the course of a five-week murder trial.

In 1935, in her best "daddy's-favorite-daughter" style, she managed to charm her way up to Bruno Hauptman's defense attorney and land an exclusive interview with the suspected killer of the Lindbergh baby. In so doing, less than four years after she had been hired as a summer college intern, Kilgallen had managed to scoop Damon Runyon, Arthur Brisbane, and her own father, Jim Kilgallen.

Kilgallen became huge. In later years she took the inside track on the famous Dr. Sam Shepherd murder case and always maintained the good doctor's innocence. When Shepherd was found guilty, the banner headline on that evening's paper was not "SHEPHERD FOUND GUILTY" but rather "DOROTHY KILGALLEN SHOCKED." She had reached that rare and most dangerous pinnacle in American journalism: she had become bigger than most of the stories she was assigned to cover.

Kilgallen was given her own column, called "Voice of Broadway," in the grand Hearst/Runyon/Winchell tradition. She used that column to vent her well-heeled scoops and tips and also to express her increasingly shrill anti-Communist point of view. When she wrote that most unemployed domestic workers in New York City possessed a more attractive personal wardrobe than did the visiting Mrs. Nikita Krushchev, she almost instantly regretted it. A well-turned wardrobe had always been one of her better subjects, but a remark like that was out of character for a good Catholic girl. She apologized.

On the evening of November 8, 1960, Dorothy Mae completed her weekly "What's My Line" panel show, successfully detecting that the occupation of one woman guest was that of dynamite-maker, and returned to her home to write and file her regular Monday *Journal-American* column.

During the night she died in her sleep. Suicide was suspected, but almost immediately ruled out. Dorothy Mae had simply expired. In her passing, as in life, Kilgallen could be counted on not to make that much of a fuss.

—*Bob Callahan*

He: Och! 'Tis betther to be born lucky nor rich, anyhow!

She: Oh, ho! An' do ye think ye wor born lucky?

He: Well, ain't I lucky not to be worryin' becase I wasn't born ayther way?

His Argument (1900) *by Rose O'Neill*
A gifted illustrator, novelist, sculptor and poet, Rose O'Neill drew heavily on her urban Irish background for the superb cartoons she drew for *Puck* magazine at the turn of the century.

THE YELLOW KID AND HIS NEW PHONOGRAPH.

MICKEY DUGAN, THE YELLOW KID

Between 1895 and 1898, Mickey Dugan took the city of New York by storm. Initially drawn by Richard Felton Outcault as a background figure in a weekly *New York World* color comic feature called "Hogan's Alley" —a raucous, grungy newsprint gander at Manhattan slum kids in comic pratfalls—the Dugan named Mickey caught the public eye, fired up some comment around town and led Outcault to pull him forward, nightshirt, bare feet, bald head and all, to the center of the Sunday panel. Mickey began to make spicy comments on regular "Hogan's Alley" activities across the front of his nightshirt which, after having been shown as green, red and blue, became a permanent bright yellow, leading his growing public to call him "The Yellow Kid." His audacious, cocky posture and remarks—not only was the Kid to survive the slums, but he was going to revel in them—amazed and delighted huge segments of the New York newspaper public. The *World's* sales soared, and the Kid's likeness was seen everywhere—on gum, cigars, penny arcade machines, books, magazines and the Broadway stage, and even in the experimental nickelodeons of the day. He was America's first great Sunday color comic hit.

Accidentally (and in keeping with the Kid's off-the-wall, thumb-to-nose attitude and behavior), Outcault's feature also became the world's first definitive comic strip shortly after the Kid's transfer, at a hefty increase in pay, to the *World's* great rival, William Randolph Hearst's *New York Journal*. In one of "The Yellow Kid" episodes drawn for the *Journal* of October 25, 1896, Outcault made dialogue balloons a crucial part of the narrative point, the first time they had ever been used in a cartoon feature with a recurrent character. Previously, printed captions had been used for explicatory purposes. Although it provoked no immediate follow-up, this vital episode planted a seed that was to blossom everywhere come the turn of the century.

—*Bill Blackbeard*

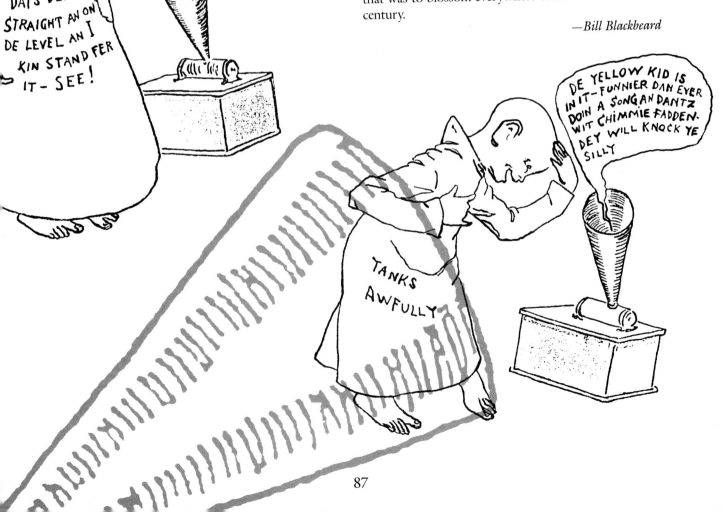

Catherine McGurk, Bat Masterson's mother, was born in the north of Ireland of good solid, frontier Presbyterian stock. So was S.S. McClure. John Sloan could trace his own heritage back to similiar Scots-Irish roots. In journalism, as in most other areas of the American cultural experience, the working-class Irish Protestant was swept into the same land of limited opportunities awaiting all Irish people of little, or no, property. Orange shoulders, or green, the shovel weighed just about the same. Success in the New World awaited Paddy, provided he or she could dance, carry a rifle, tell funny jokes, sweep floors or learn how to write or sing. Save for those privileged by birth, the dollar sign on the outer door equalled out just about everything.

THE BAT MAN

By Robert K. DeArment

Bat Masterson was no ordinary newspaperman. He came to journalism with extraordinary credentials—Bat was a former gunfighter, buffalo hunter, and frontier lawman, who had been Wyatt Earp's colleague-in-peacekeeping around Dodge City. Later, when he went into eastern newspapering, it was with a publication whose character was as unique as Bat's own background. This was the *New York Morning Telegraph.* Heywood Broun, who preceded Masterson at the *Telegraph* just after the turn of the century, recalled the paper in terms that explain why Bat would have felt at home there:

I doubt whether any newspaper in New York ever had quite the intimate atmosphere of the old *Telegraph.* It was like a tough *Emporia Gazette.* The city room was always cluttered up with people who didn't seem to have any business there. Very often you couldn't get to your desk because there would be a couple of chorus girls sitting there waiting for a friend who was finishing up an editorial. Everybody wrote editorials. They were not regarded as very important because the *Telegraph* had no policy about anything except that it was against reformers.

Bat moved into the newsroom of the *Telegraph* as if it had been his home throughout his life. By 1907, he had been made a staff writer and was turning out a lengthy column three times a week. The column, appearing in Tuesday, Thursday, and Sunday editions and later headed "Masterson's Views on Timely Topics," dealt chiefly with pugilistic activities, a subject with which Bat had remained in close contact. Frequently, Bat interlarded his ring news with personal observations on the state of the world as he reviewed it, and these typically outspoken asides provide our clearest picture of the crusty old frontiersman's philosophy in his later years.

As a longtime professional gambler who had his ups and downs, Bat spoke from experience when he referred to life as a great gamble:

A good sport is a good loser and takes his medicine when … the "kirds" are against him. This applies as well to one line of human endeavor as to another. Pretty much everything we do is more or less of a gamble.

Bat made enemies in New York, as he had in Dodge City and Denver, but he made a horde of friends as well. His favorite eating was Shanley's Grill, a popular steak house at Broadway and Forty-third Street. There he could be found almost every evening, hunched over a thick, sizzling steak, surrounded by a crowd of admirers who never tired of hearing his tales of the Old West. Later, Bat would usually adjourn to the Metropole Bar, run by the sons of John Considine, a former gambler from Seattle. This establishment, at Broadway and Forty-second, long was a favorite hangout of the sports, theatrical and gambling gentry. Among the habitués of the Metropole was Irvin S. Cobb, then a rewrite man for the *Morning World.* Cobb recalled how imperfectly Bat's appearance fitted the stereotyped picture of a western lawman:

Mr. Masterson was sawed-off and stumpy legged, with a snub nose and a tedious sniffle; wore a flat-topped derby … and in doubtful weather he carried an umbrella. He was addicted to seltzer lemonades and tongue sandwiches; and in general more nearly approximated the conception of a steam-fitter's helper on a holiday … than the authentic person who'd helped to clean up Dodge City and Abilene with a Colt forty-five for his broom. Two things betokened the real man: his eyes. They were like smoothed ovals of gray schist with flecks of mica suddenly glittering in them if he were roused. But you might not notice the glint in those eyes unless you looked closely—it came and instantly was gone. And some of the men who faced him through the smoke fogs of cow-town melees hadn't lived long enough to get a good look.

Among Bat's intimates were Tom O'Rourke, who had moved in the same boxing circles with Masterson since the days of John L. Sullivan; William Muldoon, another crony who traced his friendship with Bat back to bare-knuckles days and who was later boxing commissioner of New York; Tex Rickard, the greatest fight promoter of all time; Alfred

Henry and William E. Lewis; Val O' Farrell, ace sleuth of the New York police force, who in later years managed one of the nation's largest private-detective agencies; and a young reporter named Damon Runyon.

A decade later, when Runyon was achieving national fame with his humorous short stories of Broadway characters, he published a tale called "The Idyll of Miss Sarah Brown." The central character was a gun-toting, high-rolling gambler from Colorado named Sky Masterson. The story was the nucleus of a hugely successful Broadway musical and motion picture, *Guys and Dolls*, a generation later. Sky Masterson had been patterned after the real-life Bat Masterson, whom Runyon had heard spin yarns of gun-toting, high-rolling Colorado gamblers in a corner of Shanley's Grill.

On Tuesday, October 25, 1921, Bat Masterson sat at his desk, writing the column that would appear in the *Telegraph* the following Thursday. He had contracted a severe cold the previous week and had stayed home from his office. Now he was catching up on his report of local fistic affairs. He wrote with pen and ink, rapidly, stabbing out the words as thoughts crossed his mind. As usual, his reportorial items were flavored with pointed personal opinions:

Lew Tendler received little more than $12,000 for his scrap with Rocky Kansas at the Garden a week ago. Not so bad for a job like that.... No wonder these birds are flying high when they get that kind of money for an hour's work. Just think of an honest, hard-working farmer laboring from daylight to dark for forty years of his life, and lucky if he finishes with as much as one of these birds gets in an hour. Yet there are those who argue that everything breaks even in this old dump of a world of ours.

I suppose these ginks who argue that way hold that because the rich man gets ice in the summer and the poor man gets it in the winter things are breaking even for both. Maybe so, but I'll swear I can't see it that way....

A member of the newspaper's staff, concerned about the old man's cold, looked in at the door and asked how he was feeling. "All right," Bat said, scratching away at the paper.

Those were the last words he ever spoke. When an assistant came into the office several minutes later, Bat Masterson was no longer breathing. The heart of the sixty-seven-year-old fighting man, who'd survived a charge of 500 attacking Indians at the Battle of Adobe Walls, had simply stopped breathing. ❧

◀

Wild West gunfighter and New York journalist, Bat Masterson.

Sam McClure Invents Muckraking

The origin of what was later called the "muckraking" movement was accidental. It came from no formulated plan to attack existing institutions, but was the result of merely taking up in the pages of my magazine some of the problems that were beginning to interest the American people.

When I began to feel the necessity to handle economic questions, I soon realized that most of our journalists were unaccustomed to going into a question very thoroughly, and the trained students of the subject either could not write clearly or were warped by some special prejudice and devoted to some particular aspect of the subject. I decided, therefore, to pay my writers for their study rather than for the amount of copy they turned out—to put the writer on such a salary as would relieve him of all financial worry and let him master a subject to such a degree that he could write upon it, if not with the full authority of a specialist, at least with such

S.S. McClure as photographed by Arnold Genthe.

accuracy as could inform the public and meet with the corroboration of the experts.

The articles produced under this new system were generally called "McClure articles," and they were from the first recognized as authoritative. The preparation of the fifteen articles which made the Standard Oil series took Miss Tarbell five years. The articles were produced at the rate of about three a year and cost the magazine four thousand dollars each. Mr. Lincoln Steffens averaged about four articles a year, and each article cost us about two thousand dollars.

It so happened that the January 1903 number of *McClure's*, which contained the third article of Miss Tarbell's Standard Oil series, also contained Mr. Steffens' Minneapolis article and Mr. Ray Stannard Baker's article on the anthracite coal strike of 1902. It is generally conceded that the "muckraking" movement in American journalism began with that issue of my magazine.

—*S.S. McClure with Willa Cather*

Reading in the Subway (1926) *by John Sloan*
Pigeonholed as an "Irish humor illustrator" by a number of turn-of-the-century magazines, John Sloan had a true gift for immigrant street life which began to emerge in his work as early as 1905.

STREET TALK

By Neil A. Grauer

Jimmy Breslin is in the grand tradition of Finley Peter Dunne—though, in Breslin's case, you sometimes get the sense that a character like Martin Dooley could in fact be one of Breslin's long-lost Queensborough cousins.

On the surface at least, William Buckley seems to be a whole other story: an Irishman grown more Anglo than even the English themselves. Do not let appearances fool you. Both Jimmy Breslin and William F. Buckley are fictions created by their real-life authors in an attempt to outfox their critics in a world where Irish Catholics still tend to wear masks no matter if the coast really is clear at last. For a more accurate picture of Irish political journalism, you are probably better off reading "Pogo," the immortal comic strip which was finally translated into Gaelic just last year.

Jimmy Breslin enjoys telling interviewers that he is "an unlettered bum" who has read few books and took five years to get through high school without ever obtaining a diploma. Despite this small gap in Breslin's secondary education, a friendly basketball coach somehow got him admitted as a student at Long Island University, since the *Long Island Press*, the first newspaper he worked for, "only wanted college guys."

"So I went there and took a few courses [and] now the Long Island University claims I graduated from there!" Breslin exclaims, rolling his brown eyes upward and chuckling. "I mean, you could look it up—I didn't take but four courses. They want to list me as an a-lum-nus, whatever you call it. They want my name on letterheads, I mean, it's a gag.... I don't know what I took."

Perhaps. Breslin's old friends James G. Bellows and Richard C. Wald once wrote that facts about his education "are hazy because he lies so much about it," and he himself has written that "reminiscences are to be enjoyed, not authenticated." If he were as uneducated, uncultured, and illiterate as he claims, it would have required the kind of miracle nuns used to tell him about in elementary school for him to have written from London on the day Winston Churchill died:

The rest of London was quiet and empty in the wet Sunday morning. Lord Nelson stood on his spire, high over the black lions and water fountains of Trafalgar Square. The Duke of Wellington glared down at the taxicabs and delivery wagons moving around his plaza. Queen Victoria sat grandly on her throne, surrounded by angels, her back turned on Buckingham Palace. The water dripped from Gladstone, who was stationed by Saint Clement Danes Church. And at 8:05 A.M., on January 24, 1965, in the rear first-floor bedroom of No. 28 Hyde Park Gate, the old man in the green bed jacket died with the curtains drawn and a lamp turned on and he became England's last great statue.

Sir Winston Spencer Churchill, who saved his nation, saved, perhaps, the entire English-speaking world, stepped into history with its scrolls and statues, and he will be the last who ever will do it as he did because the world never again can survive the things that had to be done in the years he lived.

He died wordlessly. He was a man who put deep brass and powerful strings into words, and then built them up to a drumroll to reach out and grab people and shake them by the shoulders and in their hearts. But he had not uttered a word for ten days when he lay dying in a coma, while his heart throbbed and struggled to throw it off....

Such is not Breslin's usual subject matter, and his style more often is considerably less lyrical. His regular beat is New York, a city he still loves passionately despite the growing decay, inequities, and racism he finds there; and increasingly the people he writes about are the homeless, the unemployed, or the troubled, not the colorful, famous, or powerful.

In recent years, Breslin has been referred to disparagingly as "Runyon on welfare." If what Breslin wrote was often described as "Runyonesque," then there must have been a writer named Runyon who did some of the things that Breslin later emulated. (When asked if he ever read Runyon when he was a kid, Breslin replies with a wonderful non sequitur: "No, and he was terrible, too, by the way. He got away with murder.")

There was, of course, a Runyon—a "snap-brim merchant of marzipan and machismo," as Heywood Hale Broun once described him. He is best remembered for his Broadway stories, peopled with characters who are the direct ancestors of the "friends" who appeared three decades later in Breslin's columns and early books. Runyon knew, or contrived, the likes of Nicely-Nicely Jones, Dave the Dude, Sam the Gonoph, Harry the Horse, and Big Jule. Breslin has known the likes of Jerry the Booster, Klein the Lawyer, Bad Eddie, and others. Breslin, minus the snap-brim, may have written

about a low-life behemoth such as Fat Thomas, a 350-pound bartender-bookmaker, or Big Jelly Catalano, an inept Mafia hit man, but Runyon was there first with a fellow named Earthquake:

Earthquake is a guy of maybe six foot three, and weighing a matter of two hundred and twenty pounds, and all these pounds are nothing but muscle....

When he is in real good humor, Earthquake does not think anything of going into a nightclub and taking it apart and chucking the pieces out into the streets, along with the owner and the waiters and maybe some of the customers, so you can see Earthquake is a very high-spirited guy and full of fun.

Big Jelly, a character from *The Gang Who Couldn't Shoot Straight*, was just as tall as Earthquake, weighed a lot more, and benefited from an easing of the rules of what was suitable in print:

Big Jelly ... is 425 pounds slabbed onto a 6-foot-3 frame and topped by a huge owl's face with a mane of black hair. He looks at the world through milk-bottle eyeglasses. What he thinks the world should be has made him, at thirty-two, a legend in South Brooklyn. In grammar schools, with 280 pounds of him lopping over both sides of his seat and blocking the aisles, he spent his years with his hands covering his mouth while he whispered to the girls:
"Sodomy!"
"Period!"
"Come!"
Since that time he has done so many bad things that Judge Bernard Dubin, Part 2B, Brooklyn Criminal Court, one day was moved to observe, "If this man ever could fit on a horse, he would have been a tremendous help to Jesse James."

When Breslin began his column, there was a spirited debate over whether the stock characters he used were real persons or fictional composites. The same questions could have been raised, but weren't, about many of Runyon's figures. A Runyon biographer, John Mosedale, provided some insight into how Runyon worked by describing a tour of New York he gave a young friend. While on the tour, Runyon introduced the new arrival to a seedy character he called Dr. DeGarmo. "'I have deposited Dr. DeGarmo right here,' he said. And he tapped his brow with a well-manicured finger. 'Locked up tight, right here. Money in the bank. The Runyon Savings and No-Loan Bank.'" Breslin undoubtedly has opened up his own branches of a similar depository. ❧

THE JOURNALIST AND THE PRESIDENT

The legendary William F. Buckley, Jr., writes—and speaks—in a prose so rococo you can almost see grottoes forming inside it. Buckley is the principal spokesperson for the "Anglo-Irish" American Irish tradition. Although by inclination he is strictly a Tory, Buckley's sense of showmanship, his extraordinary gift for neo-academic blarney and his maddening contentiousness nonetheless set him apart from the various English traditions, manners and masters he so dearly loves to emulate.

From the time of the publication of *God and Man at Yale* to the heyday of the *National Review,* to his pioneering television opinion show, "Firing Line," Buckley has created an intellectual agenda for the New Right which has had profound consequences in contemporary American life.

When a declining Hollywood actor—with a warm and attractive personality and a real gift for the modern arts of telecommunication —came along with a similiar conservative bent for politics, Buckley threw all his weight behind the popular General Electric spokesman and conservative banquet speaker, Ronald Reagan, providing the future candidate with a detailed ideological checklist in his successful drive for, first, the governor's mansion in California, and then the White House.

On more than a handful of important political issues, Buckley still serves as the intellectual power broker behind Ronald Reagan's Teflon throne.

"Reagan has been doing disconcertingly well in his campaign for governor of California," Buckley wrote in 1965, "to the distress of those who would dearly like to see him foam at the mouth and come out for the repeal of the internal combustion engine."

Ronald Reagan, of course, would never be caught foaming at the mouth; more, his sense of repeal would be directed almost entirely toward social justice government programming. Buckley did not invent Ronald Reagan, of course. Jack Warner and three thousand years of Irish history helped to do that. Yet, in the long and illicit history between the press and the politicians, no relationship remains more curious than that which came to pass between this particular Irish-American showman and journalist and this particular Irish-American politician and actor.

—*Bob Callahan*

Yay! Team! (1948) *by Walt Kelly*
A "funny animal" cartoonist since 1935, Walt Kelly "broke form" somewhat to draw a series of sharply rendered political cartoons in 1948-1949 for the short-lived *New York Star.*

The Wild West Show

▶

*John Wayne, Claire Trevor,
Andy Devine, John
Carradine and fellow riders
are whisked across the
Monument Valley desert floor
in the 1939 United Artists
production of John Ford's*
Stagecoach.

STERMER

JESSE & FRANK JAMES

JUDGEMENT FOR JESSE

BEING AN ANONYMOUS
REPORT FILED TO THE
ST. JOSEPH WESTERN NEWS,
APRIL 3, 1882

SHOCKING DETAILS
REVEALED AT DEATH HOUSE
AT LAFAYETTE AND
THIRTEENTH STREETS

"WE ARE ALL GRIT,"
MURDERER SAYS

When we approached the door leading into the front room, our eyes beheld a man lying on the floor, cold in death with the blood still oozing from his wound. From the few who had gathered around the door more out of curiosity than anything else, we inquired what was the cause of the shooting. None of them knew but said we could find out from the man's wife who was in the rear room.

Walking into the room and around the dead man's body, we opened the door leading into a kitchen where we found a woman with two small children, a boy and a girl.

When she discovered us with notebooks in hand, she began to scream and said: "Please do not put us into the paper!"

At first she refused to say anything about the shooting but after a time she said "the boys" who had killed her husband had been living with them for some time and their name was Johnson. Charles, she said, was a nephew, but she had never seen the other, Robert, until he came to the house with her husband a few weeks ago. When asked what her husband's name was, she said it was Howard.

"Where was your home before coming here, Mrs. Howard?"

"We came from Baltimore and intended to rent a farm and move to the country but so far we have been unsuccessful."

"Had your husband and the Johnson boys had any difficulty before?"

"Never. They have always been on friendly terms."

"Why did they do this deed?"

It could be called the Antrim predilection. "As the class to which William and Henry James sank from importance in the United States through lack of courage," the great Thomas Beer has written, "there was a slight but sure alteration toward the religious standards of the other James brothers, Jesse and Frank, who intermittently attended church in Missouri between spells of brigandage and were judged good Christians by their neighbors." Jesse and Frank's father was, in fact, a Protestant minister. The boys' mother, a Cole, was a Catholic whose distant roots could also be traced back to Ireland.

▶ **An early depiction of the murder of Jesse James.**

"That is more than I can tell. Oh, the rascals!"

At this point she began to cry and begged God to protect her.

"Where were you when the shooting was done?"

"I had been in the kitchen and Charles had been helping me all morning. He entered the front room and about three minutes later I heard the report of a pistol. Upon opening the door I discovered my husband lying in his own blood upon the floor.

"I ran to the front door as Charles was getting over the fence but Robert was standing in the front yard with a pistol in his right hand.

I said, 'Oh, you have killed him!' And Charles said, 'No, we didn't kill him' and then turned around and walked back into the kitchen and then left with Charles who was waiting outside the fence."

At this juncture the Johnson boys made their appearance and gave themselves up to the officer and told them the man they had killed was Jesse James and now they claimed the reward.

Those who were standing nearby drew their breath in silence at the thought of being so near Jesse James even if he was dead.

Marshall Craig said, "My God, do you mean to tell us this is Jesse James?"

"Yes," answered the boys in one breath. "This is Jesse James and we have killed him and don't deny it. We feel proud that we have killed a man who is known all over the world as the most notorious outlaw who ever lived."

"How are we to take your word?" asked the marshall.

"We don't ask you to take our word. There is plenty of proof. The confession of the wife will be enough."

The marshall then took the woman who called herself Mrs. Johnson into another room and he told her the name of her dead husband was not Johnson. She denied it at first, and after the marshall left, the *News* reporter entered the room with three other gentlemen and a lady who was present.

Walking up to her, the *News* man said, "Mrs. Howard, it is said your name is not Howard but James and that you are the wife of Jesse James."

"I cannot help what they say," she replied. "I have told you the truth."

"The boys who killed your husband have come back and say your husband is Jesse James."

"Oh, is it possible they have come back? I can't believe it!" she cried. Then she placed her arms around the shoulders of her little boy and girl and wept bitterly.

The *News* man and others present then told her it would be much better for her to tell the truth, that the public would think more of her and she would not want for anything.

Then walking through the room where her dead husband lay, she caught sight of the men who had ki!led her husband. Screaming at the top of her voice she called them cowards and asked, "Why did you kill the one who had always befriended you?"

Then turning to the body of Jesse she prayed that soon she and her children might be in the hands of Death's cold embrace.

She then left the room followed by the reporter who told her that the boys were not mistaken that the dead man was her husband, Jesse James.

She uttered not a word but the seven-year-old son standing at her side said: "God Almighty may strike me down if it is not my Pa."

"The boys outside say their names are Ford and not Johnson as you said," the reporter told her.

"Do they say that? And what else do they say?" she said.

"That they killed him to get the reward money."

Then holding her little children to her bosom, she said, "I cannot shield them much longer. Even after they shot my husband who has been trying to live a peaceful life, I tried to withhold his name. But it is true. My husband is Jesse James and a kinder hearted and truer man to his family never lived."

The confession from the wife of the most notorious outlaw who ever lived created a profound sensation in the room. The thought that Jesse James had lived for six months within our city and walked our streets daily caused one to shudder with fear.

"Jesse has been accused of being engaged in nearly all the robberies committed in the United States."

"Yes, that is true. But he was not half-bad a man as his enemies have reported. He has endeavored to lead an honest and peaceful life but wherever he went he was hunted down by a lot of scoundrels who were not better than himself. We lived in Kansas City and Jesse was not discovered by anyone."

"Where is Frank?"

"I don't know. I have not seen or heard of Frank in a long time."

At this point the officers began prowling around the house and Mrs. James said: "I wish they would quit. They have no business with my dead husband's outfit."

The reporter then went outside and interviewed the Ford brothers. They were both young, the oldest not more than twenty-one years of age. When we asked them why they had killed Jesse James they said they wanted the reward.

"You are young but gritty."

"We are all grit," said Charles. "You never expected to see the body of Jesse James in St. Joseph but we thought we would create a sensation and put him out of the way."

❧

THE SAD DEMISE
OF WILD BILL CODY

By Gene Fowler

Bonfils and Tammen were bargain hunters. They had developed a circus from a dog-and-pony show, and now they coveted Buffalo Bill's famous Wild West concern. They set out to ensnare it in 1913, at a time when Colonel Cody was harassed by debt, entangled in a partnership with Major Gordon W. Lillie ("Pawnee Bill") and confused by those sad and disillusioning truths that descend with the snows of old age.

The celebrated Colonel's biographers have made him a Sir Galahad of the plains, an Indian fighter and scout superior to the rugged Kit Carson. His critics have gone to the other extreme, portraying him as a bellowing faker, a butcher of buffaloes, a glutton for rum and romance. The man himself is lost between legend and calumny. All agreed, obviously, that, demigod or satyr, Buffalo Bill was an institution.

Perhaps the handsomest Amercian of all time and a symbol of adventure, he was envied by men, beloved and spoiled by women and emulated by growing boys. He sat on his white stallion like a dream prince, and every time he shook his long curls, the lassies of many towns suffered the amatory jitters. In one respect, the Colonel's tresses were a godsend to mothers who persisted in the most villainous hoax ever perpetrated on the lads of America—the infliction of the Lord Fauntleroy coiffure on screaming boys.

"You look like Buffalo Bill," these addled mothers would plead. It was a telling argument, heaven forgive! For Bill was the pied piper of the trails.

Both obstinate and sentimental, the Colonel drove through all obstacles to the fortunes which he never could hold. Indiscreet, prodigal, as temperamental as a diva, pompous yet somehow naive, vain but generous, bigger than big today and littler than little tomorrow, Cody lived with the world at his

The Irish-American experience, believe it or not, was never merely confined to certain neighborhood activities inside the metropolitan centers of Boston, Chicago and New York. Feeling trapped and unwelcome in these large cities, many new Irish immigrants took Dion Boucicault seriously when he advised one young friend: "Go west, young man, and change your name." Indeed, many of the Irish who did move west not only changed their names, they also changed their religion. If more orange now than green, the American West was in good part Irish nonetheless. Bill Cody, for example, became George M. Cohan on horseback. Gene Fowler caught up with Cody at the sad tail end of his career.

99

feet and died with it on his shoulders. He was subject to suspicious whims and distorted perspectives, yet the sharpers who swindled him the oftenest he trusted the most.

Cody's record on the frontier was that of an intelligent, brave and capable scout. The five-cent Buffalo Bill novels of Ned Buntline and the paeans of press agents led the public to believe that Cody had slain thousands of venomous hostiles and almost single-handed had won the West.

Foremost among his exploits was the victory over Chief Yellow Hand at Warbonnet Creek in the summer of 1876. Circus Homers described Yellow Hand as having been an aboriginal Goliath. Cody's Denver critics sought to belittle the whole affair and Scout Wiggins, grizzled disciple of Kit Carson, held that Yellow Hand was in the last stages of tuberculosis at the time, or, as sportsmen say, a setup for Cody.

The Colonel himself usually refrained from speaking of the Yellow Hand fracas. Pressed by Bonfils to give the details, he declared that Yellow Hand was anything but an invalid.

"I was chief of scouts for General Merritt," the Colonel said. "I had been guiding the Fifth Cavalry to cut off a band of Sioux and Cheyennes under Yellow Hand and Crazy Horse on their way from the Red Cloud Agency. The news of the Custer Massacre had reached us only a few days before, and we sought to prevent Yellow Hand and his band from reinforcing Sitting Bull, author of the Custer debacle.

"Custer had been my friend. I had served with him at Pilot Knob and elsewhere during the Civil War. I wanted revenge for my friend. I reported that we were across the line of march of the redskins, and General Merritt ordered his men to lie in wait. I went out to scout and happened on an immigrant train. I escorted them to our lines, but in so doing revealed our presence to the enemy. It could not be avoided.

"Immediate plans were made for an engagement. The Indians were on the other side of the valley. Warbonnet Creek separated us from them. I was in advance of our troops. Suddenly I saw an Indian ride forward, shouting and waving a white cloth. My interpreter, Little Baptiste, translated the shouts:

"'He says that Yellow Hand is the greatest of their warriors and would like to fight Pahaska [Buffalo Bill], as he is the bravest of palefaces.'

"I said: 'That suits me fine,' and put spur to my horse. The herald retired, and now a huge and fiercely painted chief—Yellow Hand—came charging from the Indian lines. There was a great whoop from his warriors and a cheer from my comrades.

"When we had come within about fifty yards of each other, we simultaneously raised our rifles and fired. My horse stepped a forefoot into a gopher hole and turned a complete somersault. I fell and rolled, losing my rifle. I was on my feet immediately, however, and shouted to let my comrades know I had been uninjured. I ran forward, drawing my bowie knife. I noticed now that Yellow Hand also was on foot. My shot had killed his horse, and the Chief had been thrown and lost his rifle. He was brandishing a tomahawk.

"As we closed in, I crouched to get inside the arc of his blow. He had left his hand extended to ward off any thrust I might make. Instead of stabbing at him, however, I feinted and dashed inside the arc of his blow, just as his tomahawk began its descent. I then sank my bowie between his ribs, beneath the left armpit. He fell, his mouth open and his eyes staring."

Mr. Bonfils suspected further details. "Didn't you scalp him?"

The Colonel was somewhat embarrassed. "I regret to say that I did. I was carried away by the thought of Custer. I jerked off Yellow Hand's Big Bonnet, grasped his war-lock and cut it off."

"It was a bloodthirsty thing to do," said Bonfils.

"Yes," said the Colonel. "And that is why I seldom refer to the duel. I sent the scalp to my wife, and when she saw what it was she fainted."

Colonel Cody told Bonfils this story in January of 1913. It prefaced a plea for a loan. Buffalo Bill for some time had been in a circus partnership with "Pawnee Bill" (Major Lillie) under the title "Buffalo Bill's Wild West and Pawnee Bill's Far East Show." Of late they had encountered a deficit. They owed for lithographs and other matters.

Bonfils and Tammen lent the show twenty thousand dollars, payable in six months at six percent interest. It was the beginning of much trouble, of litigation, and perhaps hastened the end of Buffalo Bill's glamorous career.

In lending that enterprise the twenty thousand, it was understood that Cody would split company with his partner, "Pawnee Bill," and throw his name and his Wild West interests into the Sells-Floto camp.

And now began a legalistic stampede destined to wreck the Cody-Lillie organization. The *Post*'s owners got what they were after—Buffalo Bill, in name and in person. The confused Colonel gallantly kept at the business of shooting smoke balls from the saddle of his white horse, McKinley, to keep himself from the poorhouse and his charger from the boneyard. His spirit was broken in the manner which usually seems to please one's critics immensely, but his pride remained with him to the grave.

To enumerate all the litigations arising from the Cody-Lillie split-up, would be endless. Suffice that the hand of the *Post* was felt, if not seen, in much of the court-storm. Bonfils and Tammen had set out to get what they wanted, for little more than the "loss" of their twenty-thousand loan. They hardly accomplished that aim, for Major Lillie managed to escape with his buckskin pants, his horse and a few thousand dollars. Not so the gallant Colonel. His creditors realized about fifty cents on the dollar from the sale, but from now on Cody was virtually a chattel of the Sells-Floto Circus.

His fight to retain his pride was a much harder battle for Cody than had been his struggle against Chief Yellow Hand. His heart was cutting up, and uremic poisoning was spreading through his system. He tried baths at one of Colorado's spas, but knew that death was not far off. He didn't seem to care much about death, one way or another, except that he wanted to meet his end in Wyoming.

He was disappointed in this. Shortly after his family had breakfasted on January 10, 1917, at the home of Cody's sister, Mrs. L. E. Decker of Denver, he called out that he was going to die. An hour later he was unable to speak. He resorted to the sign language he had learned among the Indians. He died in the early afternoon at the age of seventy-two years. &

Pointing a revolver at Buffalo Bill's head, the traitor cried wildly: "Release me, Cody, or I'll kill you this instant."

▲ Cover of *Buffalo Bill Stories* from 1906.

▼ Lettering from *Scouts of the Prairie* stage production starring Buffalo Bill in 1872.

THE LINCOLN COUNTY WAR — THE CREATION OF BILLY THE KID —

JOHN CHISUM.. TEXAS CATTLE BARON IN CONFLICT WITH THE SMALL RANCHERS FOR THE PUBLIC LANDS.. HE ALSO IS IN COMPETITION WITH ..

" THE HOUSE OF MURPHY.. THREE IRISHMEN.. MURPHY, DOLAN AND RILEY.. THEY RUN THE LOCAL GRAFT.. AND WILL KILL TO KEEP IT ..

.. CHISUM GOES INTO PARTNERSHIP WITH JOHN TUNSTALL .. A YOUNG ENGLISHMAN WHOSE ASSASSINATION WILL START THE WAR .. AND ALEXANDER McSWEEN, A BIBLE THUMPING SCOTS LAWYER .. THEY BUILD A NEW STORE ACROSS THE STREET FROM THE MURPHY STORE .. TUNSTALL ACCUSES THE MURPHY STORE OF TAX FRAUD .. DOLAN THREATENS TUNSTALL'S LIFE ..

A MURPHY POSSE, APPOINTED BY THE MURPHY JUDGE TO SERVE A WARRANT FOR EMBEZZLEMENT FOR McSWEEN, MEETS TUNSTALL ON THE ROAD AND MURDERS HIM ..

TUNSTALL'S MURDER IS WITNESSED BY AN 18-YEAR OLD COWBOY RECENTLY HIRED AND BEFRIENDED BY TUNSTALL ..

.. HIS NAME .. HENRY McCARTY.. BORN 1859, NEW YORK CITY .. HIS PARENTS ARE MICHAEL AND CATHERINE McCARTY, NATIVES OF IRELAND .. WIDOWED, SHE MOVES TO NEW MEXICO .. MARRIES WILLIAM ANTRIM.. REMEMBERED AS A " JOLLY IRISH LADY", SHE DIES OF TB IN 1874.. HENRY IS ON HIS OWN AT 14 ..

HENRY IS IN ARIZONA .. 17 YEARS OLD .. GOADED INTO A FIGHT WITH AN ARMY BLACKSMITH, HE KILLS THE BLACKSMITH IN SELF DEFENSE .. TO AVOID A LYNCH MOB, HE ESCAPES TO NEW MEXICO .. NOW CALLING HIMSELF WILLIAM BONNEY, HE HIRES ON WITH TUNSTALL SOME MONTHS BEFORE THE ENGLISHMAN'S MURDER ..

ENRAGED BY THE SHOOTING OF TUNSTALL, HE SAYS," I'LL GET EVERY SON OF A BITCH WHO HELPED KILL JOHN IF IT'S THE LAST THING I DO !!" THE REGULATORS, A POSSE OF TUNSTALL-McSWEEN RIDERS STRIKES BACK ..

MURPHY RIDERS ARE KILLED ..

GUERRILLA WAR BETWEEN THE MURPHY-DOLAN CLAN AND McSWEEN REGULATORS CULMINATES IN A 5 DAY BATTLE IN LINCOLN .. THE KID AND 14 OTHERS UNDER SEIGE BY DOLAN AND A HUGE POSSE.. McSWEEN IS KILLED .. THE KID ESCAPES.

OUTLAWED BY THE MURPHY CONTROLLED GOVERNOR, BILLY CONFRONTS CHISUM .. REMINDS CHISUM OF HIS PROMISE TO BACK McSWEEN AND TUNSTALL .. BILLY DEMANDS $500 FOR THE REGULATORS AS PAYMENT FOR FIGHTING IN CHISUM'S INTERESTS ..

CHISUM TURNS BILLY DOWN .. NO DEAL .. FINE, SAYS THE KID .. I'LL STEAL YOUR COWS UNTIL WE'RE EVEN ..

THE BOLIVIAN CONNECTION

By Percy Seibert with James D. Horan

The mystery of Butch Cassidy and the Sundance Kid continues to this day. Cassidy's "Hole in the Wall" gang was, of course, the stuff of legend—a fact not lost on the producers of the famous Cassidy film starring Paul Newman, Robert Redford, and Katherine Ross as the redoubtable Etta Place. But did Cassidy actually die in that small Bolivian pueblo, as Percy Seibert recounts? The answer is no, according to the outlaw's sister, Lula Parker Betenson. Butch escaped, Lula claims, went on to fight in the Mexican Revolution and finally returned to the Pacific Northwest where, under the alias of William Thadeus Phillips, he died in his sleep in Spangler, Washington, in 1937. Which version is correct? This is a cowboy story. You are free to take your pick.

I first went to Bolivia around the turn of the century to serve as the Commissioner General of the Bolivian Railroad Supply Company allied to the Concordia Tin Mines.

The building of the Bolivia Railroad was one of the most difficult engineering tasks in the world; the route had to be hacked out of a jungle, across mountains, deep valleys, and span incredible rivers. The heat and the weather were indescribable: it took men of great physical strength who could endure enormous hardships to build that railroad. Men of many nationalities were drawn to the job and of course no questions were asked. They included not only adventurers but also fugitives from the law of many lands, including the American West. By 1903 there were outlaw bands in the interiors of the South American countries and before long we began to hear of western-style train and bank robberies.

In 1906, it was Christmas week I believe, I arrived in La Paz. As was his custom, Clement Rolla Glass, Superintendent of the Concordia Tin Mines where I was now employed as his assistant, closed down the mine and led all the men—Americans, Welshmen, English remittance men, Spanish, and Indians—down to the square of La Paz. Here everyone toasted each other, calling out Merry Christmas as the bells of Our Lady of Guadelupe pealed out.

Glass and my old friends at the mine gave me a wild welcome and then Clement started making the rounds with me, introducing the new men who had joined the mine since I had been away. I noticed one fellow, in his thirties, blond and stocky, who seemed to edge away every time I approached. This irritated me and finally I pushed my way through the crowd, held out my hand, and said "I'm Percy Seibert, Mr. Glass' assistant. I don't think we met."

He hesitated a moment, then put out his hand. "I'm Jim Maxwell," he said. "Mr. Glass hired me and my partner," he pointed to a smaller man, also with blond hair, who was in a crowd but seemed to be watching us intently.

"And what's his name?" I persisted.

"Enrique Brown," he said with a slight smile, then nodded and moved away. Not very sociable, I thought

Butch Cassidy in Bolivia.

to myself.

The day after Christmas, on the way back to the mine, I asked Glass about Maxwell and Brown. He was silent for a moment, then looked around and said he would talk to me later at the mine. That night he carefully closed his office door and sat down facing me across his desk.

"Perce," he said, "what I tell you now must remain confidential."

"Of course," I said somewhat puzzled.

"About Maxwell and Brown," he continued. "Have you ever heard of Butch Cassidy and the Wild Bunch, you know, that gang of outlaws in the West?"

"Of course," I told him. "In fact, just before I left New York I saw a movie in Coney Island about him."

"Well, Maxwell is Butch Cassidy," he said, "and Brown is Harry Longbaugh, the Sundance Kid."

I guess I looked stunned because he packed his pipe and poured us a drink.

Butch and the Kid would disappear periodically. Word eventually would get back to the mine that a bank or a train had been robbed. It was a delicate situation; Cassidy and the Kid were, of course, prime suspects in our minds but we didn't have definite proof. In any event, the law back in La Paz didn't seem to be very anxious to do anything about them. It must be recalled that the Bolivian interior of that time was a rugged country and, as in American West, the law was usually what hung on a man's hip.

Somehow Cassidy took to me. Perhaps it was because I knew something of the West and the cattle business—also I never asked questions.

Cassidy was quite popular in the countryside, particularly with the Indian children. Whenever he went to La Paz he would always come back with the sticks of candy which he gave to the children. I can still see him coming up the trail to our place, followed by a pack of yelling, laughing kids, who called him Don Max.

I also realized that Cassidy was shrewdly making friends with the Indians who would never betray him....

In contrast to Butch, the Sundance Kid was almost taciturn.

I found Butch an amiable man with a fatalistic philosophy: "I know how it's going to end, Perce," he said once. "I guess that's the way it's got to be."

We talked generally of the West and ranching, and gradually as he came to trust me, he spoke of his life as an outlaw—never naming names of men who had ridden with him—and his technique so to speak.

"I came down to South America with the idea of settling down," he said. "In the States there was nothing but jail, the noose, or being shot by a posse. I thought maybe I could change things but I guess things at this late date can't be changed."

One day when the Kid wasn't with him, he told me about Etta Place. He described her as "the best house-keeper in South America but she has the heart of a whore."

One day, he said, Etta had severe stomach pains. They got worse and finally the Kid took her to the nearest doctor, who diagnosed her condition as acute appendicitis. He wanted to put her in the local hospital but Etta refused. Frankly, I didn't blame her. Medical conditions were crude and unsanitary, and you were often at the mercy of a native doctor who did everything from treating mules to pulling teeth.

Etta begged the Kid to take her back to the States; finally Cassidy and the Kid agreed that had to be done. The Sundance Kid and Etta went back to Denver, where Etta entered the hospital. The next day the operation was to be performed. That night the Kid went on a high lonesome and came back to his boardinghouse roaring drunk. He woke up with a terrible hangover and shouted for someone to bring him a cup of coffee. Of course, no one did. Then he grabbed one of his guns, which hung in a holster at the side of the bed, and fired a few rounds into the ceiling.

The Kid had forgotten he wasn't in a cow camp twenty-five years before. Denver was no longer a frontier town. The outraged landlord shouted that he was going to call the police. The Kid realized suddenly he would make a fine catch, so he threw on his clothes and ran out to hire a carriage to take him to the railroad station, where he finally got connections back to New York and a steamer to South America, where he rejoined Cassidy.

When I asked if they had ever heard of Etta again, he just shook his head.

One winter Cassidy and the Kid selected the Chocaya Tin-Silver Mine for their next holdup. What took place was told to me by Mr. Roberts, general manager of the Companio Aramayo, whose payroll was taken.

The payroll was for the tin mine of Aploca and was en route to Aploca from Cachisla, where the general offices were located. It was in a *petaca*, or small straw suitcase, tied on the back of a pack mule led by a *mozo*, or native guard, who was riding a large silver-gray mule. On the flank of this particular mule was the mine's brand.

They were heading along the trail when they were held up by Cassidy and the Sundance Kid; Cassidy also took the *mozo*'s silver-gray mule.

The bandits then struck out for San Vincente, which is about thirty-five miles from where the robbery had taken place. This trail leads from Atocha, a small village near the Bolivian-Argentine border.

After he had been robbed, the *mozo* rode the remaining pack mule to Atocha where he notified the local authorities, who recruited a band of Bolivian soldiers, not more than five, who were camped nearby. At the time the Bolivian soldiers were only peons, pressed into service, many times without shoes or even bullets for their rifles. But these men were armed.

They arrived at San Vincente as dusk was falling. The village was walled, with a corral inside. The *mozo* and his soldiers entered by the large open wooden gate and the *mozo* found his mule in the corral.

Cassidy and the Kid were in an adobe hut in the opposite corner of the barrio, cooking over a small beehive baking oven. By the time the soldiers appeared they had a candle.

When the Americans had entered, they had stripped the mules and placed their rifles, ammunition and saddles against the wall, some distance from the entrance of the hut.

When the *mozo* found his mule he told the soldiers. One shouted to the outlaws to surrender.

The order was still echoing in the gathering darkness when one of them, believed to have been Cassidy, fired, hitting the soldier in the neck. He clutched his neck, stumbled outside the gate, and died. The others poured after him and started to fire from the wall.

Shots were exchanged, followed by silence. The *mozo* and the soldiers patrolled the barrio, occasionally shouting demands to surrender, or firing, but there were no answering shots. Meanwhile a messenger had been sent to Atocha for reinforcements.

When dawn came the soldiers fired a few more rounds at the hut but there was only silence.

Then about ten o'clock, when no reinforcements had appeared, the soldiers sent in an Indian woman carrying a baby. As the soldiers and the *mozo* watched, she walked across the open ground and entered the hut. In a few moments she reappeared crying that the *bandidos Yanqui* were dead. When the soldiers and the *mozo* entered the hut they found Cassidy lying on the floor and the Kid squatting on his haunches on a wide adobe bench that circled the room. He had been shot through the eyes. Roberts told me that one had been critically wounded making a dash for their rifles and the other had committed suicide.

Roberts came from Atocha with the reinforcements, saw the bodies and got the story of what had happened from his *mozo* and the soldiers. The officer in charge ordered his men to bury the pair in the Indian graveyard not far from the village. This officer took Cassidy's and the Kid's rifles and side arms and a small gold watch which one of them had carried. I met this officer many times on the La Paz stage and he never tired of telling me the story and showing me the small gold watch.

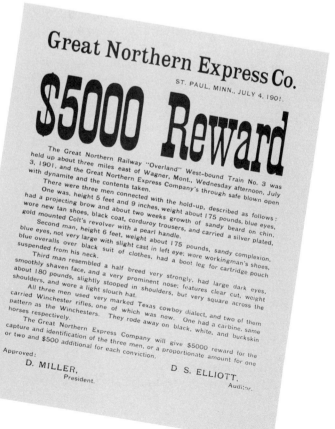

Great Northern Express Co.

ST. PAUL, MINN., JULY 4, 1901.

$5000 Reward

The Great Northern Railway "Overland" West-bound Train No. 3 was held up about three miles east of Wagner, Mont., Wednesday afternoon, July 3, 1901, and the Great Northern Express Company's through safe blown open with dynamite and the contents taken.

There were three men connected with the hold-up, described as follows:

One was, height 5 feet and about 9 inches, weight about 175 pounds, blue eyes; had a projecting brow and about two weeks growth of sandy beard on chin, wore new tan shoes, black coat, corduroy trousers, and carried a silver plated, gold mounted Colt's revolver with a pearl handle.

Second man, height 6 feet, weight about 175 pounds, sandy complexion, blue eyes, not very large with slight cast in left eye; wore workingman's shoes, blue overalls over black suit of clothes, had a boot leg for cartridge pouch suspended from his neck.

Third man resembled a half breed very strongly, had large dark eyes, smoothly shaven face, and a very prominent nose; features clear cut, weight about 180 pounds, slightly stooped in shoulders, but very square across the shoulders, and wore a light slouch hat.

All three men used very marked Texas cowboy dialect, and two of them carried Winchester rifles, one of which was new. One had a carbine, same pattern as the Winchesters. They rode away on black, white, and buckskin horses respectively.

The Great Northern Express Company will give $5000 reward for the capture and identification of the three men, or a proportionate amount for one or two and $500 additional for each conviction.

Approved:

D. MILLER,
President.

D. S. ELLIOTT,
Auditor.

106

WHERE THE COTTONWOODS GROW

By Joan Didion

A good deal of bad poetry has been made out of the facts that the Celtic hinterlands were Europe's "Wild West," that the Celts were Europe's Apache, and that the oldest sagas of Ireland provide the story of a series of interminable cattle raids. However the irony of history, the American West was very, very Irish/Scots-Irish indeed. It was only fitting, then, that when the story of the West began to be portrayed larger than life on the silver screen, Irish-American actors were called upon to play those key roles. William S. Hart was the first great Western film star, while the greatest Western film hero of them all was the tall, strapping Morrison kid who had taken the name John Wayne.

▼

The Duke and the Ladies, out where the cottonwoods grow, from the 1943 Republic production of *War of the Wildcats.*

In the summer of 1943 I was eight, and my father and mother and small brother and I were at Peterson Field in Colorado Springs. A hot wind blew through that summer, blew until it seemed that before August broke, all the dust in Kansas would be in Colorado, would have drifted over the tar-paper barracks and the temporary strip and stopped only when it hit Pikes Peak. There was not much to do, a summer like that: there was the day they brought in the first B-29, an event to remember but scarcely a vacation program. There was an Officer's Club, but no swimming pool; all the Officer's Club had of interest was artificial blue rain behind the bar. The rain interested me a good deal, but I could not spend the summer watching it, and so we went, my brother and I, to the movies.

We went three and four afternoons a week, sat on folding chairs in the darkened Quonset hut which served as a theatre, and it was there, that summer of 1943 while the hot wind blew outside, that I first saw John Wayne. Saw the walk, heard the voice. Heard him tell the girl in a picture called *War of the Wildcats* that he would build her a house, "at the bend in the river where the cottonwoods grow." As it happened I did not grow up to be the kind of woman who is the heroine in a Western, and although the men I have known have had many virtues and have taken me to live in many places I have come to love, they have never been John Wayne, and they have never taken me to that bend in the river where the cottonwoods grow. Deep in that part of my heart where the artificial rain forever falls, that is still the line I wait to hear.

I tell you this neither in a spirit of self-revelation nor as an exercise in total recall, but simply to demonstrate that when John Wayne rode through my childhood, and perhaps through yours, he determined forever the shape of certain of our dreams. It did not seem possible that such a man could fall ill, could carry within him that most inexplicable and ungovernable of diseases. The rumor struck some obscure anxiety, threw our very childhood into question. In John Wayne's world, John Wayne was supposed to give the orders. "Let's ride," he said, and "Saddle up." "Hello, there," he said when he first saw the girl, in a construction camp or on a train or just standing around on the front porch waiting for

somebody to ride up through the tall grass. When John Wayne spoke, there was no mistaking his intentions; he had a sexual authority so strong that even a child could perceive it. And in a world we understood early to be characterized by venality and doubt and paralyzing ambiguities, he suggested another world, one which may or may not have existed but in any case existed no more: a place where a man could move free, could make his own code and live by it; a world in which, if a man did what he had to do, he could one day take the girl and go riding through the draw and find himself home free, not in a hospital with something going wrong inside, not in a high bed with the flowers and the drugs and the forced smiles, but there at the bend in the bright river, the cottonwoods shimmering in the early morning sun.

"Hello, there." Where did he come from, before the tall grass? Even his history seemed right, for it was no history at all, nothing to intrude upon the dream. Born Marion Morrison in Winterset, Iowa, the son of a druggist. Moved as a child to Lancaster, California, part of the migration to that promised land sometimes called "the west coast of Iowa." Not that Lancaster was the promise fulfilled; Lancaster was a town on the Mojave where the dust blew through. But Lancaster was still California, where desolation had a different flavor: antimacassars among the orange groves, a middle-class prelude to Forest Lawn. Imagine Marion Morrison in Glendale. A Boy Scout, then a student at Glendale High. A tackle for University of Southern California, a Sigma Chi. Summer vacations, a job moving props on the old Fox lot. There, a meeting with John Ford, one of the several directors who were to sense that into this perfect mold might be poured the inarticulate longings of a nation wondering at just what pass the trail had been lost. "Dammit," said Raoul Walsh later, "the son of a bitch looked like a man." And so after a while the boy from Glendale became a star. He did not become an actor, as he has always been careful to point out to interviewers ("How many times do I gotta tell you, I don't act at all, I re-act"), but a star, and the star called John Wayne would spend most of the rest of his life with one or another of those directors, out on some forsaken location, in search of the dream.

Out where the skies are a trifle bluer
Out where friendship's a little truer
That's where the West begins.

Nothing very bad could happen in the dream, nothing a man could not face down. But something did. There it was, the rumor, and after a while the headlines. "I licked the Big C," John Wayne announced, as John Wayne would, reducing those outlaw cells to the level of any other outlaws, but even so we all sensed that this would be the one unpredictable confrontaion, the one shoot-out Wayne could lose. I have as much trouble as the next person with illusion and reality, and I did not much want to see John Wayne when he must be (or so I thought) having some trouble with it himself, but I did, and it was down in Mexico when he was making the picture his illness had so long delayed, down in the very country of the dream.

It was John Wayne's 165th picture. It was Henry Hathaway's 84th. It was number 34 for Dean Martin, who was working off an old contract to Hal Wallis, for whom it was independent production number 65. It was called the *Sons of Katie Elder*, and it was a Western, and after the three-month delay they had finally shot the exteriors up in Durango, and now they were in the waning days of interior shooting at Estudio Churubusco outside Mexico City, and the sun was hot and the air was clear and it was lunchtime. Out under the pepper trees the boys from the Mexican crew sat around sucking caramels, and down the road some of the technical men sat around a place which served a stuffed lobster and a glass of tequilla for one dollar American, but it was inside the cavernous empty commissary where the talent sat around, the reason for the exercise, all sitting around the big table.

And there was Wayne himself, fighting through number 165. There was Wayne, in his thirty-three-year-old spurs, his dusty neckerchief, his blue shirt. "You don't have too many worries about what to wear in these things," he said. "You can wear a blue shirt, or, if you're down in Monument Valley, you can wear a yellow shirt." There was Wayne, in a relatively new hat, a hat which made him look curiously like William S.

Hart. "I had this old cavalry hat I loved, but I lent it to Sammy Davis. I got it back, it was unwearable. I think they all pushed it down on his head and said O.K., John Wayne—you know, a joke."

There was Wayne, working too soon, finishing the picture with a bad cold and a racking cough, so tired by late afternoon that he kept an oxygen inhaler on the set. And still nothing mattered but the Code. "That guy," he muttered of a reporter who had incurred his displeasure. "I admit I'm balding. I admit I got a tire around my middle. What man fifty-seven doesn't? Big news. Anyway, that guy."

He paused, about to expose the heat of the matter, the root of distaste, the fracture of the rules that bothered him more than the alleged misquotations, more than the intimation that he was no longer the Ringo Kid. "He comes down, uninvited, but I ask him over anyway. So we're sitting around drinking mescal out of a water jug."

He paused again and looked meaningfully at director Henry Hathaway, readying him for the unthinkable denouement. "He had to be assisted to his room."

They argued about the virtues of various prizefighters, they argued about the price of J & B in pesos. They argued about dialogue.

"As rough a guy is, Henry, I still don't think he'd raffle off his mother's Bible."

"I like a shocker, Duke."

They exchanged endless training-table jokes. "You know why they call this memory sauce?" Dean Martin asked, holding up a bowl of chili.

"Why?"

"Because you remember it in the morning."

"Hear that, Duke? Hear why they call this memory sauce?"

They delighted one another by blocking out minute variations in the free-for-all fight which is a set piece in Wayne pictures; motivated or totally gratuitous, the fight sequence has to be in the picture, because they so enjoy making it. "Listen—this'll be really funny. Duke picks up the kid, see, and then it takes both Dino and Earl to throw him out the door—how's that?"

They communicated by sharing old jokes; they sealed their camaraderie by making gentle, old-fashioned fun

of wives, those civilizers, those tamers. "So Senora Wayne takes it into her head to stay up and have one brandy. So for the rest of the night it's 'Yes, Pilar, you're right, dear. I'm a bully, Pilar, you're right, I'm impossible.'"

"You hear that? Duke says Pilar threw a table at him."

"Hey Duke, here's something funny. That finger you hurt today, get the Doc to bandage it up, go home tonight, show it to Pilar, tell her she did it when she threw the table. You know, make her think she was really cutting up."

They treated the oldest among them respectfully; they treated the youngest fondly. "You see that kid?" they said of Michael Anderson, Jr., "What a kid."

"He don't act, it's right from the heart," said Hathaway, patting his heart.

"Hey kid," Martin said. "You're gonna be in my next picture. We'll have the whole thing, no beards. The striped shirts, the girls, the hi-fi, the eye lights."

They ordered Michael Anderson his own chair, with "BIG MIKE" tooled on the back. When it arrived on the set, Hathaway hugged him. "You see that?" Anderson asked Wayne, suddenly too shy to look him in the eye. Wayne gave him the smile, the nod, the final accolade.

"I saw it, kid."

Since that summer of 1943 I had thought of John Wayne in a number of ways. I had thought of him driving cattle up from Texas, and bringing airplanes in on a single engine, thought of him telling the girl at the Alamo that "Republic is a beautiful word." I had never thought of him having dinner with his family and with me and my husband in an expensive restaurant in Chapultepec Park, but time brings odd mutations, and there we were, one night that last week in Mexico. For a while it was only a nice evening, an evening anywhere. We had a lot of drinks and I lost the sense that the face across the table was in certain ways more familiar than my husband's.

And then something happened. Suddenly the room seemed suffused with the dream, and I could not think why. Three men appeared out of nowhere, playing guitars. Pilar Wayne leaned slightly forward, and John Wayne lifted his glass almost imperceptibly toward her. "We'll need some Pouilly-Fuisse for the rest of the table," he said, "and some red Bordeaux for the Duke." We all smiled, and drank the Pouilly-Fuisse for the rest of the table and the red Bordeaux for the Duke, and all the while the men with the guitars kept playing, until finally I realized what they were playing, what they had been playing all along: "The Red River Valley" and the theme from *The High and the Mighty*. They did not quite get the beat right, but even now I can hear them, in another country and a long time later, even as I tell you this.   ❧

SHOOT-OUT AT THE LAMBS CLUB

In April 1925, the Lambs Club asked me to appear at their annual gambol in New York. In the dressing room were John Philip Sousa, Al Jolson, John Drew, and General Black Jack Pershing. Outside, the greatest dancers of ages were doing acts that could not be duplicated. It was colossal!

I was terrified. I had intended for my solo appearance to do some little Western recitations. I now realized, if I made such an appearance, I would be judged next door to ridiculous.

But what could I do? I could draw guns quickly and fire them rapidly—I would do just that on the stage in front of my audience! Yet, after the war, the manufacturers of ammunition got in the habit of using very poor ammunition in their blank cartridges. A blank cartridge when discharged will sometimes swell, and if it does .... good night!

I left the dressing room sweating.

Someone took me by the arm and led me to the big curtains. I started talking.

I told how, in 1869, at Abilene, Kansas, there was a marshall, Bill Hickok, a great gunman; how his enemies, the bad element, imported from Texas a celebrated desperado, named Phil Cole, to kill him; how Cole's men waited for Hickok to enter the local

▶

**William S. Hart,
pioneering
western film star.**

saloon; how eight gunmen, bad men, followed; how Hickok stood with his back to them; how Hickok's two guns came from nowhere and leaped into life....

At the proper moment my own guns leaped into life. My cartridges did not swell. It was one of the proudest moments of my life.

An hour later, at the little round table in the rear of Dinty Moore's, Will Rogers grinned at me and said:

"Bill, what in thunder did you do to those folks out in front tonight—whatever it was, they sure thought you was marvelous!"

—*William S. Hart*

The Strip Artists

The first definitive comic strip, Richard Felton Outcault's "The Yellow Kid," appeared in William Randolph Hearst's New York Journal on October 18, 1896. "The Yellow Kid" portrayed the ongoing adventures of Mickey Dugan and his regular gang of Irish street urchins, as set in a mythical slum called Hogan's Alley. Although Outcault was German, it would not be long before Irish-Americans began to experiment with these unique new possibilities for comic art. Irish-American artists would eventually pen many of the masterpieces in the history of this most popular of all American pop art forms. ❧

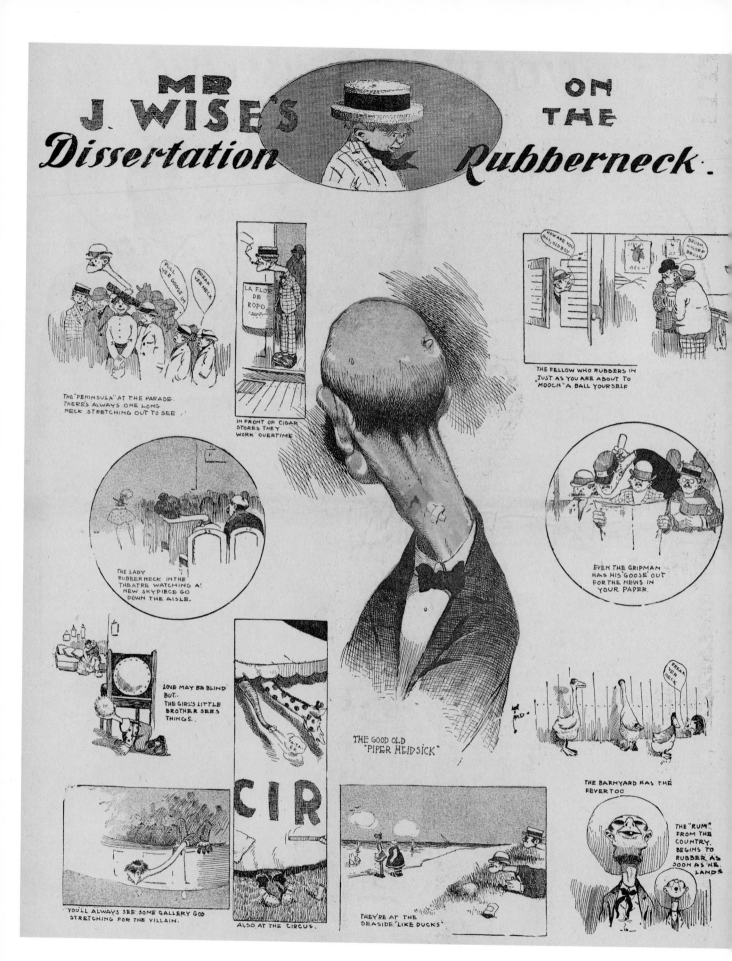

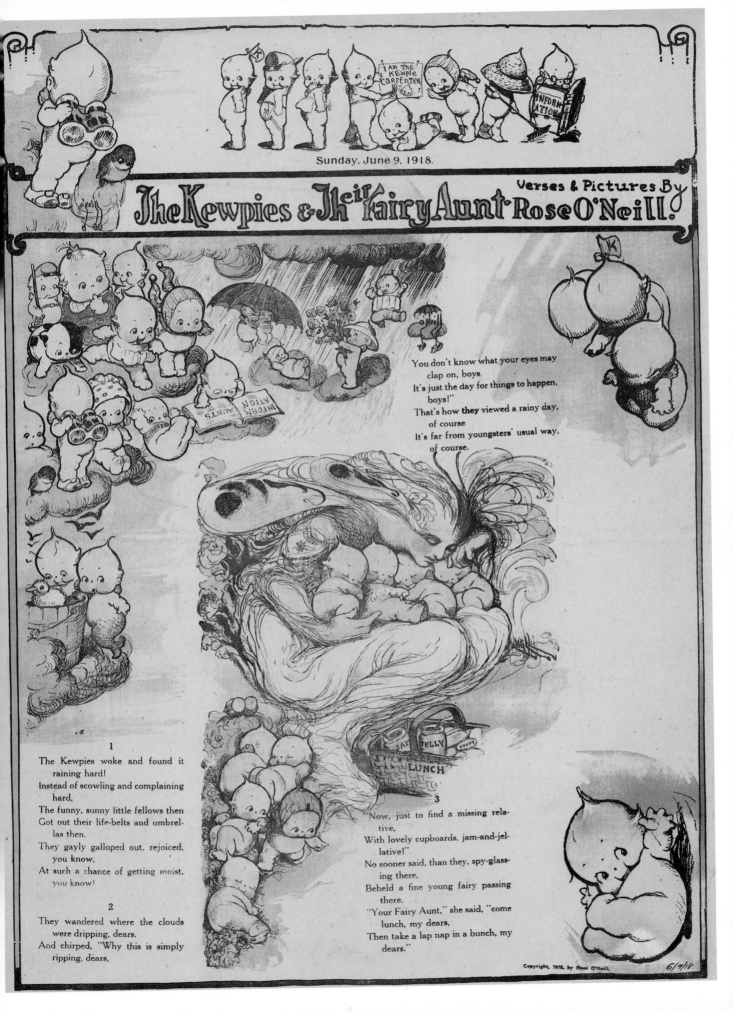

Sunday. June 9, 1918.

The Kewpies & Their Fairy Aunt

Verses & Pictures By Rose O'Neill

You don't know what your eyes may
    clap on, boys,
It's just the day for things to happen,
    boys!"
That's how they viewed a rainy day,
    of course
It's far from youngsters' usual way,
    of course.

1

The Kewpies woke and found it
    raining hard!
Instead of scowling and complaining
    hard,
The funny, sunny little fellows then
Got out their life-belts and umbrel-
    las then.
They gayly galloped out, rejoiced,
    you know,
At such a chance of getting moist,
    you know!

2

They wandered where the clouds
    were dripping, dears,
And chirped, "Why this is simply
    ripping, dears,

3

"Now, just to find a missing rela-
    tive,
With lovely cupboards, jam-and-jel-
    lative!"
No sooner said, than they, spy-glass-
    ing there,
Beheld a fine young fairy passing
    there.
"Your Fairy Aunt," she said, "come
    lunch, my dears,
Then take a lap nap in a bunch, my
    dears."

ND THE WORLD WITH THE YELLOW KID.

BY RUDOLPH BLOCK.

BLARNEY KASSIL.—Dere Mrs. Cassidy, here I am in d' land uv me ansessters, and, o, wot a luvly country it aint not nit. D' hole gang wuz ded stuck on goin' to Ireland but no sez I, no me frends, let us go su mware else.

bekause we got trubbils enuff an' wot's d' use uv borrowin' sum uv Ireland's trubbils. But d' gang wuz stubborn an' dey went an' Liz went an' where Liz goze I go. but say, dey regret it. Shure dey regret it an' if we get out alive we wont get caut again.

De land uv me ansessters aint wot it's crakked up t' be an' I don't blame 'em fer gaw'n t' Noo Yaurk witch is a sinch cumpaired wid Ireland. I cauled on yure ansessters Mrs. Cassidy an' I guv 'em yure luv an' I had an elligint scrap wid a little Cassidy boy, o how I dun him up.

foist we went t' Dublin where Mr. Kelly went out wid a soljer wot had a luvly unifaurm on an' cum home wid two soljers wot wuz carryin' him on a board. O he had a peetch. I t'ink it wuz Dublin stout but I aint shure, he never had one like dat befaur. We put him t' bed an' he sed it wuz all rite all rite but I don't know wot he ment.

Den we went t' d' laiks o' killarny. I wish we had dem laiks in Sentril Park dey're fine. D' coon went swimmin' an' d' laiks wuz full o' ded fishes d' nex. day 'cause dey'd never saw a coon befaur.

We're havin' grate spaurt wid d' coon, dere aint no coons in Ireland nothin' but trubbil an' fites.

I met d' Markwiss uv Londonderry in Killarny an' he inwited me to his pallis wot's in Ulster, say I know a man wot's got his Ulster in a pallis wot belongs t' simpson but I didn't spring dat gag on d' Markwiss 'cause me an' him is grate frends. Dere aint no flize on d' nobillity uv Ireland, dey aint got much munny but dey've got sand.

Markwiss I sez wot's d' matter wid Ireland ennyway, wot? wel Mickey he sed Ireland is strugglin' t' be free. Hooze keepin' it back I sed. He guv me d' wink an' sez, wisper Mickey, it's d' Queen. Ye can't fool me Markwiss I sed, I'll bet d' Queen knows better. Ennyway I'm gaw'n t' rite to d' Queen about it an' see wot I c'n do fer Ireland. D' Queen is me frend an' she'll do wot she can fer me. I fergot t' say in me last letter dat she wants t' be rememburd t' Mr. Cassidy.

we stopt at d' hotel waldorf witch wuzn't d' name uv d' hotel but say Mrs. Cassidy ye'd orter seen d' bil wot dat hotel keeper sprung on us. It wuz an orful nerve, we guv him enuff munny t' feed d' starvin' poor in Ireland fer ate years. Wen Slippy Dempsy seen dat hotel bil he sed o mommer I'd be afraid t' fall awf dat bil it's too high.

Den we went t' Blarney Kassil. say dat's d' funniest game wot I ever run up aggenst. If ye kiss d' stone wot's pasted up on d' top uv d' kassil where ye can't get at it ye c'n lie like a pollitishun an' noboddy gets on t' ye. I tride t' kiss d' stone but it wus no go, I neerly broke me nek.

Slippy Dempsy tride t' kiss it but he slipt an' fel. o he's a lukky boy he fel on his hed.

I red a luvly story in me gide book about d' Blarney Kassil an' de odder nite I sprung it on Liz. we went out fer a walk t' pick shamrox an' w'en we got t' d' kassil I told Liz how mutch I luvved her. Liz I sed on dis spot a grate nite wunst made luv to a prinsess wot livved in d'

Kassil. Her old man had munny t' boin an' d' nite had sum connexshun wid a match faktory but de ole man wuz ded leery on him. Me luv sed d' nite let's giv de ole man d' rinky dink.

nay nay sed d' princess 'cause he's me only father an' I wil never giv him d' shake. But wot'll we do sed d' nite, he wont giv his consent to our marrij an' I luv you an' you luv me. How c'n we fly, nit jentle nite sed d' prinsess, I cannot fly but I c'n die.

Den let's die sed d' nite an' dey went an' stood in d' shadder uv d' lonely Kassil. Jest as dey wuz gettin' dere daggers reddy t' do d' job de ole man cums out. ah ha he sed, traterous retch, I hav caut thee. An' wid dem woids he kills d' nite.

Den I waited fer Liz t' ask wot he did wid d' chippy, but Liz jest kept on chewin' gum so I had t' finnish d' tale. Dat luvly maden wuz locked up in d' Kassil til she dide an' on dis spot we're standin' now. o come awf, sed Liz. Mrs. Cassidy dat goil has no sentiment in her sole.

don'tche beleev it Liz I sed? no sed Liz, I red dat story in d' gide book meself. Goils aint so foolish. If a nite ever got stuk on me she cudn't lose me.

I gess I'll drop Liz, ever since she's stakked up aggenst de Yooropean nobillity she's been gettin' fresh. Wel ennyway we went back to d' hotel an' I sed where's Mr. Kelly an' everyone in d' joint sez here I am. No I sez, I want Mr. Kelly wot belongs to our party. Is dis him dey sed, liftin' a bundle from under d' table. poor Kelly, it wuz him.

I wont rite no more Mrs. Cassidy 'cause I'm sleepy. We wuz gaw'n t' Donnybrook but it's too oily fer d' fare an' t'ings is too quiet. I gess next week we're gaw'n to Parris. I shal always hav tender memmeries about Ireland but I don't want t' go back. Yure luvly frend.

MICKEY.

P. S. Mr. Kelly sez dat story about St. Patrick is a fake.

R. F. Outcault

Johnny Wise by T.A.D.

Thomas Aloysius Dorgan, aka "T.A.D.," the articulate creator of both "Indoor Sports" and "Outdoor Sports," was born in San Francisco in 1877. Dorgan's early "Johnny Wise" pages began to appear in the San Francisco Bulletin when "T.A.D." was merely nineteen years old.

The Kewpies
by Rose O' Neill

An accomplished avant-garde artist and a poet preoccupied with the themes of Celtic folk religion, Rose O'Neill created "The Kewpies" in 1905. Her full-page "Kewpie" adventures were first syndicated in 1917.

The Yellow Kid
by R.F. Outcault

Most of "The Yellow Kid" was set in Hogan's Alley. On one occasion, however, Outcault took the entire Hogan's Alley gang on a tour of Europe. The lads seem something less than reverential on arriving back in the land of their ancestors' birth.

Teenie Weenies
by Wm. Donahey

Along with Rose O'Neill's "Kewpies," Wm. Donahey's "Teenie Weenies" represent Irish America's other major contribution to the saga of the "wee people." The "Teenie Weenies" first appeared in the Chicago Tribune in the 1920s and continued to circulate into the early 1960s.

Happy Hooligan
by Frederic Opper

As drawn by Frederic Opper—who had already made a good deal of money depicting Irishmen as apes and monkeys for the pages of Puck—"Happy Hooligan" gave the "wild Irish" a new American name. Opper's "Hooligan" flourished from 1900 until 1932 in Hearst newspapers all across the country.

Our Boarding House
by Gene Ahern

Gene Ahern was born on Chicago's South Side in 1895. Featuring the suspiciously English braggart Major Hoople, Ahern's "Our Boarding House" was drawn under his own hand from 1923 until 1936.

Bringing Up Father
by George McManus

The most Irish of all the major American comic strips, George McManus' unfolding stories of the travails of Jiggs and Maggie appeared on the front page of Puck: The Comic Weekly from 1917 until 1954.

Dick Tracy
by Chester Gould

The Depression era produced a number of detective strips with Irish-American lead characters, but none of them were quite as inventive as Chester Gould's "Dick Tracy." Gould sold his first "Dick Tracy" to Captain Patterson's syndicate in October 1931.

Plastic Man
by Jack Cole

A marvelous, early parody of the virtues of superhero cartoons, Jack Cole's "Plastic Man"—which began in 1941—told of the transformation of detective Eel O'Brien into the most elongated and wily crime fighter of all time.

Captain Easy
by Roy Crane

The premier comic adventure strip, Roy Crane's "Captain Easy" reached the pinnacle of its full-page, four-color Sunday glory in the 1930s. After the Second World War, Crane began to turn his attention to the adventures of "Buz Sawyer."

Terry and the Pirates
by Milton Caniff

Milton Caniff's graphic and narrative skills have made "Terry and the Pirates" the most compelling and realistically drawn adventure story in the entire history of the American comic strip.

The Fenian Invasion
by Dan O Neill

With R. Crumb, Dan O'Neill is one of the most significant artists to emerge from the "underground comix" rebellion. O'Neill's "The Fenian Invasion," based on actual historical events, was drawn exclusively for this collection.

Pogo
by Walt Kelly

The son of "Krazy Kat" and the father of "Doonesbury" and "Bloom County," Walt Kelly's "Pogo" provided ongoing commentary on the aberrations of American political and social life from 1948 until Kelly's death in 1973.

Blue Collar Tales

▶

*Jack Kehoe (Sean Connery)
leads his unit of rebel "Mollys"
out of the coal mines of western
Pennsylvania in the 1970
Paramount production of*
The Molly Maguires.

*"I guarantee to survive, and I guarantee that my bones,
dissolving into chalky dust, will fight them from the grave."*
—James T. Farrell, 1965

FARRELL

By Pete Hamill

Famine Ireland provided nineteenth-century America with a huge, new, English-speaking, industrial working class. From 1820 through 1870, five out of ten Irish immigrants found themselves employed as either unskilled laborers or domestic servants. The building trades— the plumbers, structural ironworkers, steam fitters, masons, etc.—soon became very Irish. The Irish also poured into dock work and the metal trades. In time Irish accents could be regularly heard down at the local police and fire departments, and over in the teacher's cafeteria at the local public schoolhouse. The American writer who possessed the most accurate, least romanticized feeling for these people was of course James T. Farrell of Chicago. Ruth McKenney, better known for her lighter work such as My Sister Eileen, *also wrote two neglected classic labor novels back in the 1930s.*

Growing up in Brooklyn during World War Two, two books helped change my life. One was *The Adventures of Huckleberry Finn,* which opened for me a lyrical vision of American freedom. Somehow, reading Mark Twain's great novel for the first time, I sensed that my parents, Catholics from Belfast, had crossed the cold indifferent Atlantic for one essential reason: to get up on that raft with "Nigger Jim," and like Jim, armored with courage and defiance and a lust for freedom, find the great good place. Of course, in the tenements of my neighborhood, a lot of us were always missing Cairo in the fog; but others determined, as Huck did, that sooner or later we would have to light out for the territory. It was no accident, I thought, that Finn was an Irish name.

The other book was *Studs Lonigan.*

Turning the pages of the paperback edition, I found myself abruptly and suddenly in the world outside my door and seeing it for the first time. It was all there: the aloof unforgiving Church, the whispering fear of sex, the hard drinking, the swaggering macho codes, the pervasive sense of sin. This familiar world was at once defined and revealed in words that seemed to have been hammered onto the page. I studied the small blurb on the back of the book. James T. Farrell. Another Irish name, the name, in fact, of the grandest bar in my neighborhood, up on Ninth Avenue, a block from Holy Name Church. Born in Chicago. The son of a Teamster. His face battered, tough, the kind of face I saw every day on the streets of Brooklyn. But a writer.

I was a twelve-year-old kid then. I had not yet formed the foolishly romantic notion of becoming a writer. I wanted to draw a comic strip like Milton Caniff, or play left field for the Brooklyn Dodgers, or become an archaeologist unearthing lost cities in the heart of the Yucatan. But I know now how important Farrell was to my nascent vocation. He taught me and other city writers to look with pity and terror and compassion at the people we knew and at ourselves, to give value to the casualties of the urban wars, to speak in some way for those who have no voices. Many of his people were Irish-Americans; and, in sum, their collective story showed that even for the second and third generation, the journey to freedom and dignity could

▲

The great James T. Farrell, author of *Studs Lonigan*.

in protest. His credo was simple: "Neither God nor man is going to tell me what to write." This was no easy choice. "Farrell traveled a lonely road," Murray Kempton has said. "Ten years later, Albert Maltz, facing expulsion from the Communist Party, would declare that he did not wish to share Farrell's fate. Farrell's fate, the unspeakable, was to walk alone."

Farrell must have known, during the fierce ideological wars of the Depression and its aftermath, that he might someday pay a price for walking alone. And of course he did. After the war, his brand of American realism fell out of fashion; he sometimes complained bitterly about the narrow powers of the literary establishment, their punishing elitist zeal. In one 1954 lecture, he spoke firmly against the idea that "if a writer has a kind of vision, a way of seeing life, in which he looks at life directly and sees the meaning of experience in the experience itself ... he is inherently to be criticized by the various critics, called the New Critics, because he is not producing myths and allegories." Farrell's position was not anti-intellectual; it was rather a plea for pluralism, for a generosity of vision that most of his critics could not allow. So he journeyed on alone, seeing the world his way and writing about it as he found it, free of fad or fashion. In the last two decades of his life, he was ignored. He was not the first American writer to be cast into such brutal oblivion (think of Melville, Algren, James, Tennessee Williams, to mention only a few). He will not be the last in a country where critics are still trained to be mere literary prosecutors.

To struggle for the value of your own work—to ask that it be allowed the chance to live and not be murdered in its crib—is not the same thing as self-pity. Farrell hated that emotion. That is why his characters, including Studs and Danny O'Neill, remain interesting and complicated, long after the world they inhabited has changed forever. In essays, speeches, and interviews, Farrell made clear his belief that human beings were responsible for their own lives; they could not cop out with the complaint that the world made them what they were. That is why the Communists, in the end, could not abide him; he wouldn't blame the fates of his characters on History or Capitalism or America.

still be a passage across a mine field. More than fifty years later, Studs still speaks to us, the fearful tale reminding us that the world is a hard and dangerous place. The young still die badly on 58th and Prairie.

Farrell wrote more than the *Studs Lonigan* trilogy, of course. Decade after decade, his work came in a steady stream: essays and short stories and many more novels. In his late twenties and thirties, riding on the fame given him by Studs, he was a combative and engaged writer, briefly a Depression Communist who battled the Stalinists without ever surrendering his own individual freedom to the Trotskyites. When the literary commissars of the day insisted that he and other radical writers must produce a proletarian literature that could be used as a weapon in the class struggle, Farrell rose

He knew that victims were not heroes. If men and women didn't struggle against the world they never made, they were not truly living their lives, they were living mere apologies. And he obviously believed passionately that literature was one of the most extraordinary tools devised by humans to make themselves more human.

"The world is a mystery," Farrell said in a 1950 speech to high school students. "There are mysteries on all sides of us. And the beginning of the mystery of life is the mystery of ourselves. Along with the mystery of ourselves, there is the mystery of other people. We don't know ourselves too well, and we don't know other people very well. Novels in which there is some kind of truth help us to explore the mystery, help to give us the feeling that life is a little less mysterious, that life is a little less awesome and fearful."

For any writer, this is not a small goal; for Farrell, it was his most lasting accomplishment. Today almost all of his work is out of print. But those books will be back again, when people want to see what life was actually like during this awful century. When that happens, they'll almost certainly discover that James Thomas Farrell of Chicago also spent his life and career up on that raft with Huck and Jim. 🙥

MY SISTER EILEEN

In the decade immediately following James T. Farrell's first blue-collar tales—and F. Scott Fitzgerald's plunge into the Jazz Age, fast-cash myth and legend—Irish-American literature turned rather swiftly to the security and comfort to be found in old-fashioned, ethnic neighborhood romances. To put it mildly, in the wake of Farrell and Fitzgerald, Irish-American literature seemed to have lost its nerve.

A few important authors, but no more than a few, would try to buck this trend. John O'Hara was every bit as *noir*—if not more—than Farrell. James M. Cain was positively blistering.

Of the few other important authors of this period, Horace McCoy and Ruth McKenney are among the most interesting. McCoy has at least enjoyed something of a revival due to the film success of his story, *They Shoot Horses, Don't They?* But nobody—nobody—ever speaks much about Ruth McKenney anymore.

This is very strange. After the publication of her first book, it once seemed as if Ruth McKenney would soon have the whole world eating out of her hand.

Ruth McKenney was born in Mishawaka, Indiana, on November 11, 1911. If you have never heard of Mishawaka, Indiana, you probably already have some idea of Ruth McKenney's background: strictly small-town, Midwest and also very, very Irish. McKenney's childhood, particularly her relationship with her only sister, became the subject of her first book, the runaway best-seller, *My Sister Eileen*.

Published in 1938, *Eileen* was quickly turned into an award-winning 1940's Broadway play; a popular 1942 movie (for which Rosalind Russell would be nominated for an Academy Award); and, in 1956, an obligatory movie musical—a movie only partially redeemed by Jack Lemmon and dance-master Bob Fosse appearing in supporting roles.

McKenney, in short, was a smash.

Ruth McKenney, however, had a different agenda in mind. To evaluate her work based on *Eileen* would soon prove to be entirely misleading.

Six years before the publication of *My Sister Eileen*, McKenney had gone to work as a features writer on the *Akron Beacon Journal*. In this capacity, she covered the great Akron, Ohio labor wars—the period, during the early 1930s, when Akron's leading employers, Goodyear, Goodrich and Firestone, were locked in mortal combat with their largely middle-European, immigrant workers.

McKenney's coverage would lead to her 1939 labor classic, *Industrial Valley*, a novel that fascinates today through its pioneering use of newspaper clippings (many of them, her own), a technique that can't help but remind the reader of the work of McKenney's midwestern neighbor, John Dos Passos, in his *U.S.A. Trilogy*.

McKenney would follow *Industrial Valley* with a second labor novel, *Jake Hone*, loosely based on the lousy Sacco and Vanzetti business. By 1940, the author had clearly wandered center-stage left. During the year, she became editor of *The New Masses*, the most powerful left-wing literary journal of its time.

Did the editor of *The New Masses* find it slightly odd that her earlier work, *My Sister Eileen*, was becoming the darling piece of the bourgeoisie precisely at the same time her novels were being considered vanguard in terms of proletariat literature in this country? How far can any author push it in this country, before the whole act really starts to wobble? As far as we can tell, no interviewer ever stopped to ask McKenney these questions.

In her later life, McKenney went on to churn out a few more books largely in the *Eileen* mode—which may, or may not, be the answer— but, on one occasion, she did attempt to join her talent for cornball sentiment with her talent for hardball politics. The book is called *The Loud Red Patrick*. In it, McKenney attempts to memorialize her Grandfather Flynn much in the same manner she once had turned her sister, Eileen, into something of a period legend. This time, however, the public wanted no part of it. An avowed socialist, an unrepentant noncon-formist and a flaming Sinn Feiner, Grandfather Flynn proved entirely too much rough trade for a public that, by then, had already fallen in love with the midnight romance of Bing Crosby.

Nonplussed, Ruth McKenney continued her writing career, selling short stories to magazines such as *Harper's* and *The New Yorker*, and main-taining a regular column in the *New York Post* up until her death, in New York, on July 25, 1972. In our own time—when a woman's work is valued far more than it was in hers—it can't be much longer before someone comes along and launches a full-scale Ruth McKenney revival.

—*Bob Callahan*

One of the most unusual aspects of the Irish wing of the American Labor Movement was the leadership roles secured by Irish women by the end of the nineteenth century. Mary Harris of County Cork became a national institution as the resolute "Mother Jones." Harris was hardly a token. Kate Mullaney became known for her organizational work among the collar laundresses of Troy. Mary Elizabeth Lease soon went to bat for small farmers. Lenora O'Reilly organized the garment workers of New York City. Augusta Lewis became identified with the plight of women printers. And, in Oakland, California, Kate Kennedy unionized the public schoolteachers—a first in the history of American labor. These women left a legacy still being maintained—often by Catholic nuns—in the depressed areas of many modern American cities today.

THOSE MULES WON'T SCAB TODAY

By Mother Jones

Lattimer was an eyesore to the miners. It seemed as if no one could break into it. Twenty-six organizers and union men had been killed in that coal camp and in previous strikes. Some of them had been shot in the back. The blood of union men watered the highways. No one dared go in.

I said nothing about it but made up my mind that I was going there some night. After the raid of the women in Coaldale in the Panther Creek, the general manager of Lattimer said that if I came in there I would go out a corpse. I made no reply but I set my plans and I did not consult an undertaker.

From three different camps in the Panther Creek I had a leader bring a group of strikers to a junction of the road that leads into Lattimer. There I met them with my army of women again.

As I was leaving the hotel the clerk said, "Mother, the reporters told me to ring their bell if I saw you go out."

"Well, don't see me go out. Watch the front door carefully and I will go out the back door."

We marched through the night, reaching Lattimer just before dawn. The strikers hid themselves in the mines. The women took up their position on the door steps of the miners' shacks. When a miner stepped out of his house to go to work, the women started mopping the step, shouting, "No work today!"

Everybody came running out into the dirt streets. "God, it is the old mother and her army," they were saying.

The Lattimer miners and the mule drivers were

afraid to quit work. They had been made cowards. They took the mules, lighted the lamps in their caps and started down the mines, not knowing that I had three thousand miners down below ground waiting for them and the mules.

"Those mules won't scab today," I said to the general manager who was cursing everybody. "They know it is going to be a holiday."

"Take those mules down!" shouted the general manager.

Mules and drivers and miners disappeared down into the earth. I kept the women singing patriotic songs so as to drown the noise of the men down in the mines.

Directly the mules came up to the surface without a driver, and we women cheered for the mules who were first to become good union citizens. They were followed by the miners who began running home. Those that didn't go up were sent up. Those that insisted on working and thus defeating their brothers were grabbed by the women and carried to their wives.

An old Irish woman had two sons who were scabs. The women threw one of them over the fence to his mother. He lay there still. His mother thought he was dead and she ran into the house for a bottle of holy water and shook it over Mike.

"Oh for God's sake, come back to life," she hollered. "Come back and join the union."

He opened his eyes and saw our women standing around him.

"Sure, I'll go to hell before I'll scab again," says he.

The general manager called the sheriff who asked me to take the women away. I said, "Sheriff, no one is going to get hurt, no property is going to be destroyed, but there are to be no more killings of innocent men here."

I told him if he wanted peace he should put up a notice that the mines were closed until the strike was settled.

The day was filled with excitement. The deputies kept inside the office; the general manager also. Our men stayed up at the mines to attend to the scabs and the women did the rest. As a matter of fact the majority of the men, those with any spirit left in them after years of cowardice, wanted to strike but had not dared. But when a hand was held out to them, they took hold and marched along with their brothers.

The bosses telephoned to John Mitchell that he should take me and my army of women out of Lattimer. That was the first knowledge that Mitchell had of my being there.

When the manager saw there was no hope and that the battle was won by the miners, he came out and put up a notice that the mines were closed until the strike was settled.

I left Lattimer with my army of women and went up to Hazelton. President Mitchell and his organizers were there. Mr. Mitchell said, "Weren't you afraid to go in there?"

"No," I said, "I am not afraid to face any thing if facing it may bring relief to the class that I belong to."

The victory of Lattimer gave new life to the whole anthracite district. It gave courage to the organization. Those brave women I shall never forget who caused those stone walls to fall by marching with tin pans and catcalls.

THE TERENCE POWDERLY LEGACY

Terence Powderly was General Master Workman of the country's largest labor organization, the Knights of Labor, in 1883. At that time he was also mayor of Scranton, Pennsylvania, and a vice-president of the Irish National Land and Industrial League of the United States. After the Philadelphia convention, at which that organization had given way to the new Irish National League of America, Powderly presided over a rally in Scranton, at which Thomas Brennan from Ireland was welcomed to the city. Many Knights of Labor local assemblies and nationalist clubs marched in the grand parade, but it was headed by the Parnell Rifle Club.

Powderly was also a national leader of the Clan na Gael. From his letters we learn that in city after city, leading activists of the trade unions and the Knights were also members of that secret, militant, nationalist group. In the little rolling mill town of Woods Run, adjacent to Pittsburgh, for example, forty workers and the priest of St. Andrew's Catholic Church belonged to the Land League, forty-five people had contributed to the Fenian "skirmishing fund," and twenty-one members belonged to the Clan na Gael.

These personal links embedded the causes of Irish nationalism and land reform deeply within the American labor movement. They also reinforce the conclusion that one simply cannot rest content with the conception of the late nineteenth-century Irish-American community as divided into an upwardly mobile middle class and a disreputable "underclass" of drunkards, thieves, and Fenians—however popular that segment may have become, it is misleading to interpret everyone's history in its terms.

The iron puddlers and rollers of Woods Run produced their own leaders, men and women of broad political vision, and all of them staunch trade unionists. The cultural legacy which they had brought from Ireland blended with the experiences they gained in countless factories, and factory towns, to produce a complex and resilient new working-class ideology, which was their ultimate gift to all of American labor.

—*David Montgomery*

THE MOLLY MAGUIRES

THE ANTHRACITE COAL REGIONS OF EASTERN PENNSYLVANIA .. DURING AND AFTER THE CIVIL WAR .. THE SCENE OF THE EARLIEST AND MOST SAVAGE OF THE CONFLICT BETWEEN CAPITAL AND LABOR ..

JAMES McPARLAN .. ALIAS JAMES McKENNA , IN THE EMPLOY OF THE PINKERTON DETECTIVE AGENCY, IS SENT INTO THE COAL FIELDS TO INFILTRATE THE MOLLY MAGUIRES .. McPARLAN , BORN CATHOLIC IN ARMAGH , 1844 , MAKES FRIENDS EASILY ..

.. WITH HIS FELLOW CATHOLIC IRISH .. HE IS SOON ACCEPTED INTO THE ANCIENT ORDER OF HIBERNIANS, AND INTO THE DEEPER ORDER .. THE MOLLY MAGUIRES ..

FRANKLIN B. GOWEN .. FORMER DISTRICT ATTORNEY IN THE COAL REGION .. NOW PRESIDENT OF THE PHILADELPHIA AND READING RAILROAD ..

GOWEN HAD SOUGHT A MONOPOLY OF THE COAL BEDS . HIS REDUCTION OF LABOR COSTS WITHOUT REGARD FOR THE HUMAN NEEDS OF THE MINERS WAS DONE TO COVER THE COST OF HIS EXPANSIONIST POLICIES .

DEEPLY IN DEBT, THE RAILROAD CANNOT AFFORD LABOR TROUBLE. VIOLENCE AGAINST THE MINE OPERATORS BREAKS OUT. THE ATTACKS ARE RUMORED TO BE THE WORK OF THE MOLLY MAGUIRES .. A SECRET ORGANIZATION WITHIN THE FRATERNAL ANCIENT ORDER OF HIBERNIANS ..

ALLAN PINKERTON
HEAD OF THE PINKERTON DETECTIVE AGENCY IN PHILADELPHIA .. IT IS HIS OPERATIVES IN MISSOURI THAT HAVE THROWN A BOMB INTO THE HOME OF JESSE AND FRANK JAMES' MOTHER, THE EXPLOSION TEARING THE ARM FROM THE MOTHER AND KILLING A SMALL CHILD. THE COUNTRY IS HORRIFIED BY THE PINKERTONS' TACTICS .. HE DESPERATELY NEEDS A PUBLIC RELATIONS SUCCESS ..

JAMES McPARLAN ..

HAVING AN AGENT INSIDE THE MOLLIES IS NOT ENOUGH FOR GOWEN AND PINKERTON .. McPARLAN IS ENCOURAGED TO LEAD THE MOLLIES INTO A MURDER PLOT AGAINST THE MINE OPERATORS .. GOWEN AND PINKERTON FEEL ONLY A MASS EXECUTION WILL STOP THE LABOR UNREST ..

EDWARD COSGROVE, A MOLLY MAGUIRE, IS KILLED BY GOMER JAMES, A WELSHMAN.. JAMES IS TARGETED FOR MURDER.. McPARLAN WARNS JAMES TO LEAVE THE AREA..

JAMES IS SHOT AT A PICNIC BY THOMAS HURLEY.. MOLLIES THEN SHOOT THOMAS SANGER, A COLLIERY BOSS.., AND WILLIAM UREN, A MINER.. McPARLAN'S EVIDENCE.. AT THE TRIALS, IS ALL HEARSAY.. HE WAS NOT PRESENT AT THE SHOOTINGS..

AFTER THE KILLINGS, THE MOLLIES ARE ARRESTED.. ON McPARLAN'S TESTIMONY, WITH ONLY THE TESTIMONY OF TWO OTHER INFORMERS, KERRIGAN AND LAWLER, WHO WILL SWEAR ANYTHING TO AVOID THE ROPE, TWENTY MEN ARE CONVICTED OF MURDER AND TEN WILL HANG ON ONE DAY..

KERRIGAN.. ONE OF THE INFORMERS..

McPARLAN.. AS JAMES McKINNA ENCOURAGED, PLOTTED, AND HELP CARRY OUT MURDER, AND THEN GAVE EVIDENCE TO HANG HIS FELLOW MOLLIES..
THE LINE BETWEEN DETECTIVE AND ACTIVE PARTICIPANT IN MURDER IS BLURRED..
A MEMBER OF THE ANCIENT ORDER OF HIBERNIANS IS NOW BY PUBLIC HYSTERIA..
.. A MOLLY MAGUIRE ..

1 JOHN DONOHUE 2. EDWARD J. KELLY 3. ALEXANDER CAMPBELL 4. MICHAEL J. DOYLE 5. THOMAS DUFFY 6. JAMES CAMPBELL 7. JAMES ROARITY 8 HUGH McGEHAN 9. JAMES BOYLE 10. THOMAS MUNLEY 11. ANDREW LANAHAN

THE KING OF THE MOLLY MAGUIRES

JACK KEHOE.. IS CONVICTED OF MURDER.. EIGHT YEARS EARLIER, WITNESSES TESTIFY HE THREATENED A VICTIM THREE WEEKS BEFORE THE ASSAULT.. ALTHOUGH HE CAN PROVE HIS PRESENCE ELSEWHERE THE DAY OF THE MURDER, HE IS FOUND GUILTY.. KEHOE IS CONSIDERED THE KING OF THE MOLLY MAGUIRES AND MUST HANG TO SATISFY GOWEN AND PINKERTON.

.. WERE THERE REALLY MOLLY MAGUIRES IN PENNSYVANIA..?

FOR THE SAKE OF THOSE LIVES PAST, IN THE BENEVOLENT GRIP OF YOUNG AMERICAN CORPORATIONS, WE CAN ONLY HOPE SO..

FRANKLIN GOWEN, ON FRIDAY THE 13TH, 1889, IN GOOD HEALTH, AGE 53, PUT A BULLET THROUGH HIS HEAD IN A WASHINGTON D.C. HOTEL ROOM.. REMORSE FOR HIS ROLE IN THE HANGINGS WAS SPECULATED.. NO NOTE ..

WHAT DO WE KNOW?.. WE KNOW A MILITANT ORGANIZATION OF WORKINGMEN, OF ONE NATIONALITY AND ONE RELIGION WAS DISPERSED BY EXECUTION OF ITS LEADERS..

WE KNOW THE PROSECUTIONS WERE CONDUCTED BY LAWYERS IN THE EMPLOY OF THE LEADING CORPORATIONS IN THE REGION..
DID THE CORPORATIONS ENTER A CONSPIRACY WITH THE PINKERTONS TO MANUFACTURE EVIDENCE WITH WHICH TO CONVICT THEIR ENEMIES..? WHY DID GOWEN KILL HIMSELF.. IN 1907, McPARLAN WILL BE DISCREDITED BY CLARENCE DARROW IN THE TRIAL OF BIG BILL HEYWOOD.. FOR MANUFACTURING EVIDENCE ..

CONNOLLY IN THE BRONX

By Elizabeth Gurley Flynn

In 1907, during the campaign to free Moyer, Haywood and Pettibone, I was invited to speak at a meeting, in Newark, New Jersey, arranged by the Socalist Labor Party. There was protest against my acceptance by the New Jersey Socialist Party, which either had not been invited to participate or had refused. I felt I should go anywhere to speak for this purpose. Our rostrum was an old wagon, set up in Washington Park. The horse was inclined to run when there was loud applause, so he was taken out of the wagon shafts. This meeting was an unforgettable event in my life because it was here I first met James Connolly, the Irish Socialist speaker, writer and labor organizer who gave his life for Irish freedom nine years later in the Easter Rising of 1916 in Dublin.

At the time I refer to he worked for the Singer Sewing Machine Company of Elizabeth, New Jersey, and had a hard struggle to supply his wife and six small children. He lost his job when he tried to organize a union in the plant. He was short, rather stout, a plain-looking man with a large black mustache, a very high forehead and dark sad eyes, a man who rarely smiled. A scholar and an excellent writer, he used speech that was marred for American audiences by his thick, North of Ireland accent, with a Scotch burr from his long residence in Glasgow. On the Washington Park occasion someone spilled a bottle of water in his hat, the only one he possessed undoubtedly, and with a wry expression on his face he shook it out and dried it, but made no complaint.

Connolly and I spoke again in 1907 at an Italian Socialist meeting early one Sunday morning. I wondered then why they arranged their meetings at such an odd hour but discovered it was a substitute for church among these rabid anticlericals, and happily did not interfere with their sacred ritual of the big spaghetti and vino dinner later on. I asked Connolly, "Who will speak in Italian?" He smiled his rare smile and replied, "We'll see. Someone, surely." After we had both spoken, they took a recess and gave us coffee and cake behind the scenes, a novel but welcome experience for us. Stale water was the most we got elsewhere! Then we returned to the platform and Connolly arose. He spoke beautifully in Italian to my amazement and the delight of the audience who "viva'd" loudly.

Later he moved his family to Elton Avenue in the Bronx and the younger children of our families played together. Once, Patrick Quinlan, a family friend who had left a bookcase with a glass door at Connolly's house, was horrified to find all the books on the floor and the Flynn-Connolly children playing funeral, with one child beautifully laid out in the bookcase. "Who's dead?" Connolly asked. "Quinlan," they replied serenely. Needless to say, the children did not like Quinlan.

Connolly worked for the International Workers of the World and had an office at Cooper Square. He was a splendid organizer, as his later work for the Irish Transport Workers, with James Larkin, demonstrated.

Elizabeth Gurley Flynn (1890-1964) was one of America's most radical and articulate labor organizers. Throughout her life, Flynn remained a spellbinding platform orator. Here is how Theodore Dreiser described her first "performance" in 1906: "Her name is Elizabeth Gurley Flynn, and she is only a girl just turned sixteen.... It was in January last that she made her first appearance on the lecture platform and electrified her audience with her eloquence, her youth, and her loveliness." What the mildy patronizing Dreiser failed to mention was that Flynn was more Marxist than Karl and also tough as nails. She was the American link with James Connolly, James Larkin and the class-intelligent labor movement back in Ireland. Flynn was the Bernadette Devlin of her time.

He felt keenly that not enough understanding and sympathy was shown by American Socialists for the cause of Ireland's national liberation, that the Irish workers here were too readily abandoned by the Socialists as "reactionaries" and that there was not sufficient effort made to bring the message of Socialism to the Irish-American workers. In 1907 George B. McClellan, mayor of New York City, made a speech in which he said: "There are Russian Socialists and Jewish Socialists and German Socialists! But, thank God! there are no Irish Socialists!" This was a challenge to Connolly, my father and a host of others with good Irish names, members of both the Socialist parties. They banded together as the Irish Socialist Club, later known as the Irish Socialist Federation. James Connolly was chairman and my sister Katherine was secretary. She was then fifteen years old. Connolly was strong for encouraging "the young people."

The Irish Socialist Federation caused great protest among the other existing federations. The others insisted we didn't need a federation because we weren't foreign-speaking. We wanted a banner we could fight under. The Unity Club required us to be too placating, too peaceful. The Federation was born one Sunday afternoon at our house in the Bronx. Connolly, Quinlan, O'Shaugnessy, Cooke, Cody, Daly, Ray, all the Flynns, were there; also our faithful Jewish friend, Sam Stodel, who was sympathetic to our proposal.

He went into the kitchen and said to my mother, "Have you anything for this bunch to eat?" She confessed she had not, so he went around the corner and bought ham, cheese, corned beef, beer, crackers, etc., to feed the doughty Irish when their session was over. Nourished by Sam, we went forth to battle. The Federation arranged street meetings to show that Mayor McClellan was an ignoramus and a liar, especially in Irish neighborhoods where such meetings had never been held. It had a large green and white banner, announcing who and what it was, with the Gaelic slogan, Faugh-a-Balach (Clear the Way) in big letters surrounded by harps and shamrocks. The meetings were stormy but finally accepted at many corners. A German blacksmith comrade built the Federation a sturdy platform that could not easily be upset, with detachable iron legs that could be used as "shillelaghs" in an emergency. These helped to establish order at the meetings, and won a wholesome respect for the Federation.

The Federation issued a statement of its purposes (written by James Connolly): "To assist the revolutionary working-class movement in Ireland by a dissemination of its literature, to educate the working-class Irish of this country into a knowledge of Socialist principles and to prepare them to cooperate with the workers of all other races, colors, and nationalities in the emancipation of labor." James Connolly wrote one book, *Labour in Irish History*, one play and many pamphlets.

His extensive writings were spread out over many years in various workers' papers and magazines.

He published a monthly magazine, *The Harp*. Many poems from his own pen appeared. It was a pathetic sight to see him standing, poorly clad, at the door of Cooper Union or some other East Side hall, selling his little paper. None of the prosperous professional Irish, who shouted their admiration for him after his death, lent him a helping hand at that time. Jim Connolly was anathema to them because he was a "So'—cialist."

He had no false pride and encouraged others to do these tasks by setting an example. At the street meetings he persuaded those who had no experience in speaking to "chair the meeting" as a method of training them. Connolly had a rare skill born of vast knowledge, in approaching the Irish workers. He spoke the truth sharply and forcefully when necessary, as in the following from *The Harp* of November 1900:

To the average non-Socialist Irishman the idea of belonging to an international political party is unthinkable, is obnoxious, and he feels that if he did, all the roots of his Irish nature would be dug up. Of course, he generally belongs to a church—the Roman Catholic Church—which is the most international institution in existence. That does not occur to him as atrocious, in fact he is rather proud than otherwise that the Church is spread throughout the entire world, that it overlaps the barriers of civilization, penetrating into the depths of savagedom, and ignores all considerations of race, color, or nationality.... But although he would lay down his life for a Church which he boasts of as "Catholic" or universal, he turns with a shudder from an economic or political movement which has the same characteristics.

Connolly published *The Harp* here as the official organ of the Irish Socialist Federation, and moved it to Dublin in 1910.   ❧

JAMES LARKIN IN AMERICA

One day in the spring of 1914 a knock came on our door at 511 East 134th Street in the Bronx. We lived up three flights of stairs and the bell was usually out of order. There stood a gaunt man, with a rough-hewn face and a shock of graying hair, who spoke with an Irish accent. He asked for Mrs. Flynn. When my mother went to the door, he said simply: "I'm Jim Larkin. James Connolly sent me." He came regularly after that to drink tea with my mother, whom he called "my countrywoman." He had come to raise funds for the Irish Citizens' Army and the labor movement there. He had been a founder, with Connolly, of the Irish Transport Workers Union and a fiery leader of its great strike in 1913. Once he was out of Ireland, the British government did everything in its power to prevent his return. He remained throughout World War I, was jailed here during the Palmer raids and finally deported.

He was very poor and while in New York he lived in one room in a small alley in Greenwich Village, called Milligan Place. It ran diagonally from Sixth Avenue through to 11th Street and faced the old Jefferson Market Court. He had a small open fireplace and a tea kettle was ever simmering on the hearth. The tea was so strong that it tasted like medicine to us. His way of life was frugal and austere. He was bitterly opposed to drink and denounced it as a curse of the Irish. Once he was with a group of us at John's Restaurant on East 12th Street, which we frequented from 1913 on. He asked for tea. They had none, but out of respect for him, they sent out for tea and a teapot, and he taught them how to make it.

He was a magnificent orator and an agitator without equal. He spoke at antiwar meetings, where he thundered against British imperialism's attempts to drag us into war. My mother gave him the green banner of the Irish Socialist Federation and he spoke under it innumerable times, especially on the New York waterfront. It finally was lost somewhere on the West Side by an old Irish cobbler who used to take care of it in his shop—but visited taverns en route. When Connolly and his comrades were shot down in the 1916 Easter Rising, Larkin aroused a tremendous wrath of protest here, especially when he roared against the professional Irish, mostly politicians, who tried to explain away an actual armed uprising of the Irish people. He went to Paterson with us after we won our free speech fight, and spoke to a large gathering of silk workers who contributed a pathetic collection of pennies, nickels and dimes to help the Irish, in response to Jim's appeal "for bread and guns." Many an Irish cop turned the other way and pretended not to hear when Jim made this appeal.

James Larkin was the nephew of one of the Manchester martyrs, hanged by the British government in 1867. He boasted of his family tree, amid cheers of approval from Irish audiences, that "a man was hung in every one of four generations, as a rebel." Connolly and Larkin represented a remarkably effective combination in the struggle for Irish freedom, the building of an Irish labor movement and the establishment of a socialist movement. They complemented each other and were loved and respected in Ireland—and respected each other. I am proud I had the opportunity to count both of these truly great sons of Erin as my comrades and friends.

—*Elizabeth Gurley Flynn*

It is no longer possible, of course, to put the Irish in labor—or anywhere else, for that matter—inside one particular political basket. The Communist activist William Z. Foster was Irish, but so was the conservative Frank Fitzsimmons. Raymond Donovan is of Irish descent, but so is Democratic Socialist Michael Harrington. You would undoubtedly be in for a hair-raising and heated evening if you invited Patrick Buchanan and Alexander Cockburn over for tea to discuss the fate of the American Labor Movement today. It is a long, complex and fascinating history—and still, should the discussion turn to the prototypical Irish labor leader in the old, grand style, you could do far worse than to consider the "underground" legend of Michael J. Quill.

MIKE QUILL
By Jimmy Breslin

For the last fortnight, a distinguished group of twenty transportation trade unionists from Ireland have been in New York to watch the methods, the warking methods, of Mr. Michael J. Quill, president, International Transport Workers Union, and while it has been forty years since Mike Quill left Ireland, he goes back every so often to charge the battery and keep friendships growing. Yesterday was the last day that his friends from the unions in Ireland would be around to see him operating. So Mike Quill, sitting there with twenty of them from the Old Country peering right over his shoulder, gave them a grand show for their last day.

At noon Quill called a press conference. He announced he was calling a subway and bus strike for the entire City of New York at 5 A.M. on December 15. His union's contract does not run out until the end of the month. And Mike never has strikes. It's been so long since he was on a picket line that he wouldn't even know which way to turn at the end of the walk. But every other year at this time, with the transit workers' contract coming up, Mike Quill becomes the enemy of the city and anything he says sets everybody off to blathering.

By three o'clock in the afternoon he had the whole city even more upset than it was the day before, which was very upset, and the twenty Irishmen who were watching him had something more to take back with them, and God help the bus company in Dublin. "What else would you have the man do?" they were saying. "This is the way warkers fight for their rights." And then they all took Michael out and threw him a party.

"Will you have a small one?" Jerry Monks of Dublin said while the seating was going on in the restaurant at the Sheraton-Atlantic Hotel.

"It's a little early in the day yet."

Michael J. Quill of the
city of New York,
1941.

"Accardin' to the man," Monks said.

"That makes it too early, then."

"Will you mind if I have a small one?" Monks said.

"I'd be honored if you'd have one without taking it as an insult that I don't have one with you."

"Thank you, thank you," he said. He picked up a bottle from the portable bar set up by the table and he poured enough whiskey into the glass to put a house-painter in business.

While Mr. Monks set the tone for the trade unionists from Ireland, Mr. Michael J. Quill sat up at the other end of the table. He was waiting on his pea soup. He had in front of him a softcover book, *1913: Jim Larkin and the Dublin Lock-Out*, which is printed by the

Workers' Union of Ireland, 29 Parnell Square, Dublin I, and which contains on its pages this tribute to scabs who went to work for the Dublin Tramway Company during the strike:

You can tell him 'midst a thousand by his crime and by his crawl,
   For of dignity or courage he possesses none at all.
   In the aleshop he's a sponger, in the workshop he's a spy;
   He's a liar and deceiver with low cunning in his eye.

Sitting next to Michael was Jim Larkin, Jr. It was his father who was involved in the Dublin strike in 1913 and who then came over here and in 1919 was put

143

into Sing Sing prison for four years on charges growing out of union activity. Now this is a long time ago, but it was fresh in everybody's mind yesterday.

"I remember him tellin' me he'd been in jail in probably every state of the country," Jim Larkin, Jr., was saying.

"He probably was, he was arganizing everywhere," Quill said.

And then Larkin got up and as a memento of the visit to this country he gave Mike Quill a plaque and on the plaque was a red hand, O'Neill of the Red Hand, and if you don't know what that stands for let Michael himself who got up on his feet explain it to you.

"I've seen the red hand before," he said. "Many years ago, a prince and a fellow both wanted to claim some land and they had a boat race for it and the prince saw he was losing, so he took out his sword and cut off his hand and threw it onto the land and claimed it. And that's the spirit with which warkers fight for their rights everywhere in the world."

Michael then recalled 1913, when he took on the tramways in Dublin. "They told us the chairman of the board of impliers was an English Jew, but he turned out to be a good solid West Cork man named William Martin Murphy and what he didn't kill in Dublin he starved in the streets and of course he went to Mass the next day and that made it all right. Kill 'em first and then go to Mass. Then the English warkers sent us a boatload of food and they offered to take the children for us and the powers that be told us that they'll all be atheists when they come back. That's what they told us. But we know that the warkers are the same all over the world, boundaries make no differences."

With this spirit, he sat down to his steak and green beans. It is very good that he was lunching, not bargaining with the city's new "implier," John Lindsay, because Quill has had strong thoughts running through his mind for the last two weeks, while he's had the people from Ireland here, and they left last night at

THE IRISH UNDERGROUND RAILWAY

On leaving Ireland during the 1920s we were given a transfer from the Irish Republican Army to Clan na Gael in the United States. This organization helped us financially and in getting jobs. I became active on arrival and at the monthly meetings met with subway workers who were members of the I.R.A. and were now active in the Clan. Among these was one man in particular whom I got to know well—Michael J. Quill of the Austin Stack Club. Following our Clan meeting in Tara Hall on 66th Street, we would go to a restaurant and have coffee and discuss incidents in Ireland, conditions on the job, a good place for rooms (or digs as we called them), etc.

On one particular occasion Mike Quill and Michael Lynch mentioned the possibility of organizing a union. Quill suggested that we begin to think about the possibility of picking out reliable workers in our different departments with whom we would meet in our own homes, in a manner something along the lines of the I.R.A. in Ireland. Quill explained how previous efforts to organize the Union were always beaten by the Company Beakies (undercover company police), who got to know the most active members before the movement got organized and had the key men fired.

Quill also explained that James Connolly had tried to organize a union on the subway and was unable to obtain the support needed. Following Quill's advice, we began to get groups and small branches organized all over the subway. For almost a year our key members held meetings in the home of Vic Bloswick, a machinist in the 168th Street yard who lived on Kelly Street. Bloswick's boss was a Mr. Gregory who was suspicious of Bloswick's activities on recruiting for the Union. Gregory kept transferring Bloswick from midnight to A.M. shifts, then to days, hoping, as he thought, to keep him out of touch with the men.

Years after Gregory met Bloswick as a Transport Workers Union officer and said, "Well, Bloswick, you did a great job in organizing the Union." Bloswick replied, "No, you did, Mr. Gregory." Gregory asked what he meant by that and Bloswick said, "By changing my shifts all the time, I met many more men than I would have if I had stayed on one shift."

In 1933 Jim Graelton, a retired World War I veteran who had been living in Ireland, was deported from there for Socialist activities. On arrival here he organized Irish Workers Clubs in the Bronx, Brooklyn and Manhattan. These clubs arranged for lectures and publication of the teachings of James Connolly, who was executed by the British in 1916. The membership of these Clubs was helpful in giving out leaflets at subway terminals and bus depots.

It was then suggested by Tom O'Shea that we visit the Communist Party headquarters at 13th Street. Our committee got an appointment with the Executive Officers of the Party—William Z. Foster, an old-time active official of the Industrial Workers of the World, Israel Amter, Rose Wortis and their Party officials.

William Foster knew all about the failures of

9 P.M. and New York's contract with the transit workers can be handled perhaps a little more easily.

"Have you ever had occasion to meet Lindsay?" he was asked.

Michael reached out for green beans with his fork. He took up a few and put them into his mouth. He chewed on them. Then he put the fork down.

"I've had no occasion to meet Lindsay," he said.

He picked up the fork again. Mr. Quill always has been pictured in the newspapers as some sort of loud mouth. This is fantasy because he is silent Irish who sits and waits and then is very good at answering, which is one of the great arts.

"You called Lindsay a coward. Do you find that language goes further than all these diplomatic terms which everybody has come to use these days?"

This time he reached out for a piece of steak. He cut it and put it into his mouth. Then he put the knife down.

"It does, it does."

"What's the favorite thing you've called people over the years?"

He chewed the steak for a long time. Then his jaw stopped moving.

"Bastard."

Michael reached for the steak again and the twenty trade unionists from Dublin said sure, if a man is a bastard why then you call him a bastard. They all finished lunch and went home last night, which is good because if those men stayed around, the feeling is that the whole city would be walking by New Year's Day. ❧

trying to organize the subways—1905, 1910, 1926, etc. He agreed that Quill's idea on organizing was marvelous to get the movement going. It was agreed at the time that we would get financial aid to start the organization of the Transport Workers Union.

In the months that followed, we began invading the Company Union meetings and, under the leadership of Michael J. Quill, began taking over the meetings. The president of the Company Union was Paddy Connelly and at one of the big Company Union meetings, which was held in Anderson Hall where we were in the majority, Connelly called down from the platform, "Don't you know your leader Mike Quill, sitting there, is a Red?" Quill stood up and said to Connelly, "I'd rather be a Red than a rat."

—*Gerald O'Reilly*

Vaudeville Days

▶

Gordon MacRae gets a lift in the 1950 Warner Brothers production of The Daughter of Rosie O'Grady.

THE HUMAN MOP

By Buster Keaton with Charles Samuels

I f I say I "officially joined" my folks' act in 1899 it is because my father always insisted that I'd been trying to get into the family act unofficially —meaning unasked, unwanted, and unbilled— practically from the day I was born.

Having no baby-sitter, my mother parked me in the till of a wardrobe trunk while she worked on the stage with Pop. According to him, the moment I could crawl I headed for the footlights. "And when Buster learned to walk," he always proudly explained to all who were interested and many who weren't, "there was no holding him. He would jump up and down in the wings, make plenty of noise, and get in everyone's way. It seemed easier to let him come out with us on the stage where we could keep an eye on him.

"At first I told him not to move. He was to lean against the side wall and stay there. But one day I got the idea of dressing him up like myself as a stage Irishman with a fright wig, slugger whiskers, fancy vest, and oversize pants. Soon he was imitating everything I did, and getting laughs.

"But he got nothing at all at the first Monday show we played at Bill Dockstader's Theatre in Wilmington, Delaware. Dockstader told me to leave him out of the act. But he had a special matinee for kiddies on Wednesday and suggested that children, knowing no better, might be amused by Buster's antics."

On Wednesday Bill noticed that their parents also seemed amused and suggested I go on at all performances. Pop said he didn't want to use me in the night show as I had to get my rest like any small child. Dockstader then offered to pay the act ten dollars a week extra. My father agreed to try it. I had no trouble sleeping through the morning and played night and day with the act from then on.

Even in my early days our turn established a reputation for being the roughest in vaudeville. This was the result of a series of interesting experiments Pop made with me. He began these by carrying me out on the stage and dropping me on the floor. Next he started wiping up the floor with me. When I gave no sign of minding this he began throwing me through the scenery, out into the wings, and dropping me down on the bass drum in the orchestra pit.

Much like German and Jewish immigrants, blacks and Native Americans, Paddy was also reduced to a stereotyped cartoon character by the turn of the century. Yet, costumed comedy at least did bring its own rewards. If nothing else, it sure beat carrying around all those red cement bricks. Just about every Irish-American entertainer—from Shakespearean actresses to flagpole sitters— grew up on the vaudeville stage. Buster Keaton was no exception. The Great Stone Face was already entertaining three-a-day crowds before he was even eight years old.

▶

Joe, Myra and Little Buster Keaton—"The Three Keatons" on stage.

148

The people out front were amazed because I did not cry. There was nothing mysterious about this. I did not cry because I wasn't hurt. All little boys like to be roughhoused by their fathers. They are also natural tumblers and acrobats. Because I was also a born ham-bone, I ignored any bumps or bruises I may have got at first on hearing audiences gasp, laugh, and applaud. There is one more thing: little kids when they fall haven't very far to go. I suppose a psychologist would call it a case of self-hypnosis.

Before I was much bigger than a gumdrop I was being featured in our act, The Three Keatons, as "The Human Mop." One of the first things I noticed was that whenever I smiled or let the audience suspect how much I was enjoying myself they didn't seem to laugh as much as usual.

I guess people just never do expect any human mop, dishrag, beanbag, or football to be pleased by what is being done to him. At any rate it was on purpose that I started looking miserable, humiliated, hounded, and haunted, bedeviled, bewildered, and at my wit's end. Some other comedians can get away with laughing at their own gags. Not me. The public just will not stand for it. And that is all right with me. All of my life I have been happiest when the folks watching me said to each other, "Look at the poor dope, wilya?"

Because of the way I looked on the stage and screen the public naturally assumed that I felt hopeless and unloved in my personal life. Nothing could be farther from the fact. As long back as I can remember I have considered myself a fabulously lucky man. From the beginning I was surrounded by interesting people who loved fun and knew how to create it. I've had few dull moments and not too many sad and defeated ones.

In saying this I am by no means overlooking the rough and rocky years I've lived through. But I was not brought up thinking life would be easy. I always expected to work hard for my money and to get nothing I did not earn. And the bad years, it seems to me, were so few that only a dyed-in-the-wool grouch who enjoys feeling sorry for himself would complain of them.

My parents were my first bit of great luck. I cannot recall one argument that they had about money or anything else when I was growing up. Yet both were rugged individualists. I was their partner, however, as well as their child. From the time I was ten both they and the other actors on the bill treated me not as a little boy, but as an adult and a full-fledged performer. Isn't that what most children want: to be accepted, to be allowed to share in their parents' concerns and problems? It is difficult, of course, for a man of my age to say with certainty what he felt and thought and wanted as a little kid. But it seems to me that I enjoyed both the freedom and privileges of childhood, certainly most of them, and also the thrill of being treated as full-grown years before other boys and girls. 🐦

149

THE GREAT STONE FACE

eaton's face ranked almost with Lincoln's as an early American archetype; it was haunting, handsome, almost beautiful, yet it was irreducibly funny; he improved matters by topping it off with a deadly horizontal hat, as flat and thin as a phonograph record. One can never forget Keaton wearing it, standing erect at the prow as his little boat is being launched. The boat goes grandly down the skids and, just as grandly, straight on to the bottom. Keaton never budges. The last you see of him, the water lifts the hat off the stoic head and it floats away.

No other comedian could do as much with the deadpan. He used this great, sad, motionless face to suggest various related things: a one-track mind near the track's end of pure insanity; mulish imperturbability under the wildest of circumstances; how dead a human being can get and still be alive; an awe-inspiring sort of patience and power to endure, proper to granite but uncanny in flesh and blood. Everything he was and did bore out this rigid face and played laughs against it. When he moved his eyes, it was like seeing them move in a statue. His short-legged body was all sudden, machinelike angles, governed by a daft aplomb. When he swept a semaphorelike arm to point, you could almost hear the electrical impulse in the signal block. When he ran away from a cop, his transitions from accelerating walk to easy jog trot to brisk canter to headlong gallop to flogged-piston spring —always floating, above this frenzy, the untroubled, untouchable face—were as distinct and as soberly in order as an automatic gearshift.

—*James Agee*

◄

Buster Keaton gets a lift from the local "Paddy" wagon.

TALES OF THE MULLIGAN GUARD

By Samuel G. Freedman

The theater critic William Dean Howells spent much of his life searching for indigenous American drama, and in 1886 he announced he had found it in the person of one Edward Harrigan. Here was a man, Howells declared, who wrote, directed, acted and managed his works in the manner of a Shakespeare or a Moliere. Here was a social realist on the order of Dickens or Zola.

Such accolades must have surprised Howells' highbrow readership, for Harrigan was not the product of a university or a conservatory, but rather the self-educated son of a seaman. He had grown up in Manhattan's Irish slums and had run away to sea in his teens. His plays carried the cheapest ticket in town and their most devoted spectators were the orphaned newsboys whom New York had by the thousands.

But with his featured actor Tony Hart and his songwriting partner Dave Braham, Harrigan created plays that were unsentimentally true to the New York of the immigrants. From the 1870s through the 1890s, as much American theater was imitating European farce or the English music hall, Harrigan evoked the city of pushcarts and tenements, landlords and ward heelers. The accents heard on his stage came from the mouths of Irish, German, Italian and Jewish immigrants and the blacks streaming to the urban north after the Civil War.

Beyond the importance of his themes, Harrigan also laid the groundwork for what would become American musical comedy, particularly in his use of songs to advance the stage action. Harrigan—and perhaps to a greater degree Hart—also represented one of the beginnings of an American popular theater based on an individual performer's comic brilliance. The variety circuit that spawned Harrigan and Hart would metamorphose into vaudeville, burlesque and silent films, the training ground for such comedians as Bob Hope and Milton Berle and the influence on such modern theater artists as the mime Bill Irwin.

For all that, Harrigan has remained largely a footnote in American theatrical history, quite overshadowed as an innovator by the man he influenced, George M. Cohan. The Harrigan legacy, however, has somehow lingered on.

When asked in 1889 why he dealt so often with the subject of runaway black slaves and Irish immigrants, Edward Harrigan replied that these were the two peoples who cared the most about the tradition of song and dance. Harrigan's own song and dance career began in San Francisco where, by 1861, he was already singing duets with the legendary Lotta Crabtree. Harrigan's influence on the first generation of Irish-American vaudevillians was enormous. For people like George M. Cohan, Harrigan (H-A-DOUBLE R-I, G-A-N spells HARRIGAN) would always remain the real Chairman of the Boards.

▲

Edward Harrigan and Tony Hart, the original Mulligan Guard.

AN ORIGINAL SKETCH AND SONG BY ED. HARRIGAN.

MUSIC BY

DAVID BRAHAM.

SUNG WITH IMMENSE SUCCESS BY

HARRIGAN & HART.

NEW YORK.

◀

**Harrigan and Hart turn out
for the St. Patrick's
Day Parade.**

Harrigan tried to explain that legacy in an essay in 1903, eight years before his death. "I have sought above all," he wrote, "to make all my plays like pages from actual life. I have depicted some painful types, I am well aware, and some have been shockingly realistic.... My slum and beggar types, my tramps, are not the burlesque caricatures that appeal to the mirth of spectators by absurd and implausible exaggeration.... I examine the general effect of every character with the closest scrutiny."

It is impossible to understand Harrigan without understanding his times, his milieu. He grew up near what is now the Manhattan side of the Brooklyn Bridge when the neighborhood was so thick with Irish immigrants that, as he once observed, Gaelic was the prevailing language. Some two million Irish immigrants came to America between 1840 and 1860; by 1850, twenty-six percent of the population of New York—133,000 of 513,000—had been born in Ireland.

Their lives were harsh. As one newspaper of the time put it, "There are several sorts of power working at the fabric of this Republic—water power, steam power and Irish power. The last works hardest of all." The men worked twelve or fourteen hours a day of manual labor for perhaps fifty cents and many of the women hired themselves out as maids for one dollar a week. There was a truism that you never saw a gray-haired Irishman—because so many died in their thirties or forties. From that phenomenon came the orphan newsboys who so adored the Harrigan and Hart shows.

Harrigan literally found much of the material for his plays on the streets. He observed and eavesdropped on the landlords, the Tammany Hall politicians, the social clubs. "He would ride the streetcars," recalls Nedda Harrigan Logan, the youngest of Mr. Harrigan's ten children and the wife of producer Joshua Logan. "He would go and sit in Battery Park. He'd follow people around, learn their walks, see where they lived. He would buy clothes off of people's backs to use for costumes, so they would look authentic. He met Ada Lewis, one of his actresses, walking in the street and he put her onstage in the clothes he found her in."

The most important of Harrigan's alliances, however, was with Tony Hart. They met in 1871 when both were working the variety circuit, precursor to vaudeville. As Harrigan expanded his writing from skits into full-length plays, Hart was his most gifted and brilliant interpreter. Hart was so especially skilled at playing women that the producer Augustin Daley could write to Harrigan in 1881, "I know of no leading women who could even touch the hem of his petticoat in the part." But after Harrigan and Hart split up in 1885, their lives took opposite courses. Harrigan continued to work in the theater, growing more established and affluent. Hart, suffering from syphilis, failed as an actor and died in a madhouse in 1891, at the age of thirty-six.

But the results of their fifteen-year partnership were both popular and, in time, critically respected. Twenty-three of Harrigan's plays, including those that starred Hart, ran for more than one hundred performances on Broadway. Harrigan and Braham wrote more than two hundred songs, including such period hits as "Maggie Murphy's Home." The most famous and successful of the Harrigan-Hart-Braham shows were the Mulligan Guard series, oriented around an Irish social club named the Mulligan Guards. Harrigan was savvy enough to know an effective formula when he had it, and he recycled the Mulligan characters season after season. But the plays also had serious underpinning, touching on such subjects as political corruption, race relations, Irish-German intermarriage, evictions and upward mobility. "Mr. Harrigan," William Dean Howells explained in an 1886 essay, "shows us the street cleaners and contractors, the grocery men, the shysters, the politicians, the washerwomen, the servant girls, the truckmen, the policemen, the risen Irishman and Irishwoman of contemporary New York."

These plays tell something about their times in the way American popular culture often has—whether it is the Horatio Alger novels explaining the American success mythology or Lieber and Stoller's rock and roll songs describing 1950's suburbia. The vaudeville shows that followed Harrrigan and Hart by a generation borrowed the pair's topicality, lampooning such targets as Prohibition and the Ku Klux Klan and even including "social betterment" lectures—*The History of Steel* was on the bill at one Chicago vaudeville house in 1910, along with the song-and-dance teams and animal acts.

"Plays like the Harrigan and Hart plays are not favored by critics who mistake the solemn for the serious," said Ralph G. Allen, a professor of theater at Queens College and the author of *Sugar Babies,* an homage to vaudeville. "But there is in these plays a uniquely American kind of drama that bears reviving more than the pretentious plays that are in the anthologies. There is a great deal more vitality in these 'lower forms' than in the 'higher forms.'"

The Harrigan-Hart-Braham shows also represented a step toward modern musical comedy. They dealt with realistic rather than fantastic characters and situations; in their somewhat primitive way, they used songs to advance the action or to develop characters. It is significant that Harrigan thought of himself not as someone who wrote musicals but as someone who wrote dramas that happened to have songs.

Harrigan and Hart were also prototypes of entertainers who could hold an audience as much by performance as by material. Indeed, their spectators would often shout salutations to both men by name, regardless of their costume or character. What Brooks Atkinson wrote about vaudeville in 1939 would probably have been equally true of Harrigan and Hart's variety shows fifty years earlier: "Far from being an inferior form of entertainment, as some people snobbishly assume, it is a distinctive style with laws of its own. It requires performers magnetic enough to dominate an enclosed area on stage. They must be so exuberant or skillful that they can capture an audience's attention and hold it until the act is over." 🐌

IS THAT MR. RILEY?

Pat Rooney (father of Pat Rooney II and grandfather of Pat Rooney III) was an Irish singles act who relied on jauntiness, originality, and charm. In his first routine Rooney appeared in cutaway coat with tight sleeves, fancy waistcoat, pants with large plaid checks, a plug hat, and all-around whiskers called "Galway sluggers." In this costume he sang "Owen Riley," "The Day I played Baseball," "The Sound Democrat," and the highly popular "Biddy the Ballet Girl."

Then Rooney would change to knee pants, sack coat, ballet shirt, flowing tie, soft hat, and go into a deft song and dance such as "Pretty Peggy" or "Katy Ryan," both of which are still played as instrumental numbers.

Incidentally, during World War I a controversy raged over the origin of the song "Is That Mr. Riley?" A number of people in America, and even in Europe, claimed authorship. Indeed, the great American composer Charles Ives even managed to work the song's refrain into his own composition, "The Side Show." Pat Rooney could have settled the question of origins had he lived, for it was published under his name in sheet music form back in the 1880s.

Rooney's graceful performance and attractive personality were an important influence in changing (but not too fast) the early Irish kick-in-the-bowels comedy to something slightly more genteel—if that is the right word. A change that aided Rooney in this regard was that he came into vaudeville at the time male and female audiences were being seated together for the very first time. It is doubtful that he would have achieved the measure of success that was justly his had he been forced to play the free-and-easies with their previously all-male raggle-taggle audiences.

—*Douglas Gilbert*

▶

Pat Rooney, Sr., asks, "How can you tell that I'm Irish?"

GALLAGHER AND SHEAN

Linked forever in the public fancy by their famed "'Positively, Mr. Gallagher?' 'Absolutely, Mr. Shean'" exchange for the Ziegfeld Follies of 1922, Ed Gallagher and Al Shean actually played together for less than eight years during separate comic careers that spanned half a century. They first frolicked on the vaudeville circuit as a team between 1910 and 1912 with their fast-action gag exchanges and their modest song and dance, eventually winding up a considerable hit in a musical comedy called *The Rose Maid*. Ten years later, Shean wrote a comic song for Ziegfeld's 1922 epic, and contacted Gallagher as the ideal foil in a joint singing of the lyrics. The song was a smash hit. For thirty or forty verses a show, Gallagher and Shean would make coy and cocky exchanges on the order of that quoted by Joe Franklin in his definitive piece on the team:

Shean: *Oh, Mr. Gallagher, Oh, Mr. Gallagher!*
If you're a friend of mine please lend me a couple of bucks.
I'm so broke I'm badly bent,
I haven't got a cent,
I'm as clean as if I'd just been washed with Lux!

Gallagher: *Oh, Mr. Shean, Oh, Mr. Shean!*
You don't mean to say you haven't got a bean?
On my word as I'm alive
I intended touching you for five!

Shean: *Positively, Mr. Gallagher?*

Gallagher: *Absolutely, Mr. Shean!*

Commanding top salaries now, Gallagher and Shean toured with the 1925 *Greenwich Village Follies* and starred in a 1926 comedy titled *In Dutch*, after which they broke up for good.

As drawn by Jo Swerling, a comic strip portraying a number of the Gallagher and Shean lyrics became a major newspaper hit in the mid-1920s.

—*Bill Blackbeard*

In the modern era, television shows such as "David Letterman" and "Saturday Night Live" have kept the old zany tradition of vaudeville alive. Some of the very best, early "Saturday Night Live" skits were penned by the very demented Michael O'Donaghue. Both Bill Murray and Jane Curtin performed in the best manner of so many of the old Irish vaudeville troupers. Billed as Chevy Chase's replacement, Murray did not have a particularly easy go of it when he first joined the show.

THE STREET DOG AND THE SUBURBAN PRINCE

By Doug Hill and Jeff Weingrad

Bill Murray joined "Saturday Night Live" on January 15, 1977, five shows after Chevy left. Producer Lorne Michaels had kept Billy waiting in the wings to help him avoid as much as possible the onus of being Chevy Chase's replacement, but there was plenty of resistance anyway. NBC didn't care for the choice of Bill Murray at all: After the comforting accessibility of Chevy, Billy looked to Aaron Cohen and others at the network like some Irish Catholic street dog. Which was pretty much what he was.

Billy was such a brawler even John Belushi was wary of him. John knew Billy and his brother Brian from Second City in Chicago—Belushi had roomed with Brian when he first came to New York, and John later hired Bill for "The National Lampoon Show." When Billy arrived in New York, John and Bob Tischler, the producer of the "Lampoon Radio Hour," on which Billy also worked, felt it was necessary to sit down with him to chat about his propensity for rowdy behavior. Cool it, they told him. Some on "Saturday Night" think Lorne didn't push harder to hire Billy for the first season because he knew Billy's reputation and decided he had enough machismo on his hands with John and Danny Ackroyd.

Billy's fashion sense, like John's and Danny's, bordered on the anarchistic. He favored outlandishly baggy pants and wrinkled shirts that looked as if they'd been picked out of a pile in his closet, which they probably had been. He was a drinker, not a drugger. He could toss down a half-dozen beers before the first-quarter buzzer sounded at a Knicks game, and he sometimes swigged from a fifth of Irish whiskey as he walked around 8H during blocking, a practice NBC tried to discourage.

He had a physical exuberance that always threatened to cross over into violence, even when he was being friendly. Soon after he arrived on the seventeenth floor he got into the habit of throwing the women down on a couch or the floor and tickling them unmercifully into hysterics. Other times he'd simply pick up a passing woman and bite her on the rear end. Another favorite trick was to stand up in the green room during dinner break and squeeze sandwiches through his fingers.

He had a deeper, mystical side to him as well, what Tom Schiller called "an itinerant monk actor kind of thing." Schiller shared a set of secret code initials with Billy. "T.E.," for Total Enlightenment. But outwardly Bill Murray was anything but sedate. Before a show, people would see him standing in a corner backstage warming up, hopping from one foot to the other, swinging his arms, doing chin-ups. "It was a dangerous energy," says Neil Levy. "You were almost afraid to go over to him for fear he'd attack you."

Billy's assimilation into "Saturday Night Live" was so bruising that for his first season he all but breathed fire. He once told *Rolling Stone* he was hired initially on a trial basis for three shows; Lorne denies this, saying Billy was simply given the job. In any case, he had a great first show, but after that it got difficult.

Once hired, Billy had to put up with a flood of vicious letters from fans of Chevy's who assumed Billy was responsible for his departure and who took the trouble to write, telling Billy how much they hated

Chevy Chase and Bill Murray on "Saturday Night Live."

him for it. Billy saw some of the letters before Tom Davis started intercepting them, and Davis says he couldn't believe how ugly they were. "You suck" was a common motif.

Chevy Chase returned to "Saturday Night" for the first time as its host in February of the third season. Chevy was apprehensive about coming back. He'd been out of touch since he left, so he wasn't sure what to expect. When he arrived on the seventeenth floor, he immediately discovered that the atmosphere had been, as he saw it, "poisoned" against him. Whatever support he'd had when he left had been all but evaporated by the stories that circulated about the circumstances of his departure. "Something had happened in the matrix there," Chevy said later, "and people had talked." Chevy didn't doubt that Lorne was one of the "leprechauns" responsible for spreading what Chevy considered to be lies about him, and that John was the other. Bill Murray, who hadn't gotten along that well with Chevy even in the "Lampoon" days, was probably on edge to begin with at the news of Chevy's return, and the stories he was hearing only made it worse.

Chevy's attitude that week seemed to confirm everything that people had been saying about him. He took up where he'd left off, acting the part of the big star coming back to show the kids how it should be done. He kept interrupting people, giving them directions, and talking about his decision to leave the show. "I know what you're going to say," he kept repeating.

"You all think I made a bad career move."

The friction between Chevy and Billy started sparking before the dress rehearsal on Saturday. Chevy was sitting in Franken and Davis' office when Billy burst in and told Chevy what an asshole he'd been while he was on the show. Chevy said later he was shocked—this was the first time anyone had confronted him directly with what they thought, and he knew then why everybody had been treating him so badly. They started shouting and finally Chevy told Billy to get out. There was more tension during the recess, while they were rehearsing a sketch together called "Celebrity Crack-Up," and more words exchanged after dress in the hallway outside 8H. It had gotten around that Chevy was having troubles at home with Jackie Carlin, and Billy twisted the knife. "Go fuck your wife," he said. "She needs it."

Chevy came back with a put-down about Billy's face, saying it looked as if Neil Armstrong had landed on it. Their shouts echoed through the eighth and ninth floors.

Billy and Chevy came to the notes meeting between dress and air furious but contained. Five minutes before air, though, it boiled over. Chevy found Billy in John's dressing room and called him out.

"Let's go, sucker," he said. The thought ran through Chevy's mind as he put up his fists that maybe he'd made a mistake, since, as Chevy put it later, Billy was from a tougher side of the tracks than he, and Billy liked to fight.

Billy didn't have to be asked twice, and he came at Chevy swinging. "This is my show now!" he yelled.

Belushi somehow wedged himself between them, and Brian Murray grabbed at Chevy's arms. Gilda Radner and Laraine Newman tried to get out of the way; Tom Schiller did nothing, since he was pinned behind the dressing room door. Both Chevy and Billy were throwing punches, most of which hit John. They were quickly pulled apart and everyone went out, shaken, to get in place for the show.

The acrid air of the fight hung over 8H as the show went on. The studio audience gave Chevy a standing ovation when he entered, but to those backstage he'd clearly been thrown off his stride. Lorne, watching on his monitor and saddened by what had occurred, whispered to no one in particular as he watched, "Chevy doesn't have it tonight."

At the end of the show, as Chevy stood onstage with the rest of the cast members waving good night, Billy paced back and forth behind the group with a menacing smile on his face, like a tiger pacing a cage, looking as though he might jump over them all to throttle Chevy as soon as the camera went off. Danny and John slipped back from the front of the stage to stand beside him. The show scored its highest rating ever to that point.

WHAT KELLY WON'T DO NEXT

Raised in New York's Hell's Kitchen, Alvin "Shipwreck" Kelly joined the Navy at an early age. By the mid-1920s he was broke, and on the bum, traveling the Midwest in search of employment. He watched a man climb a building in St. Louis as a stunt—"human flies" were then the craze—and he suddenly got the idea that sitting atop a flagpole would provide infinitely more thrills than a man edging himself up the facade of a bank. The manager of a St. Louis hotel also thought flagpole sitting might be a good idea; the stunt would attract crowds to his hotel and drum up needed business. He hired Kelly to climb the flagpole on his hotel roof and sit there as long as he could. Kelly not only drew enormous crowds to watch him sway back and forth on the pole twelve stories above the street, but he also set a new record for flagpole sitting of seven days and one hour. Kelly was hailed as a modern-day St. Simeon Stylites, a saintly hermit who squatted atop a pillar to do penance and preach to the heathens in the fifth century. If Kelly was praying for anything up on that pole, it was for light wind and warm weather, and for the Jazz Age never to come to an end.

—*Jay Robert Nash*

◄
The world's greatest flagpole sitter, "Shipwreck" Kelly, awaits the oncoming storm.

TO BE IN VAUDEVILLE YOU JUST HAD TO BE BORN

By Fred Allen

Why a man with the perfectly good name of John F. Sullivan, born and raised in the perfectly good town of Boston, Massachusetts, would eventually choose to change his name to Fred Allen is somewhat less of a mystery than it appears to be on the surface. Young Jimmy Sullivan desperately wanted a job on the old B.F. Keith vaudeville circuit, and soon found that the door could be pushed open if he billed himself "Freddy St. James: The World's Worst Juggler" and claimed to have just returned to the Boston area after having received rave reviews out west. Sullivan-St.James-Allen went on to write "the finest comedy in the history of radio broadcasting," according to his friend, author Edwin O'Connor, but his radio career was entirely shaped by his twenty some odd (very odd) years on the vaudeville stage.

▶

Radio's most gifted comic writer, Fred Allen (aka John F. Sullivan).

Vaudeville is dead. The acrobats, the animal acts, the dancers, the singers, and the old-time comedians have taken their final bows and disappeared into the wings of obscurity. For fifty years—from 1875 to 1925—vaudeville was the popular entertainment of the masses. Nomadic tribes of nondescript players roamed the land. The vaudeville actor was part gypsy and part suitcase. With his brash manner, flashy clothes, capes, and cane, and accompanied by his gaudy womenfolk, the vaudevillian brought happiness and excitement to the communities he visited. He spent his money freely and made friends easily. In the early days, the exact degree of prosperity the small-timer was enjoying could be determined by taking inventory of the diamonds that adorned his person. If he was doing well, the small-timer wore a large diamond horseshoe in his tie and two or three solitaires or clusters on his fingers; his wife, dripping with necklaces, rings, earrings, and bracelets, looked as though she had been pelted with ice cubes that had somehow stuck where they landed. The small-timer's diamonds didn't have to be good. They just had to be big. What difference if the eight-karat ring was the color of a menthol cough drop as long as the stone soaked in the spotlight during the act? To the small-timer, a diamond represented security. It impressed the booker, the manager, and the audience, but more important, the diamond was collateral. Confronted with a financial crisis in a strange community, the small-timer didn't have to embarrass himself by attempting to convince a tradesman or a hotel manager that his credentials were valid. To obtain emergency funds, he merely stepped into the nearest pawnshop, slipped the ring from his finger, and consummated a legitimate business transaction. When his diamonds were temporarily on location, the small-timer avoided his friends and his usual haunts, knowing that the absence of his Kimberley gravel was an admission that the panic was on. The instant his luck changed, the diamonds were redeemed and returned to their customary places. Back in the spotlight with the horseshoe pin and the rings sparkling, the small-timer's necktie and his ring fingers resumed strutting their stuff.

The herd instinct was a dominant impulse in the vaudeville actor's behavior pattern. When the season closed, the small-timers congregated at vacation resorts to revel in each other's company. The small-timer lived in another world. He thought and talked only about his act and about show business. Nothing else interested him. If you said to him, "Do you remember the Johnstown flood?" he would probably reply, "Remember the Johnstown flood? Are you kidding? I and the wife were playing Pittsburgh that week. Eva Tanguay was the star. Walter Kelly was next to closing. After the first show the manager comes running back and says 'You kids is the hit of the bill!' He moves us down to next to closing for the rest of the week. Kelly is blowing his top. All week long I and the wife murder them!" Everybody in Johnstown could have been swept out of town: the small-timer wouldn't know or care. He had nothing in common with anybody who was not in his profession.

Vaudeville could not vouch for the honesty, the integrity, or the mentality of the individuals who collectively made up the horde the medium embraced. All the human race demands of its members is that they be born. That is all vaudeville demanded. You just had to be born. You could be ignorant and be a star. You could be a moron and be wealthy. The elements that went to make up vaudeville were combed from the jungles, the four corners of the world, the intelligentsia, and the subnormal. An endless, incongruous swarm crawled over the countryside dragging performing lions, bears, tigers, leopards, boxing kangaroos, horses, ponies, mules, dogs, cats, rats, seals, and monkeys on their wake. Others rode bicycles, did acrobatic and contortion tricks, walked wires, exhibited sharpshooting skills, played violins, trombones, cornets, pianos, concertinas, xylophones, harmonicas, and any other known instruments. There were hypnotists, iron-jawed ladies, one-legged dancers, one-armed cornetists, mind readers, female impersonators, male impersonators, Irish comedians, Jewish comedians, blackface, German, Swedish, Italian, and rube comedians, dramatic actors, Hindu conjurors, ventriloquists, bag punchers, singers and dancers of every description, clay modelers, and educated geese: all traveling from hamlet to town to city, presenting their shows. Vaudeville asked only that you own an animal or an instrument, or have a minimum talent or a maximum of nerve. With these dubious assets vaudeville offered fame and riches. It was up to you.

The small-timer, as he trudged through the seasons, always felt that he was getting closer to his goal. Every vaudeville actor dreamed of his personal utopia. Weekly sums were banked or mailed home against the day the small-timer "quit the business." Then he would open his restaurant, filling station, real-estate office, chicken farm, dancing school, or other project that he had envisioned supporting him through his remaining years. Very few small-timers saw their dreams take dimension.

As the vaudeville monologist would explain it, "A funny thing happened to my savings on the way to my utopia." Sickness, relatives, going into businesses he didn't understand, meeting real-estate salesmen, joining collapsible building and loan clubs, gambling, lending money to other actors who never repaid him, playing the stock market, and a thousand other mishaps dissipated the small-timer's savings and shattered his hopes. The few that did realize their ambitions found that after the travel and excitement of vaudeville, the dull and sedentary routine imposed on them as they tried to run some picayune enterprise in a small town was boring.

The small-timer was never happy in retirement. Had it been within his power, the vaudeville performer would have been a timeless wanderer, spanning the generations by using the bridge of his talents.

But vaudeville is dead. Vaudeville was more a matter of style than of material. It was not so much what the two- and three-a-day favorites said and did, as how they said and did it. For fifty years vaudeville's minstrels found their way into all lands, preaching their gospel of merriment and song, and rousing the rest of the world to laughter and to tears. A few diehards who knew and enjoyed vaudeville hover over their television sets, hoping for a miracle. They believe that this electronic device is a modern oxygen tent that in some mysterious way can revive vaudeville and return its colorful performers of yesteryear to the current scene. The optimism of these day and night dreamers is wasted. Their vigils are futile. Vaudeville is dead. Period.

Parish Life

▶

*Barry Fitzgerald tries to spell
the word "brouge" as Father
Bing Crosby and Father
James McHugh look on, in
the 1944 Paramount
production of* Going My Way.

REQUIEM FOR AN ANARCHIST

By Michael True

Most Irish people have never needed a Jerry Falwell or a Cardinal Spellman to remind them that, in this world at least, religion turns into politics at just about every turn. The two major churches of Ireland—the Catholic and Presbyterian— remain at base populist in character. Outlawed by Anglican authorities at various times in their history, both religions have been sustained under the threat of state punishment by the popular will of the Irish people. A man such as Ammon Hennacy demonstrates the continuity of this tradition and provides us with a fascinating profile of the modern Irish religionist as a contemporary political rebel.

His latest leaflet, with the headline "Thou Shalt Not Kill!" and a scribbled note on the back ("Good TV coverage this campaign—Love Ammon"), arrived on January 9. Like many previous fliers, it announced a protest against capital punishment: "Picketing the Board of Pardons at the Capitol (in Salt Lake City) at noon, from Monday through Friday, January 5 to February 5, 1970."

But within the week, the local papers carried a brief excerpt from the *Times* obituary, saying that Ammon Hennacy, graying *enfant terrible* and one-man revolution, at seventy-seven, was dead.

We met four years ago when he and Joan arrived to stay with us during a swing east, before the closing of Joe Hill House. Although I had read his column in the *Catholic Worker*, for which he served as associate editor during the 1950s, my knowledge of his goings and doings came principally from the first edition of his own story, *The Autobiography of a Catholic Anarchist*, an item in a bibliography in Mark Harris' dissertation on Randolph Bourne. Ammon loved to repeat Bourne's famous statement, "War is the health of the State." He had given his bed over to Bourne when the social and literary critic visited Madison, Wisconsin, in 1915; they shared a common ideology, socialist and anarchist, even in those pre-World War I days, before Ammon served his first prison term for refusing to go to the army in 1917.

Since that initial sentence, Ammon had been returned to jail over thirty times: in Atlanta, where a note from a fellow anarchist, Alexander Berkman, restored his courage and determination to live, even in "the hole"; in New York City, at the request of various Roman Catholic clergy, for selling the *Catholic Worker* outside downtown churches after Mass; in Arizona, while picketing against war bases and atomic blasts in the desert. His descriptions of these experiences have become standard anthology pieces on anarchism and nonviolence in America, particularly that initial journey to Christian anarchism made many years ago:

"I had passed through the idea of killing myself. This was an escape, not any solution to life. The remainder of my two years in solitary must result in a

"Am I not a wonder?"—the great Ammon Hennacy.

clear-cut plan whereby I could go forth and be a force in the world.... Gradually I came to gain a glimpse of what Jesus meant when he said, 'The Kingdom of God must be in everyone'—in the deputy and the warden, in the rat and the pervert—and now I came to know it in myself.... To change the world by bullets or ballots was a useless procedure.... Therefore the only revolution worthwhile was the one-man revolution within the heart. Each one would make this by himself and not need to wait on a majority."

The uncompromised principles and the practical wisdom, the idea and the deed, appear side by side in his autobiography, as they do in the book he was writing at the time of his death: a collection of portraits of his fifteen great Americans from John Woolman, Tom Paine, and Thomas Jefferson (the only president in the group) to Malcolm X, Helen Demoskoff, and Dorothy Day, with selections from their writings and reflections on their lives and times. One of the best tributes to him would be for his friends and admirers to see that that book is brought to a large and appreciative reading public. His associates at the *Worker* and in Salt Lake, I am sure, are working on it already.

In the meantime, we are left with memories: the sight of the gray-haired, slightly stooped, but still virile man in a dark shirt, with a western, Indian-decorated tie (the picture in the recent bulletin of the War Resisters League, which named him pacifist of the year last spring); the witty, even bawdy remarks, barbed comments, and critiques of friends and enemies, particularly when the former didn't measure up to his (or was it their) principles. He could excuse ignorance; but once a man drew the line, Ammon expected him to hold fast. And he always cautioned people against drawing too fast and then "chickening out." He thought Eugene Debs was probably the greatest American, but he admired several of the younger radicals, too. At Christmas, he always sent cards to young men in prison for conscience's sake, from Fort Dix stockade to Sandstone and beyond.

It would be ridiculous, however, to romanticize him. Ammon was a crusty old Irishman—cantankerous, gregarious, stubborn—constantly confronting his listener with his attitude on diet ("on fish, flesh, or fowl") or his own favorite sayings on sometimes obtuse subjects. He advised reading the morning paper "to find out what the bastards are up to today." Even last spring, he carried through a busy schedule of a radio talk show, a peaceful protest supporting the Catonsville 9, and a speech before local college students, in one day. He liked poetry, and he talked precisely about books he had read in any discipline.

He is a chapter in the history of American radicalism, indomitable, singular, humane. I loved him. 🙢

THE TAX PROBLEM

I first met Ammon Hennacy in Milwaukee where I was speaking at a big social action rally. The auditorium was almost as large as Madison Square Garden. I was the only woman on the platform. When the local bishop had invited me to speak, I had asked if he was aware of our stand on the Spanish Civil War (which had ended shortly before). He said he was, so I spoke, bringing in our principles on nonviolence, the general strike, and nonpayment of income tax as a means to effect social change. Judging from the applause, I don't think the audience realized the implications of what I was saying. But Ammon Hennacy did, and as I was getting into a car afterward to go to a friend's home for coffee, he squeezed in between me and a stout club-woman prominent in Catholic circles, and started to talk at once—beginning, as he usually did, with the story of his life.

He wanted me to know that he was a Tolstoian Christian, having become one in prison.

"And what jails have *you* been in and how long did *you* serve?" he wanted to know, to establish an intimacy between us at once. My record was modest: sixteen days in a Washington jail during the suffrage years,

and a long weekend in a Chicago jail when they were raiding I.W.W. headquarters during the Palmer red raids after World War I.

Ammon clung to us all that evening. He was well acquainted, he informed me, with the Catholic Worker group in Milwaukee. He didn't think our people there had much gumption. None of them had even been in jail. Ammon had been inside more than one jail. (It is much easier to go to jail if you are poor. You can be sentenced for vagrancy, for sleeping on a park bench or in the subway, for begging, for selling neckties or toys on street corners without a license, even for walking through the park after midnight.)

Ammon had presented us all with a problem. What kind of work can we do for which we need not pay federal income tax? Even if we try not to pay it, there are the withholding tax and the hidden federal taxes on tobacco, liquor, the theater, etc.

Ammon found his solution first in working in the Southwest. He irrigated, picked cotton, and did other farm work around Phoenix, Arizona, and was paid by the day. He lived, like the early church fathers, in the desert, on vegetables and bread. He sent his money to his two daughters, so that they could finish their education at Northwestern University's music school. He fulfilled his moral obligations, and his daughters were graduated. Then, in 1952, when he came to New York and joined our staff, he worked for board and room, as the rest of us do, and so did not have to pay federal income tax here, either.

Ammon made an impression on New York. Over the years he got a great deal of publicity. The *New York Times* and the *New York Post* would sometimes give space to his exploits. When this would happen, much like Barrie's Sentimental Prince, he would often crow, "Am I not a wonder?"

—Dorothy Day

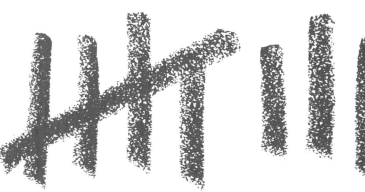

166

Raymond Chandler's mother was born in Waterford, Ireland. Writing about his mother's family to Charles W. Morton, an editor at the Atlantic Monthly, *in 1945, Chandler stated: "An amazing people, the Anglo-Irish. They never mixed with Catholics socially.... I grew up with terrible contempt for Catholics, and I have trouble with it even now.... My uncle's snob housekeeper wouldn't have a Catholic servant in the house, although they were probably much better than the trash she did have." Mary McCarthy encountered a comparable intolerance growing up in her grandmother's house in Washington. However rooted in the class history of Ireland, it was just this kind of intolerance that eventually led young Margaret Higgins Sanger to seek social justice outside the confines of the American Irish church.*

IN MY GRANDMOTHER'S HOUSE

By Mary McCarthy

Whenever we children came to stay at my grandmother's house, we were put to sleep in the sewing room, a bleak, shabby, utilitarian rectangle, more office than bedroom, more attic than office, that played to the hierarchy of chambers the role of a poor relation. It was a room seldom entered by the other members of the family, seldom swept by the maid, a room without pride; the old sewing machine, some cast-off chairs, a shadeless lamp, rolls of wrapping paper, piles of cardboard boxes that might someday come in handy, papers of pins, and remnants of material united with the iron folding cots put out for our use and the bare floor boards to give an impression of intense and ruthless

167

temporality. Thin white spreads, of the kind used in hospitals and charity institutions, and naked blinds at the windows reminded us of our orphaned condition and of the ephemeral character of our visit; there was nothing here to encourage us to consider this our home.

Poor Roy's children, as commiseration damply styled us, could not afford illusions, in the family opinion. Our father had put us beyond the pale by dying suddenly of influenza and taking our young mother with him, a defection that was remarked on with horror and grief commingled, as though our mother had been a pretty secretary with whom he had wantonly absconded into the irresponsible paradise of the hereafter. Our reputation was clouded by this misfortune. There was a prevailing sense, not only in the family but among storekeepers, servants, streetcar conductors, and other satellites of our circle, that my grandfather, a rich man, had behaved with extraordinary munificence in allotting a sum of money for our support and installing us with some disagreeable middle-aged relations in a dingy house two blocks distant from his own.

We, as a matter of fact, were grateful to the point of servility. We made no demands, we had no hopes. We were content if we were permitted to enjoy the refracted rays of that solar prosperity and come sometimes in the summer afternoons to sit on the shady porch or idle through a winter morning on the wicker furniture of the sun parlor, to stare at the player piano in the music room and smell the odor of whiskey in the mahogany cabinet in the library, or to climb about the dark living room examining the glassed-in paintings in their huge gilt frames, the fruits of European travel: dusky Italian devotional groupings, heavy and lustrous as grapes, Neapolitan women carrying baskets to market, views of Venetian canals, and Tuscan harvest scenes —secular themes that, to the Irish-American mind, had become tinged with Catholic feeling by a regional infusion from the Pope. We asked no more from this house than the pride of being connected with it, and this was fortunate for us, since my grandmother, a great adherent of the give-them-an-inch-and-they'll-take-a-yard theory of hospitality, never, so far as I can remember, offered any caller the slightest refreshment, regarding her own conversation as sufficiently wholesome and sustaining. An ugly, severe old woman with a monstrous balcony of a bosom, she officiated over certain set topics in a colorless singsong, like a priest intoning a Mass, topics to which repetition had lent a senseless solemnity: her audience with the Holy Father; how my father had broken with family tradition and voted the Democrat ticket; a visit to Lourdes; the Sacred Stairs in Rome, bloodstained since the first Good Friday, which she had climbed on her knees; my crooked little fingers and how they meant I was a liar;

a miracle-working bone; the importance of regular bowel movements; the wickedness of Protestants; the conversion of my mother to Catholicism; and the assertion that my other grandmother must certainly dye her hair. The most trivial reminiscences (my aunt's having hysterics in a haystack) received from her delivery and from the piety of the context a strongly monitory flavor; they inspired fear and guilt and one searched uncomfortably for the moral in them, as in a dark and riddling fable.

Luckily, I am writing a memoir and not a work of fiction, and therefore I do not have to account for my grandmother's unpleasing character and look for the Oedipal fixation or the traumatic experience which would give her that clinical authenticity that is nowadays so desirable in portraiture. I do not know how my grandmother got the way she was; I assume, from family photographs and from the inflexibility of her habits, that she was always the same, and it seems as idle to inquire into her childhood as to ask what was ailing Iago or look for the error in toilet-training that was responsible for Lady MacBeth. My grandmother's sexual history, bristling with infant mortality in the usual style of her period, was robust and decisive: three tall, handsome sons grew up, and one attentive daughter. Her husband treated her kindly. She had money, many grandchildren, and religion to sustain her. White hair, glasses, soft skin, wrinkles, needlework—all the paraphernalia of motherliness were hers; yet it was a cold, grudging, disputatious old woman who sat all day in her sunroom making tapestries from a pattern, scanning religious periodicals, and setting her iron jaw against any infraction of her ways.

Combativeness was, I suppose, the dominant trait in my grandmother's nature. An aggressive churchgoer, she was quite without Christian feeling; the mercy of the Lord Jesus had never entered her heart. Her piety was an act of war against the Protestant ascendancy. The religious magazines on her table furnished her not with food for meditation but with fresh pretexts for anger; articles attacking birth control, divorce, mixed marriages, Darwin, and secular education were her favorite reading. The teachings of the Church did not interest her, except as they were a rebuke to others; "Honor thy father and thy mother," a commandment she was no longer called upon to practice, was the one most frequently on her lips. The extermination of Protestantism, rather than spiritual perfection, was the boon she prayed for. Her mind was preoccupied with conversion; the capture of a soul for God much diverted her fancy—it made one less Protestant in the world. Foreign missions, with their overtones of good will and social service, appealed to her less strongly; it was not a *harvest* of souls that my grandmother had in mind.

CHRISTMAS IN CORNING

Born in Ireland, Michael Hennessy Higgins was a nonconformist through and through. All other men had beards or mustaches—not he. His bright red mane, worn much too long according to the family, swept back from his massive brow; he would not clip it short as most fathers did. Actually it suited his finely modeled head. He was nearly six feet tall and hard-muscled; his keen blue eyes were set off by pinkish, freckled skin. Homily and humor rippled uneasily from his generous mouth in a brogue which he never lost. The jokes with which he punctuated every story were never lost. When I was little they were beyond me, but I could hear my elders laughing.

The scar on father's forehead was his badge of war service. When Lincoln had called for volunteers against the rebellious South, he had taken his only possessions, a gold watch inherited from his grandfather and his own father's legacy of three hundred dollars, and had run away from his home in Canada to enlist. But he had been told he was not old enough, and was obliged to wait impatiently a year and a half until, on his fifteenth birthday, he had joined the Twelfth New York Volunteer Cavalry as a drummer boy.

Immediately upon leaving the Army, father had studied anatomy, medicine and phrenology, but these had been merely for perfecting his skill in modeling. He made his living by chiseling angels and saints out of huge blocks of white marble or gray granite for tombstones in cemeteries. He was a philosopher, a rebel and an artist, none of which was calculated to produce wealth. Our existence was like that of any artist's family—chickens today and feathers tomorrow.

Christmases were on the poverty line. If any of us needed a new winter coat or pair of overshoes, these constituted our presents. I was the youngest of six, but after me others kept coming until we were eleven. Our dolls were babies—living wriggling bodies to bathe and dress instead of lifeless faces that never cried or slept. A pine beside the door was our Christmas tree. Father liked us to use natural things and we had to rely upon ingenuity rather than the village stores, so we decorated it with white popcorn and red cranberries which we strung ourselves. Our most valuable gift was that of imagination.

—Margaret Sanger

► **Suffragette and family-planning pioneer, Margaret (Higgins) Sanger.**

FATHER COUGHLIN'S FATAL CAMPAIGN

By Sheldon Marcus

Irish Catholic social teaching has been considered a starting point for left-wing political activists like Ammon Hennacy. Yet the church has also provided a home for right-wing Evangelicals and anti-Semites, such as the late Father Coughlin. A bigot in populist clothing, Coughlin was ancestral to so many of our contemporary broadcast Evangelicals and one of the most dangerous figures to have moved across the political landscape of his time.

Coughlin was ready to begin in earnest. He startled the audience by roaring out, "Martin Sweeney, stand up and tell them where you stand on the Democratic party." Sweeney jumped to the microphone and played Charlie McCarthy to Coughlin's Edgar Bergen. "Because Roosevelt is a double-crosser, Father, I stand with the National Union for Social Justice." This interlude over, Coughlin continued, his booming voice catching the fancy of the Townsendite listeners. They cheered and applauded his criticisms of Roosevelt and the New Deal. Each round of applause sparked Coughlin to greater criticism of the president. By the time he reached the conclusion of the talk, he was almost shrieking at the crowd. He was completely immersed in its reaction to him. He had the crowd eating out of his hand.

His notes were forgotten. He reminded the audience that F.D.R. stood for "Franklin Double-crossing Roosevelt." Most of the crowd cheered this remark, but a number of people started to boo. Dr. Townsend quickly strode to the podium and said in a soft voice, "Will the sergeant-at-arms put those booers out." Frank Arbuckle, the convention chairman, then shouted at the audience, "There is no place here for that." The booing subsided. When Father Coughlin resumed his talk he asked why it was that the Communists were supporting Roosevelt. He then ripped off his Roman collar and in an almost hysterical voice labeled the president of the United States a "liar" and "betrayer." The crowd was frenetic. It was going wild. Coughlin was on the verge of physical exhaustion, but it had been worth it.

The Vatican failed to see how Coughlin's intemperate remarks and his direct involvement in politics could improve the image of the Church. It instructed its Apostolic Delegate to the United States, Ameleto Cicognani, to inform Father Coughlin that an apology was to be made immediately to President Roosevelt and that his political activities were to be "toned down." Coughlin made his apology and then promptly continued to lambaste the president, although not in such language as he had used in Cleveland.

After his apology, Coughlin embarked on another series of public appearances. First, he went into upstate

▼

The Little Flower of Fatima, Father Charles E. Coughlin.

New York. Then, in Hamburg, a suburb of Buffalo, he made it abundantly clear that his apology to the president was behind him and that "I have no apologies to offer the gentleman in the White House who lies on the rotten meat of broken promises."

From New York, Coughlin moved on to Hankinson, North Dakota, for a rally. Several thousand farmers heard Coughlin tell them that if Roosevelt were re-elected they "should repudiate their debts, and if anybody tries to enforce them, repudiate them also." Later, Coughlin denied that he had urged the repudiation of farm debts, and blamed the poor public address system for distorting what he had said.

In early August, Coughlin campaigned in Massachusetts and Rhode Island, where he was greeted by large crowds that cheered him when he launched his tirades against Roosevelt and Landon.

In September, twenty thousand followers in his eastern stronghold of Brooklyn turned out to greet Coughlin. From Brooklyn it was on to New Haven, Des Moines, St. Louis and Cincinnati. As always, he

was greeted at the train platform by crowds of well-wishers who surged forward in an effort to touch his coat, while shouting words of devotion and encouragement to him. And as always there was a considerable number of special police on hand to protect Coughlin because of the usual number of crank calls threatening his life. As the campaign tempo increased, he became exhausted, sick and irritable. He refused to talk to reporters. "I am a very sick man. I need to see a doctor rather than reporters."

The instructions to "tone down" Coughlin's activities were apparently not being interpreted strictly enough to satisfy the Vatican. The Vatican now felt compelled to restrict Coughlin's activities. It sent Eugenio Cardinal Pacelli, Vatican Secretrary of State (later elected Pope Pius XII), to confer with Archbishop McNicholas, the powerful and highly respected head of the Cincinnati archdiocese, about the political and social ramifications within the United States of any decision made concerning Coughlin. His work done, Pacelli returned to Rome to report to Pope Pius XI and Coughlin continued his political campaigning.

Coughlin seemed shaken. "The arm of Jim Farley is long," he told an associate. "Mr. Roosevelt has served notice on the Pope that he will not send the Church a fraternal delegate to Rome unless Father Coughlin is silenced."

But Coughlin continued his offensive in a Boston press conference when he labeled as Communists both David Dubinsky and Felix Frankfurter. John Barry, a reporter for the *Boston Globe*, who knew Frankfurter well, took exception to this description of the Harvard law professor. There was some additional verbal give and take between the two men before the press conference concluded. Soon after, Coughlin met Barry by chance at the Hotel Biltmore in Providence, where he had delivered a speech. Tired and overworked, he berated the Boston newspaperman and then suddenly lunged at him. He ripped off the reporter's glasses and punched him in the face before Thomas O'Brien finally succeeded in restraining him. Barry said that since Coughlin "was a priest of the Catholic Church there was nothing for me to do but stand and take it."

The next morning, upon his return to Boston, Coughlin was still fuming as he told reporters, "If I had him here I'd choke ... If I see that fellow I'll tear him to pieces." The Boston police department assigned six policemen equipped with tear gas bombs and guns to Coughlin. Whether they were to guard him or to restrain him was not made clear. ❧

It is impossible to underestimate the weight of family and clan in the whole of Irish social and spiritual history. The enduring nature of this heritage has contributed to the preoccupation of Irish literature, on both sides of the Atlantic, with the powerful love between mothers and daughters and the terrible love between fathers and sons. The weight of these concerns can become so unbearable that at times it is difficult to witness a play by Eugene O'Neill or finish a novel by James T. Farrell. In our own time, Pete Hamill has handled one aspect of this theme with poetry and grace in his wonderful novella, The Gift.

CHRISTMAS IN BROOKLYN

By Pete Hamill

Christmas really did mean something in Brooklyn if you were poor and Irish. The Depression was still a fact there, lingering like the roaches after the rest of the town had raised the money for an exterminator. My mother had arrived in America on the day the stock market crashed; my faher came in 1923, on the lam from anti-Catholic bigotry in Northern Ireland. They were the Irish without property, and in the early 1950s, there seemed little hope that they would ever really own anything. So Christmas became one of those brief seasons of celebration, when you held back the dark fact that you had moved through another year.

My father worked for the Globe Lighting Company, on the third floor of the old Ansonia Clock Factory, which had been for a while the largest factory in America and was now a dirty red-brick pile. I remember hearing him come up the stairs, one step at a time, humming quietly some fragment of an old song. He was a short, compact man then, with glossy black hair, and there was a picture on the wall of one of the bedrooms that represented all the mystery of him to me. The photograph was brown and beginning to fade, and it was a group portrait of young men in soccer uniforms who played for a team of Irish exiles called St. Mary's Celtics. One of them was my father.

In 1951, I had worked for a year in the sheet metal shop at the Brooklyn Navy Yard, and men there told me about how good my father had been, when he was young and playing soccer. He was fierce and quick, possessed of a magic leg, moving down those Sunday playing fields as if driven by the engines of anger and exile, playing hardest against the British teams, the legs pumping and cutting and stealing the ball; hearing the cheers of strangers, and everybody drinking after the games until the later hours in the speakeasies, singing songs they learned across an ocean. Until one day, in one hard-played game, a German had come out of nowhere and kicked, and the magic leg had splintered and my father fell as if shot, and someone came off the bench and broke the German's jaw with a punch, and then they were pulling slats off the fence to tie against the ruined leg and waited for an hour and a half for the ambulance to come from Kings County Hospital while

they played out the rest of the game. And then at the hospital he was dropped in a bed, and there were no doctors, and across the room detectives were questioning a man whose stomach had been sliced open in a fight, and the ceiling reeled and turned, and there was no feeling left in the magic leg. When the doctors finally showed up the next morning, the leg was thick with gangrene, and they had to slice the football off with a razor, and in the afternoon they took the leg off above the knee. When he talked about it later, he never mentioned the pain. What he remembered most clearly was the sound of the saw.

And so I had grown up with his presence in the house but never had the kinds of things other kids had with fathers. We never went out to play baseball or kick a football around a field. He was a stranger I had come to love from a distance. He drank a lot in Rattigan's across the street, and at night he would come in with some of his friends and they would sit in the kitchen and talk about fights, with my father illustrating Willie Pep's jab on the plastic knob of the lamp cord or throwing Ray Robinson hooks into the wash on the kitchen line. He loved to sing, and I always liked the outrage and the passion that he would force into the lines from "Galway Bay," about how the strangers came and tried to teach us their ways, and scorned us just for being what we are.... We were what we were in that neighborhood, and we didn't care what the strangers thought about us. I loved the hard defiance, and I would lie in the next room listening to them, as they brought up the old tales of British malignance and murders committed by the Black and Tans. But I didn't really know him: he had left school at twelve to work as a stonemason's apprentice and had struggled for a while at night school at Brooklyn tech; but he didn't really know how to deal with me when I tried to do my homework, and in many ways he was still Irish and I was an American. I loved the way he talked and the way he stood on the corner with a fedora and raincoat on Sunday mornings, an Irish dude waiting for the bars to open, and I loved the way he once hit a guy with a ballbat because he insulted my mother. I just never knew if he loved me back.

THE SERMON OF
THE DOCKS

By Budd Schulberg

The tradition of the "Soggarth Aroon," or the "Good Priest," is another Irish tradition that crossed the Atlantic and stood the Irish immigrant community in America in good stead during those first decades in the New World. Father Edward McGlynn of New York City was one of the first of America's "Soggarth Aroons," championing the cause of Irish freedom in the early 1870s and using his office to publicly endorse the single tax theories of social reformer Henry George. A more recent champion of the people, the "Waterfront Priest," Father John Corridan, lived to see a Waterfront Commission established for the Port of New York before he died in New Jersey in 1986.

▼

Karl Malden plays Father John Corridan, "The Waterfront Priest," in the 1960 Columbia Pictures production of *On the Waterfront*.

Civil war was raging through New York harbor in 1952 when director Elia Kazan and I were there to film *On the Waterfront*. Insurgent longshoremen, backed by the American Federation of Labor, were battling the then mob-infested International Longshoremen's Association which had just been expelled from the A.F.L. in a bitterly fought election campaign to determine which branch of the union would bargain for the 40,000 men who annually moved more than $6.5 billion dollars of cargo through the port of New York.

I had first entered this crime-ridden world with the help of the Reverend John Corridan, the celebrated "waterfront priest." Father John had revolutionized my attitude toward the Church. In Father John, a tall, fast-talking, chain-smoking, hardheaded, sometimes profane Kerryman, I had found the perfect antidote to the stereotyped Barry Fitzgerald-Bing Crosby "Fahther" so dear to Hollywood hearts. In West Side saloons I listened to Father John, whose speech was a unique blend of Hell's Kitchen, baseball slang, an encyclopedic grasp of waterfront economics, and an attack of man's inhumanity to man based on the teachings of Christ as brought up to date in the papal encyclicals on the reconstruction of the social order.

Father John had ticked off for me the various mobs controlling different sections of the harbor, named the hiring bosses with criminal records and described the evils of the shape-up hiring system. He gave me chapter and verse on the wholesale pilferage from ships' cargoes and explained how

I.L.A. hoodlums extorted payoffs from the shipping companies, highly vulnerable to threats of work stoppages since idle ships earn no money. He sketched other dockside rackets—narcotics, gambling, loan-sharking—and he introduced me to a sawed-off longshoreman named Brownie who would guide me for a look at harbor conditions.

That night Brownie took me on a tour of the bars that face the docks. "Keep ya ears open and ya mouth shut," he warned me. I got a close, hard look at the loan sharks, the bookmakers and their muscle, who took their bread out of the envelopes of longshoremen. In the neighborhood of the luxury-line berths were the enforcers who had moved in through bank-robber Mickey Bower's notorious "Pistol Local" 824: the reptilian-eyed John Keefe, "Apples" Applegate and "Sudden Death" Ward. These men may sound like extravagant creations of the late Damon Runyon, but they were there in the flesh—although invisible to the tourists waving happy good-byes from the decks of passenger ships like the *Ile de France*, the *Queen Elizabeth* and the *United States*.

Moving into the railroad flats of longshoremen, I felt I was living my way into the jungle-world of the waterfront. I began to identify myself with the group of longshoremen who had been coming to St. Xavier's Labor School after dark, for advice from Father Corridan.

"Father John knows the score" had become a popular saying by the time I came to know him well. And as the influence of the Corridan group spread through the harbor, so did the violence. One member of the group, Joey Cuervo, was sitting with his children watching TV when a shot was fired into his living room. Christy Doran, hiring boss on Pier 42, another member of the cleanup movement, fell to his death from a cliff at a church picnic. "*Fell?* That's a hot one," said Brownie, my guide.

On notorious Pier 32, Michael Brogan, an assistant hiring boss, disappeared shortly after his local, 895, voted 5-1 to quit the I.L.A. Three weeks later Brogan's body was found floating in the river. He had talked openly of breaking with the old crowd and of his troubles with the gunman Ackalitis. With the federally sponsored union election on its way, most of the West Side Irish rebels interpreted Brogan's death as "a McGrath-Ackalitis election maneuver." Eddie McGrath, an I.L.A. organizer for fifteen years and a mob leader with a record of twelve arrests for crimes ranging from petty larceny to murder, had fled to Florida after his brother-in-law and gang partner, John (Cockeye) Dunn, was executed for murder in 1949. But he was reported still to be running the rackets on the lower West Side piers by remote control from Miami—and one of those piers was Pier 32.

Intimidation, beatings and murders dominated this whole campaign, for the racketeers were fighting for survival on the waterfront. But on election night, May 26, 1954, the rebels were in a victory mood. With no union hall of their own, thousands of them gathered at the Seafarers International Union Hall in Brooklyn to await the election returns.

At first it seemed that the graft-ridden I.L.A. was finally being pried loose, but by midnight it was creeping up on the rebels. And by early morning, when the returns were in, the I.L.A. had polled 9,110 votes to 8,791 for the reform movement. A mere 319 votes separated the old order from the new. In Jersey City alone, buses scheduled to carry anti-I.L.A. dockworkers to the polls failed to show up. One of the A.F.L. organizers responsible for this transportation was promptly rewarded by the I.L.A.—promoted to hiring boss. That one defection—and there were others—cost this tragic photo-finish defeat.

What happened to the nearly 9,000 longshoremen who gambled their livelihood, and some their lives, only to blow it by less than two percent of the total vote? Scores had to ship out as sailors to escape mob vengeance. Our dock boss in the film had shouted down the rebels as "living dead men," and that's what the stand-up guys of the narrowly defeated movement soon became. Men I had come to know in battle for the harbor were starved out. Some threw in the sponge and turned to other jobs—a stagehand, a helper on a truck. The demoralized drifted off into alcoholism. But there were diehards strong enough to stick it out on the docks, unsung heroes in the long upward struggle for freedom from degradation, crime and corruption on the waterfront.

Ten years later I returned to the waterfront to see how much had changed. A new Waterfront Commission had been formed. The criminal shape-up system had been abolished. And, led by Teddy Gleason, a more reform-minded leadership now ran things at the I.L.A. Had the New York waterfront improved? Yes, particularly in the daily lives of longshoremen. Did the racketeers still control the docks? Yes, although control had now been shaded down to *influence*, less obvious than ten years ago, more sophisticated, more subtle, perhaps even more dangerous.

Father John Corridan, considered by old harbor hands the father of the Waterfront Commission, was now teaching theology at St. Peter's College in Jersey City. "Not until we can bring the spirit of Almighty God into our daily economic, political and social lives can our city prosper," he said when I talked with him on the phone. It was the same flash point in a very old rebellion.

John McNulty is the absolute master of the eternal vagaries of Irish Catholic parish life. As James Thurber has stated: "American writing in our time has developed few men with so keen an eye and so sharp an ear. Nothing, however commonplace, that he touched with words remained commonplace, but was magnified and enlivened by his intense and endless fascination with the stranger in the street, the drinker at the bar and the bartender behind it, the horseplayer, the cab driver, the guy at the ball game, the fellow across the room, the patient in the next hospital bed." The neighborhoods, and neighborhood characters, that John McNulty clearly loved are gone now. And yet, as the accomplished writer and contemporary rock star Jim Carroll points out, Christmas in California is just not the same thing.

CAN'T SLIP ANY DRUGS TO SISTERS ON FIFTH AVENUE

By John McNulty

A nun stumbled on the sidewalk on Fifth Avenue, near Forty-seventh Street. There was a bad place in the sidewalk and the nun had stepped on it while walking along with another nun. This happened in the middle of a busy afternoon, and the sidewalks were crowded.

A man in a yellow polo coat grabbed the nun's arm, helpfully. The other nun grasped her other arm and looked into her face, which was pale. The two nuns were not used to crowds and milling around, and both looked scared over the trivial mishap.

The man jerked his hat off before he spoke, solicitously, to the nun who had stumbled. He had a cauliflower ear and his hat was a Madison Square Garden kind of hat.

"Is something the matter, Sister?" he said, leaning toward the nun. "Something happen? You hurt yourself, Sister?"

The nun spoke so softly, out of embarrassment, that the man could not hear what she said. Another man, with his hat off, was there by then, and the two nuns and two men made a small clump in the middle of the busy sidewalk. Still another man stood still, only a few feet away, watching them.

"Begging your pardon, Sister," the cauliflower man said, being very careful to use the highest-class language he could figure out, "I thought something happened you're like in distress. I mean taken or something, or hurt your foot, if you'll excuse me."

From under the black hood and starched linen of her religious garb, the nun looked timidly and kindly at him. "I-I-I slipped," she said, and looked appealingly at the other nun.

"I think Sister is all right now," the other nun said. "Her foot slipped, I think. Are you all right, Sister Veronica?"

"Yes. I twisted my—I twisted my ankle a little," Sister Veronica answered. She took a step or two, carefully. The cauliflower-ear man put on his hat, helped her that step or two, then let go of her arm, and took his hat off as the two nuns went on slowly and anxiously down the Avenue.

"Jeez, I thought something happen to her, I don't know what," said the cauliflower-ear man. He put on his hat again, looking back at the departing nuns, then started up the street, almost in stride with the second man.

At that minute, the third man, the onlooker, joined them, and the three moved along, almost as if they had known each other before this.

"Look, see what I got—amyl nitrate," the third man said, opening his gloved hand and showing a capsule in it. "I was just going to slip it to her if she—"

"I think she's all right," the second man said to him.

"Slip what to her?" the cauliflower-ear man said, almost angrily, checking his stride.

"The amyl nitrate," the fellow answered. "I have it for my old man. He gets attacks. He got a bad heart, my old man, so I have to have it, and I was right there. I thought the nun maybe had a heart at—"

"Whaddaya mean slip it to her. You ain't going to slip no amble nitrites to her," the cauliflower-ear man said. "You ain't slipping no drugs to no nuns on Fifth Avenue. Whaddaya mean?"

"My father," the fellow said, and by now all three were walking together again up the sidewalk, "he's liable to collapse any minute while I'm with him. So I got this—Look it's to keep your heart going if you get a heart attack like my father does." He showed the capsule again, and then put it back in his coat pocket.

"Yeh, I know what he means," said the other man. "He thought maybe the Sister had a heart attack, and he wanted—"

"Oh, oh," the cauliflower-ear man said, but only partly satisfied, it seemed by the tone of his voice and the way he looked at the amyl-nitrate man.

"Oh, yes. Yes, that's what I thought. She maybe had a heart attack when I saw you two there helping her. I meant I was ready to slip her the amyl nitrate and bring her to," the man said.

"Yuh? But what if it wasn't?" the cauliflower-ear man asked, only a little placated. "Maybe something else instead of heart attack and that stuff be exactly the wrong thing to slip her? I don't like the idea, slipping drugs to Sisters on Fifth Avenue. You can't go slipping drugs to Sisters on Fifth Avenue, what I mean."

"I can tell if it would be the right thing," the man said. "My father—"

QUEBEDEAU '87

"I see't you mean, you meant well all right, but I don't like the idea slipping even well-meant drugs to a Sister on Fifth Avenue," the cauliflower-ear man said. Then, just before he turned west, he summoned it up. "Anyway, the Sister made out all right. All's well ends well."

"Yeah. So long," the amyl-nitrate man said, turning the other way at the corner. "Just the same, lucky I was there, in case it was a heart attack. That stuff I showed you save my old man's life many a time. So long."

The cauliflower-ear man went west, the amyl-nitrate man went east, and the third man went straight up the Avenue, looking back, but there was no sign of the two nuns, who were a couple blocks away by then, probably.

CHRISTMAS IN CALIFORNIA

Spending Christmas last week in California seemed a bit absurd, the climate and surroundings evoking none of my youthful remembrances. In a sense, that was a good thing ... Christmas has given me nothing but a flair for inventive suicides since I passed the sad years of that holiday at the age of nine. Out here in the mecca of Clorox, the date just slid by with a surreal thievery. The smell of eucalyptus permeating these roads does not do much for me in the way of wintry nostalgia, except recollections of cough drops and seasonal colds and that frightful balm my mother would heat and rub on my chest while I was laid up in bed on the big day, while I heard my brother out in the living room running down the batteries on my toys, if not wrecking them outright.

Even the nativity scene at the local church here seemed suspect. When I passed by I saw the straw in the manger under serious attack by these monstrous turkey buzzards, who had knocked flat two adoring shepherds and Joseph's donkey and whose truly enormous wingspans threatened to decapitate a wise man as they scattered at my approach.

There was one effect I had not bargained on and which I cannot explain, but without the trappings of snow, bogus Santas and fir trees in vacant lots being hawked for outrageous markups, I found myself thinking of it more as a holyday than a holiday, taking in Mass and, more importantly, not feeling a hypocrite for it. The rest of the day, as I recall, I spent the better part of three hours climbing two adjoining trees in the fault-line ravine to rescue one of my cats.

—*Jim Carroll*

THE CALVARY
CEMETERY STRIKE

By John Cooney

Francis Cardinal Spellman was undoubtedly the most powerful Irish Catholic spokesman in America from the time of the Korean "conflict" through the high tide in Asia now known as the Vietnam War. In his time Spellman had only one authentic rival, Bishop Fulton J. Sheen. Sheen had the television ratings, but Spellman had the power. Besides, Spellman would whisper, I hear that Fulton is something of a closet liberal. "Uncle Fultie" was destined never to advance all that far in Cardinal Spellman's New York Catholic church.

The March 1949 day was raw, and the cold chilled the men pacing slowly in front of the heavy metal gates at the entrance to Calvary Cemetery in the borough of Queens. Others stood in knots around trash cans bright with fire. They were grave diggers, members of United Cemetery Workers Local 293, who had been on strike since mid-January. Suddenly, a large bus rumbled up to the gate. The first person to alight was Cardinal Spellman, his clerical collar peeking above denim overalls, who stood by the front door, impatiently waving his right hand and saying, "Come on! Come On!" Dozens of youths in windbreakers and khaki pants tumbled into the icy air. They were from St. Joseph's Seminary, at Dunwoodie, Yonkers, and Spellman defiantly led them past the strikers into the cemetery. The Cardinal was using seminarians as scabs.

Spellman's step wasn't undertaken lightly, but he saw the need for dramatic action. Labor was a constant headache for him because the archdiocese was an employer on a monumental scale. Each year, Spellman paid out some $30 million in wages just to the building-trade unions that constructed his many projects. The archdiocese spent millions more on salaries for priests, teachers, hospital workers, grounds keepers, maids, and hosts of other tradespeople. The Cardinal had always been opposed to unions, but, against his better judgment, he had accepted the collective bargaining of the cemetery workers three years earlier when they had joined their local, an affiliate of the Food, Tobacco, Agricultural and Allied Workers Union of America.

The Cardinal was encouraged by Monsignor George C. Ehardt, his director of cemeteries. A stocky, balding cynic who always had a cigar jutting from the corner of his mouth, Ehardt was as dogmatic as Spellman. When the workers' contract expired on December 31, Spellman had told him to hold the line on the wages. Ehardt had taken that as a mandate to insult the grave diggers as well. When the negotiating team sat down with Ehardt and his assistant, a quiet priest named Henry Cauley, the Monsignor placed a crucifix in the middle of the bargaining table. The first union contract had been signed in 1946. Now, three years later, the grave diggers petitioned for more than the $59 a week they earned and a five-day, forty-hour week, instead of their six-day, forty-eight-hour week. The meeting concluded when the men made their demands. It was during the second meeting that Ehardt made the archdiocese's first, and final, offer. Again Cauley was at his side, looking uncomfortable. "The most we can do is a dollar a week," Ehardt said. "Take it or leave it." He added pointedly, "The Cardinal's behind me."

The grave diggers were dumbfounded. At first, they thought the Monsignor was joking, but they swiftly realized he was not. Sam Cimaglia, one of the negotiators, began arguing. He believed he had a strong case, since he had read a lot of labor literature, including papal encyclicals, on the rights of workers. "The Pope says that a worker with a family of four should get about sixty-eight dollars a week," he began.

"Where'd you read that?" Ehardt interrupted.

Cimaglia told him in *The Sign*, a publication of the Passionist Fathers.

"The Passionists," Ehardt retorted. "Why do you listen to those guys? They're a bunch of bandits."

Cimaglia and his men were all devout Catholics. Many of them went to Mass every morning. Never having heard a priest refer to other priests in such a fashion, they were shocked. "You're a man of God," Cimaglia said. "You can't believe that."

Ehardt didn't heed him. "You guys are so religious, why don't you be like God?" he said. "He worked six days a week."

Stonewalled and dismayed, the workers took the only recourse they believed was available. "Put away your rosary beads and go out," Cimaglia recalled Edward Ruggieri, their leader, saying. The sour experience made them realize an aspect of working for the archdiocese that they hadn't previously accepted. "They are just bosses," Ruggieri stated.

The grave diggers' savings quickly evaporated; the help they expected from other unions never materialized, and the lesson they learned was bitter. At first, representatives of labor organizations approached them, including teamsters and stevedores, but they quickly disappeared. The only financial assistance the cemetery workers received was a $5,000 check from the transport workers, and even that was awkward. Mike Quill demanded that the grave diggers keep his union's gift quiet. "We were up against the Powerhouse," Cimaglia related. "Everybody was afraid to touch us." Dorothy Day was one of the few who publicly supported the union. She and some of her staff from the *Catholic Worker* passed out leaflets in front of the Cardinal's residence and were arrested. The police forbade the grave diggers to picket Spellman's house.

Spellman met Ehardt to determine their best course of action. Their next step was much more serious and calculated to lose all sympathy for the union: they accused the local leadership of being Communists. In light of the times the charge was particularly vicious.

The grave diggers were shocked by the charge and were dismayed when many people apparently believed the Cardinal. Spellman, however, also lost support by the move. Some people who had sympathized with him, thinking him concerned about the families of the mounting numbers of unburied, now thought he acted maliciously.

Thus, when Spellman led the seminarians into the graveyard, there was a great deal of bitterness on both sides. He wanted to see how everything went the first day. The second day, he called in the press; reporters and photographers swarmed over the cemetery, and Spellman always found time for an interview. The strike, he contended, had reached "crisis" proportions. He said he was considering formal burial squads at parishes around the archdiocese. "I could have put an unlimited number of volunteers to work," he claimed, surveying the seminarians as they dug graves. "But this won't be necessary. My boys will return to Calvary daily until the job is finished and everything is normal." &

THE POWERHOUSE

Francis Cardinal Spellman was not particularly well known when he arrived in New York. Besides, unlike most members of the Irish-American hierarchy, he did not look particularly imposing, appearing to most people who met him for the first time rather like a middle-aged cherub. "I never did come up to expectations," he said, although this did not stop the high Irish in New York for a moment.

Spellman had inherited an archdiocese that was made up of all New York City except the boroughs of Brooklyn and Queens, and included the counties of Westchester, Putnam, Dutchess, Orange, Sullivan and Ulster. It was $28 million in debt, and, Cardinal O'Connell's reservations aside, the times really did demand a priest who was something of a bookkeeper.

In the twenty-eight years that Spellman was in New York, the archdiocese would spend more than $500 million on construction alone, and from the beginning Spellman would lean heavily on his Irish laity for advice about it. John Burke, the president of B. Altman & Company, Harry Haggerty, the president of Metropolitan Life, and John Coleman, a former president of the New York Stock Exchange, became his closest counselors, and among the other high Irish they became known as "The Blessed Trinity," ready to help Cardinal Spellman whenever they could. Coleman, who had been a poor boy raised in Hell's Kitchen, even got to be known as something of a gray eminence. This was because New York politicians have always

Francis Cardinal
Spellman.

called the chancery "the Powerhouse," although when questioned about it, the politicians, fearful of offending someone, tend to deny that they have as much as heard of the chancery. Still, in each administration at city hall, the chancery, or "Powerhouse," has at least one ambassador who makes the Cardinal's views known, and one of the pastimes among city hall reporters and lesser politicians is to guess the identity of the ambassador. Under Spellman it was decided that that position belonged to John Coleman. Because the chancery always had great political power attributed to it, Coleman had great political power attributed to him, too.

—*John Corry*

War Heroes

*The Brothers Sullivan bid one
last goodbye in the 1944
Twentieth-Century Fox
production of*
The Fighting Sullivans.

The struggle against colonialism has bound together Irish people on both sides of the Atlantic for the last two centuries. The father of the American Navy, Captain John Barry, was born in Wexford. The father of the Irish Free State, Eamon De Valera, was born in New York City. The Irish Republican Brotherhood was created in America. The Fenian Movement became so intense that, in an attempt to form a second front, thousands of armed veterans of the Civil War in America crossed the border and attacked British forts in Canada between 1866 and 1871. This is still unfinished business. With the death of Bobby Sands a few years ago, tensions were brought back to the boiling point again.

MR. DE VALERA AND MR. HEARST
By Bob Callahan

Winsor McCay's drawing, "He Died for His Country," mourned the executed Irish rebel leader Sir Roger Casement.

D ressed in a seaman's sweater and dungarees, Eamon De Valera, revolutionary head of the new outlaw Irish government, boarded the twin-screw steamer SS *Lapland* in Liverpool harbor at some point during the middle of the night. The date was June 2, 1919. The tall, gaunt Irish rebel leader was beginning a journey that would take him back to the land of his birth.

On June 11, 1919, the *Lapland* reached New York harbor. Dev was quickly taken off the ship and escorted to Liam Mellow's apartment on East 59th Street. He was now but twelve blocks away from the hospital in which—on October 14, 1882—he had been born.

Eamon De Valera had come to America with two purposes in mind. He would attempt to hammer together the various Irish-American factions behind the goals of the recent Irish revolution—itself, an impossible task— and he would try to raise American public opinion to the cause of a free and independent Ireland. America was profoundly skeptical. It was fun to sing Irish rebel songs in bars, but Great Britain remained America's greatest ally. America had just recently fought, and won, a war in Europe with Great Britain at its side.

When De Valera finally surfaced in New York, he was subjected to immediate political attack. The governor of Alabama called for his deportation. The Irishman was a fugitive from British justice, the governor argued, and America owed it to its greatest ally to help put this man inside a British jail. In the city of Los Angeles, newspapers suggested that De Valera's public meetings be mobbed. Bowing to such pressure, plans to use the Shrine Auditorium for Dev's forthcoming visit were quickly canceled.

With President Woodrow Wilson nervously—squeakingly—neutral, De Valera was uniquely dependent upon the American press. The press, however, was openly pro-British. One newspaper syndicate alone would prove the exception. That syndicate was owned by William Randolph Hearst.

By 1919 Hearst had become the most powerful and controversial journalist in America. One in every four Americans read his newspapers each and every day. It is hard to overrate the significance of that fact in an age

184

◄

Eamon De Valera and members of the San Francisco Irish community on the steps of San Francisco's city hall, 1919.

before the full development of either radio or television. Not counting woodchoppers and paper mill workers, Hearst had slightly more than 38,000 people on his regular, weekly payroll. Those mill hands were important. As W.A. Swanberg has pointed out, Hearst was easily the biggest user of paper in the world.

Hearst's sympathy for the Irish cause had come to a head with the execution of Sir Roger Casement, the Irish rebel leader. On the editorial page the following Saturday, August 5, 1916, the Hearst papers attacked the British government in near scalding terms.

"The record of the English Government's dealing with the Irish people for the last three hundred years," the editorial read, "has been one long history of tyranny and almost incredible stupidity. And we believe that the sober judgment of history will rank the hanging of Sir Roger Casement among the chiefest of the governmental crimes and blunders which have stained the long, sorrowful story of English oppression and Irish wrongs and sufferings....

"The Ministry had Sir Roger Casement in its grip. It was resolved to put him to a felon's death. It did that very thing. The hangman performed his loathsome function. And that day the British Empire lost Ireland forever."

The editorial writer was a New York Irishman by the name of Philip Francis. With Hearst's full blessing, Francis commenced to turn himself into Padraic Pearse.

"Sir Roger Casement is not dead," the editorial continued. "That poor, fettered, hooded, ghastly thing that dangled at the end of the rope was not he. No. Sir Roger Casement still lives.... The English jailors can bury his body. But the Man lives on. And he lives free. He has escaped his captors. No warrant can reach him now. No Scotland Yard can lay hands on him. He lives in history, a patriot and a martyr. He lives in Irish hearts, a hero and a savior...."

Francis' editorial was only the half of it. The entire editorial page that Saturday was devoted to similiar sentiments and supporting materials. Poems by Easter Rising leaders Joseph Plunkett and Thomas MacDonagh were reprinted. So was Pearse's famous letter to his mother. In the center of the page was an editorial cartoon, titled "He Died for His Country," drawn by Winsor McCay, creator of the truly odd and wonderful "Little Nemo" comic strip, and perhaps the finest American editorial cartoonist of this century. The entire page, in short, was truly shocking—quite worthy, in fact, of the young publisher who had once walked Harvard Yard with a crocodile on a leash.

Before the ink was even dry, the British Embassy in Washington telegraphed London. Hearst, it was reported, was now completely out of control. On October 11, 1916, the British government reacted by banning the Hearst papers from the use of its cables and its mails. Hearst's papers were soon banned from Canada. Thereafter, as W.A. Swanberg has written, a Canadian caught reading Runyon, or Jiggs and Maggie, was subject to a $5,000 fine or up to five years in prison.

Hearst apparently was thrilled. Eamon De Valera couldn't have known this, but the other Chief was just waiting for him the day he arrived. Dev would be welcomed as a conquering hero by all of the Hearst newspapers as he began his American tour.

With the Hearst papers parting the waters before him, Eamon De Valera began to move west. The ostensible focus of the tour was an Irish bond drive, but it was clear from De Valera's message that he was trying to win the rebellion against Great Britain here on American shores.

On Friday, July 18, 1916, the *San Francisco Examiner* was filled with news of Dev's arrival in the Bay Area. "De Valera welcomed by City," the front-page headline read. "Crowds Roar Greetings to Erin's Chief," the lead article proclaimed.

The next day, Saturday, July 19, 1919, Dev spoke before a crowd estimated as "in excess of 12,000" at the Civic Auditorium. The event, covered by seven different *Examiner* reporters, occasioned still another blistering anti-English, pro-Irish editorial cartoon. The editorial stated just what De Valera had come to America wanting to hear. "We are told," the *Examiner* proclaimed, "that we must not sympathize with or aid the Irish Republic, because that would constitute interference with the internal affairs of Great Britain.

"And so it would.

"But if we read history correctly, that is exactly how our fathers gained our independence—by interfering with the internal affairs of Great Britain.

"President De Valera, the *Examiner* salutes you as the rightful representative and head of your people and their free nation!

"God save the Republic of Ireland!"

Over at the St. Francis Hotel on Union Street, Captain Arthur Swagge, R.N., an attaché at the British Embassy, packed his bags and moved down the street upon learning that the hotel had just chosen to run an Irish tricolor from the roof. The naval captain's tardy maneuver was also dutifully reported on the front page of the *Examiner*.

Eamon De Valera would continue to tour America for the next eighteen months. From time to time he would be asked to write a guest article for one of the various Hearst newspapers. His Irish Fund campaign netted some $6 million. American public opinion had been aroused—thanks in part to Hearst—but it had not been aroused enough to cause either the Republican or Democratic Party to write a strong "pro-Ireland" plank into their respective 1920 presidential platforms.

In Ireland, the Anglo-Irish war was entering into a new and deadly phase. Griffith had been seized and jailed. So had Terence MacSweeny, the Mayor of Cork, who soon died in his jail cell on a hunger strike. And the British had introduced a new and particularly brutal weapon into the campaign—the "Black and Tans," auxiliary regiments made up of scum drawn from British prisons, a militia soon to be known for its torture and, even by wartime standards, its criminal behavior.

Eamon De Valera's American mission was over. Once more he made ready to run the British border. This time, however, the British made a concerted effort to stop him. Machine guns were trained on the docks of the SS *Pontia*, out of New York, when it docked in Dublin harbor. Dev, however, was aboard the *Celtic*, bound for Liverpool. When the *Celtic* drifted up the Liverpool quay, he was stored in a bin filled with potatoes by friends with an obvious sense of humor. Once again dressed in a seaman's garb, Dev made his way back from Liverpool to Manchester, then to Dublin. He was reunited with Michael Collins for dinner in Ireland on Christmas Eve, 1920.

MEAGHER OF THE SWORD

By Tom Clark

The front of the state capitol of Montana might seem the last place you'd find an equestrian statue commemorating a flamboyant Irish revolutionary, a man whose oratorical skills and fiery temper once led him from the shadow of a scaffold at Clonmel jail to political exile in Australia, and then later from a successful career as lecturer, lawyer and editor in New York to military heroism at the bloody Civil War battle of Fredericksburg. Yet there he sits, before the capitol dome at Helena, proudly poised on his restless charger, saber held high —General Thomas Francis Meagher, the legendary "Young Man of the Sword."

The college-educated son of a well-to-do Waterford mercantile family, Thomas Meagher abandoned his legal studies in order to respond in the mid-1840s to Daniel O'Connell's "Repeal" campaign which was aimed at winning legislative separation from England. Within a year or two, however, Meagher found himself a leader of the "Young Ireland" faction, a group opposed to O'Connell's nonviolent policies—and dedicated, instead, to seizing freedom by the gun and by the sword. His dramatic rise to political prominence, and the crisis of

In most Irish-American families, a military career is still widely considered an honor equal to a career in law or literature, and second only to a "calling" from the Church. This is a very ancient heritage. The leaders of early Irish Gaelic society were the brehon lawyers, the druid priests, the shanachie storytellers and, of course, the old clan chieftains. This tradition survived in Ireland for millennia and was successfully transplanted to America during the middle of the nineteenth century when the survivors of famine-ridden Gaelic Ireland began to arrive in this country en masse. An early leader of the "Fighting 69th," Thomas Meagher was just such a soldier.

▶

General Thomas Francis Meagher, leader of the Irish Brigade during the American Civil War.

the "physical force" versus "moral force" debate, came at the O'Connell Association's Conciliation Hall in Dublin on July 28, 1846, when this small, blue-eyed, twenty-two-year-old orator aroused an outnumbered "Young Ireland" constituency with fighting words. To the parliamentary authorities of the time, Meagher's appeal to the sword was barbed with a special poison tip, dipped in the still-fresh blood of the American Revolution. "Abhor the sword—stigmatize the sword?" the youthful speaker asked rhetorically. "No, my lord, for at its blow, a giant nation started from the waters of the Atlantic, and by its redeeming magic, and in the quivering of its crimson light, the crippled colony sprang into the attitude of a proud Republic—prosperous, limitless and invincible!"

Meagher became a founding member of the Irish Confederation and went to Paris as its delegate, seeking French support for an Irish revolution. On his return, in March 1848, he defiantly carried two inflammatory speeches which were recorded in shorthand by government agents. Arrested for seditious libel, he was sentenced to be hanged and beheaded, with his body to be "divided into four quarters, to be disposed of as Her Majesty shall think fit." Before Victoria could bethink herself on the subject, however, Meagher's sentence was commuted by her colonial court; on June 1, 1849, he was banished for life to Tasmania.

Australia couldn't hold the fiery Meagher for long. In May of 1852 he escaped to America. His fame as an Irish patriot had clearly preceded him there: the day following his arrival he applied for work at a New York law firm, and there was serenaded by several companies of the 69th (Second Irish) Regiment of the New York State Militia; within an hour a crowd of 7,000 wildly cheering Irish-Americans had gathered, crying out for a speech, which Meagher duly supplied.

"Meagher of the Sword" soon won a national reputation as a barnstorming lecturer and founding editor of New York's *Irish News,* but when the Civil War ripped his adopted nation apart in 1861, this libertarian's native instincts were clearly divided. When his American father-in-law spoke of the Southern insurrectionists as "rebels," Meagher strongly objected that the proper term should be "revolutionists." In private he proclaimed, "My sympathies are entirely with the South!" Still, the American republic had given him a home and a career; even more influential, perhaps, was the chance that an Irish-American army, recruited in the North, might one day be brought across the sea to liberate his mother country. After some weeks of agonizing deliberation, Meagher chose his side. He took out a newspaper ad soliciting "one hundred young Irishmen —healthy, intelligent and active" to form a company of Irish Zouaves attached to the 69th Regiment.

Meagher's volunteers were typical of the 69th New York: the enlisted men dressed casually and there was a relaxed tolerance throughout the ranks, with officers being elected by a democratic poll of the enlisted men. Beneath its green silk banner, with the harp and sunburst emblems, and under Meagher's command, the New York unit saw its first action in July 1861, at the first Battle of Bull Run. Thirty-eight men of the 69th died there; Meagher ended up thrown from his horse and shaken. He later had to defend himself and his troops against criticism by his rival, Colonel W.T. Sherman, who suggested that the Irish-American soldiers were a rabble and that Meagher himself was unfit to lead them.

Meagher returned to New York and reorganized his Irish Brigades, recruiting fresh regiments from that city, Boston and Philadelphia. Within thirty days filled with feverish public speaking he had raised an army of 5,000 men. Appointed a brigadier general, he joined his troops to Sumner's Army of the Potomac in the Peninsular campaign of early 1862. The Irish Brigades engaged McClellan's army at Malvern Hill, sustaining massive losses. In July Meagher returned to New York for emergency recruiting. Back in action that fall, his brigades led the successful attack at Antietam, again suffering huge losses. Meagher was reported to have died in action. But he survived and in December led his men in the doomed attack on Marye's Hill at Fredericksburg, where their heroic but suicidal charge left the Irish Brigade in tatters. In sympathy, the Irish-American press charged that "unjust discrimination" had befallen the Irish-American armies throughout the war, marking them off as cannon fodder.

Meagher's war was at an end. After Chancellorsville, in April 1863, where his decimated units were reduced to a supporting role, he resigned his command "of this poor vestige and relic of the Irish Brigade."

"The Young Man of the Sword" was put out to pasture. In 1865 he became acting governor of Montana. Southern gunmen with a score to settle made life nervous for him in that wild territory. One night, ill and seeking refuge (from real or imagined dangers) on a Missouri River steamboat, he fell overboard. At the age of thirty-eight, the man who had escaped an Irish gibbet, an Australian banishment and two years of Confederate gunfire, tumbled to a watery death a world away from his beloved Erin home. ❧

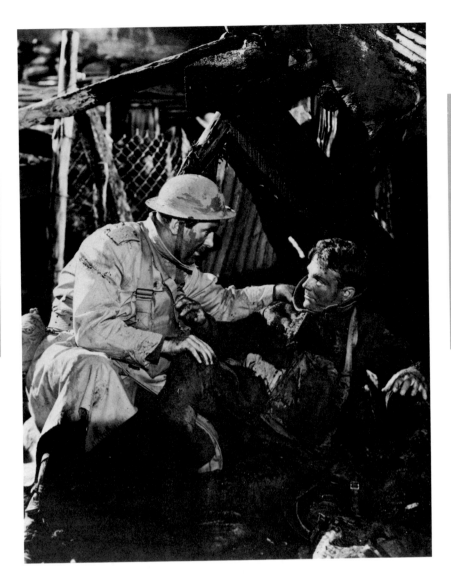

◄

Father Francis
Duffy and "Wild
Bill" Donovan
portrayed in the
1940 Warner
production, *The
Fighting 69th.*

JUST PLAIN HUMAN

Meagher's "Fighting 69th" retained its ethnic identity in World War I, serving heroically in France under the military leadership of Colonel William ("Wild Bill") Donovan and the spiritual guidance of its well-loved chaplain, Father Francis Duffy. Leading his "Micks" into battle on the western front, Donovan realized a boyhood dream inspired by the lines of the Irish bard James Charles Mangan:

> *Twas there I first beheld, drawn up in fire and line,*
> *The brilliant Irish hosts; they came, the bravest*
> *of the brave ...*

"Wild Bill" was wounded in action three times and awarded the Distinguished Service Cross, the Distinguished Service Medal, the Congressional Medal of Honor, a Purple Heart with two oak leaf clusters and the Croix de Guerre (honors that paved the way, incidentally, to a political career in the Republican Party and a World War II position as head of the Office of Strategic Services, predecessor of the C.I.A.). "Fighting Father Duffy" became almost equally famous for his bravery in the face of danger, frequently delivering last rites on the battlefield with an apparent indifference to enemy gunfire. (Two of Duffy's fellow Roman Catholic ministers, Timothy Murphy and Simon O'Rourke, became the first army and navy chaplains to die in the war.) The courage of men such as Donovan and Duffy went a long way toward earning America's "Micks" the respect of their countrymen; as Father Duffy said in the preface to his autobiography, he and most of the men in his regiment may have been Irish, "but normally and let alone, we are just plain human."

—Tom Clark

189

The Speech

One Sunday in 1944, Milton Caniff devoted a page to an idea that had been in the back of his mind for sometime. He had written the "balloons," visualized the drawings, and then waited for the right point in his narrative into which to insert it. It had the spontaneous effect of a Gettysburg speech, a Message to Garcia. The next day newspapers were republishing the speech Caniff put into the mouth of Flip Corkin, in their editorial pages. That Monday, without prompting, Representative Carl Hinshaw of California called Congress' attention to the Caniff page. "It is deserving of immortality," he said, and expressed regret that the accompanying Caniff drawings in color could not also be inserted into the *Congressional Record*.
—*Rick Marshall*

M GOING TO MAKE A SPEECH—AND LL BE THE LAST ONE OF ITS KIND CAPTIVITY—SO DON'T GET A SHORT CUIT BETWEEN THE EARS...

NO, SIR

WELL, YOU MADE IT...YOU'RE A FLIGHT OFFICER IN THE AIR FORCES OF THE ARMY OF THE UNITED STATES...THOSE WINGS ARE LIKE A NEON LIGHT ON YOUR CHEST...I'M NOT GOING TO WAVE THE FLAG AT YOU—BUT SOME THINGS YOU MUST NEVER FORGET...

D SOME SMART SLIDE RULE JOKERS AT IT OUT OVER DRAWING BOARDS GIVE YOU A MACHINE THAT WILL P YOU UP THERE SHOOTING ... I OMMENDED YOU FOR FIGHTER AIRCRAFT I WANT YOU TO BE COCKY AND SMART PROUD OF BEING A BUZZ—BOY...

...BUT DON'T FORGET THAT EVERY BULLET YOU SHOOT, EVERY GALLON OF GAS AND OIL YOU BURN WAS BROUGHT HERE BY TRANSPORT PILOTS WHO FLEW IT IN OVER THE WORST TERRAIN IN THE WORLD! YOU MAY GET THE GLORY—BUT THEY PUT THE LIFT IN YOUR BALLOON!..

KAY, SPORT, END OF SPEECH...WHEN YOU UP IN THAT "WILD BLUE YONDER" THE SONG KS ABOUT—REMEMBER, THERE ARE A LOT GOOD GUYS MISSING FROM MESS TABLES HE SOUTH PACIFIC, ALASKA, AFRICA, BRITAIN, A AND BACK HOME WHO ARE SORTA NTING ON YOU TO TAKE IT FROM HERE! GOOD NIGHT, KID!

This way to TOKIO! Next stop U.S.A.

ONE SUMMER
IN SPAIN

By Bill Bailey

In response to their own experiences with colonialism, Irish-Americans have become involved in the struggle against various forms of tyranny around the globe. During the Mexican Revolution, a brigade of Irish-Americans, known to history as the "San Patricios," played a pivotal role on behalf of the victorious rebel forces. Irishmen have been active in liberation movements in Africa and South America as well. In the 1930s, Irish-Americans also joined with the rebel Abraham Lincoln Brigade to attempt to overthrow Fascism in Spain. An Irish-American seaman, Bill Bailey of San Francisco, was only one of a number of Irishmen to take part in that particular rebellion.

We had gone as far as the train would take us. The Fascists had uprooted the tracks past the point we had reached.

"All out. All out," a commanding voice shouted. "Move it out. On the double."

Some 650 Americans, who made up the Abraham Lincoln Brigade, quickly jumped out of the rickety boxcars, throwing to the ground blankets, rifles, ammo belts and knapsacks. We were in a strange part of the country. The air was hot and the countryside was dry. We could sniff a whiff of burnt gunpowder in the hot breeze. We were glad to leave the boxcars that had been our home for the last day and a half.

We were now only two kilometers away from the Fascist Army. Only a small hill blocked our view of our objective, the town of Quinto. Nearby our artillery batteries had dug in with their two antitank cannons and two French 75's. The shelling had started early that morning. For the first time in my life I was within twenty feet of a cannon as it went off.

Our pace quickened as we charged towards the front. The town's only church suddenly appeared in view. Surrounding the church clustered the town of Quinto, a town of cobblestone streets and two-storey houses—a town superbly fortified, or so the Fascists had boasted.

To the Republicans, Quinto was the front door to the more important

▼

Bill Bailey, San Francisco labor activist and member of the Abraham Lincoln Brigade.

cities of Belchite and Zaragoza, a town that had to be won.

As we got over the hilly rise our company paused for a moment. We watched a group of light bombers, flying in a low wing-to-wing formation, drop their bombs in unison on a heavily fortified position. The thundering sound, and the smoke and dirt rising into the sky, dispelled any illusion that this was not the real thing.

Our pace quickened. We were running. Far to our left, we could hear the loud yelling of an American infantry company advancing to the first line of Fascist trenches.

Bullets were whistling past us, making their crackling, popping noise as we neared the line of fire where we could be observed by entrenched Fascists and picked off easily.

Bill McCarthy, an ex-altar boy, an ardent anti-Fascist and my close buddy, found a gully that headed towards town. A Spanish soldier from another company crisscrossed our path. We heard the crack of the bullet and the soldier fell flat on his face. McCarthy and I ran to see if he was dead. The Spaniard looked stunned, then tried to get up. As he lifted his head from the ground, blood started to flow from his jaw in the same manner as wine would flow from a keg once the plug was pulled. McCarthy jumped on him, holding him down. To stand up would guarantee a target for a sharpshooter.

The mass of blood on the Spaniard's clothing, face, hands, and even in his hair, made it appear that his life was over. He must have felt that way too. Using every available word we could muster in Spanish, McCarthy and I tried to assure him. He would be ok. We would get him to a hospital, then, home. . . .

The sight of the dead has a psychological effect. Nobody lectured us about what they would look like. Even the noise—the sound of a ricocheting shell twirling aimlessly through the air—can frighten the most experienced soldier. I felt like urinating. At this moment I would have welcomed being submerged in a bathtub filled with ice cubes.

I tried to find humor in the situation by asking myself what the hell was I doing here, going through this torture, when I could be safe at home with an easy task like passing out leaflets seeking support for the Spanish people's cause, or even stuffing envelopes. Where did it start?

Was it back when that cop slugged me on the picket line during my first attempt to help build a union . . . or was it during the reform school riot when the guards forced me up against the wall with my hands raised over my head, and made me watch as they proceeded to club into unconsciousness many of my friends?

No, it went farther back than that. Perhaps it was when I was clutching fast the handle of the baby carriage . . . maybe it went all the way back to those tiny hands trying to clutch those handles. . . .

SOMEWHERE IN SPAIN:
IN THE EVENT OF MY DEATH,
WILL THE FINDER PLEASE
MAIL THIS LETTER TO MY MOTHER.

Dear Mom

I wish I could be near you to hold your hand and to explain in some detail the reasons for my death. I know at this point that it has fallen upon you in a way that I wished would not have happened. I wanted to explain the night before I left New York where I was really going, and the reasons why I was going to Spain. But I knew that no matter what I might have told you, it would have never made sense to you, and I found that trying to explain would be an impossibility. I am sorry for that.

Don't let anyone mislead you, Mom, by telling you that all this had something to do with Communism. The Hitlers and Mussolinis of the world are killing Spanish people who don't know the difference between Communism and rheumatism. And it's not to set up a Communist government either. The only thing the Communists did here was show the people how to fight for what is rightfully theirs.

Just remember one thing, Mom, I love you dearly, and warmly, and there never was a moment when I didn't feel that way. I was always grateful and proud that you were my Mom,

Your son,
Will

I never had to have this letter mailed, although there were plenty of times when I thought I would.

I realized I had not recognized my mother's understanding of what was taking place when, one day that summer, I heard she had joined a contingent of mothers who proudly marched up Fifth Avenue in New York City behind a banner which said:

"Support our sons who are fighting in the Lincoln-Washington Brigade trying to keep Spain free." ❧

AN HONORABLE MAN

A big, big crowd in Berkeley of what's left of the Left celebrated yesterday those rare birds known as premature anti-Fascists, who fought a half century ago in the Spanish Civil War. One kid wanted to know whether premature anti-Fascist was a gynecological term. That's how hip Berkeley is these days.

Bill Bailey sat like a brick in the audience. Bill Bailey was one of the Americans who went Over There, to Spain, to fight during the bloody 1930s. He was among the Americans who had the sense and the courage to fight the good fight against the Nazis and their paper-duck Franco before the rest of the country wised up. For that, they were later smeared as Reds.

Bill Bailey is without question one of the great men of San Francisco and one of the grander men of our time. He has wise eyes and a ski-jump nose and lives in a surviving 1906 earthquake shack on Telegraph Hill. He is, belatedly, becoming something of a media star, but he still spends too much of his valuable time answering stupid questions from people about what a premature anti-Fascist was.

Yesterday, his mind was going back, not to Spain in 1937 and 1938, but to another event, in which he starred in 1935, which may explain what men like Bill Bailey are all about much better than any treatise on the Left's various glories and follies.

This was back in July 1935, when Bailey had the singular glory of being the first man in the United States of America to rip down a Nazi flag.

When he told me the story, it was like watching an old Movietone Newsreel. The luxury liner *Bremen*, pride of the German fleet, was tied up in New York harbor. Young Bill was an idealistic sailor in league with a bunch of other (mostly Irish) Lefties out to get the Swine. They decided to steal the Nazi flag.

"Hitler had opened up his terror campaign against the Jews, but nobody was doing anything about it. They had the swastika on the bow—it was a big, ugly S.O.B. of a flag. I thought it stood for everything rotten in the world.

"Patty Galvin [he fought for the I.R.A. and was later killed fighting for the United States in the Battle of the Bulge] and I and eight other guys went aboard the liner. Another Irish guy named Low Life McCormick led a diversionary party and walked up to the German sailors, who put out their hands to say hello to the Americans, and belted the stuffing out of the Krauts.

"Sirens went off and guys in gold braid were screaming 'Achtung! Achtung!' from the bridge and we fought our way to the bow. I was the only guy who made it. It was one of my lucky days. Suddenly, I was there staring at this swastika above me and I realized I didn't know how to haul it down. I was futzing with the halyard when I saw a pair of hands appear on the seabreaker I was standing on. I figured it was a German guy and was about to stomp his feet when he yelled out in Irish brogue—it was Adrian Duffy, another harp."

Duffy gave Bailey a knife and told him to cut the rope.

"The guy had fought his way through all these Germans to give me the knife. I cut it and grabbed the flag and a bunch of Nazis were crawling up toward me and I threw it in the water and it sunk like a rat.

"You should have heard the cheers from the people on the dock.

"I jumped back onto the deck and they got me good—they kicked me and stomped me and beat the rest of us until the New York cops swarmed aboard, and then *they* started beating us.

"We spent the night in the cooler and the next day the Nazis went nuts. Goebbels got so crazy that he said such a thing could only happen to the Nazi flag in a city where the mayor was half-Dago and half-Jew. That got Fiorello La Guardia mad as a hornet and when the Nazis demanded more protection for the *Bremen*, he sent only Jewish cops to protect the ship. It was great. The sides were drawn."

Drawing sides is what Bill Bailey has been about all his life. He has fought on the Left for right and reason from the Battle of the *Bremen* to the current hassle of Ronald Reagan's wish to recreate the nineteenth century in Nicaragua. He was chased by the F.B.I. from job to job when his sailor's ticket was yanked in the oppressive 1950s for undesirable patriotic activities.

He has no regrets for fighting the Good Fight. But when a retired F.B.I. agent who used to hound Bailey out of his jobs by telling his employers he smoked dynamite happened to call recently—and left a recorded apology and good wishes on his telephone answering machine—Bill Bailey, tough guy, was moved to tears of compassion.

"To think that all these years this guy was doing what he really didn't believe in," he said. "What a terrible way to have to live."

Bailey actually felt sorry for the bum. These old Lefties are often softies at heart.

—Warren Hinckle

A WAR STORY

By Robert J. Casey

I was working as a rewrite man on the *Chicago Daily Journal* when I first heard of Tom O'Malley. A couple of my schoolmates, Marcellus Donigan and Eugene Quay, who had a law office in La Salle Street, had discovered him in Joliet penitentiary and had taken him over as their personal property. They were interested, as the classic phrase has it, in "springing" him.

Gene wandered into the office one afternoon with a neatly docketed history of the case and it made an interesting story. Old Tom had been in the stir more than half his life, notwithstanding which about everything had happened to him that could have happened to any two men in the same length of time, locked up or not.

Tom, so far as Gene could discover, had been born somewhere in Pennsylvania, and Fate had started to play horse with him when he ran away to be a drummer boy in the Civil War. At the age of twelve he found himself attached to a battery of field artillery with Grant's army in the Wilderness.

He was a gay youngster, bright for his years and popular with the men. Partly because of these traits and partly because the hardy cannoneers didn't trust one another overmuch, he was given custody of the battery fund which he carried around in a knapsack.

The battery was emplaced on a knoll near the right end of the Federal trenches. As was the custom in those days it was squarely in the infantry line. The Feds had been in position for several days in which the only sounds of war came from far away. There had been some skirmishing over on the left where Grant was trying to feel out the enemy's strength and position. Once in a while patrols came to grips in the woods beyond the clearing in front of them. But most of their days were passed in lazy peace with the men on their backs in the grass asleep or sitting in little clusters playing cards.

They had no warning when the gray cavalry came bursting out of the woods. The little clearing had been empty, shimmering in the sunlight, and then, suddenly, it was cluttered up with charging horses. The shock was too much for the comfortable boys in blue. With one accord they got up and ran, infantrymen and can-

From the time of Private Miles O'Reilly's Civil War dispatches to the Herald Tribune, *Irish America has provided a number of fine war correspondents. Robert J. Casey's reports from Europe during the Second World War are considered classics in this genre. As Ben Hecht has written in the introduction to a collection of Casey's better columns and writings: "The Casey who fought, hitchhiked, and wrote his way through wars and revolutions never became an 'expert.' Bob Casey's writings are as unflaggingly the utterances of the original Bob Casey as Mark Twain's are of him."*

noneers together, and panic swept across regiment after regiment in the line to the left.

O'Malley ran with the rest a few feet and stopped. He had left his knapsack with the battery fund in it hanging to the knob on the butt of one of the guns. He hurried back up the hill to get it. The Confederates were well out of the woods, filling the world with frightful yells and coming ahead at the gallop, when he reached the crest. He snatched up his knapsack and then rediscovered what he had known all along. Every one of the dozen cannons in the line—those of his own battery and those adjoining—was laid and loaded and ready to fire.

There seemed to be no sense in leaving them that way, so young Tom started down the line pulling lanyards as he went. A rain of grapeshot struck the charging horsemen full in the center and sent them reeling back in confusion.

That didn't end the fight. Foot soldiers in gray uniforms were swarming out of the woods behind the cavalry and they were too far away to be much affected by the artillery blast. But they hesitated while the horsemen were reforming to renew their attack. And in the interval, the Federals, shaken from their mass hypnosis by the sound of the firing, came streaming back.

Not all of them came back, but enough to hold up a fanatic onslaught for ten minutes. Then the Federal cavalry came charging around the right flank in an enveloping movement that ended with the Confederates in full flight.

O'Malley, some time in the late 1870s, came to a Chicago just getting started again after the great fire, a raw, roaring town where money was plentiful and life cheap. All the riffraff of the world was gathering here and graft in the high places had taken on proportions of a major industry. There was never a night without its murder, never a morning when a couple of floaters failed to give employment to the river patrol. The lethargic populace, which for years had been accepting such things along with disaster, typhoid epidemics and bitter winters as a sort of unavoidable visitation, stopped roaring and began to mutter. A hamstrung chief of police and his dizzy police force became aware of the wrath to come.

Such was the situation in which the unsuspecting young Tom O'Malley found himself as he walked one night along Lake Street looking for lodgings.

His story, as it appears in the court record of his trial, is that a man, a total stranger, had been walking about two hundred feet ahead of him for perhaps a block when another total stranger suddenly popped out of an alley. There was a pistol shot. The first man fell to the sidewalk. The second man dashed back into the alley. O'Malley, with more courage than sense, ran forward. The man on the sidewalk was dead. The murderer's pistol lay beside the corpse. O'Malley picked it up. It was still in his hand when the police arrived.

Why the youngster from Pennsylvania wasn't expeditiously hanged is something one doesn't perceive from the records. One gathers that he must have told his own story amazingly well, for the evidence in the case was simple, direct and damning. But there must have been some doubt in the minds of the jurors—a doubt which under the law should have brought him an acquittal. Unwilling to hang him and yet not entirely convinced of his innocence, they found him guilty of murder in the second degree. A judge, who appears to have been just as confused as the jury, gave him a life sentence.

Along in the 1890s, when the town had quieted down a bit, somebody remembered Tom O'Malley and started a campaign to prove him the victim of a ghastly mistake. A petition for his release was signed by the judge who had sentenced him and by all the jurors who

had found him guilty save two who had died. In the midst of this Fate played him another horrible trick. By some legal mumbo jumbo before a political judge, he was turned loose on parole. Three weeks later somebody discovered a mistake had been made in the order and he went back to Joliet again, this time for about thirty years. But in the brief interim of his freedom he had suddenly and ironically become a man of considerable means.

It happened this way. Strolling past the express office one morning he saw a sign advertising a sale of unclaimed baggage and other articles. For lack of something better to do, he went inside. He had only a casual interest in the proceedings until a trunk was put up for auction and he thought he might need a trunk. He bid two dollars, then three and finally bought it for three and a half. When he pried it open in his furnished room that night he found that it contained a lot of women's clothing and twenty-five thousand dollars' worth of negotiable bonds. So with a fortune in his hands he went back to the penitentiary to finish a life sentence.

But the supreme joke was yet to come. In one of the dusty cubicles of the war department, some gnome got down to the bottom of a pile of Civil War correspondence that had been waiting for years to be properly filed. In the mess his eyes caught a letter bearing the signature of Ulysses S. Grant. The note was in the general's own handwriting and addressed to Abraham Lincoln, President of the United States, and so far as the gnome could decipher the scrawl it had something to do with one Thomas O'Malley who virtually unassisted had saved the Union Army from a disastrous rout in the Battle of the Wilderness and it recommended that the said Thomas O'Malley be awarded the Congressional Medal.

The gnome passed this document to the head of his department and the head of the department took it over to the White House. President Theodore Roosevelt, with a fine eye for the spectacular, took immediate action and a grateful republic somewhat belatedly decided to honor a forgotten hero. In the course of a few weeks the secret service picked up Tom O'Malley's trail and the medal was delivered to him in his cell on Joliet penitentiary.

"And here it is," said Mr. Quay, and with some effort he got it out of his coat pocket.

Fashions have changed in medals. Nowadays the honors showered by the grateful republic would bring very little in a pawnshop. But there was nothing paltry about this one. It was a circular medallion about four inches in diameter and about half an inch thick and seemed to weigh a good half pound. It was solid gold.

"I'll tell you quite frankly that Marcellus and I hope to get old Tom out of the clink," said Mr. Quay. "He'd have been out long ago if he'd had a good press agent.

And if you can get this story into print we ought to have clear sailing with the parole board and the governor. I don't believe any governor could refuse a pardon if we can get the complete history of the case in front of him. What do you think?"

"I think it's the damndest story I ever read since *Les Miserables,*" I told him ... and I still think it was.

I took the case history to Dick Finnegan, the managing editor, and when he read it he almost jumped out of his chair. In the *Journal,* as in most newspapers, few stories were ever given more than a column of space. But the barriers were down on this one.

"Take all the space you want," Finnegan told me. "A page if you need it—and don't leave out a single detail."

So I wrote it for about ten thousand words.

Few stories ever got the play in Chicago that the tragic history of Tom O'Malley did. We had one of the best morgues in town and out of it we got a few clippings of O'Malley's printed history. They weren't too informative but they supplied some dates and the names of the men who had been connected with the case. The judge had been dead for several years but we found a photograph of him. We found some line drawings of city officials at the time of the trial and any number of pictures of Chicago as it had looked at that period, including a pretty good view of the part of Lake Street where the murder had occurred. The art department rallied around to produce an impressive spread and the next day the whole country heard about Tom O'Malley.

We were pretty proud of our performance. The story was so startling that the other papers couldn't ignore it. And it brought results almost immediately. Tom O'Malley got his pardon and stepped out into a world that he hardly recognized.

We saw a lot of him between that time and his death some ten or twelve years later. With two other old lads whom he had recruited God knows where, he organized a musical act with which he toured the three-a-day circus until vaudeville expired. It was a pretty good act. The trio appeared in G.A.R. uniforms and delivered a lot of good old Civil War music with much volume and verve, on fife, drums and cornet. There was nothing elaborate about the act. They were just three nice-looking old gents with exceptional skill and the audiences loved them. They got top billing for quite a long time.

O'Malley came to the *Journal* office to see Dick Finnegan on the day of his release and wept as he thanked him. I have never witnessed a scene so touching in a newspaper office. Every time he was in town after that he repeated his visit—a routine that was still going on when I left the *Journal* and probably continued until the paper reorganized as the *Daily Times* and afterward.

I was working on Frank Knox's Chicago *Daily News* when the old man died. I dusted off the clips and revived his tragic story in a two-column obituary. I had just finished it when one of the press associations sent in a story about arrangements for the funeral. In it I learned that Old Tom had a sister living in one of the suburbs and that she intended to have him buried privately in a local cemetery.

"The place to bury Old Tom is the National Cemetery at Arlington," I said to John Craig. "And he is entitled to full military honors with all the trimmings. That's the way he'd want it and I think he has enough friends to see that his wishes are carried out."

So we wired Paul Leach, chief of the Washington bureau, outlining the particulars of the case and asking him to see what could be done about arranging for a military funeral. Late that afternoon the reply came:

"No record to show Thomas O'Malley ever served with Grant in Battle of Wilderness. No record to show Thomas O'Malley ever served in Union Army. Can't find Grant's letter concerning service. No record Congressional Medal ever issued to Thomas O'Malley. Military funeral at Arlington unauthorized unless you can supply further details."

So we left Old Tom's remains to the quiet ministrations of his family and that night I paid a call on Mr. Quay.

"Where did Old Tom get that medal?" I inquired without too much preliminary conversation.

"It was in that trunk he bought at the express company sale," he said. "There wasn't any citation with it so I fixed one up myself. Why?"

I told him why and he seemed hurt. "What are you kicking about?" he wanted to know. "The old guy was certainly innocent and he got ten or twelve years out of life that he'd never have had if that story hadn't been printed. As far as you're concerned it was a good story even if it wasn't exactly true. And your conscience is clear and you can forget about it."

"That's just it," I told him. "I can't forget it." And I can't.

The Sporting Arena

▶

Shoulders somewhat ajar, the Gipper, quarterback George Gipp (Ronald Reagan), watches from the backfield as Knute Rockne (Pat O'Brien) walks his Notre Dame team through the x's and o's in the 1940 Warner production, Knute Rockne: All American.

Gentleman Jim Corbett was born in San Francisco on September 11, 1866. During Corbett's youth, San Francisco was still very much a small Irish-dominated village. The Donahue brothers had built, and ran, both the ironworks and the gas company. The amazing Christopher Buckley controlled city hall from his Den of Thieves over on the Barbary Coast. The great minstrel, Billy Emerson, regularly shuffled and swooned for turn-away crowds at Tom MacQuire's Opera House, and the young Elizabeth Gilbert from Galway, having changed her name to Lola Montez, regularly incurred the wrath of local ministers each time she performed her immortal "Spider Dance" on the San Francisco stage. The king of all of these eccentric Paddys was Gentleman Jim Corbett. Boston may have had its John L. Sullivan, but San Francisco was more than happy with the legend of Gentleman Jim.

RINGSIDE SEAT

By Ring Lardner

Mr. Corbett tells you in his quaint patois that he is sixty years of age. The record books back him up. But when you see him, which you can hardly help doing, as he butts in everywhere, you say to yourself, "Why, he hardly looks old enough to be Zelma O'Neal's daughter-in-law. He simply can't be sixty!" Then a bystander, reading your thoughts, points out that he must be, because he had just attained his majority in 1891, when he had that sixty-one-round workout with Peter Jackson, the Eskimo, and was only a year older when he won the championship from John L.

Well, the thing is mystifying till you learn the truth, which is that way back yonder there was a federal law preventing a pugilist from performing in public before he was twenty, and to circumvent this, Jim had to lie about his age. He was actually seven when he knocked Sullivan for a row of empty pints.

Four years ago Jim published his autobiography and a short time after it came out we all took part in one of Gene Buck's benefits at Great Neck, Long Island. Whenever Gene isn't rehearsing a show or drilling a squad of pallbearers, he is staging a benefit for some-body, usually a stranger. At this benefit, which was for a wealthy lunch-wagon proprietor, I followed Jim in a series of brief speeches by people nobody wanted to hear, and naturally, I made a reference to his book, *The Roar of the Crowd*.

What I said was that the book had derived its title from people who had paid $2 for it. The audience was dumb with merriment over this mot.

But what I want to say now is that I didn't mean it. I had read the book and liked it so much that I suspected a ghost writer, perhaps Gertrude Atherton. It is one of the best-written and most entertaining volumes of its kind and is still selling up in the dozens.

I think my favorite chapter in the book is the one dealing with the Mitchell fight in Jacksonville, Florida. Jim got his man, and confesses that he had trained on champagne. There is an athlete after my own heart and I believe if the Sharkeys, Striblings and Maloneys of today would do their preliminary work in Guinan's Gymnasium, they might be mad enough to fight when the time came, especially if they were obliged to pay the checks.

The bout ended in Round Three with Mitchell eating resin sandwiches, but the second round lasted four minutes because they forgot the intermission. You wouldn't catch fighters of today doing that; it's the only part of the fight they enjoy. Jim, it seems, heard the gong and started unwillingly for his corner. The Britisher ran after him and cracked him viciously behind the ear. Jim, realizing that the blow was too hard to have come from the referee, Honest John Kelly, turned around and retaliated with a stiff punch to Charley's jaw and they kept going at full speed, with no objection from the crowd or Honest John, through the full minute usually set aside for meditation and prayer.

The gong sounded again, making it legal. Mitchell's unconventional disregard of recess had not left him in robust health and in another minute he was lying face down on the canvas with absolutely no idea of repeating the surprise attack during the next truce.

Parts of Jim's book read as if he had copied them from the collected works of Supergentleman Gene Tunney, but on page 208, we find a sentence he couldn't have plagiarized from the recently retired champion because it was written before Tunney took the nuptial veil:

"I owe all my success and happiness to her." Meaning Mrs. Jim.

Well, that is a nice sentiment and I have no reason to doubt the "happiness" part, but the late Mr. Sullivan told a few of us in strict confidence that the person who hit him in the jaw was not Mrs. Corbett.

Jim says that many of the ring tactics in usage today were originated by him. If I were he, I would keep that to myself, though it can't hurt his reputation very much, because you can go to Madison Square Garden, Ebbets Field or the Stadium seven nights a week and never see a tactic. What you do see is a fiery display of lethargy from a ringful of 200-pound Irishmen, Lithuanians, Georgians and Swedes, praying to God that they won't get as good as a draw.

But Jim was original in his treatment of the bandages which are worn under a boxer's gloves, ostensibly to protect his hands. Most boxers used to have a trick of soaking the bandages in plaster of paris, thus softening them to the texture of a brickbat and removing all doubt from the opponent's mind as to whether he had been hit or not. Mr. Corbett ascertained through his scouts what was the favorite perfume of the wife or sweetie, or both, of the man he was going to fight; then he would buy a gallon of it and smear his bandages so liberally that the other fellow could never get his mind on his work.

Unfortunately for Jim, his operatives fell down on their assignment prior to the champion's first bout with Tom Sharkey; they didn't discover until too late that Tom's gal's favorite scent was Plymouth gin and, as a result, Tom earned, or at least was given, a draw. It was different, but just as unfortunate, in the fatal Fitzsimmons encounter. The information was correct; Mrs. Fitz preferred Nuit de Noel. Jim inquired the price per gallon and decided to fight fair.

The Mitchell brawl was followed by a trip abroad, Jim taking his old folks back to their native land. Returning to this country, he toured it with a theatrical troupe, winding up in his hometown, San Francisco, where he kept in shape a couple of weeks by attending banquets and drinking *vin rouge et blanc*. It was while in a state of coma that he agreed to go four rounds at the Olympic Club with a youngster named Tom Sharkey.

In the second round, Jim hit the sailor in the right eye. This was the only blow struck. The gong sounded for Round Three. Sharkey rushed out of his corner like a defensive halfback, tackled Jim around the ankles, threw him on his back and then tossed the referee onto his stomach, which was not at its best. Between that round and the fourth, Jim sat in his corner with his head on his knees. The sailor started the fourth with another dive, but missed his tackle and the big chief of police jumped into the ring and stopped the bout before Tom had a chance to throw the champion again and perhaps smother him by piling spectators on his recumbent figure. The referee called it a draw, deciding that Sharkey's black eye offset Jim's agonized giblets.

Our Gentleman, as you may recall, lost his title to Ruby Robert, then came to New York and opened the Place at the corner of Thirty-fourth Street and Broadway. Across the street from the Place was the old Manhattan Theater, where high-class plays were performed by high-class players. High-class players usually drink in moderation, say three quarts a day, and most of them patronized Jim. According to his own confession, six of the greatest actors in the world went off their nut right before his eyes. The hams remained sane.

The atmosphere of the Place finally got the proprietor himself, and he challenged Jeffries, the current champion.

But the story of the six great actors who went loony from contact with Jim is so fresh in the minds of modern thespians that when Jim is sitting in the Lambs Club, the good ones who happen in seek tables as far from his as they can get, while the hams go right up and sit down beside him.

Fight writers and sporting men in general are in the habit of saying that the way to bet on a fight is to back the guy Jim picks to lose. In Jim's book he points out that this is unjustifiable kidding and boasts of his prediction that Dempsey would knock out the Orchid Man of France. That was prophesying to be proud of, when you consider that all the great fight critics in the world—Bernard Shaw, Neysa McMein, Miss Garrity of the handkerchief department at Lord and Taylor, Harry Thaw, Peggy Joyce, Peaches Browning and Upton Sinclair—were confident their Greek God would slaughter the Fragile Manassa Molar. To give Jim full credit, he did select the right round, but I suspect a witch told him. Plenty of witches knew about it in advance. None of them told me, but I had seen Georges "train," so I predicted he would go under a general anesthetic in Round One. And nothing can convince me—

Besides being rated the greatest boxer of all time, Gentleman Jim is easily the best, you might almost say the only, actor ever recruited from the flagrant realms of pugilism. Soon after beating Sullivan, he toured America in two successful plays (not simultaneously) and in recent years he has worked in one Follies and on the big time in vaudeville.

Audiences like him not only because he is Jim Corbett, but because he can troupe. He has a partner in vaudeville, always a good one. They wisecrack and do a burlesque boxing match. Then Jim recites all of Eddie Guest's poems while he shadowboxes, and winds up with a series of Jewish folk songs, accompanying himself on a blowpipe.

He is a country gentleman, living at Bayside, Long Island. His mammoth estate has many streams and small rivers, well stocked with trout, herring, deer, shad roe and bacon. When he is not on the stage or doing road work at the Lambs or Friars, he keeps in condition fishing, hunting and playing with his pets, which include 139 police dogs and an owl.

Before his first bout with Jeffries, he trained for a long time in secret. I hope he is doing it now. I am crazy to see him fight Uzcudun, the greatest Basque heavyweight of this, or any other, time. ❧

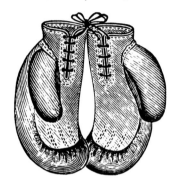

THE SULLIVAN-CORBETT FIGHT

It would take another Irishman, William Inglis, to place Jim Corbett's extraordinary 1892 victory over John L. Sullivan into a proper, traditional perspective. "The old Irish bards," Inglis writes, "certainly knew how to tell about a fight. When Cuchuillin and another hero whose name has smashed through my memory were battling for the mastery of all Ireland, one bard—I think it was Jeremiah Curtin—commented: 'And where they tore up the earth in their struggles they made hills where there had been hollows, and hollows where there had been hills, and one of the clods of turf from their heels flew off a million miles and blinded one eye of the hag who sits spinning in the eastern sky.' And that's the sort of a fight they had when Jim Corbett beat John L. Sullivan for the championship of the world."

That's also more or less the origin of the Irish-American sports-writing tradition.

In the New World the old sagas were soon surpassed by sports stories, and gangster legends, and tales of iron-willed union leaders, charming yet thoroughly corrupt ward bosses, and the occasional battling inner-city parish priest attempting to overturn entrenched Yankee power. It was, and it was not, Ireland all over again.

James Corbett and John L. Sullivan became early heroes in this brand-new folklore—these New World Fenian Tales. In many Irish homes east of the Mississippi, Jim Corbett—that awful dandy from San Francisco—would never be forgiven for having beaten the first, and perhaps the greatest, of a long line of great Irish prizefighting champions. Corbett did soften the blow somewhat, however, by later confessing, "I could have never taken John if I hadn't caught him at the tail end of his career." Maybe. That's certainly, however, the reason why they called him Gentleman Jim.

His boxing career already behind him by the turn of the century, Corbett turned to vaudeville, and the verities of the music hall life. He also wrote a fair, occasional sports column for that other San Francisco native, William Randolph Hearst. Yet Corbett's attempt to graduate from comic skits to serious melodrama brought a short, sharp end to his reign as a matinee idol. His work in Dion Boucicault's *After Dark* was deemed passable by the critics, but he met his Waterloo in the leading role in George Bernard Shaw's *Cashel Byron's Profession*. The critics, quite simply, roasted him alive. "Exchamp Corbett had a row with Bernard Shaw last night," one scribe commented in the following morning's newspaper. "Shaw knocked him cold within three rounds."

Gentleman Jim Corbett's legendary New York saloon was located on the current site of Saks Fifth Avenue.

—*Bob Callahan*

THE FIGHTING IRISH

By Jimmy Cannon

In my old neighborhood football was a mysteriously elegant ritual of the affluent practiced in remote places. We yearned to be baseball players or pugs when I was a kid. Football belonged to the wealthy.

But we were proud of Notre Dame, and what's happening to them would have depressed the people in the Irish slum. They were beaten 24–7 by Southern California Saturday and on Tuesday were dropped from the stack of top-ten teams compiled by the A.P. The fall of the national champions would have provoked as much grief on the West Side as a Republican being elected alderman.

We were flattered because they were called the Fighting Irish, and we exempted them from the contempt we had for college boys. Culture wasn't very big where I came from. There wasn't a bookstore in the district. Young men took cards out at the Public Library because a lot of girls spent the afternoon there doing homework. It was easier to pick them up there.

On the cobbled streets men from the old country kicked a ball around on cold Sundays after Mass after choose-up games of soccer. They also slashed at each other with curved sticks in a sort of gutter hockey called hurling. It was a sport that identified the immigrant. American-born kids played stickball with a hollow rubber ball and a sawed-off broomstick with a sewer cover for home plate.

The six-day bike races fascinated us. My old man took me to one in Madison Square Garden when I was very small. I recollect Reggie McNamara, a sallow rider with a swirl of black hair. I rooted for him. So did my old man.

The six-day tournament was a carnival of thieves. Gold watches were proof of affluence in my neighborhood. But men left them in the bureau drawers when they went to the bike race. They kept their overcoats on. Only hicks took them off because the larcenous sneaks were so clever they could pluck them off a guy's lap.

Music pluggers stood on pianos in the infield and shouted popular songs. The trou-

Great sports writing is every bit as much a part of the Irish-American sporting tradition as the teams and players whose exploits are now the stuff of legend. The greatest of the modern Irish sportswriters, Jimmy Cannon, grew up in a cold-water flat on the lower West Side of New York, the child of a union of the Cannons (his father was a minor Tammany politician) and the Monahans. "I'm an F.B.I.," he said, "Full-Blooded Irish." As Red Smith would later comment, "The mother tongue behaved for Jimmy as it behaved for hardly anyone else." Cannon's piece on Notre Dame first appeared in the New York Journal-American *during the fateful football season of 1967.*

▼

Pat O'Brien in his leading role in *Knute Rockne: All American*, the film that costarred Ronald Reagan in the role of George Gipp, "The Great Gipper."

badours usually quit when a jam started. I remember one of them, a hunchback, trying to finish a torch song as Oscar Egg attempted to steal a lap. It was as if a mute was silently forming words for a convention of lip readers who ignored him.

We were gambling people in our neighborhood, and men bet on horses and fights. The bookmakers didn't have a line on football then. The bookplayers took their action on street corners which were congested with players. The cop on beat would break a player's head if an argument over a bet drifted toward violence.

Our card game was Bankers and Brokers. Kids could tell you the odds on tens and fours in dice before they could recite the multiplication table. But I can't remember anyone ever putting a cigar up on Notre Dame.

Football was never important. But Notre Dame became a cherished symbol. We honored Knute Rockne in our small talk, but his skills were beyond us. What Red Grange accomplished didn't excite us. I skipped the stories Damon Runyon wrote in the old *American* when he covered football. It was Yale and Harvard and Princeton then. It seemed to be happening in another country when you lived in a tenement. But the saloons bought rounds for the house when Notre Dame beat Army.

We were proud when we read about the sidewalk alumni of Notre Dame. That, we figured, was us. But I never knew anyone in the neighborhood who had seen Notre Dame play except in the newsreels. Men made trips to the hockshops to raise the money to go to the fights and baseball games. But even Notre Dame couldn't get them to go up to the Polo Grounds where the men in my neighborhood spent as many afternoons as they could afford watching the baseball Giants.

The Giants were the New Yorkers' team. The Yankees got the tourists because of Babe Ruth. But we thought more of Frankie Frisch, and we put John McGraw in the genius category with Edison and Marconi. The Brooklyn Dodgers were a road club that crossed the bridge to play the Giants. We didn't regard them as a New York team but Notre Dame in South Bend, Indiana, was our college, although no one from our neighborhood ever went there.

Photographs of Rockne were pasted on gin-mill mirrors and pictures of the Notre Dame team were enshrined among the fighters and baseball players in the barroom galleries of sports. The Notre Dame team, in a way, became like the gold watches. They were proof the Irish were doing good.

I assumed that everyone who played for Notre Dame was Irish, and poor. It didn't seem to be a college like Harvard or Princeton or Yale. Doing good was to work steadily as a truck driver or a longshoreman.

In that neighborhood, where education meant graduating from grammar school, the Notre Dame football players were the perfection of our kind. We hadn't a president yet, and Al Smith had been beaten because he was one of us. On our mean streets no bands played, and a pennant never waved when Notre Dame won. But we were as much a part of that distant university on the prairies as though we had a diploma to prove it. That's why the A.P.'s top ten is a bad list this week.

MR. LEAHY

On one occasion, I watched a posse of powerful brutes going through a scrimmage before a big Notre Dame game. Afterwards, I asked Notre Dame's famous coach, Frank Leahy, where he located such powerful specimens. My tribute to his recruiting skills seemed to offend him.

"We really have a small squad," he said.

"Yeah," I remarked, "you've come up with a race of super midgets."

Football players come to Notre Dame in eager droves and 1953 is not any different from any other year. No other school in the country falls heir to such abundance. Leahy has the edge before the season starts. But he is not expected to lose; he must win, despite the presence of a harping throng of anti-football priests on the Notre Dame faculty. He is responsible for me correctly picking the score of the last Army-Notre Dame game. I met him in the corridor of the Oliver Hotel in South Bend on my way to Western Union to file my copy. He asked me what I thought the game would be like and I showed him my column.

"James, you will make yourself ridiculous. The lads are not capable of defeating the United States Military Academy by such a score," he said.

I took my pencil and corrected the score. He thought I had lowered the margin, but I had raised it by a touchdown.

"Your attitude convinces me," I said. "Notre Dame is seven points better than I thought."

"James," Leahy said, "you'll regret this." But the score was exactly what I made it. Any time Frank Leahy admits that he has a team populated by cripples, dim-witted children and assorted humpty-dumpties, you can safely sit down and write that he won't be beaten all season.

—*Jimmy Cannon*

T.A.D.

By Damon Runyon

The music has stopped. "Tad" is dead! A ray of sunshine across this old world has been turned to shadow. A peal of joyous laughter has been suddenly hushed.

He was sleeping, they say, at his home in Great Neck when Death whispered that he was never again to open his eyes.

In a fighter, or a ball player, or any other athlete, "Tad" admired gameness more than anything else.

Game? Say, they never made 'em any gamer than this long, lean fellow from the "South of the Slot" out in San Francisco, where his name and memory will always be revered. He was a great man. He was a great, great man.

"Tad" had a penchant for nicknames. I always thought it was because of his habit of mind to take a shortcut to what he wanted to say, a habit that was best expressed in his writings. He would always cut out a lot of superfluous "*a*'s" and "*the*'s." I have for years been the—shall I say victim?—of one of his nicknames.

He picked up the expression, "hard-boiled egg," years ago, and made it famous long before anyone quite understood what it meant, and incidentally, he gave it to me as a tag, shortening it to just "Eg." He took one glance at Tom McNamara, the cartoonist, and Thomas was thereafter "Rubber Nose."

He called his mother "Flynn" because of her Irish ancestry, and he adored her. He used to give a dinner downtown on the occasions of her birthday, and "Flynn" would have to go through a routine of trick glasses and

The most interesting cartoonist and social commentator of his era, Thomas Aloysius Dorgan, aka "T.A.D.," left his native San Francisco in 1905 to go to work for William Randolph Hearst at the New York Journal. *By 1915, Dorgan was sharing a desk in the* Journal *sports department with columnist Damon Runyon—also out of the west—and a very strange, young artist from New Orleans by the name of George Herriman. Dorgan and Runyon would often be sent out on the road together to cover the major sporting events of the time, while Herriman would be left behind to develop his brilliant, but thoroughly gnomic, new cartoon, "Krazy Kat." Winsor McKay was also drawing editorial cartoons for the* Journal *during this period, and Ring Lardner was writing a regular weekly feature. Dorgan, Runyon, McKay, Herriman and Lardner appeared each Sunday for Hearst in the weekly "City Life and Drama, Editorial Section." The following piece was written by "Tad's" desk-mate on the evening of May 2, 1929. Some fifty-eight years later, it is republished here for the first time.*

206

similar contrivances that "Tad" would acquire for her surprise and his own amusement.

"Tad" was a staunch friend, but he was also a good hater. Long ago, when he was a youngster, he was sent to interview John J. McGraw, manager of the Giants, and McGraw rebuffed him in some manner. "Tad" never forgot, and if McGraw has ever wondered at the industry "Tad" exerted in former years to hold him up to public laughter, this may enlighten him.

Arthur Brisbane, the mightiest of the modern journalists and the man who brought "Tad" out, and by suggestion and direction made the cartoonist the foremost figure of his field, once said that a great writer was spoiled when "Tad" picked up a drawing pencil, and that estimate is undoubtedly true.

As a writer of the text to go with his cartoons, "Tad" displayed an amazing literary style, a sort of staccato, running comment, generally couched in a humorous vein, that startled those who thought of him only as a cartoonist.

Again, in covering a fight or other sports event, "Tad" would cut loose with a flow of descriptive writing that spread the picture before the eye and the mind of the reader beyond the power of any other newspaper writer of our times.

From Brisbane, "Tad" undoubtedly learned much of his manner of thinking, and some of his manner of writing, but "Tad" would convert the clear and beautiful English used by the editorial writer into the vernacular of the day.

Some of the slang and many of the quaint expressions that "Tad" either originated or made famous through his cartoons are almost a part of the language. The story of how a couple of songwriters picked up his

"Yes, we have no bananas," and made a fortune, is well known. His "Daffydills," his "Judge Rummy," his "Yum —he never had a chance," his "Indoor Sports" and "Outdoor Sports" added to his fame.

It will be a long time before we see another "Tad" as a cartoonist. It will be a longer time before we see another "Tad" as a man. And if I have seemed fulsome here at any stage, I hope the reader will bear in mind that I write of him from a full heart. He was my friend.

JOHN MCGRAW'S GREATEST FIGHTS

By Tom Clark

Billy Martin, a tough kid from across the tracks
in West Berkeley, is baseball's Bad Boy of
the second half of the twentieth century.
Martin stands out because he's a throwback,
an exception to the credit-card, investment-profile uni-
formity of today's major league baseball image. What
Broadway Billy's actually a throwback to is the days of
John McGraw—when aggressive competitiveness wasn't
a freak variant, but the central strain of professional
sports.

John McGraw's mother, stepsister, and three sisters
all died of diphtheria when he was twelve. His Irish-
immigrant father, a mostly unemployed railroad section-
hand in upstate New York, suffered from the same
delimiting horizons common to so many "Sons of the
Sod" whose vision stopped at the top of the bar. As the
story has it, he whaled away at his offspring for breaking some windows, and John, then 17, took off and
became first a railroad candy salesman, then a $40-a-
month ballplayer.

Though closer to five feet than six in height, young
McGraw quickly scrapped his way to the big leagues
and was soon player-manager of the old Baltimore
Orioles, with whom, in the '90s, he developed his
"inside" game as Ring Lardner admiringly termed it.
McGraw's "inside" game included several features that
grew into accepted baseball strategy (the bunt, the
steal, and especially the hit-and-run, which McGraw
invented and worked to perfection with Wee Willie
Keeler) and also several that didn't (like McGraw's trick
of taking advantage of the early one-umpire system by
hooking his fingers in the belts of baserunners "tagging
up" after fly balls).

McGraw had two nicknames. One was "Muggsy,"
first applied by a Baltimore journalist who likened his
behavior to that of a roughneck ward politician named
Muggsy McGraw; McGraw regarded the appellation

with great hatred, more than once knocking down an
unsuspecting acquaintance who used it in jest. The
other was "Little Napoleon," pinned on him not long
after he took over the New York Giants in 1902.

McGraw's Giants were a reflection and extension of
the personality of the cocky, imperious little manager.
Like his military namesake, "Little Napoleon" saw life
as a field of battle. He was a grand strategist who
controlled the entire operation of the club, from the
positioning of fielders, calling of pitches, summoning
of relief pitchers and pinch hitters to the signing and
trading of players, minor league operations, management of the park and even grounds keeping. McGraw
dominated the National League as Napoleon had dominated Europe—he won pennants in ten of his first 22
seasons as manager—and he was similarly loved and
feared at home and despised abroad. Indeed, he loved
thinking of himself as a field general. Contrary to the
custom of the times, he managed not from the field but
from the bench, where he could survey the action from
a better vantage, transmit signals constantly, and exhort
his troops with his merciless tongue. He "rode" his
players harder than any other manager.

One of them, shortstop Al Bridwell, once socked
the manager in the jaw and had to draw a two-week
suspension, but later praised McGraw as "a wonderful
man, a real fighter. Anybody who wanted to argue, he
was ready."

McGraw lost far more fights than he won. "A man
can ad lib himself into a lot of K.O.'s by not picking
spots," Damon Runyon later suggested, "and McGraw
was noted for getting himself flattened. He was a cho-
leric and pugnacious little man and healthy and strong,
too, but he couldn't fight a lick. Yet he was always
fighting. Even when he was in his middle years and had
a paunch he was slugging it out with ball players, um-
pires, spectators, and innocent bystanders."

In 1913 the ever-ready McGraw punched out southpaw pitcher Ad Brennan of the Phils, but the next
spring a minor league manager (Pat Newman of Houston) followed him under the stands after an on-field
dispute and knocked him on his back. A few years later
McGraw himself used the same trick on Bill "Lord"
Byron, an umpire who'd dispatched him from a game
for arguing. After waylaying Byron under the grand-
stand McGraw got a $500 fine from the league and a
suspension. While under suspension he dropped a
unanimous decision to Honest John Kelly, operator of
a Broadway gambling club (Kelly got his nickname
when he found and returned the glass eye of famous
gate-crasher "One-Eye" Connolly). The papers ran
comic summaries of McGraw's "ring record."

Runyon called McGraw a "Cafe Gladiator." One of
his haunts was the theatrical club, the Lambs. ("Com-
paratively late in life," wrote Runyon, "Mac discovered
the Lambs Club and easier picking among the actors

than on the ball fields and on Broadway.") On a hot August night in the depressing Prohibition summer of 1920, with Giants out of first place and McGraw feeling nasty about it, he did some drinking in the grill room of the Lambs and then directed what his lawyer, William Fallon, later termed "third baseman's language" at the back of a man he took to be actor Walter Knight. But when the object of his curses turned around it was a different actor, the large and sturdy Bill Boyd (later to become famous on TV as Hopalong Cassidy). Boyd told McGraw to shut up or the cleaning lady might hear him. McGraw persisted, so Boyd bashed him with a water jug. McGraw was revived and brought home to West 109th Street by friends in a taxi, but when they got there McGraw wanted to argue about who ought to pay the cab fare. One of the friends, a veteran of the musical comedy named John C. Slavin, wound up with a skull fracture, a concussion, a cut lip, and two broken teeth. McGraw got out of it with only a battered nose and a black eye. A month or so afterward another Lambs Club pal, the dramatic star and noted conversationalist Wilton Lackaye, went to see McGraw to "give him some friendly advice," as it was reported. Lackaye came away with either a broken leg or a broken ankle, according to varying reports.

Slavin filed suit. Fallon settled out of court for McGraw. The Lambs Club expelled McGraw, but accepted him back after only three seasons (the members missed their free Polo Grounds passes).

Under "Little Napoleon" the Giants barnstormed around the world. In February 1914, they were in Paris. Damon Runyon took McGraw to Napoleon's tomb. "Where are we, boyo?" asked McGraw. Runyon told him, and McGraw beamed with pleasure, his first real smile since losing the previous year's World Series to Connie Mack's Athletics. When Runyon wrote up the episode for the Hearst papers he added a creative touch: "I, too, met the Duke of Wellington," Runyon has McGraw saying, "only his name was Connie Mack."

Cornelius McGillicuddy of the Philadelphia Athletics, the impeccable Connie Mack.

MR. MACK

Connie Mack (né Cornelius McGillicuddy, 1892-1956) was the other great manager of McGraw's day—and was "Little Napoleon's" opposite, the patrician gentleman of the game as vs. McGraw's brawling street fighter. Connie built up two great "dynasty" teams with his Philadelphia Athletics—and then tore them down, sending his greatest players away for money. He won nine American League pennants (to McGraw's ten National League championships) and five World Series (to McGraw's three). He managed in his Sunday duds and straw boater and was pipestem-lean, tall, austere and stately. In close combat with McGraw in three World Series, his teams won two of them. Mack never smoked, drank, or swore, but nonetheless had great success with "problem" players like the talented, erratic southpaw pitcher Rube Waddell. His quiet, gentle demeanor masked a will of steel, as players who defied him quickly learned. "Mr. Mack" became the game's grand old man, his career as player and manager spanning every Presidential administration from Grover Cleveland's to Harry Truman's.

—Tom Clark

HAIL AND FAREWELL, JACK, A CHAMPION LIKE NO OTHER

By Jim Murray

Jack Dempsey may have been the best, but the first great Irish-American heavyweight champion was James Morrisey, born in Tipperary, Ireland, on February 12, 1831. On October 12, 1853, Morrisey beat Yankee Sullivan in thirty-seven rounds and immediately declared himself the heavyweight champion of the world. One of the most popular figures of his time, Morrisey went on to become a powerful gambler, a saloon keeper, a labor leader, a Fifth Congressional District representative and an extravagant Saratoga racetrack millionaire. He was buried in Troy, New York, on May 2, 1878. Fifteen thousand people, the local newspapers claimed, followed his coffin to the cemetery in the pouring rain.

He fought out of a crouch. But he was the most stand-up guy you'd ever want to meet in the rest of life.

"Dempsey!" The very name inspired shivers in the fight game. It was a name like "Hogan!" Like "Geronimo!" and "Attila!" It was a name that was not much fun to hear. A name to inspire fear. A lion-is-loose! name. It was a name caked with history.

Whenever I hear the name Dempsey I think of train whistles on a hot summer night on the prairie. I think of a tinkling piano coming out of a kerosene-lit saloon in a mining camp. I think of an America that was one big roaring camp of miners, drifters, bunkhouse hands, con men, hard cases, men who lived by their fists and their shooting irons and the cards they drew. It was the America of the Great Plains buffalo, the cattle drive, the fast draw, the jailhouse dirge. America at high noon.

More than a man died with Dempsey. He took an era with him. Dempsey came out of the core of the America that had Buffalo Bill, Kit Carson, Billy the Kid, Ned Buntline, Butch Cassidy, the Sundance Kid, Wyatt Earp, Bat Masterson, Wild Bill Hickok and the man who shot Jesse James, men who carried their lives in their saddles and their law in their holsters. Dempsey was part of our heritage like Dan'l Boone, Davy Crockett or Honest Abe. Dempsey came out of covered-wagon America. He reinforced our image of ourselves, this black-browed, curly-haired, bronze young giant with fists like paving blocks and the savage fighting style of a recently uncaged and hungry panther.

America loved him. Never mind that "slacker" nonsense in World War I. Dempsey was what we thought we were. His fighting style was modeled after the timber wolf's. He pioneered the bob-and-weave, move-in-and-hook style of fighting. He was exciting to watch even against a punching bag. All his fights had the elemental fury of two stags rutting in a medieval forest. Tex Rickard, the promoter, was always afraid Dempsey would kill somebody.

Dempsey retired the word "Champ!" with him. "Dempsey" meant "Champ!"

When he went down, he got up. When he got hit, he hit back. When he bled, he laughed. When he got hurt, he attacked. When he got beat, he shrugged. If

▲

The champion takes to the ring: Jack Dempsey in 1923.

that doesn't mean champ, you tell me what does.

He was as gentle outside the ring as he was savage in it. He'd punch you on the arm occasionally to remind you who you were with. You might get cayenne pepper in the sugar jar. But there was no real malice in Dempsey. He gave away money the way some men give advice. Dempsey never gave advice, only friendship.

He was not a fearless man but a brave one. There's a distinction. The places Dempsey dropped off in his early hobo years, fear rode shotgun. Dempsey hurled himself at fear.

I used to meet Dempsey with his longtime friend, and mine, the great author, Gene Fowler. One of the great moments of my life was when Gene arranged a lunch at Romanoff's for me and his son, Will, with Jack Dempsey, Rube Goldberg and Grantland Rice. It was like spending an afternoon in King Arthur's court. A writer's Camelot.

Gene and his wife, Agnes, took Dempsey in when he was a young hobo in Denver. But Gene, the master biographer, would never touch Dempsey's story. He knew too much about it. That his first wife was a whore and his first job was as a bouncer in her fancy house, for instance.

Dempsey rose above his hardscrabble beginnings in Manassa, Colorado. He liked to describe himself as "a jack Mormon," but the teachings of Celia Dempsey and the hard practicalities of his father, Hiram Dempsey, were never far from the son. Dempsey was a kindly man. One time, I had just done an interview with Jess Willard, the giant Dempsey battered into a blood clot one hot July 4th in Toledo, Ohio, in a fight so ferocious men still gasp at the fury of it.

Forty-five years later, the day I interviewed him, Willard was bitter. He pointed to a massive indentation in the bone above his temple. "Does that," he demanded, "look to you as if it were made by a gloved fist?"

Whatever it was, it did not. Willard had contended for years that Dempsey's manager, Doc Kearns, had put a "load" in his fighter's gloves. He claimed Dempsey's manager had hired a band to play outside Willard's window the night before the fight so he could get no sleep.

Dempsey was amused at the charges. But he had tolerated them over the years (until a magazine published them after Kearns' death, and then he finally sued).

At that time, Dempsey laughed. "Jess has been going around telling that story for years," he said. "You know, one time when he was down on his luck, I gave him a job promoting my whiskey in some bars down in Florida. All he had to do was go in, buy the house a drink and promote sales."

"You know what he did?" Dempsey laughed again. "He would go in and tell these guys that I was a bum and if it wasn't for Doc Kearns loading the gloves and keeping him up all night, I would never have been champ!"

"Did you fire him?" I asked.

Dempsey paused. "Well, they wanted me to. He was killing off the sales of my whiskey. But shucks! Jess needed the money!"

So, ladies and gentlemen, I give you—the winner and still heavyweight champion of our world—Jack Dempsey! ❧

Kid McCoy, famous for his corkscrew punch.

THE REAL MCCOY

A great boxer of the classic era, Kid McCoy (né Norman Selby) once knocked out a saloon impersonator who claimed to be him, giving rise to the popular expression "the real McCoy." The Kid fought in the ring, too, both as middleweight and welterweight, earning the world championship in the latter class. He was companionable with the scribes of Broadway, especially Damon Runyon, who served, appropriately, as a character witness when the Kid was in his toughest scrape—standing trial for murder. McCoy's best weapon was his corkscrew punch, which he executed by twisting his left fist from the vertical to the horizontal plane as he drove it into the body of an opponent. He first entered a professional ring in 1891 and lasted twenty-five years in the game, remaining undefeated over the last twelve of them (his early losses came mostly at the hands of heavier fighters, such as Tom Sharkey and Jim Corbett). Once his fighting career was behind him he went into movies, made himself the proverbial million bucks, but lost it all when he died a suicide in 1940.

—Tom Clark

SON OF MARS
By Paul Gallico

Jack Dempsey was a picture-book fighter. By all the sons of Mars, he looked the part. He had dark eyes, blue-black hair, and the most beautifully proportioned body ever seen in any ring. He had the wide but sharply sloping shoulders of the puncher, a slim waist, and fine, symmetrical legs. His weaving, shuffling style of approach was drama in itself and suggested the stalking of a jungle animal. He had a smoldering truculence on his face and hatred in his eyes. His gorge lay close to the surface. He was utterly without mercy or pity, asked no quarter, gave none. He would do anything he could get away with, fair or foul, to win. This was definitely a part of the man, but was also a result of his early life and schooling in the hobo jungles, barrooms, and mining camps of the West. Dempsey fought to survive. I always had the feeling that he carried that into the ring with him, that he was impatient of the rules and restrictions and niceties of conduct, impatient even of the leather that bound his knuckles.

A Life of Crime

*James Cagney tries to raise
a little cab-fare money in
the 1931 Warner classic,
The Public Enemy.*

JACK'S ALIVE

By William Kennedy

"I really don't think he's dead," I said to my three very old friends.

"You what?" said Packy Delaney, dropsical now, and with only four teeth left. Elephantiasis had taken over his legs and now one thigh was the size of two. Ah time.

"He don't mean it," Flossie said, dragging on and then stubbing out another in her chain of smokes, washing the fumes down with muscatel, and never mind trying to list her ailments. ("Roaches in your liver," Flossie's doc had told her. "Go on home and die at your own speed.")

Tipper Kelly eyed me and knew I was serious.

"He means it, all right," said Tipper, still the dap newsman, but in a 1948 double-breasted. "But of course he's full of what they call the old bully-bullshit because I was there. You know I was there, Delaney."

"Don't I know it," said the Pack.

"Me and Bones McDowell," said the Tip. "Bones sat on his chest."

"We know the rest," said Packy.

"It's not respectful to Bones' memory to say he sat on the man's chest of his own accord," Tipper said. "Bones was the finest reporter I ever worked with. No. Bones wouldn't of done that to any man, drunk or sober, him or Jack the corpse, God rest his soul. Both their souls, if Jack had a soul."

"He had a soul all right," said Flossie. "I saw that and everything else he had too."

"We'll hear about that another time," said Tipper, "I'm now talking about Bones, who with myself was the first up the stairs before the cops, and Jack's wife there in the hallway, crying the buckets. The door was open, so Bones pushed it the rest of the way open and in he snuck and no light in the room but what was coming in the window. The cops pulled up then and we heard their car door slam and Bones says to me, 'Come inside and we'll get a look before they kick us the hell out,' and he took a step and tripped, the simple bastard, and sprawled backward over the bed, right on top of poor Jack in his underwear, who of course didn't feel a thing. Bones got blood all over the seat of his pants."

"Tipper," said Packy, "that's a goddamn pack of lies

and fell,' says Bones. 'Don't be swearing on your mother at a filthy time like this,' says Barney, 'you ought to be ashamed.' 'Oh I am,' says Bones, 'on the grave of me mother I am.' And then Barney threw us both out, and I said to Bones on the way down the stairs, 'I didn't know your mother was in the grave,' and he says to me, 'Well, she's not, the old fart-in-the-bottle, but she oughtta be.'"

"You never got a good look at the corpse," Packy said to Tip, "and don't tell me you did. But you know damn well that I did. I saw what they did to him when he was over at Keenan's the undertaker's for the autopsy. Thirty-nine bullets. They walked in there while he was sleeping and shot him thirty-nine times. I counted the bullet holes. You know what that means? They had seven pistols between the pair of them."

"Say what you will," I told them, savoring Packy's senile memory, remembering the autopsy myself, remembering Jack's face intact but the back of his head blown away by not thirty-nine but only three soft-nosed .38-caliber bullets: one through his right jaw, tearing the neck muscle, cutting the spinal cord, and coming out through the neck and falling on the bed; another entering his skull near the right ear and moving upward through his brain, fracturing his skull, and remaining in the fracture; and the third entering the left temple, taking a straight course across the brain and stopping just above the right ear.

"I still don't think he's dead."

I had come to see Jack as not merely the dude of all gangsters, the most active brain in the New York underworld, but as one of the truly new American Irishmen of his day; Horatio Alger out of Finn McCool and Jesse James, shaping the dream that you could grow up in America and shoot your way to glory and riches. I've said it again and again to my friends who question the ethics of this somewhat unorthodox memoir: "If you liked Carnegie and Custer, you'll love Diamond." He was almost as famous as Lindbergh while his light burned. "The Most Picturesque Racketeer in the Underworld," the *New York American* called him; "Most Publicized of Public Enemies," said the *Post*; "Most Shot-At Man in America," said the *Mirror*.

Does anyone think these superlatives were casually earned? Why he was a pioneer, the founder of the first truly modern gang, the dauphin of the town for years. He filled the tabloids—never easy. He advanced the cause of joyful corruption and vice. He put the drop of the creature on the parched tongues of millions. He filled the pipes that pacify the troubled, loaded the needles that puncture anxiety bubbles. He helped the world kick the gong around, Jack did. And was he thanked for this benevolence? Hardly. The final historical image that endures is that corpse clad in underwear, flat-assed out in bed, broke and alone.

and you know it. You haven't got the truth in you, and neither did Bones McDowell."

"So in comes big Barney Duffy with his flashlight and shines it on Bones sitting on poor Jack's chest. 'Sweet mother of mine,' says Barney and he grabbed Bones by the collar and elbow and lifted him off poor Jack like a dirty sock. 'Haven'tcha no manners atall?' Barney says to him. 'I meant no harm,' says Bones. 'It's a nasty thing you've done,' says Barney, 'sittin' on a dead man's chest.' 'On the grave of me mother I tripped

That's what finally caught me, I think: the vision of Jack Diamond alone, rare sight, anomalous event, pungent irony. Consider the slightly deaf sage of Pompeii, his fly open, feet apart, hand at crotch, wetting surreptitiously against the garden wall when the lava hits the house. Why he never even heard the rumbles. Who among the archeologists could know what glories that man created on earth, what truths he represented, what love and wisdom he propagated before the deluge of lava eternalized him as The Pisser? And so it is with Jack Diamond's last image. It wouldn't matter if he'd sold toilet paper or milk bottles for a living, but he was an original man and he needs an original epitaph, even if it does come four and a half decades late. I say to you, my reader, that here was a singular being in a singular land, a fusion of the individual life flux with the clear and violent light of American reality, with the fundamental Columbian brilliance that illuminates this bloody republic. Jack was confusion to me. I relished his company, he made me laugh. Yet wasn't I fearful in the presence of this man for whom violence and death were

well-oiled tools of the trade? Yes, ah, yes. The answer is yes. But fear is a cheap emotion, however full of wisdom. And, emotionally speaking, I've always thought of myself as a man of expensive taste.

I chose the Kenmore to talk to Packy, Tipper, and Flossie because if Jack's ghost walked anywhere, it was in that bar, that old shut-down Rain-Bo room with its peeling paint and its glory unimaginable now beneath all that emptiness. In the 1920s and 1930s the Kenmore was the Number One nightclub between New York and the Canadian border. Even during the Depression you needed a reservation on weekends to dance in evening clothes to the most popular bands in the country: Rudy Vallee and Ben Bernie and Red Nichols and Russ Morgan and Hal Kemp and the Dorsey Brothers and all the rest who came before and after them. Naturally, limelighter that he was, Jack lived there. And so why wouldn't I choose the place to talk to three old friends, savor their memories and ring them in on my story?

I called Flossie first, for we'd had a thing of sorts

between us, and I'll get to that. She was pretty back in those days, like a canary, all yellow-haired and soft and with the innocence of a birdsong, even though she was one of the loveliest whores north of Yonkers: The Queen of Stars, she called herself then. Packy's Parody Club had burned years before and he was now tending bar at the Kenmore, and so I said we can meet there and can you get hold of Tipper? And she said Tipper had quit the newspaper business finally but would be on tap, and he was. And so there we were at the Kenmore bar, me looking up at the smoky old pair of David Lithgow murals, showing the hunt, you know. Eight pink-coated huntsmen on horseback were riding out from the mansion in the first mural, at least forty-five hounds at their heels, heading into the woods. They were back indoors in the second painting, toasting and laughing by the fire while one of their number held the dead fox by the tail. Dead fox.

"I was sitting where you're sitting," Packy said to me, "and saw a barman work up an order for Jack's table, four rum Cokes. All he poured was one shot of rum, split it over the top of the four and didn't stir them, so the suckers could taste the fruit of his heavy hand. 'I saw that,' I told him after the waiter picked the order up, 'and I want you to know Jack Diamond is a friend of mine.' The thieving bastard turned green and I didn't pay for another drink in this joint till Jack died."

"His name had power," Tipper said.

"It still does," I said. "Didn't he bring us together here?"

And I told them I was writing about him then, and they told me some of their truths, and secret lies, just as Jack had, and his wife Alice and his lovely light o' love, Kiki, had years ago. I liked all their lies best, for I think they are the brightest part of anybody's history.

I began by recalling that my life changed on a summer day in 1930 when I was sitting in the second-floor library of the Knights of Columbus, overlooking Clinton Square and two blocks up from the Kenmore bar. I was killing time until the pinochle crowd turned up, or a pool partner, and I was reading Rabelais, my gift to the library. It was the only book on the index in the library and the only one I ever looked at.

That empty afternoon, and that book, gave me the insight that my life was a stupendous bore, and that it could use a little Gargantuan dimension. And so I said yes, I would take Jack Diamond up on his telephone invitation of that morning to come down to his place for Sunday dinner, three days hence. It was the Sunday I was to speak at the police communion breakfast, for I was one of Albany's noted communion breakfast intellectuals in those days. I would speak, all right, and then I would walk down to Union Station and take the west shore train to Catskill to listen to whatever that strange and vicious charmer had to say to an Albany barrister. ❧

"Brother Ed" Murray, a minor Irish Broadway petty criminal, gained an easy immortality in the stories of Damon Runyon. Runyon was influenced by his close friend Tad Dorgan, especially T.A.D.'s ear for American street language. Unlike T.A.D., Runyon did not invent language for his characters. Nor did he ever heighten or burlesque the speech of the figures he wrote about—Irish or otherwise. With a high degree of insight, he caught the literal tone and phrase of the gangsters and con men who populated New York's wicked streets.

DEATH FOR SOME LAUGHS

By Damon Runyon

I happened to think of "Brother Ed" because I just read an article about one William Stanley Sims, a professional hoaxman, which was "Brother Ed's" only role, only "Brother Ed" was an amateur. He was the master ribber of all time.

This Sims makes a business of appearing at banquets and other gatherings public and private in various guises for the purpose of laughs. He is an entertainer in the manner of Lou Barnett of Pittsburgh, who may not have originated that peculiar profession but who certainly made it famous.

I have seen Barnett work as a waiter and send fellows like Jim Corbett and Babe Ruth off into violent rages. I have seen him play the part of a Polish editor to the befoolment of a festive board of journalistic brains. They tell me Lou's son, Vince Barnett, is pretty good at this weird racket, too.

But "Brother Ed" was the peer of them all. I think his first name was Hiram and his surname may have been Murray; I am not sure. We all spoke of him as "Brother Ed" because of the character he created. It is my recollection that he came out of New England, maybe Providence.

He was a smallish, rural-looking chap, with the most guileless expression you ever saw on a human kisser. Sims and Barnett performed for hire, but "Brother Ed" took no fee. He was strictly for the amusement of our set. And where the audiences of Sims and Barnett were usually doctors and lawyers and the like, "Brother Ed" pegged at some of the toughest guys that ever wore shoe leather.

The first time I ever saw him in action was in front of Billy Lahiff's tavern on West 48th Street one evening. The Diamond brothers, tubercular and peevish Eddie and truculent Jack, afterwards called "The Clay Pigeon" because of the number of times he was shot, though just then not as hot with the cops as he later became,

had just come out of the tavern and were standing on the sidewalk when Hiram sidled up to them.

"Where's my brother Ed?" he asked of Jack, plaintively.

"What are you talking about?" demanded Jack, roughly.

"You know what I'm talking about," replied Hiram. "I'm talking about my brother Ed. I saw you go into the bank over there with him this afternoon and he had $4,000 with him. Ten dollars of it was mine. I haven't seen him since. What have you done with him?"

Now Jack's first impulse was probably to belt the guy, but on second thought he no doubt reflected that here was a daffy citizen who nonetheless produced something of a situation with his story of "Brother Ed" and the $4,000 that could call for a lot of explaining if it reached the cops. So he tried placating Hiram with soft words, all the time trying to shake him off and depart, but Hiram stuck close to him asking over and over for his "brother Ed."

Finally he suddenly fell forward grabbing Jack's lapels with froth issuing from his mouth as if in a fit, and the way the tough Diamonds left that vicinity was the talk of the neighborhood for a long time. Whereupon Hiram spat out a mouthful of soap and recovered from his fit and all hands hee-hawed like sixty.

There was a lammister out of K.C., finger man of the Machine Gun Kelly mob, I believe, who was subsequently cold cooked out west, but who was so alarmed by Hiram's "Brother Ed" routine that he got Hiram into a doorway and pressed a $100 bill on him to let him alone. And what do you suppose became of Hiram?

Well, I understand he died of heart failure, superinduced largely by his exertions in his supposed fits. In short, he died for laughs. ❧

222

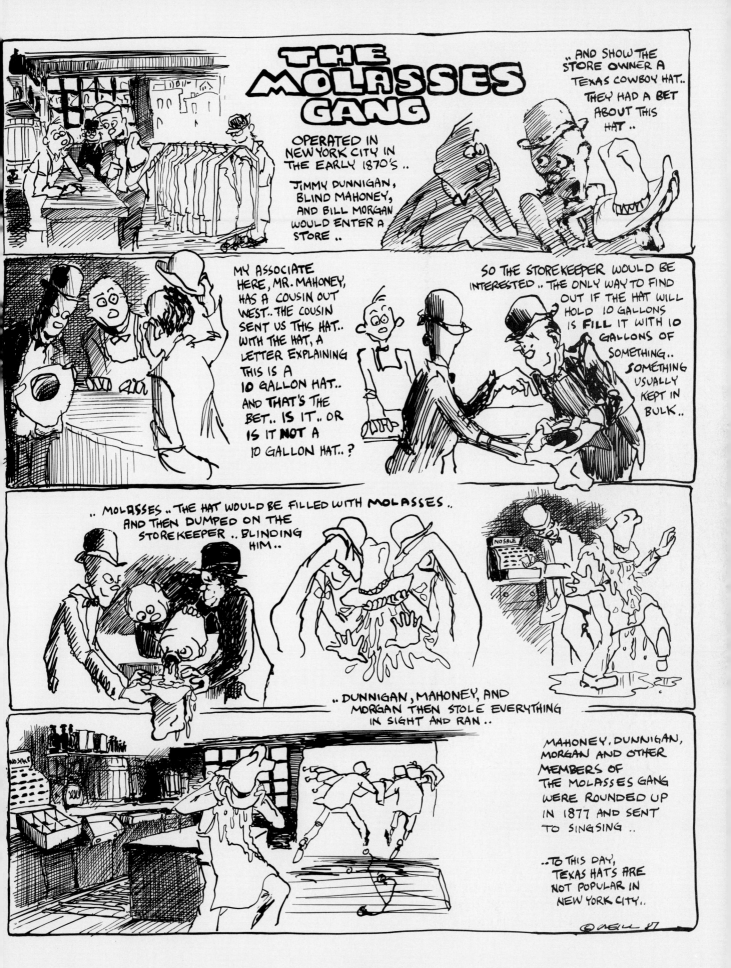

THE ROBBERY

By James M. Cain

"Good evening."

"I guess we've seen each other a couple of times before, haven't we? Me and my wife, we live downstairs."

"Yeah, I know who you are. What do you want?"

"Just want to talk to you about something."

"Well—come in."

"No. Just close that door behind you and we'll sit on the steps."

"All right. That suits me. Now what's the big idea?"

"Today we was robbed. Somebody come in the apartment, turned the whole place inside out, and got away with some money, and my wife's jewelry. Three rings and a couple of wristwatches. It's got her broke up pretty bad. I got her in bed now, but she's crying and carrying on all the time. I feel right down sorry for her."

"Well, that's tough. But what you coming to me about it for?"

"Nothing special. But of course, I'm trying to find out who done it, so I thought I would come around and see you. Just to see if you got any idea about it."

"Yeah?"

"That's it."

"Well, I haven't got no idea."

"You haven't? That's funny."

"What's funny about it?"

"Seems like most everybody on the block has an idea about it. I ain't got in the house yet before about seven people stopped me and told me about it, and all of them had an idea about who done it. Of course, some of them ideas wasn't much good, but still they was ideas. So you haven't got no idea?"

"No. I haven't got no idea. And what's more, you're too late."

"How you mean, too late?"

"I mean them detectives has been up here already. I mean that fine wife of yours sent them up here, and what I had to say about this I told them, and I ain't got time to say it over again for you. And let me tell you something: You tell any more detectives I was the one robbed your place, and that's right where the trouble starts. They got laws in this country. They got laws against people that goes around telling lies about their neighbors, and don't you think for a minute you're going to get by with that stuff no more. You get me?"

"I'll be doggone. Them cops been up here already? Them boys sure do work fast, don't they?"

"Yeah, they work fast when some fool woman that has lost a couple of rings calls up the station house and fills them full of lies. They work fast, but they don't always work so good. They ain't got nothing on me at all, see? So you're wasting your time, just like they did!"

"What did you tell them, if you don't mind my asking?"

"I told them just what I'm telling you: that I don't know a thing about you or your wife, or your flat, or who robbed you, or what goes on down there, 'cepting I wish to hell you would turn off that radio at night once, so I can get some sleep. That's what I told them, and if you don't like it you know what you can do."

"Well, now, old man, I tell you. Fact of the matter, my wife didn't send them cops up here at all. When she come home, and found out we was robbed, why it got her all excited. So she rung up the station house, and told the cops what she found, and then she went to bed. And that's where she's at now. She ain't seen no detectives. She's to see them tomorrow. So it looks like them detectives thought up that little visit all by their-self, don't it?"

"What do you mean?"

"I mean maybe even them detectives could figure out that this here job was done by somebody that knowed all about me and my wife, when we was home, when we was out, and all like of that. And 'specially, that it was done by somebody that knowed we had the money in the house to pay the last installment on the furniture."

"How would I know that?"

"Well, you might know by remembering what time the man came around to get the money last month and figuring he would come around the same day this month, and that we would have the money here waiting for him. That would be one way, wouldn't it?"

"Let me tell you something, fellow: I don't know a thing about this, or your furniture, or the collector, or nothing. And there ain't nothing to show what I know. So you ain't got nothing on me, see? So shag on. Go on down where you come from. So shut up. So that's all. So good-bye."

"Now, not so fast."

"What now? I ain't going to stay out here all night."

"I'm just thinking about something. First off, we ain' got nothing on you. That sure is a fact. We ain't got nothing on you at all. Next off, them detectives ain't got nothing on you. They called me up a little while ago and told me so. Said they couldn't prove nothing."

"It's about time you was getting wise to yourself."

"Just the same, you are the one that done it."

"Huh?"

"I say you are the one that done it."

"All right. All right. I'm the one that done it. Now go ahead and prove it."

"Ain't going to try to prove it. That's a funny thing, ain't it? Them detectives, when they start out on a thing like this, they always got to prove something haven't they? But me, I don't have to prove nothing."

"Come on. What you getting at?"

"Just this: Come on with that money, and come on with them jewels, or I sock you. And make it quick."

"Now wait a minute ... Wait a minute."

"Sure. I ain't in no hurry."

"Maybe if I was to go in and look around ... Maybe some of my kids done that, just for a joke—"

"Just what I told my wife, old man, now you mention it. I says to her, I says, 'Them detectives is all wrong on that idea. Them kids upstairs done it,' I says, 'just for a joke.'"

"I'll go in and take a look—"

"No. You and me, we set out here till I get them things in my hand. You just holler inside and tell the kids to bring them."

"I'll ring the bell and get one of them to the door—"

"That sure is nice of you, old man. I bet there's a whole slew of them robberies done by kids just for a joke, don't you? I always did think so." ❧

FAT THOMAS'
FRIENDS AND
DALE CARNEGIE

By Jimmy Breslin

Much has been made of the darkness of the Irish-American crime writer—from Carroll John Daly, who invented the hard-boiled detective novel, through the definitive age of James M. Cain and Raymond Chandler, to George V. Higgins and many of the other fine crime writers of our age. Jimmy Breslin's criminals are, however, often rather comic. On occasion, Breslin still writes very funny tales about merely petty thiefs. We have taken our language—the American language—from our crime writers, our journalists and our sports reporters—as well as from the various "sporting" characters they have traditionally written about. These writers should be celebrated. They have given us something lively, colorful and unique. They have given us back a language equivalent to the way in which we actually speak.

Among the great education achievements of the year not commented upon by such as Dr. James B. Conant was the performance of Fat Thomas' brother in the Dale Carnegie course at Attica State Prison. Fat Thomas' brother was awarded the Dale Carnegie Gold Pencil for Achievement. He is doing a short bit in Attica for poor usage of a gun.

"They tell me he was beautiful," Fat Thomas says.

"He was a very good pupil," Harry Kindervatter, of the Dale Carnegie staff in Buffalo, says. Kindervatter donates his time to Attica, just as the Peace Corps people do in Mesopotamia, and he is to be similarly applauded.

"We feel our course has tremendous value to these boys," Kindervatter says. "Few of them ever stood up before crowds and had to speak." This is understandable. Criminals who talk too much in public usually wind up among the missing dead. The last great public speaker we had around here was Abe Reles. They threw him out a hotel window.

"With this course of ours," Kindervatter says, "the boys get confidence."

"Confidence?" Fat Thomas yelled. "He's up there to get straightened out, not to become a confidence man."

According to the Dale Carnegie people, talking has become quite the rage in better prisons throughout the

The most imposing figure in the history of New York gangs was a leader who flourished in the 1840s, and captained the old Irish gangs in the most important of their punitive and marauding expeditions. His identity remains unknown, and there is excellent reason to believe that he may be a myth. Under the simple sobriquet of Mose he has become a legendary figure of truly heroic proportions.

Mose was at least eight feet tall

Mose

THE BOWERY BOY

nation. Courses are given in nearly all New York institutions and one of the best in the land is conducted at Leavenworth.

There are, of course, severe problems attached to this great work. A guy named Cousin brought this up during a small party Fat Thomas threw in honor of his brother's achievement. Cousin is an expert on the subject. Some years ago he was subject to deep personal embarrassment when police found a machine gun in the trunk of his car. Cousin insisted he had no intention of using the gun, although, when discovered, it was not packed in Cosmoline for storage. The judge, for some reason, did not listen to Cousin.

So one night he wound up filing into a room in the Trenton State Prison in New Jersey to attend his first Dale Carnegie course.

"It got you out of the cell for a couple of hours," Cousin was saying, "so if you had any brains you had to go for it. Besides, they gave you half a pack of cigarettes if you came.

"Well, you know how the Dale Carnegie course operates. They get you up and you talk about something in your past. It's easier talking about something you know about and you have lived with than it is to stand up there and read from a book or something.

"But for openers, the guy running the course tells us to stand up and say what kind of work you did before you got here. 'What is he, crazy?' I said to myself.

"Nobody would get up. So then he changed it. He said to talk about something from way back in your past. That was better. It gave you a chance to talk about some legitimate thing you did when you was a kid.

"So up pops this one old guy who came off the East Side. He can't wait to talk. 'When I was a kid,' the guy says, 'we stood up-a on the roof and wait for cops to come by. Then we push-a the chimney over and the bricks, they fall five stories on the cop's head. Serve him right. He was-a always beat us on the shins.'

---

and broad in proportion, and his colossal bulk was crowned by a great shock of flaming ginger-colored hair. In his lighter moments it was Mose's custom to lift a horse car off the tracks and carry it a few blocks on his shoulders, laughing uproariously at the bumping the passengers received when he set it down. So gusty was his laugh that the car trembled on its wheels, the trees swayed as though in a storm, and the Bowery was filled with a rushing roar like the thunder of Niagara.

Sometimes Mose unhitched the horses and himself pulled the streetcar the length of the Bowery at a bewildering speed; once, if the legend is to be credited, he lifted a car above his head at Chatham Square, and carried it, with the horses dangling from the traces, on the palm of his hand as far as Astor Place.

Mose could swim the Hudson River with two mighty strokes, and required but six for a complete circuit of Manhattan. But when he wanted to cross the East River, Mose scorned to swim the half mile or so: he simply jumped.

Mose was scarcely cold in his grave before Chanfrau immortalized him by writing *Mose, The Bowery B'hoy*, which was first performed before a clamorous audience at the old Olympic Theatre in 1849.

—*Herbert Asbury*

"I yell at him, 'Shut up, you jerk.' But he thinks I'm doing this heckling business that's part of the course. He keeps going. He got the bit in his mouth and he won't let go. Before the instructor got him down, he tells the whole class, and an assistant warden sitting in the back, about two more homicides and a good stickup.

"I don't know what happened to the bum. I can tell you this. I cut the next two classes."

"I don't understand all this talking," one of the guys at Fat Thomas' table said. "I come up different. When I got grabbed by the F.B.I. the last time I just sat down in the room and I says, 'Sir, I don't want to insult your intelligence with a lot of smart talk. So I'm not going to answer no questions.'

"And the guy says, 'Fine,' and that was it. Now what's the matter with that? How much more talkin' do you need to get by with?"

He was wrong. The Dale Carnegie people have found that few people with prison addresses are able to communicate with words efficiently. This gives them a tremendous problem. So to gain recognition, which was not available by word, they went out and pulled off some fine heists. And this search for recognition extends even to the prison yard.

"What are you in for?" a close friend asked a newcomer to the population at Danbury one day.

"Big bank robbery," the new guy said. "The cops busted in right in the middle of it. I was all set to shoot it out, but one of them nailed me from behind. You must of read it in the papers."

The next day an inmate-clerk made a small check of the newcomer's record. He was in for what is known as a Slow Walker. This is a person who follows the mailman around and steals checks out of mailboxes. But at Danbury he felt he needed a more romantic background in order to gain that recognition.

"When I left the place," my friend recalls, "the Slow Walker still was telling about his big bank robbery."

Dale Carnegie people, and prison officials, feel they can combat this type of problem by teaching inmates how to get up and talk to others. It is a fine idea. And Fat Thomas feels its usefulness goes far beyond even this.

"My brother don't need recognition," he said. "They run his picture page one when he got nailed. What he needs is a trade so he can be paroled. Now he got one. He is going to be an after-dinner speaker." 🐾

New York had Owney Madden, and the free-lance artistry of Jack "Legs" Diamond. Chicago had Dion O'Banion, and the very lucky Bugs Moran. Like Madden, O'Banion was also a criminal ward boss. On Chicago's North Side, it was risky business to move even a jukebox without O'Banion's explicit approval. Then came Al Capone. In Chicago, Bugs Moran functioned more or less like Madden's Big Frenchy DeMange. Moran controlled the artillery. As the body count mounted, simple Bugs became a figure of something more than mere comic relief.

DION O'BANION: ALTAR BOY GONE WRONG

By Paul Sann

"....and he never left home without telling me where he was going or kissing me good-bye."

—Viola O'Banion, the wife

"We're businessmen without high hats," Dion O'Banion used to say, and it was sort of true. He had a flower shop in Chicago and he could furnish wreaths and garlands in any quantity. If the floral pieces were for a funeral and you were shy a corpse, he could furnish that, too, if he was so minded. That's how diverse his business was, and flowers and cadavers were only a sideline. Dion O'Banion also ran the bootleg liquor and manned the gambling traps for the Gold Coast and the slums north of the Loop; he wouldn't dream of limiting his public services to the carriage trade when the other side of the tracks teemed with decent, honest, hard-working citizens equally in need of diversion. He was poor himself before he went wrong. The elder O'Banion, a plasterer, had a time scraping together the few dollars for the lad's surplice and cassock back at the turn of the century when he was in the choir at the Holy Name Cathedral.

Nobody could say how bright little Dion—called Dean or Deanie and sometimes "Gimpy" because an accident had left him with a limp—got off the straight and narrow. Maybe it was because he grew so fast. Even in his teens he had enough brawn to take a job in McGovern's Saloon in the Little Hell section, running beer and sentimental ballads to some very tough customers. Before long, he was an apprentice stickup man and safe-blower, and a muscleman in the Chicago newspapers' early circulation wars. He did time in Bridewell for burglary in 1909 and for assault in 1911. He was caught tampering with somebody else's vault in the Postal Telegraph building once but beat that rap. He

228

got into the trade in stamp-free liquor fairly early, using hijacked supplies because his capital was low. Come Prohibition's golden flow, he was a fairly well-established tradesman and his firm abounded in such true and trusted chums of his young manhood as Hymie (The Pollack) Weiss, George (Bugs) Moran, Vincent (Schemer) Drucci, Louis (Three-Gun) Alterie, and assorted PFC's. Once this happy-go-lucky set was caught borrowing 1,750 barrels' worth of prewar bonded Kentucky bourbon from a warehouse, but the proprietors and even the police guard appeared to be helping them with the million-dollar haul, so that case never got to the annoying courtroom stage.

When Johnny Torrio inherited Big Jim Colosimo's throne, he summoned O'Banion. Deanie was not above heisting an occasional truckload of his liquor, so Torrio explained to him that this form of poaching would be frowned on in the new and more formal organization of the underworld empire. He said O'Banion and his playmates could have the whole North Side preserve for their very own exploitation, plus some brewery interests, but they would (A) have to cease all hijacking and (B) observe the territorial rights of their underworld neighbors. Otherwise, trouble. O'Banion got in line and, while he lived, it proved to be a good idea.

The exchoirboy tied up the loose ends in the retail liquor outlets in his barony, not overlooking the drugstores, and tightened his grip on the varied gambling activity. He passed up the prostitution industry, having a decided aversion to the love-for-sale bit. Even without this lush sideline, O'Banion got so rich that he shed his former coloring as a hoodlum and brawler. He dressed better—but conservatively—and got his nails manicured. He married Viola Kaniff, a nice girl with some book learning, and had her dress up their Pine Grove Avenue love nest with good paintings. He put in a $14,000 player piano and a console radio. He had some tuxedos made (with special pockets for artillery). He went to Mass regularly. He made pilgrimages to his boyhood streets in Little Hell and spread odd sums among the needy. ("I am a very swell fellow," Dean might say, "a very swell fellow.")

Dion and Viola O'Banion.

And he acquired half a touch of responsibility by buying a half interest in William F. Schofield's flower shop on North State Street, right by the Holy Name Cathedral. He loved flowers. He would spend lots of time in the shop.

For all his outward Peace of Mind, Dion O'Banion, Baron of the North Side, had a king-sized assortment of headaches, tabled below:

1—He talked vaguely about retreating from Chicago to more genteel environs and got Johnny Torrio to buy his $500,000 interest in the giant Sieben brewery. Then Reform Mayor William E. Dever ordered a police drive on illegal beer operations, and both O'Banion and Torrio were arrested when the raiding forces got around to Sieben's. Torrio didn't mind the

229

pinch so much but couldn't shake the nagging feeling that Deanie—always well-connected in official circles—knew the crackdown was coming before he sold his piece. This sort of dark suspicion in the racket empire's throne room wasn't calculated to do O'Banion any good.

II—He took to feudin' with the Genna Brothers, also known as The Terrible Gennas. He said they were selling their corn-sugar alcohol—home-cooked in hundreds of friendly tenements—in his bailiwick for three dollars per gallon, while his had a six dollar to nine dollar price tag. The Gennas, so affluent that they had five police captains and four hundred patrolmen on their payroll, drawing $350,000 a month in "ice," charged in turn that O'Banion had fallen into his old habits and was hijacking liquor out of their West Side domain. Hymie Weiss suggested to O'Banion that the Gennas were most excitable fellows and might get violent. Deanie cast off his new-found respectability for a moment. "Aw," he said, "to hell with them Sicilians." It was not a nice way to talk in Chicago in 1924.

III—He got into an intermob squabble over a matter of $30,000 in IOU's spread around the syndicate's Cicero gambling casino, The Ship, by Angelo Genna. Al Capone wanted to write off Genna's losses as trifling, but Deanie insisted that a man should pay his debts. O'Banion paid no mind to Capone, The Ship's skipper-of-record, and told Genna to get up the thirty Big Ones or else. Again, no way to talk to people named Genna.

IV—He touched off a noisy municipal scandal, quite innocently, by filling the Guest of Honor's chair at a testimonial dinner and accepting a $2,000 platinum wristwatch set in diamonds and a smattering of rubies. Mayor Dever raised the City Hall roof the next day because the highest police brass had attended the affair, breaking bread with such celebrated O'Banion associates as Schemer Drucci, Hymie Weiss, Bugs Moran and Three-Gun Alteries. The storm didn't quiet down until Chief-of-Detectives Michael Hughes turned in his badge and gun, all the while protesting that he left the affair "almost at once" when he learned to his dismay that it was a memorial to the living O'Banion.

Mike Merlo, first president of the Unione Siciliana, passed away in Chicago on November 8, 1924. He died of natural causes, an unusual avenue of exit for the society in which he dwelt. It was a nice thing, in a way, because it meant there would be no recriminations in the underworld, no petty finger-pointing, no hard feelings. Everyone could get together to give Mike Merlo a funeral befitting his exalted station. Thus, the next day, orders for floral tributes poured into the O'Banion-Schofield flower emporium in unprecedented quantities. John Torrio selected a $10,000 display. Al Capone picked out an $8,000 item. Someone else told O'Banion to rustle up a floral effigy of the departed Merlo—life-size, of course. That night another party ordered an elaborate spray and said he would send around for it at noon. O'Banion said he would attend to that one himself and he was out front, clipping some chrysanthemums, when three men came in at the appointed hour.

O'Banion limped toward them—he evidently knew the trio—and extended his right hand. The man in the middle took the proffered handshake and held tight. The other two drew revolvers and pumped fire into O'Banion until he slumped to the floor. Then the trio hurried to an undertaker's limousine waiting at the curb. When the police arrived to inspect the remains, they found that the executioners had held their guns so close that there were powder burns among the six gaping holes ripped into the husky gangster's head and torso. The shop's porter, who was on the premises during the O'Banion demise, had no idea what the three messengers of death looked like. Nor could anyone in the noonday crowd outside throw any light on this point. With O'Banion's own hard lips and blue eyes forever closed, the usual fruitless investigation followed. The police called in everybody, more or less, and let them all out again. Torrio and Capone were invited downtown, along with Mike Genna, Albert Anselmi and John Scalisi. The latter two, the most accomplished torpedo men in The Terrible Gennas' troop, were widely credited with the deed. Others said that Frankie Yale, né Uale, a citizen of Brooklyn but a dear friend of Torrio, was in on the job. In any case, nobody was held long enough to delay the funeral—and Dion O'Banion, departing at thirty-two, got a $100,000 send-off that made the Mike Merlo obsequies look like the services for any Skid Row bum. 🙦

THE LUCK OF THE IRISH

The phrase "The Luck of the Irish" is an overused piece of marlarky. It is also often untrue.

The case of Bugs Moran was different—he indeed was blessed with the luck of the Irish.

Moran, through a combination of instinctual tardiness and criminal wariness, was the guy who showed up late for the St. Valentine's Day Massacre. That little bit of luck added twenty-eight years to his life.

A little background music, with a drumroll of staccato machine-gun sounds:

George Moran was the offspring of Polish and Irish immigrant parents. Born in 1893 in Minnesota, Bugs grew up in North Side Chicago. He learned his craft early, logging twenty-six stickups before he was legal to drink.

It was during those formative years that he met his model, Chicago gangsterism's No. 2 guy, Dion O'Banion. The latter, an accomplished thief, safecracker, liquor distributor and florist, was the only "could have been contender" for Al Capone's throne.

Moran, as Dion's right-hand man, served his master well, even to the point of doing five years in the Crowbar Hotel for a crime O'Banion masterminded.

In 1924 Capone dealt O'Banion his Aces and Eights hand. Moran was now in charge of the O'Banion boys. And the Chicago gang wars were at their height.

In 1926 Moran ordered the infamous machine-gun motorcade that redesigned Capone's Hawthorne Hotel.

That attack was the last straw for Capone.

On Feburary 14, 1929, Big Al sent four men to massacre Moran and his gang at a garage at 2122 North Clark Street. The Moran gang, expecting a hooch drop, was caught with its guard down when the four Caponeists (two dressed as cops, two as civilians) marched in.

The "policemen," led by Machine Gun Jack McGurn, had the boys spread 'em, and then they bled 'em. Seven men died. Only Moran escaped.

Bugs had seen the "cops" arrive. Figuring it was a shakedown, he had hung back. That instinct was his best Valentine's Day present.

Machine Gun McGurn was shot down in 1936; Moran was a suspect, but never fingered. The North Clark Street bloodletting was pretty much curtains for Bugs. He pulled a few more small-potatoes bank jobs in Ohio, and was arrested by the F.B.I. in 1946. He did ten years, was released, then started another stretch for another bank heist. He died of cancer in Leavenworth.

His death date was February 25, 1957. "The Luck of the Irish," which had ridden with Bugs, held for exactly twenty-eight years and eleven days after the St. Valentine's Day Massacre.

—J.P. O'Shea

◄ The Lucky Irishman, Bugs Moran.

The Silver Screen

▶

*Sunset descends on
"the most witty and knowing
spoof of Hollywood
movie-making of all time"
in the 1941 Paramount
production of Preston Sturges'*
Sullivan's Travels.

Studs Terkel's remarkable interview with James Cagney first appeared in Esquire *magazine in October 1981. As* Esquire *editor Lee Eisenberg then wrote in his note of introduction: "Cagney and Terkel met on a sunny afternoon in Cagney's modest farmhouse eighty miles north of New York City. Terkel, whose books include* Hard Times *and* American Dreams, *was*

Studs Terkel as usual: ebullient and probing. Sadly but necessarily missing from these printed pages is the sound of Cagney's voice. For even though his once-compact body had by then turned bulky, Cagney's voice remained true, unmistakably and unforgettably the one and only." James Cagney died on March 31, 1986.

IT'S ALL IN THE SCHEME

By James Cagney and Studs Terkel

Studs Terkel: *I'm thinking, well, let's go back to beginnings, that's the thing. You came from a very tough district in New York, didn't you? On the East Side?*

James Cagney: Yeah. But I didn't know it was tough. Nobody knew it was tough.

You were right in the heart of it.

Sure. My father was a saloonkeeper. A bartender.

Did you hang around the saloon?

No, not much.

What was your dream? What did you want to be?

A farmer.

Funny. Kids in tough areas always want to be firemen or cops, you know, or lawyers. Yet you, with no background at all in farming, wanted to be a farmer ... and that's what you are today, of course.

This is all I ever wanted to do.

Why, do you think? What is it ...?

Can't tell you why. It was just that the country attracted me. My Greek great-uncle and his Irish wife were country people—they had a tiny house out in what's now Flatbush, in Brooklyn. It was very easy there. No great strain. There was no great strain for anything, really.

Funny how your approach is so straight. You lived in hurly-burly turbulence.

I didn't know it.

What about some of your friends? Were they affected?

You mean the ones that went to the chair? [Laughs] *Yeah.*

Well, Bootah, he and I sat alongside each other in school.

Who was that?

Bootah. Peter Heston.

But he was called Bootah?

Yeah. Why, that I don't know. He and I sat alongside of each other in school. And anybody could lick him. But he had a gun. And he did a stickup on 102nd Street, and a cop named Riley came around the corner and saw what was going on. And without saying anything Riley just sneaked up behind Bootah. And Bootah gave him both barrels.

Bang. Killed the cop?

Right then and there. And Bootah went where we always went when we were being chased: down the cellar, through the yard, over the fence, and out in the next street. He had shot himself in the leg putting the gun away, so the cops had a beautiful trail. They found him on the fourth or fifth floor of a tenement house, in bed with the gun. But he was too weak to lift it, he lost so much blood. So they took him in.

I went to play ball at Sing Sing in 1919 and I was catching, warming up a pitcher. And this little voice beside me said, "Hello, Red." I was always called Red. We were told not to talk to the prisoners, so I just said, "Hello, how are you?" He said, "What's the matter? You gettin' stuck up?" Real, you know, New York. And I looked at him, and I said, "Bootah?" And he said, "Yeah." And I said, "How long you in?" And he said, "Five to ten." How he got away with that, I don't know.

I was going to say, only five to ten for killing a cop!

I was amazed, yes. No, wait; he didn't kill him. Pardon me, I was wrong. He killed a cop later. This cop he shot in the neck, I think—a superficial wound. Alongside him was a kid named Red Russell. I used to box with Russell in the backyard.

I'll be damned.

"Hello, Red," he said, and so on—you know, small talk. And so I got up, I went behind the batter, and the first man getting up had white hair. He was twenty-six years old. And this guy Jack—Dirtyneck Jack Dougherty—turned around and I said, "You Jack Dougherty?" He said, "Yeah." He said, "Too bad about your father." My father had died the previous fall and this was late in September when we were playing ball.

What kept you from being like them?

I had a mother who would belt us if we did anything cockeyed. Stiffened us, really. But we had other

interests, anyway. We played ball and so on.

What about your father?

A good guy. Nice fellow, you know? Drunk most of the time.

But your mother was the strong one?

Oh, yes.

That happens so often, doesn't it? Particularly in immigrant families or families that are new to a new world—the old man has a job making a living and the old lady is the tough one.

Yeah. [Laughs] She was just as tough as she needed to be. A great woman.

There were five kids?

Seven, really. Two died.

And you were where?

Second. Second eldest. Harry was the eldest.

You wanted to be a farmer. Is it true that once, when you were a young guy, you enrolled in an agricultural school?

Farmingdale School of Agriculture. [Laughs] One of the profs came over to see why the hell this kid from the East Side wanted to enroll in an agricultural school. He had real clodhopper shoes on, you know, a real farmer.

But you couldn't do it because of the lack of dough, is that it?

That was everything, eventually.

But it's funny. Even now, country people look upon city people as strange, and the reverse is true, too. You span both worlds, the country and the city.

I suppose. I'm never aware of it.

Because of your mother and your interests, you were able

235

to avoid being a guy in the pokey—being a guy like the characters you eventually played in the movies. Do you think your knowledge of these guys when you were a kid played a role in the characters you created in Public Enemy, *in* Doorway to Hell … ?

It all contributed. Some of the things I said in the movies were things people around me said. "Whattya hear, whattya say?" That was one of the …

One of the lines you had.

I put that in. There was a gal in the neighborhood, I think she was a hooker—I never found out, really—and she came out with that one day. One of her boyfriends used to say it, so I dropped it in.

You could drop in your own phrases?

Well, I knew more about the hoods than the writers did, for God's sake. They were country boys.

As the definitive gangster, you created a whole image in those movies of the thirties about the twenties. Yet it wasn't so much for the director's doing, because Milos Forman said you do things instinctually. That's always been the case with you? This instinct …

I was there when it was going on. I called on that.

What about "That's the kind of hairpin I am"? You said that in Strawberry Blonde.

That was my grandfather's line. It was something he used to say as a kid—in Norway.

Let's go back to the early years. How did you get into theater? After you were in the neighborhood.

I needed a job, and a fellow told me to go to the 81st Street Theater. That was how easy it was. I walked in, met the stage manager, and I was doing the job the next morning.

Doing what?

Dancing, singing, doing female impersonations.

Tough Jimmy Cagney doing female impersonations!

That's right.

You didn't have training as a song-and-dance man?

Oh no, none at all. But I could dance. They showed it to me, I did it. As we did it, we learned.

How about singing? Did that come naturally to you?

I couldn't sing. I never could.

Now, how did Sinner's Holiday *happen? You were a song-and-dance man and then you had …*

No, at that time I was doing a play.

A straight play.

Mm-hmm. You see, we never turned down a job. You just damn well did it, did the best you could with it.

That was always your theme.

Mm-hmm. But never consciously.

You were in Penny Arcade *with Joan Blondell.*

Yeah. And they hired her and me not knowing anything about us at all. But she was able. She'd been around for a long time.

And that's when you came to Hollywood.

Mm-Hmm. April 11, 1930.

You remember the date! So after, when did you know that you were a hit?

Let me see. After *Penny Arcade*, I did a picture called *Doorway to Hell*. We were driving down Santa Monica Boulevard and my name was up in lights. That was the first time I knew.

This is the obvious question, of course, but of all the roles you've done, is there one in your mind that was the greatest satisfaction and challenge?

Yankee Doodle.

Yankee Doodle Dandy. *So it's George M. Cohan, after all.*

Well, you see, I grew up with him. I saw him in … what the hell did I see him in? *I'd Rather Be Right*. And *Ah! Wilderness*.

Oh, he came back as a straight actor, the father in O'Neill's Ah! Wilderness, *that's right. Stunned everybody.*

Mm-Hmm. What a job he did there.

Did you ever know him, I mean, meet him?

Yeah, I met him once. He was casting a play and I went up to a hotel. He was behind a desk, and … Chamberlain Brown, you remember that name?

He was an agent.

That's right. He sent me up there. Well, apparently he had some signals with Cohan and Brown was behind me, and I said, "Hello, Mr. Cohan." And he looked over at Brown and said, "I don't think you're right for us, son."

And that was it?

Mm-hmm.

And years later you make this guy immortal as Yankee Doodle Dandy *in a film. Cohan was rough in the early days when it came to the actors' unions, Equity, I think he fought Equity.*

Oh, sure he did.

But you became one of the early presidents of the Screen Actors Guild.

That's right. You do all the things that happen, one into another.

But you're always on the side of the underdog. You even gave dough to the Abraham Lincoln Brigade in the Spanish Civil War. You helped poor cotton farmers. That got you into a little trouble for a while didn't it?

No. It's all part of the scheme. ❧

▶

James Cagney as George M. Cohan with Joan Leslie in the 1942 Warner production, ***Yankee Doodle Dandy.***

237

THE ICE PRINCESS

An era was measured, allowed to pass, and a new era began. And it all happened at the movies. In 1956 the two great Pennslyvania Kellys—Grace and Gene—were given the starring socialite roles in the very Waspish *High Society*, the musical remake of Philip Barry's marvelous play, *The Philadelphia Story*. In the movie, the role of the Irish-American reporter assigned to cover these goofy dilettantes was given to the Italian, Frank Sinatra. The demographics were churning. For a moment or so, it seemed as if all the Episcopalians had been driven out of Hollywood.

Another false dawn.

High Society turned out to be a bomb.

And yet if ever there was a simple colleen whose whole purpose in life was to confuse forever the lines separating the wealthy Catholics from the wealthy Protestants—and assert, beyond all argument, the absolute American primacy of cold, hard cash—clearly that woman was Grace Kelly.

On the moon, perhaps, it could have been otherwise.

Her uncle Walter was a bit actor and a beloved vaudevillian. Her uncle George was widely known as an underrated playwright and somewhat of a raconteur. Her father Jack—whom F.D.R. had called the handsomest man he had ever seen—fell some 47,000 votes short of becoming mayor of Philadelphia.

Poor Jack.

He had to settle instead with becoming one of the wealthiest construction contractors the Northeast coast had ever seen.

So, somewhere beneath all of that ice, some of the old Irish gris-gris must have still flowed through the system.

By the Age of Grace, however, the money was already in the bank.

Grace Kelly made her film debut in *Fourteen Hours*. The film was a clunker, but from the moment she appeared on the silver screen she became the ultimate model for that kind of impossible beauty from which later imposters, like Princess Di, would eventually be cast.

Grace Kelly became a fine, fine actress—

Grace Kelly, from the 1954 Paramount production of *The Country Girl*.

history will give her that—and Alfred Hitchcock came along and made her a bona fide Hollywood star.

Pardon, then, these irreverent remarks from that old Paddy consciousness up in the attic.

Just once, I would have liked to have seen her marching on a picket line somewhere members of her class only know from watching movies. Just once. The politics don't matter. I would be looking, only, for a simple show of vigor.

Just once I would have liked to have been able to imagine her, elbows up, buying a round of shots and beers for a fine crowd down at the local bar.

It never happened.

This is my loss, of course; but I also think it was hers.

—*Bob Callahan*

PRESTON STURGES: WHAT A LIFE!

By Andrew Sarris

Preston Sturges' natural father was Edward Biden, a Chicago collection agent. His mother was the former Mary Dempsey, who, after divorcing Biden, changed her name to Mary d'Este, claiming that she was in fact the descendant of a distinguished Italian prince who had landed in Ireland in the wake of a romantic duel. Sturges would later lampoon the epidemic name changes in his family in Palm Beach Story. *From* The Great McGinty *to* Sullivan's Travels, *many of Sturges' movies told the story of slightly eccentric, very funny Irish-Americans, wandering through the world forever confused for the want of cold hard cash. It is Sturges' love of language, however, that makes his films so sly, sophisticated and wonderfully Irish.*

▼

Barbara Stanwyck and Henry Fonda in the 1941 Paramount production, *The Lady Eve*.

Acknowledged as the foremost satirist of his time, Preston Sturges enjoyed his greatest vogue between 1940 and 1944 when his pungent wit and frenetic slapstick exploded on such topics as Tammany Hall politics, advertising, American fertility rites, hero and mother worship. Within the context of a Sturges film, a gangster could declare with ringing, heavily accented conviction: "America is a land of great opportunity." An underpaid clerk could rise to fame and fortune by coining the slogan: "If you can't sleep, it isn't the coffee, it's the bunk!" A sign in a flophouse could remind its denizens: "Have you written to mother?" Sturges repeatedly suggested that the lowliest boob could rise to the top with the right degree of luck, bluff and fraud. The absurdity of the American success story was matched by the ferocity of the battle of the sexes. In *The Lady Eve*, when Henry Fonda plaintively confesses: "Snakes are my life," Barbara Stanwyck snaps back: "What a life!" The climax of *Palm Beach Story* finds Rudy Vallee serenading Claudette Colbert's upstairs window while the object of his affections is being seduced by the subject of hers, Joel McCrea.

Sturgean comedy was influenced by the silent antics of Charles Chaplin, Buster Keaton and Harold Lloyd in the 1920s, and by the crackling verbal rhythms of Howard Hawks, Frank Capra, Leo McCarey and Gregory La Cava in the 1930s. Sturges contributed to this distinguished tradition mainly through the unusual density of his scripts. His films were noted for the hilarious side effects of character and bit actors. It was not unusual for a gravel-voiced bus driver to use the word "paraphrase," nor for a hoodlum to invoke the ruinous symmetry of "Samson and Delilah, Sodom and Gomorrah." A stereotyped performer like Eric Blore was virtually rediscovered savoring the line: "I positively swill in his ale." Similarly, Edgar Kennedy was resurrected from two-reelers to play an inspired bartender reacting to a customer asking for his first drink ever: "Sir, you rouse the artist in me." The Sturges stock company was particularly noted for the contrasting personalities of William Demarest, the eternal roughneck, and Franklin Pangborn, the eternal snob.

Sturges was criticized at the time by James Agee,

Manny Farber and other reputable critics for an ambivalence in his work projected from a childhood conflict between a culturally demanding mother and an admired businessman foster father. This unusually Freudian analysis of the director's work sought to explain the incongruity of continental sophistication being challenged by American pragmatism. Sturges himself was seen as an uneasy mixture of savant and wise guy. On the one hand, his extreme literacy, rare among Hollywood screenwriters, enabled him to drop words like "ribaldry" and "vestal" into their proper contexts without a pretentious thud. On the other, he seemed unwilling to develop the implications of his serious ideas. His flair for props and gadgets suited the popularly recalled image of the young inventor of kissproof lipstick.

His reputation today is based mainly on the eight films he directed for Paramount. *The Great McGinty*, a vigorous satire of big city politics marked by lusty performances from Akim Tamiroff as the boss and Brian Donlevy as the hobo elevated to governor, was the pilot film of the writer-director movement in Hollywood. Most directors had previously risen from the ranks of studio technicians and stage directors. After Sturges led the way, John Huston, Billy Wilder, Dudley Nichols, Clifford Odets, Nunnally Johnson, Robert Rossen, Samuel Fuller, Frank Tashlin and Blake Edwards followed from the writer's cubicle to the director's chair. *Christmas in July* lingered over a Depression mood as Dick Powell and Ellen Drew played an engaged couple trying to make ends meet on a combined salary of forty dollars a week. The vagaries of luck and the cruelty of practical jokes developed the plot in what was to be later recognized as the distinctive and disturbing Sturges manner. *The Lady Eve*, a sophisticated comedy with Henry Fonda and Barbara Stanwyck, was hailed by the *New York Times* as the best film of 1941. Sturges circumvented the censors with a rowdy blackout technique that began where the more discreet "Lubitsch touch" had left off. An adroit manipulation of mistaken identity aided Sturges in preserving the technical morality of the marriage contract. The duet in *The Lady Eve* was later enlarged into the quadrille of *Palm Beach Story* in which Joel McCrea, Claudette Colbert, Mary Astor and Rudy Vallee were perpetually confused and obsessed by the permutations of what Sturges leeringly defined as "Subject A."

Sullivan's Travels, a Swiftian glimpse of Hollywood and its occasional flirtations with social consciousness, is generally considered the most profound expression of the director's personality. Dedicating the film to the world's clowns and mountebanks, Sturges forthrightly defended the muse of comedy against the presumably more serious demands of society. Like Shakespeare's *The Winter's Tale*, the film pivots in one dancelike moment from comedy to tragedy when an old derelict is trapped in a metal jungle of switch rails and is unable to evade an oncoming train. *The Miracle of Morgan's Creek* and *Hail the Conquering Hero* represented the director's original vision of small-town America within which Eddie Bracken emerged as a Sturges folk hero. In *Miracle*, Bracken has "greatness thrust upon him" when his frolicsome V-girl sweetheart, Betty Hutton, is thoughtful enough to transcend her disgrace with sextuplets. In *Hero*, Bracken survives the ordeal of a 4-F self-exposed as a false war hero, and again he is redeemed by the generous emotions of his girlfriend, Ella Raines. Many critics were impressed by the intense performance of exprizefighter Freddie Steele, in the film an orphanage-bred marine hero with a severe mother complex.

After 1944, when he left Paramount to form a short-lived partnership with Howard Hughes, Sturges' career suffered a precipitous decline. His three subsequent Hollywood films were remote from the tastes of their time, and during his long exile in the 1950s, his one realized European project, the bilingual *Les Carnets de Major Thompson* (*The French They Are a Funny Race*), was unsuccessful. His present reputation is that of a period director who ultimately lost contact with his audience. Even at the time of his greatest success, he was overshadowed by the emotions aroused by the war and the stylistic revolution introduced with *Citizen Kane*. He received an Academy Award for the script of *The Great McGinty* in 1940, and was nominated twice in 1944 for *The Miracle of Morgan's Creek* and *Hail the Conquering Hero*, though again as a writer rather than as a director.

THE JOYS OF SCREENWRITING

The story conference is to screenwriting what crabgrass is to the lawn. It encourages the most spurious sense of collaboration: if it allows the producer to feel "creative," it makes the writer ever more aware that he is an employee. Everyone involved feels impelled to pump significance into the most banal bloodletter; rarely this side of academe does one hear more about "illusion versus reality" than one does in a story conference, usally in a story conference about a Western. Every sentence tends to begin with "What if . . . " as in "What if the young doctor blows up the boat?"

"As an existential act?"

"Right."

"The illusion-versus-reality-type-thing?"

"Right on."

"But his wife's in the boat."

"What if he only thought she was?"

"There's your illusion versus reality again."

(Break)

A studio executive came to a writer friend of mind and said he had an idea for a film. "We're all very excited about it," the executive said. "The sky's the limit on development money."

"What's the idea?" the writer said.

"Relationships," the executive said. He beamed and pulled on his pipe.

The writer stared at him for a long time, waiting for him to add something else. "You mean men and women?" he said finally.

"That'd be a part of it."

(Break)

My wife and I were once taken to lunch by a producer with a hot idea: "World War II."

"What do you want to do with it?"

"You're the writers."

—*John Gregory Dunne*

THE HIBERNIAN HALL OF FAME

By James Y. O'Perill

Left to right:

First row: Aline MacMahon, Mia Farrow, Buster Keaton, James M. Cain, Margaret O'Brien, Mickey Rourke, Pat O'Brien

Second row: Barry Fitzgerald, Alice Brady, Victor McLaglen, Art Carney, Preston Sturges, Amy Madigan

Third row: Tyrone Power, Carroll O'Connor, Billie Burke, Errol Flynn, Laurette Taylor

Fourth row: John Huston, Audie Murphy, Leo Gorcey, Maureen O'Hara, Margaret Sullavan, James Cagney, Shirley Maclaine, Jackie Gleason

Fifth row: Mary Tyler Moore, Warren Beatty, Angelica Huston, Alice Faye, John Wayne, Walter Brennan

242

243

THE MAN WHO MADE KING KONG

By Christopher Finch

Willis O'Brien was a twenty-five-year-old San Francisco stonecutter and a part-time sports cartoonist for the San Francisco Daily News *when he began to experiment with the building of small clay models in 1912. O'Brien's first models were simply of the fireplaces he intended to build, but he soon began to create a series of small clay prizefighters primarily for his own amusement. He graduated from prizefighters to dinosaurs and other prehistoric beasts, and this new interest took him to Hollywood, the creation of* King Kong *and a career as perhaps the greatest special effects technician in the history of film.*

Willis O'Brien is one of the greatest names in the history of special effects, a pioneer of stop-motion animation and a masterful coordinator of the entire arsenal of special effects available during the recent sound era. After a restless adolescence, which had seen him employed as a cowboy, a prizefighter, and a railroad brakeman, O'Brien began to experiment with model animation, one of the most trying and time-consuming ways of making a movie that has yet been devised.

On the set of a live-action film, the camera records the movement of the performers by breaking it down into twenty-four still images every second. When the film is projected at the same speed, the figures are brought back to life thanks to the phenomenon known as "persistence of vision," which causes our brains to run the succession of images together

▶
Willis O'Brien, creator of King Kong.

to produce the illusion of movement. It is possible to create this illusion from scratch by photographing a series of carefully related still images—drawings, for example—one frame at a time, with a special movie camera designed for this purpose. Animated cartoons are made this way, and such "flat" animation has its place in special effects, too.

Model animation, as practiced by Willis O'Brien, simply carries the same principle into the third dimension. Flexible figures with articulated skeletons are made to move in tiny increments. The animator simply moves them by hand, causing an elbow or a knee to bend a fraction of an inch at a time. After each minute move, the animation camera exposes one frame of film. When the exposed strip of film is developed and projected, the figures appear to move on their own. If the animator possesses the skills of a Willis O'Brien, the figures actually seem to be alive, but the work is maddeningly slow and demanding.

This technique has been known at least since 1897 (nearly a decade before the first recorded animated cartoon), but it was still no more than a novelty when Willis O'Brien, in his twenties, began to experiment with it. His first serious effort was a short titled *The Dinosaur and the Missing Link*, which he completed in 1925. This prehistoric comedy announced O'Brien's predilection for movies about the age of dinosaurs. Both of his major successes of the silent era—*The Ghosts of Slumber Mountain* (1918) and *The Lost World* (1925)—feature confrontations between man and prehistoric monsters. The set of the latter film, produced by First National, was visited by Fritz Lang on his first trip to America. He pronounced the film "a technical masterpiece," while Sir Arthur Conan Doyle premiered clips from it before the Society of American Magicians in New York. Newspaper reports of this occasion suggest that some of those present believed that the dinosaurs they saw on screen were "real."

As the 1920s came to a close, O'Brien was at R.K.O. developing *Creation*, another picture in the same vein. But when in October of 1931 David O. Selznick was appointed vice president in charge of production at the studio, one of the first things he did was to place *Creation* on hold, suspecting, perhaps, that O'Brien had gone to the well once too often. Selznick might have killed it outright if it had not been for the fact that a considerable sum had already been spent on development and production. As things stood, he had to go through the motions of evaluating the project, appointing Merican C. Cooper to look into its potential.

Cooper had made innovative documentaries and quasi documentaries in exotic locations such as Persia and Siam. While shooting in Africa he had become fascinated with gorillas and had conceived the idea of making a movie with an ape as the central character. The idea he was hawking around the studios in 1930

PIERRE BAILLY

KING KONG AMONG THE LILLIPUTIANS

The poetic qualities of *King Kong*—"the visionary, strange and horrible power of its content," as Jean Ferry has stated—proceed out of a dream—Willis O'Brien's dream—a perfect, total, complete dream. And it is this dream, animated thanks to the technology of movie-making, which gives *King Kong* its poetic impact.

King Kong may be the most remarkable—perhaps even the only—example of a man's entire dream (O'Brien's) turned into a masterpiece, thanks to technology, and thus made available to the world.

Which unconscious memories induced O'Brien to design the sequence of the gorilla appearing at the window? "For a long time," Jonathan Swift first wrote, "the terror of seeing a gorilla peering through my window haunted my childhood insomnia." Did Willis O'Brien ever possess, in his childhood library, a copy of Swift's *Gulliver's Travels* with an illustration precisely representing the gorilla kidnapping the hero "like a Baby in one of his Fore-Paws" and taking refuge at the top of the palace overlooking the city of Brobdingnag? We shall probably never know. O'Brien need not be concerned—to have dreamt the same dream as Jonathan Swift could hardly prove to be detrimental!

—*Jean Boullet*

and 1931 was for a film that would feature a real gorilla, but no one was buying, apparently thinking that in the changed conditions of the sound era the cost of location shooting would be prohibitive. At the time he signed on as a Selznick aide, Cooper was still committed to his gorilla idea and presumably looked on his R.K.O. duties as interim chores.

When Cooper was called in to assess the *Creation* project, Willis O'Brien saw the writing on the wall but took note of the fact that Cooper seemed impressed with his skills as a model animator and special effects artist. (Extensive tests had already been shot for *Creation*.) O'Brien decided to gamble. He had heard about Cooper's gorilla idea and set out to convince the producer that, with the aid of photographic effects and his stop-motion miniatures, he could place on screen an ape that would appear far more imposing than any live gorilla. Moreover, with a little imagination on the part of the scenarist, many of the expensive miniatures prepared for *Creation* could be worked into the story line.

Cooper immediately saw that a giant ape would give his proposal a new dimension and decided to persuade Selznick of its feasibility. He concocted the barest outlines of a story, then hired the British thriller writer Edgar Wallace to flesh it out. Wallace's name appears on the credits, though apparently almost nothing of the treatment he prepared found its way onto the screen. (He died shortly after delivering the first draft.) Meanwhile, O'Brien's top modelmaker, Marcel Delgado, began work on a miniature Kong. For a while Cooper insisted that Kong should be given some human characteristics, but this notion was quickly abandoned, and Delgado soon produced the prototype of the ape that was to sweep the world.

O'Brien himself had developed a miniature rear-projection system which proved of enormous value. A typical setup might involve the following elements: Nearest the camera, foreground vegetation painted on glass. Beyond this, a miniature jungle set, built in forced perspective, consisting of real and man-made plants and rocks. In the middle ground of this set, articulated puppets representing Kong and a prehistoric reptile locked in mortal combat. Beyond this miniature set, another glass painting representing background vegetation. Finally, and most unusual, a miniature rear-projection screen set into rocks, its hard edges disguised with creepers and lichens.

By projecting live action of an actor, shot on a matching full-size set, onto this rear-projection screen, O'Brien could introduce human protagonists right into his miniature world. In the end, though, it was the stop-motion miniatures that made *King Kong* a sensation in its day. The Kong figures and the dinosaurs set a standard by which all such models would be judged for decades.

Sean Aloysius O'Feeney (the Anglicized form of O'Fearna) was born on Cape Elizabeth in Maine on February 1, 1895. His father was born in Galway. His mother was from the Aran Islands. The most Irish of all of the major Irish-American artists, Ford had an ability to use the silver screen as if it were a vast, rolling canvas, an ability continually underscored by his absolute, commanding sense of the power and splendor of myth. The perfect John Ford shots—a stagecoach crossing Monument Valley, small children framed against a hill during springtime in a small Welsh village, young, gangling Abe Lincoln riding out past a broken fence onto the prairie—possess such extraordinary graphic power as to be considered equal to the finest paintings composed by an American artist in our time.

THE TALL SOLDIER: MEMORIES OF JOHN FORD

by James Cagney and Peter Bogdanovich

"We were making a picture," says cameraman Joseph LaShelle, "and the head of the studio sent his assistant down to the set to tell Ford he was a day behind schedule. 'Oh,' said Ford, very polite, 'well, how many pages would you figure we shoot a day?' 'About eight, I guess,' the guy said. 'Would you hand me the script?' Ford said, and the guy handed it to him. He counted out eight pages, and handed them to the guy. 'You can tell your boss we're back on schedule now,' he said. And he never did shoot those eight pages."

"To the Navajos, Mr. Ford was holy, sorta," says Harry Goulding, who used to own the lodge in Monument Valley where the director often stayed.

"Ev'ytime they've had a rough time, boy, this things comes outa the blue. They'd been hit pretty bad by the Depression an', by God, if an Indian'd walked into our store an' put a dollar on the counter, why Mrs. Goulding an' I'd a fainted. Well, Mr. Ford came here to make *Stagecoach*, and gave a score a jobs to the Navajos and a lotta lives was saved. Then, just after he'd finished shootin' *She Wore A Yellow Ribbon* here, we had a blizzard that left the Valley covered with 'bout twelve feet a snow. Army planes dropped food in. Thanks to that, an' the two hundred thousand dollars or so he'd left behind, why, another tragedy was prevented. An' in '63 he heard his friends was gonna have too little t'eat, an' there he was again makin' *Cheyenne Autumn*. He's been taken into the Navajo tribe, you know. They have a special name for 'im, the Navajos. Natani Nez.

That's *his* name, only his. Natani Nez. It means the Tall Soldier."

"Ford had a slightly sadistic sense of humor," James Cagney recalled. "It's hard to resist the impression he occasionally allowed things to occur in order to satisfy this inner enjoyment. One scene in *What Price Glory* required me to come out of a building, exhilarated by the thought of going on leave, jump into the sidecar of a motorcycle driven by my sergeant, and drive off.

Before the scene, Ford, smoking that tiny pipe the Irish call a dudeen, came over and said, 'Do you really want to ride with this guy?' I answered, 'Why not?'

"This guy was the actor playing the sergeant, Bill Demarest. Bill had actually driven motorcycles in combat during World War I and knew these machines down to their tiniest nut and bolt. I assured John that I saw no harm in riding with Bill.

" 'Why?' John asked, with drawn-out deliberation.

" 'The script says so.'

◄

Victor McLaglen
and Margot
Grahame in John
Ford's *The
Informer*, a 1935
R.K.O.
production.

of shooting, he got the entire cast and crew together in the middle of the set, and he brought out the producer. 'Now get a good look at this guy,' Ford said and he took hold of the man's chin. 'This is Cliff Reid. He is the producer. Look at him now because you will not see him again on this set until the picture is finished.' And that was true—we never saw him again—he just disappeared."

"I was president of the Directors Guild in the 1950s," says Joseph L. Mankiewicz, "during the McCarthy Era, and a faction of the Guild, headed by deMille, tried to make it mandatory for every member to sign a loyalty oath. I was in Europe when the thing started, but as soon as they notified me, I sent word that, as president, I was very much against anything like that. Well, pretty soon, these little items about me started appearing in the gossip columns. 'Isn't it a pity about Joe Mankiewicz? We didn't know he was a pinko.' In those days, you know, an insinuation was almost as good as a proven fact. Well, it really got serious—I began to realize my career was on the block. They called a meeting of the entire Guild, finally, and I flew back for it. The entire membership showed up. It was harrowing —deMille's group made speeches—four hours it went on. And all during this, I was wondering, and I knew quite a few others were wondering, what John Ford thought. He was kind of the Grand Old Man of the Guild and people could be influenced by him. But he just sat there on the aisle wearing his baseball cap and sneakers, didn't say a word. Then after deMille had made *his* big speech, there was silence for a moment and Ford raised his hand. We had a court stenographer there to take it all down and everybody had to identify themselves for the record. So Ford stood up. 'My name's John Ford,' he said. 'I make Westerns.' He praised deMille's pictures and deMille as a director. 'I don't think there's anyone in this room,' he said, 'who knows more about what the American public wants than deMille—and he certainly knows how to give it to them.' Then he looked right at deMille, who was across the hall from him. 'But I don't like you, C.B.,' he said. 'And I don't like what you're saying here tonight. Now I move we give Joe a vote of confidence—and let's all go home and get some sleep.' And that's what they did."

" 'Well,' he said, taking a draw on his pipe, 'you don't always do what the script calls for, do you?'

" 'No, you know I don't. But this one seems reasonable.'

" 'Well, all right. But *I* wouldn't.' And with that he turned and walked away, still sucking on the dudeen.

"When time came for the shot, I dived out of the building on cue into the sidecar, and Bill jumped aboard the motorcycle. Now Bill was wearing hobnailed boots, and what neither of us realized at the time was that the rubber had worn off the motorcycle's brake pedal. We began our ride down a steeply graded hill, and to the right just beyond the hill's curve was what we call a parallel, a stand on which lights for the scene are hung. On this occasion, a little electrician stood in front of the parallel with an arc trained for the proper illumination. Bill and I roared down toward the curve, Bill's hobnailed boot slipped as he applied the brakes. Knowing that hitting the wall would be catastrophe, he turned left and we crashed into the parallel, hitting the electrician and breaking both his legs. The motorcycle handlebar whipped around, catching Bill in the groin, knocking him silly. Luckily, I had managed to brace myself as I put both arms in front of my face. I was stunned, but Bill and the electrician had to be taken to the hospital. Once they had been taken care of, I limped up the hill to find John Ford standing there, quietly sucking on his dudeen. As I drew abreast of him, he looked meditatively at me and said, 'What'd I tell ya?' "

"Ford was always a cop hater by religion, by belief," Robert Parrish remembers. "He had a big streak of contempt for any kind of authority, any kind of paternal influence on him—all the producers, all the money— they were the enemy. On *The Informer*, on the first day

248

KING REBEL

Recent newspaper photos of John Huston show him full of tubes, suffering from emphysema, confined to a wheelchair.

Then you look closer.

The son-of-a-gun is still pumping, still working, at the age of eighty-one. All the arteries are open. The brain cells and the vision are as on point as during his directorial debut, *The Maltese Falcon* (1941).

Who else would touch writers as diverse as James Joyce (*The Dead*), Malcolm Lowry (*Under the Volcano*) and Flannery O'Connor (*Wise Blood*)?

Who else would attempt the works of that mystical trio and when the work was done comfortably say: I did them just; I gave them their due.

John Huston could say that.

In *Under the Volcano* there was a drunken street scene of Albert Finney falling on his face in a small town in the mountains of Mexico. It was right on the mark: a magical mix of the writer Lowry, the director Huston and the actor Finney all collectively saying: we know this territory very, very well.

It was just one more take in a history of stunning takes.

Some details of a life well-spent: Huston was born on August 5, 1906, in Nevada, Missouri. Family legend has it that John's grandfather won the town in a poker game. It is rumored that John Huston also likes the feel of the cards.

John Huston is the son of Walter Huston, one of the great stage and film actors of his time. His mother was Rhea Gore Huston, a newspaperwoman and a lover of horses.

Among Huston's youthful diversions was a career as a lightweight boxer in California, winning twenty-two of twenty-five fights. He would later direct *Fat City*, one of the finest fight films ever made.

He was a Parisian street artist, a newspaper reporter in New York and a screenwriter of such films as *High Sierra*, *Sergeant York* and *The Killers*.

He owns an Academy Award for the direction of *The Treasure of the Sierra Madre*; the list of other awards is as long as his life. His films include *The Red Badge of Courage*, *The African Queen*, *The Asphalt Jungle*, *Moby Dick*, *Reflections in a Golden Eye*, *The Man Who Would Be King* and *Prizzi's Honor*.

John Huston is a man of Joycean understanding.

—J.P. O'Shea

◄ **The young John Huston.**

The Music Hall

▶

The beautiful Irish melodies of Stephen Foster (Don Ameche) break one more heart in the 1939 Twentieth-Century Fox production of Swanee River, as cowritten by Phillip Dunne, the son of the creator of "Mr. Dooley."

OLD FOLKS AT HOME

By Charles Hamm

▲
Antrim's Stephen Foster, America's finest nineteenth-century popular song composer.

Stephen Foster was of Irish extraction: his great-grandfather, Alexander Foster, emigrated from Derry in about 1728, eventually settling in Pennsylvania. Stephen grew up in a family conscious of its Irish heritage. He was raised in an emotional and cultural environment shaped in particular by the poems, songs, and sentiments of the Dublin poet and songwriter, Thomas Moore. Foster's older sister, Charlotte, was the family pianist, and her repertory is known to have included Moore's "Come Rest in This Bosom" and "Flow On, Thou Shining River."

The most relevant proof of Foster's acquaintance with Moore's songs, however, can be found in Foster's own music. Many of his songs, including some of the best, show clear traces of Irish ancestry.

As early a song as "The Spirit of My Song" (1850) has a first phrase outlining a pentatonic scale, as well as characteristic Irish rhythmic patterns. A pure example of Irish melody is "Sweetly She Sleeps, My Alice Fair" (1851). Again the opening phrase of the melody is pentatonic, and the tune is strongly reminiscent of several of Moore's "Irish Melodies," among them, "Has Sorrow Thy Young Days Shaded?"

Other songs by Foster showing strong resemblance to Irish tunes include "Mother, Thou'rt Faithful to Me" (1851), "Maggie by My Side" (1853), "Little Ella" (1853), "Willie, We Have Missed You" (1854), "I See Her Still in My Dreams" (1857), and "None Shall Weep a Tear for Me" (1860).

The most popular of all of Foster's "Irish Melodies" is "Jeanie with the Light Brown Hair," written in 1854. The melody is pentatonic throughout, except for two measures in the middle where a modulation to the dominant key takes place.

The text echoes many lines by Moore:

I hear her melodies, like joys gone by,
Sighing round my heart o'er the fond hopes that die: ...
Her smiles have vanished and her sweet songs flown,
Flitting like the dreams that have cheered us and gone.

It is inconceivable that this song could have been written had there not been a Thomas Moore.

Stephen Foster's first truly popular compositions

were, of course, his minstrel songs. These songs established his fame in America and abroad, and were the first Foster composed written in a style distinctly his own.

Foster became involved in minstrel music for the first time at the age of nine, when he became a member of a neighborhood "thespian" company performing in a makeshift theater in a nearby carriage house. It was not until a decade later, however, that Foster tried his hand at writing an "Ethiopian Melody" (as minstrel songs were first called) himself. About 1845, a group of young men calling themselves the Knights of the Square Table began meeting at the Foster house twice a week to practice "songs in harmony" with piano, guitar, flute, and fiddle to support the voices. As Morrison Foster, Stephen's brother, recalls:

At that time, Negro melodies were very popular. After we had sung over and over again all the songs then in favor, Stephen proposed that he would try and make some for us himself. His first effort was called "The Louisiana Belle." A week after this he produced the famous song "Old Uncle Ned."

"Oh! Susanna" is another one of the early songs written by Stephen for his friends in Pittsburgh. This is Foster's first song to be associated with the Christy Minstrels. Foster's name does not appear on the first edition of "Oh! Susanna," but the success of several of his songs on the minstrel stage prompted Firth, Pond & Co. in New York to bring out a set of his new minstrel songs that year with a cover featuring his name at the very top:

Foster's Ethiopian Melodies ...
As sung by the Christy Minstrels ...
Nelly was a Lady, My Brudder Gum, Dolcy Jones, Nelly Bly ...

The same firm brought out a set of four new songs later that year. By 1850 Foster had published a series of minstrel songs which had quickly become a staple in the minstrel show repertory. Their young composer, still in his midtwenties, was now recognized as one of

BEAUTIFUL DREAMER

By Stephen Foster

Beautiful dreamer, wake unto me,
Starlight and dewdrops are waiting for thee.
Sounds of the rude world heard in the day,
Lulled by the moonlight have all passed away.
Beautiful dreamer, queen of my song,
List while I woo thee with soft melody.
Gone are the cares of life's busy throng,

Beautiful dreamer, awake unto me,
Beautiful dreamer, awake unto me.

Beautiful dreamer, out on the sea
Mermaids are chanting the wild Lorelei,
Over the streamlet vapors are borne
Waiting to fade at the bright coming morn.
Beautiful dreamer, beam on my heart
E'en as the morn on the streamlet and sea,
Then will all clouds of sorrow depart.

Beautiful dreamer, awake unto me,
Beautiful dreamer, awake unto me.

FOSTER'S CHILD

The rains had stopped, and the fall winds had died down just a few hours before. A relieved crowd was now pouring into the open-air Greek Theatre in Berkeley. Van Morrison was back in town. The Belfast-born Irishman was returning to a community where he had once lived for many, many years.

At around nine in the evening, Morrison took the stage. Sitting up in the back of the theater, with a blanket on the still wet grass, it was possible to see all the lights going on across the Bay in nearby San Francisco.

Van Morrison in Berkeley.

Augmented this evening by a string quartet, the Morrison band struck up a number of perfectly familiar chords. The stage lights came on and began to swirl and cross the stage, and over the first few rows of the crowd. "It's a marvelous night for a moondance," the Irish gospel singer began to growl. In the audience, everyone and their friends began to melt in the early evening glow.

Perhaps more than any other rock musician of our time, Van Morrison has created a thoroughly multicultural, American popular music. Neither solely Irish, nor blues, nor gospel, nor jazz, nor even rock and roll, Morrison's music has become a very rich blend of all of these various root traditions.

It has become, in fact, an American music in a manner previously denied to the various roots musicians who created its elements in the first place. When Morrison's string quartet crested for a moment in the melodies of Stephen Foster, it was possible to say: "Van has reached out, and now he has got it all."

On this distant Berkeley hill, in the spiritual presence of all of his musical ancestors—Irish fiddlers, Delta blues singers, mariachi performers and lost gospel choirs—Morrison picked up the occasion, turned it inside out, and, to the sound of "Danny Boy" being played up-tempo on a small alto sax, Van the Man danced his audience all the way back home.

—Bob Callahan

the leading American composers of minstrel songs of his time.

Foster's five new minstrel songs, written between 1851 and 1853, represent the peak of his inspiration in this genre. Four of these songs remain among the most popular songs he ever wrote: "Old Folks at Home" (1851), "Farewell, My Lilly Dear" (1851), "Massa's in de Cold Ground" (1852), "My Old Kentucky Home" (1853), and "Old Dog Tray" (1853).

These songs also represent the virtual end of Foster's career as writer of minstrel music. Foster wrote a mere handful of minstrel songs in the last decade of his life. "Ellen Bayne" (1854) and "The Glendy Burk" (1860) were the best of the lot, and neither rises above a rehashing of the melodic and textual formulae of some of his earliest music.

Foster spent his last years composing a series of brilliant and wistful ballads, including "Old Black Joe" (1860) and "Beautiful Dreamer" (1863). Having sold off the rights to most of his songs for next to nothing— E.P. Christy, for example, had purchased the rights to "Old Folks at Home" for fifteen dollars—America's greatest nineteenth-century popular song composer died a destitute drunk in a fleabag hotel in New York City in 1864.

THE INCOMPARABLE BING

By Gilbert Seldes

As Gilbert Seldes is the "father" of American popular arts criticism, his remarks on the Great Crooner will be of particular interest to all those who recall Seldes' classic The Seven Lively Arts. *It is pleasurable to think of Bing Crosby, as Seldes begins, as one of the few guest vocalists Duke Ellington ever invited to sing with the Duke's great Cotton Club orchestra. It is also pleasurable to think of all the great Irish-American jazz artists—from the Dorsey Brothers to Gerry Mulligan, to John McClauglin—who have learned how to swing inside this unique Afro-American art form.*

Bing Crosby, 1934.

I t is a pleasure to think about Bing Crosby.

I had known Crosby as a pleasurable voice for a long time and I had also seen a few of his forgotten two-reel movies when I became aware of him in a new phase. He was wandering aimlessly about in his radio program and suddenly he said something about Marcel Proust. I discovered later that this sort of glancing reference to the intellectual life was one of the inventions of Carroll Carroll, Crosby's chief writer at the time. What I liked was the offhandedness. It was a throwaway gag line, and it was not even meant to cause more than the faintest ripple.

There was a sort of gentlemanly ease in Crosby's approach, an indifference to effect.

And this makes it all the more remarkable that Crosby is the man who, all by himself, almost wrecked the whole radio network broadcasting system in the United States and did, in effect, profoundly alter many of that system's most cherished practices. Remarkable but entirely in keeping with the Crosby character, because Crosby wanted to be easy about a lot of things, and the network wouldn't let him. They had an idea that a radio program on the air at nine P.M., Pacific Standard Time, required the presence of the star in the studio at nine P.M., not to mention rehearsals the same day —all of which interfered with Crosby's inalienable right to pursue golf balls or fish whenever and wherever he pleased.

An invention showed Crosby how to circumvent the opposition: the machine that records sound, on a disc, on a wire, on a tape—it hardly mattered. The moment a record was made, it began to be possible for the east coast to hear Crosby at nine in the evening and for Idaho to hear him also at nine—their time, not the time of the radio bosses in New York. It became possible for Crosby's program to be spotted on one station on a Wednesday and on twenty others on Friday, if this was more advantageous to the sponsor—if, for instance, in certain regions Crosby's regular time conflicted with the broadcast of local sporting events.

Now, in those days, the managers of network broadcasting had an almost supernatural regard for the idea of a network, and they were justified in this because in a sense networks did not exist, but were in a way mythological entities. The network was a great creative force in broadcasting. Programs were created in the studios of the principal stations, and then made available to affiliates. The network became the financial web which held all of these various stations together. The network became, in fact, among the most profitable group of corporations in the entire economy. The thought, therefore, that Crosby's maverick practices might cause networks to crumble was highly displeasing.

And yet Mr. Crosby persisted. Presently it was discovered that people did not know whether the program was prerecorded or not. It was also discovered that the networks continued to thrive. Actually, Crosby had done them a good turn: he made them flexible at the point when they were threatened by a hardening of the arteries—a dreadful, but common enough, disease in the communications business.

It is pleasant to think of Bing Crosby in still another way: as the savior of the small radio station. There was a time, not so long ago, when it was truthfully said that no hour of the day or night, year after year, passed without the voice of Bing Crosby being heard somewhere on this earth; indeed, on the album with which a grateful Decca commemorated Crosby's activities, there appears the statement (which Decca should have printed in solid gold instead of mere gold ink): "The voice of Bing Crosby has been heard by more people than the voice of any other human being who ever lived." We do not always arrive at the standards of excellence by the sheer weight of numbers, but it is a satisfaction to discover an excellence so artless and so unaggressive being recognized in this statistically supreme way. There are those who are certain that Russ Columbo, had he lived, would have outstripped Crosby; there are benighted ones who think that someone else (and they made the oddest choices) actually sang better in the style than Crosby. They are, I am sure, misled, misguided and (in the theological sense) invincibly ignorant. Crosby sings best. And, as we have seen, he also sings most.

He is himself authority for the legend that a node on his vocal cords was to be removed, but the family lacked money (and it is a fair bet that the young Bing was not anxious to do anything about it). He (or a pleasant press agent) carries on the legend of a series of accidental meetings, half-formed decisions and driftings that brought him in 1926 to Paul Whiteman and his first recording, "Muddy Water." He has made over two thousand separate recordings since—not bad for an easygoing man whose artistic symbol is the half-out, many-colored sport shirt.

The radio business was just beginning to get its growth in 1926; ten years later the small stations were dotted over the land, the 250-watters, the ones they called "coffeepots," which played recordings all day long and some of them all night as well, and often played nothing but Crosby records for hours at a time. Around the Crosby records—and, for all I know, interrupting the records—the little stations brought in their endless local commercials. It was not great creative broadcasting, but presently the techniques were refined and the disc jockey became an established presence in broadcasting. The establishment of the disc jockey led, in turn, to the development of strong local personality programs in radio and, later, in television. Once again, the influence of Crosby pops up. To be sure, you can say that the stations would have used other records if there had been no Crosby—but if we go in for ifs, how do we know that the broadcasting of records would have paid off as well if there had not been this constant stream of Bing.

FIFTH AVENUE DAYS

They probably closed it down more than twenty years ago, but there once was a walk-down bar off Fifth Avenue, somewhere between East 10th and East 12th Streets, where, once a week, I would come downtown from Morningside Heights and have a few beers with a couple of home boys attending graduate school at nearby N.Y.U.

Like most, but not all, neighborhood bars, this walk-down could also be judged by the quality of its jukebox. Mostly standard fare, as I recall, with the profound exception of a single tune recorded on April 13, 1936, by Bunny Berigan and his Boys, called "I Can't Get Started with You."

Berigan still remains today somewhat of a mystery. He was Irish. He drank too much. He often sang and played trumpet like an angel. With the exception of a long Whitney Balliett piece in an old issue of *The New Yorker*, you will not find much information on him beyond mere notes on certain album covers.

Balliett respected Berigan enormously, placing him ultimately in the same class with a small number of other early jazz trumpet masters including Louis Armstrong, Bix Beiderbecke and Jabbo Smith.

256

and a white coat from the proseeds of selling the jalloppy and hocking the ring. I rehearsed with the band altho Collins the leader hates my guts and finely I talked the asst mgr into letting me do a single irregardless of the band and he did.

Well you might say I ran the opening nite. I m.c'd and they had a couple kids from a local dancing school doing tap, one of them not bad altho no serious competition for Ginger Rogers. They were only on for the first week. They also had another mouse who was with the band, living with the drummer. She tried to be like Maxine. Well she wasnt even colored, thats how much like Maxine she was. The local 400 turned out for the opening nite and inside a week I was besieged with offers to entertain at private parties which I do nearly every Sunday as the bar and ballroom are not open Sunday or at least I do not work. In addition to the job at the hotel and the private parties you probably have read about the radio job. I went on sustaining the first week and by the end of the second week I got myself a nice little commercial. I am on just before the local station hooks up with NBC Blue Network five nites a week but I dont think you can catch me in New York. Not yet! My sponsor is the Acme Credit Jewellery Company but I only have eight more weeks to go with them then I am free to negosiate with a better sponsor. Still Im not complaining. Your old pal Joey is doing all right for himself. I get a due bill at the hotel and what they pay me in additon aint hay. I also have the radio spot and the private parties. I went for a second hand Lasalle coop and I am thinking of joining the country club. I go there all the time with some of the local 400 so I figure I might as well join but will wait till I make sure I am going to stay here. I get my picture in the paper and write ups so much that I dont even bother to put them in my scrap book any more.

The crowd at the club are always ribbing me about it and accuse me of having the reporters on my payroll but I just tell them no, not the reporters, the editors. I am a little sore at one of the papers because the local Winchell links my name constantly with a very sweet kid that I go to the club and play golf with. Not that it isnt true. We see each other all the time and she comes to the hotel practically every nite with a party and when Im through for the nite we usely take a ride out to a late spot out in the country. Her father is president of the second largest bank. It is the oldest. The biggest bank was formally two banks but they merged. Her name is Jean Spencer and a sweeter kid never lived. I really go for her. But this local Winchell took a personal dislike to me and made a couple cracks about us. One was "That personality boy at a downtown hotel has aired the femme that got him the job and is now trying to move into society." Me trying to move into society! Society moved in on me is more like it. Jean was burned because she was afraid her father might see the item and when I meet her father I dont want him to have the wrong impression. I think the colyumist got the item from my ex-friend Nan. I didnt see much of her when I was rehearsing and the afternoon of opening nite she called up and said she wanted to come but what the hell could I do? Ask for a big table when they were getting $5 a head cover charge? I was glad enough to get the job without asking too many favors. Then a week or so later she called up and asked me could I let her have $50. I asked her what for and she hung up. Well if she didnt even want to do me the curtesy to tell me what for I wasnt going to follow her around begging her to take it. But I gave it a few days thought and decided to let her have it but when I phoned her they said she quit her job and left town. I understand from Schall the asst mgr that she sold her Plymouth and went to N.Y. Her name is Nan Hennessey so if you run into her anywhere youll know her. She could be worse, that is worse on the eye, a little dumb tho.

Well pally, they will be billing me for stealing all their writing paper if I dont quit this. Just to show you I dont forget I inclose $30. Ill let you have the rest as soon as possible. Any time I can help you out the same way just let me know and you can count on me. I guess you kissed that fifty goodbye but that isn't the way I do things. But I guess you know that, hey pal?

All the best from
Pal Joey

EDDIE COCHRAN

By John Tobler

The enduring memory of Eddie Cochran in most people's minds is of a fairly typical young James Dean type, an all-American boy, tall, dark and handsome, who only looked complete with a guitar slung round his neck. The reality was a little different. Despite his moody image, the real Eddie Cochran wasn't really cast in the James Dean mold, but was ordinary in most ways. Except one—he was quite a brilliant musician, composer and singer.

Eddie was born on October 3, 1938 in Albert Lea, Minnesota, the youngest of five children in a family who had been forced to move away from their previous home in Oklahoma City by the Depression. He first began to play the guitar at the age of twelve and was besotted with country and western music, teaching himself to play country hits on his instrument.

In 1953, the family moved again, this time to California, although by this time most of his brothers and sisters had left home, and the young Eddie began to practice very hard on his guitar to combat the resulting solitude, which he hadn't experienced before. This led on to the formation of a small group who played for local functions, and in 1955, he met Jerry Capehart, who later became Eddie's cowriter. Capehart organized Eddie's first recording session, for an almost unknown label,

Blackboard Jungle, *cultural historians tell us, was one of those "art events" that come along every twenty years, or so, and help kick off a new cultural revolution. The theme music for this particular revolution was supplied by Bill Haley and The Comets. The theme song was "Rock Around the Clock." Haley was Irish. So was Haley's contemporary, the far more talented and mysterious Eddie Cochran. The road that led from Bill Haley and Eddie Cochran to the contemporary music of John Fogerty and Jim Carroll is by now perfectly obvious.*

but the single that was released was an instant flop. Capehart and Cochran then began to work on making demonstration discs for a publishing company, many of these recordings being commercially released after Eddie's death. They are ample proof that even at the age of sixteen, Eddie Cochran was a guitarist to be reckoned with.

However, he plumped for stardom rather than a steady living and, after releasing another single on a minor label, signed up with the newly formed Liberty Records. The year was 1957, and Eddie had also been signed up for a cameo part in what has come to be recognized as the finest rock 'n' roll film ever made, *The Girl Can't Help It*. Strangely, the song Eddie performed in the film, "Twenty Flight Rock," wasn't his debut single for Liberty—instead, a John D. Loudermilk song, "Sittin' In The Balcony," was released, became a hit during May 1957, and was followed up by "Twenty Flight Rock," which just failed to make the top twenty. Both records have fine guitar breaks by Eddie, who was one of the very few people who played lead guitar on their own records at that time.

Cochran and Capehart came up with a song in March 1958 which finally established Cochran as a topflight star. It was "Summertime Blues," the only single that Eddie made which went top twenty in both Britain and America. In 1959, "C'Mon Everybody" did nearly as well in America, better in Britain, and Eddie began to tour on both sides of the Atlantic, developing into as big a live act as he was on record, and proving that he could do on stage everything that he did in the studio.

But by that time, Eddie was looking to the future. He was still making great records, such as "Something Else," "Hallelujah I Love Her So," "Teenage Heaven," "Cut Across Shorty" and several others. But being a rock 'n' roll star was not all that Eddie wanted—

260

hit records were desirable, certainly, but by this time he also had a steady girlfriend, Sharon Sheely, and his idea was to settle down in semiretirement before long.

Unfortunately, that wasn't to be. In early 1960, Eddie embarked on a British tour with Gene Vincent, which went so well that it was extended for several months. (George Harrison followed the caravan from city to city, watching Eddie's fingers to memorize the licks.) On April 17, 1960, he was traveling in a limousine with Gene Vincent and Sharon Sheely, when a tire burst, and the car ran hard into a lamppost. While Gene and Sharon survived the crash, Eddie sustained multiple head injuries from which he died a few hours later in the hospital without regaining consciousness.

Subsequently, Eddie Cochran scored his biggest hit, ironically titled "Three Steps To Heaven," and a couple of other singles also hit the British charts in the year following his death, "Lonely" and "Weekend." It's odd that Cochran was so much more popular in Britain than in America at the time of his death. It may have been that he perfectly fitted the British idea of the American rock 'n' roll star, a novelty in Britain but commonplace in the States—and this accounted for his relative lack of recognition in his own country. ❧

THE BIRTH OF ROCK AND ROLL

The only good thing about this new neighborhood up here in Inwood is the giant park and the woods. They've got these incredible Indian caves way in deep with all kinds of tunnels and shit you can climb around in. This fat guy got stuck in one the other day and the fire department came and popped him out. It took five big guys pulling on a rope to do it. Funny scene. Up at the caves is this old man every day, name of Bill. He gives out chocolate bars and got this big jug of apple cider we swig on and he plays the flute all day with some weird sound that carries out through the whole woods and a lot of birds come around and squirrels and he tosses bread-crumbs and nuts to them. He's like a saint. My cousin says he's been there since his old man was a little kid. There's one incredibly steep long hill called "Deadman's" that's fantastic for sleigh riding in the winter, but now it's almost summer and in some parts the green is so dense it's like tropical jungles or something. Way up top is a meadow, and past that a cliff overlooking the Hudson. I come up myself and smoke reefer when I have some (can't get it up in this lame place so I get a little off Bunky on 29th when I go down to the old neighborhood once in a while) and watch the boats going up along the Palisades. Today I smoked with Willie, the only guy from the school that smokes too, and we watched two jets moving across the sky like it was flat and they were racing on one long strip. I just want to be high and live in these woods. Screw all the rest like Saint Bill down at the caves.

—Jim Carroll

The Uillean Piper Division of the Chicago Police Department.

When the Irish arrived in America, they brought their fiddles with them. Chicago's Francis O'Neill was "the music's" first great American scholar. Count John McCormack may have been the first great Irish tenor most Americans ever heard. Michael Coleman, James Morrison and Paddy Killoran were only three of Sligo's great fiddlers to be recorded in America for the first time. This remains an active tradition. Thanks to the efforts of a brilliant generation of contemporary Irish traditional musicians, some of the finest traditional Irish music ever played is still being played in the small clubs and bars of America today.

THE POLICEMAN AND THE PIPER

By Peter O'Neill and Eddie Stack

By the turn of this century there was probably more traditional Irish music being played in America than there was back in the "Old Country." Irish music was nurtured and revered in America and it is not surprising that the most significant contribution to its survival and preservation came from the United States. It was here that the bible of Irish music was compiled, *The Dance Music of Ireland* (1907), by an Irish immigrant, Francis O'Neill.

Born in Tralibane in West Cork in 1849, O'Neill learned to play the flute early in life and was an accomplished musician by the age of fourteen. But Tralibane could not contain young Francis and at the age of sixteen he ran away from home and made his way to Cork City. Yearning to see more of the world, O'Neill went to sea as a deckhand, a career that almost came to grief when he was shipwrecked in the mid-Pacific some few years later. Finding his land legs in San Francisco, Francis said goodbye to the mariner's life and found employment in the New World. The wanderlust was still with him, though. Working as a railway clerk, schoolteacher, and even as a herdsman, he roved throughout the United States, finally reaching Chicago, where he entered the police force in 1873.

Being a major center for the Irish, Chicago had a thriving community of traditional musicians from many parts of Ireland. Francis soon became immersed in this hive of cultural activity. Before too long he realized the wealth of musical material all around him and he set about collecting it for preservation. There was one problem, though. While he had a keen ear and excellent memory for tunes, he was unable to put them down upon paper. To achieve this he turned to his fellow policeman, James O'Neill, a fiddler from County Down who could read and write music.

Initially, the tunes were noted down by James from the playing, whistling, humming, lilting, and singing of the various contributors. With the tune reproduced on paper, James would play the piece back on the fiddle, comments would be solicited, and the appropriate adjustments made. At the time there was no thought about having this work published, but as mate-

THE MINSTREL LAD FROM ATHLONE

The fact that I don't know the difference between an arpeggio and a coloratura soprano is doubtless what led to my assignment to cover John McCormack's concert in San Diego last night. City editors have an unnatural way of shoveling out stories to the reporter who knows next to nothing about the subject on hand.

◀ Count John McCormack.

Nevertheless a fellow at the theater, who had heard McCormack sing somewhere back east, told me I would enjoy the affair, that McCormack sang a number of songs we all heard in our younger days.

As to that, however, I had some doubts when I saw the program. I learned that this Irish tenor—whom the phonograph people say they made famous, much in the same way Mr. John McGraw might speak of Mr. Christopher Mathewson—was going to sing an aria by the justly celebrated Mr. Handel.

And when I heard him do this I still had some doubts, for it all sounded miles away from anything like what Souza or Cohan has written. Besides, I noticed that the most applause came from the chaps in dress suits and the ladies in dress to match. In fact, their applause was furious, not to say superior.

It was when the Irishman came back for his encore that I realized the truth of what my friend had been saying. McCormack began with some old Irish folk songs, with the lilt of the old island still in them, and love, and romance, and a bit of mischief too. Then, by and by, he sang "I Hear You Calling Me," and I went to the back of the hall because the tears had come into my eyes.

In the back I met a local musical expert. This man has a fine tenor voice, and often sings for money. Timidly I asked him how McCormack stood among the great singers. "Good Lord, man," he said, "if I had that voice—if I could only reproduce those tones—I'd give my socks, my shoes, my shirt—everything I own!"

At the end of the concert they all stood up and applauded, and McCormack came back and sang again to that great audience, one of the largest ever seen at a musical event in San Diego.

I'd go again to hear this man sing without being sent.

—*William Flynn*

Captain Francis O'Neill.

rial accumulated, the value of the publication became obvious.

The Music of Ireland appeared in 1903. Easily the biggest collection of Irish music ever published, this work contained almost 2,000 pieces, including marches, slow airs, and a staggering total of 1,100 dance tunes. More than half the collection was contributed by the Irish residents of Chicago.

Although this massive work must have been a time-consuming task, it did not interfere with Francis' political career. By 1901 he had risen to the rank of chief superintendent of the Chicago police force. His collaborator, James O'Neill, somehow achieved the rank of sergeant. It was well known that any Irish immigrant with the gift of traditional musicianship was readily accepted into the ranks of Chicago's finest.

Retiring from the force in 1905, Francis had more time to spend with his beloved music, and in 1907, the bible appeared—*The Dance Music of Ireland*. This later edition contains 1,100 dance tunes—important works from the first book are reprinted, and it includes many new tunes and variations. The book won immediate approval and ensured the survival and preservation of a music that might have otherwise perished.

O'Neill's work is probably the greatest single contribution made to Irish music in modern times. The fact that it is still the definitive reference book on Irish dance music today—eighty years after its first appearance—is in itself a fitting tribute to Chief O'Neill and the Irish musicians of America. ❧

IRISH MUSICIANS
By Terence Winch

The Irish Riviera

I wish I could remember the names
of these two old guys I used to see
when I was a kid and spent my summers
in Rockaway   which was known as The Irish Riviera
one of them played the fiddle   the other played
the accordion   and I think one of them wore
a top hat   they just wandered in and out of bars
playing for drinks   they were like bums
but I still remember how fine they sounded

Johnny Lynch's Reputation

Johnny Lynch's reputation rested on
his ability to sing
dance
and play the accordion
all at once
at the age of thirty what hair he had
was gray
he was pink and chubby
an alcoholic
simple minded
kind hearted
he said the rosary every night
he would pick up Wheeling West Virginia
on the radio at about 4 a.m.
and would kneel down by his bed
and listen to the music

Mike and Ike

my brother Jesse whose name is really James
just told me on the phone that the names
of those two Rockaway musicians were
Mike and Ike
and that they were in the great tradition
of Irish street singers

Club House Gangs

▶

*An era passes as Frank
Skeffington (Spencer Tracy)
gets the bad news in the 1958
Columbia production of John
Ford's* The Last Hurrah, *based on Edwin O'Connor's
marvelous, thinly disguised
novel on the exploits of the
great James Michael Curley.*

THE POL

By George V. Higgins

Off to the southwest behind the two-story brick building that served as the high school for Rockland, Massachusetts, in the 1940s and 1950s, there was a large patch of land with a pine grove. There on clement evenings the local swains repaired to pursue and feel up the girls who also went there, for some reason or other.

On the other side of the pine grove was the railroad track, where a contemporary of mine, it's alleged, recently murdered a fellow much younger, and beyond that was a factory that made shoes and had bats in its attic. The bats came out in the evening, too, and flew through the pine grove and did a whole lot more business than the local swains. But the bats were faster and could see in the dark, I guess, or something.

About the time I got old enough to hear, with wide-eyed wonderment, how my older acquaintances had damned near sprained their wrists in fruitless struggles with those goddamned armor-plated panty girdles, some prematurely aging genius rightfully decided that, Rockland being a football town, the otherwise unused greensward could be put to better purpose by construction of a football stadium upon it. And he was right, too, unless there was a lot more truth than I thought in what I later decided to be lies.

When they got the stadium up, they called it a memorial to Rockland's veterans and held a dedication exercise. It pretty largely bored nearly everybody—it was a very hot day, as I recall it—except one of the invited guests. His name was James Michael Curley, former mayor of Boston, former governor of Massachusetts, and former inmate of the federal correctional institution at Danbury, Connecticut (mail fraud).

Governor Curley never permitted himself a dotage, but he was certainly not in his heyday then, either, twenty-five-plus years ago, and to be frank, I wonder now why the hell he bothered to show up. For the same reason that I would be perplexed by the agitation of an old war-horse whiffing cordite.

My grandfather, for reasons that were more important then than they are now, had run for town treasurer of Rockland for many, many years, and after he won once was never defeated (he ran because he was part of an Irish-American cabal of storekeepers and lawyers, and a Swamp Yankee cabal of doctors and automobile dealers, none of whom saw any particular reason why they should take, lying down, the plain disinclination of the better classes to share the business with them). I want to make it perfectly clear that Charlie Higgins was no goddamned politician. He was my grandfather, a good and decent man who worked very hard, at never less than a couple of jobs at once, and furthermore he was a plain pushover for me. So, of course, I loved him. He was a good, tough man, dead honest, abstemious, churchgoing, and generous to a fault.

On that hot day, James Michael Curley recognized that minor town official then retired, who was my grandfather, and came over to him at Memorial Park and said to "Charlie" that it was very good to see him again after so long. Then my grandfather introduced me to the governor—I suppose I was, oh, ten or so, not much more than that—and for an embarrassingly long time after that, I thought he *was* the governor. Furthermore, since my grandfather was so plainly pleased to make that introduction, I thought that it was probably a very good thing to be governor, and that the man who was—this was long before "persons" became governors, at least around here—was therefore an admirable fellow.

Now, like the rest of us (except for Curley and my grandfather, who are dead), I am older and have more sense. In the 1960s I got less practical education than I wanted, but perhaps more than I needed, in the realities of politics. So now I know, I guess, what fools we are. What a fool I was.

The late Rep. Julius Ansel, of the Massachusetts general court, perished of a heart attack, most probably to his considerable astonishment. He was a small round man who smoked cigars and did not have his clothes pressed regularly and spoke from the corner of his mouth, and he had dozens of heart attacks, virtually all of them in public, before the one that carried him off. To Julie, who once dropped a lady off a stretcher after she'd had an attack on a plane, heart seizures were not medical problems but parliamentary devices, and it was difficult for him to take them seriously.

What he did take seriously was staying in office and being useful to the other Democrats who ran the House of Representatives. The first objective inspired him to install a VHF radio in his home in Mattapan and use

His Honor, James
Michael Curley
of Boston.

it to monitor the police band. It was that practice which got him to Logan International Airport in time to bound up the stairs before the door of the airplane was opened the night the lady from his district collapsed en route from Florida. It was that which enabled him to emerge from the plane with the leading edge of the stretcher, whereupon he became so dazzled by the lights of Channel 4 news cameras that he raised his hand to shield his eyes (not to wave as some meanly suggested) and dumped the lady about twelve feet to the Tarmac.

Both the lady, in life, and Julie, in office, survived that experience, a result which permitted Julie to continue in his conspicuous service to the House leadership, who incidentally apportioned districts, and patronage, among reps like Julie who were vitally interested in such matters. Julie did not attend the legislature in order that he might in some small way participate in advancing and maintaining the Commonwealth's position as foremost among the states of the Union (although, to be sure, if you asked him that, in those terms, and made it plain to him that you preferred an affirmation that he did, you would have gotten one); he attended and strove valiantly to keep his membership privileges, because he was a politician and that's what politicians do. He got jobs and contracts for people in his district who needed jobs and contracts. He made calls to the registry for people in his district who misplaced their driving licenses by handing them to state troopers who suspected them of driving under the influence and later proved it in court. He was sympathetic, and effectively sympathetic, to storekeepers with inspection problems, respectable citizens with unemployed offspring, lawyers who wanted to be judges (that was the hardest thing for a state rep to deliver), the lame, the halt and the blind. He got his effectiveness in part by simulating heart attacks.

Julius Ansel knew his place. Around prorogation time, when the merrier of the reps were giving each other ten pennies to rack back the hands of the clock moving toward midnight, he could discern the Speaker's signal that there was time needed for hard conversations in the cloak room and the corridors, and maybe in the pub across the street from the State House, in the old Hotel Bellevue. So he would have one of his heart attacks, rising dramatically from his seat, sometimes slumping forward, at other times of great exigency collapsing on the floor, and the Speaker would exclaim: "Brother Ansel has had a heart attack. This House will be in recess." The House would go get done what needed to be done, while Julie, miraculously, revived, accepted plaudits and refreshments in a convenient bar.

It was in the late 1950s—I am no surer of this date than I was of the others, and therefore omit it—that I was in Boston one day with three or four seventeen- or eighteen-year-olds like myself, walking along Beacon Street near the State House, leather jacketed, smoking cigarettes, wearing Levis and boots, trying god-awful hard to look tough and hoping two things: that the home-forbidden ducktails we'd put into our hair after leaving the house had not come out, and that somehow, somewhere in the sinful city, what we'd been unable to accomplish in the pine grove behind Memorial Stadium would be achieved, miraculously, on the pavements of the city. It wasn't.

Down the steps of the State House came an old man, a very old man by then as shrunken in his own suit and shirt as he'd appeared to be in the oversize suit and shirt he bought to wear before the House of Representatives to buttress his claim for clemency with an appearance of failing health. What the hell James Michael Curley was doing at the State House on that day, I do not know.

In any event, I did not recognize him. But, at the foot of the stairs, he stopped and scanned us and made us stop by coming up to me. He shook my hand and said: "How are you George?" and asked me how my grandfather was doing. I am ashamed to say that I did not know his name. He had to tell me. ❧

Jimmy Walker's Long Ride

Walker's absences from city hall were being commented upon by some of the newspapers. The *Herald Tribune* pointed out that Mayor Walker had taken several vacations during his first two years in office, for a total of one hundred and forty-three days, and had visited London, Paris, Berlin, Rome, Houston, Hollywood, San Francisco, Atlanta, Bermuda, Florida, Canada, Havana, and Louisville for the Kentucky Derby. The city as a whole, however, looked upon Walker as an ambassador of goodwill. Besides, the stock market kept riding high—with here and there a day of recession and then a swift recovery—and the voices of critics were lost in the roar of speculative trade.

Al Smith had several times endeavored to confer with Jim, but Walker, disliking lectures, had played the duck. The governor, however, did not have any moral preachments in mind. Rather, he sought to enlist Jim's aid in quieting the transit problems of the city, so that he could devote himself wholly to the larger issues of the presidential campaign.

When Al Smith called again at city hall and found that Jim was out, he said, "If you make a date with Jim in December, he will keep it next May."

The traction interests were pounding away at Smith for legislation to authorize an increase in subway fares. The governor set the day for a hearing in Albany on this matter. The noted attorney De Lancey Nicoll was to argue the case for the companies. Al Smith notified Walker to be present at the executive chamber on the appointed morning to argue in behalf of the city of New York.

Mr. Nicoll and his brief-bag bearers arrived at Albany at ten o'clock on the morning of the hearing. When Walker did not appear, Governor Smith's secretary did some telephoning. Walker had missed his train for Albany and would be an hour late.

The hearing was postponed until eleven o'clock. When the eminent Mr. Nicoll and his assistants, and as large a group of citizens as could be accommodated in the executive chamber, reappeared, Walker was still missing. Smith restrained his anger with some difficulty. A second telephone call to New York disclosed that Jim had missed another train but was surely on his way to the capitol in his town car.

It was almost four o'clock in the afternoon when Jim, looking somewhat sleepy-eyed and off the beam, reported to the governor in the anteroom of the executive chamber. Smith upbraided him privately. He inquired of Jim if he thought he was a "fit representative of a great city to be wasting the time of the governor?"

Beau James in Hollywood, with Colleen Moore on vocals.

He gruffly ordered Walker to "go in there and listen, and then speak, if you can."

It did not improve Al Smith's disposition any when the crowd applauded the tardy Jim. The dignified Mr. Nicoll pretended to be unruffled and, at a word from the governor, delivered his speech. The great lawyer spoke for an hour or so in behalf of a fare of more than five cents. When Mr. Nicoll had finished, Al Smith turned to Walker. "The mayor of the city of New York will now reply."

Jim rose, as jaunty as you please, did his usual handkerchief trick, then said in reference to the lawyer's lengthy speech, "Gentlemen, that was the longest ride I ever had on a Nicoll."

This remark set off such hilarity among the spectators that Smith had to bellow for order.

From this moment on Jim held the stage. He said that he didn't mind if the traction people charged as much as a dollar for a subway ride, provided they could and would guarantee every passenger a seat, and not crowd the citizens of New York like cattle into the filthy cars. He said that transit officials themselves had admitted to him that they could not possibly put more cars or equipment into the existing subways, and that until they remedied this condition it was useless and illogical for the subway owners to ask for higher fare for inferior service.

Mr. Nicoll left Albany a defeated man.

—*Gene Fowler*

George Washington Plunkitt was born in a shantytown called Nanny Goat Hill on Manhattan's upper West Side. He died wealthy and renowned in 1924 at the age of eighty-two. According to his biographer, Arthur Mann, Plunkitt's claim to fame derived from a series of very plain talks on certain practical political skills he gave at the turn of the century. But Plunkitt was not a writer. He was a Tammany Hall ward boss. As Mann explains, "Plunkitt became an author thanks to a chance meeting with William L. Riordon of the New York Evening Post, *who interviewed him and preserved his political philosophy for posterity." Bath House John Coughlin and Hinky Dink Kenna grew up in more or less the same school and bestowed their own Plunkitt-like wisdom upon the old First Ward in Chicago.*

ON HONEST GRAFT
By George Washington Plunkitt
with William L. Riordan

Everybody is talkin' these days about Tammany man growin' rich on graft, but nobody thinks of drawin' the distinction between honest graft and dishonest graft. There's all the difference in the world between the two. Yes, many of our men have grown rich in politics. I have myself. I've made a big fortune out of the game, and I'm gettin' richer every day, but I've not gone in for dishonest graft—blackmailin' gamblers, saloonkeepers, disorderly people, etc.—and neither had any of the men who have made big fortunes in politics.

There's an honest graft, and I'm an example of how it works. I might sum up the whole thing by sayin': "I seen my opportunities and I took 'em."

Just let me explain by examples. My party's in power in the city, and it's goin' to undertake a lot of public improvements. Well, I'm tipped off, say, that they're going to lay out a new park at a certain place.

I see my opportunity and I take it. I go to that place and I buy up all the land I can in the neighborhood. Then the board of this or that makes its plan public, and there is a rush to get my land, which nobody cared particular for before.

Ain't it perfectly honest to charge a good price and make a profit on my investment and foresight? Of course, it is. Well, that's honest graft.

Or supposin' it's a new bridge they're goin' to build. I get tipped off and I buy as much property as I can that has to be taken for approaches. I sell at my own price later on and drop some more money in the bank.

Wouldn't you? It's just like lookin' ahead in Wall Street or in the coffee or cotton market. It's honest graft, and I'm lookin' for it every day in the year. I will tell you frankly that I've got a good lot of it, too.

271

I'll tell you of one case. They were goin' to fix up a big park, no matter where. I got on to it, and went lookin' about for land in that neighborhood.

I could get nothin' at a bargain but a big piece of swamp, but I took it fast enough and held on to it. What turned out was just what I counted on. They couldn't make the park complete without Plunkitt's swamp, and they had to pay a good price for it. Anything dishonest in that?

Up in the watershed I made some money, too. I bought up several bits of land there some years ago and made a pretty good guess that they would be bought up for water purposes later by the city.

Somehow, I always guessed about right and shouldn't I enjoy the profit of my foresight? It was rather amusin' when the condemnation commissioners came along and found piece after piece of the land in the name of George Plunkitt of the Fifteenth Assembly District, New York City. They wondered how I knew just what to buy. The answer is—I seen my opportunity and I took it. I haven't confined myself to land; anything that pays is in my line.

For instance, the city is repavin' a street and has several hundred thousand old granite blocks to sell. I am on hand to buy, and I know just what they are worth.

How? Never mind that. I had a sort of monopoly of this business for a while, but once a newspaper tried to do me. It got some outside men to come over from Brooklyn and New Jersey to bid against me.

Was I done? Not much. I went to each of the men and said: "How many of these 250,000 stones do you want?" One said 20,000, and another wanted 15,000, and the other wanted 10,000. I said: "All right, let me bid for the lot, and I'll give each of you all you want for nothin'."

They agreed, of course. Then the auctioneer yelled: "How much am I bid for these 250,000 fine pavin' stones?"

"Two dollars and fifty cents," says I.

"Two dollars and fifty cents!" screamed the auctioneer. "Oh, that's a joke! Give me the real bid."

He found the bid was real enough. My rivals stood silent. I got the lot for $2.50 and gave them their share. That's how the attempt to do Plunkitt ended, and that's how all such attempts end.

I've told you how I got rich by honest graft. Now, let me tell you that most politicians accused of robbin' the city get rich the same way.

They didn't steal a dollar from the city treasury. They just seen their opportunities and took them. That is why, when a reform administration comes in and spends a half-million dollars in tryin' to find the public robberies they talked about in the campaign, they don't find them.

The books are always all right. The money in the city treasury is all right. Everything is all right. All they can show is that the Tammany heads of departments looked after their friends, within the law, and gave them what opportunities they could to make honest graft. Now, let me tell you that's never goin' to hurt Tammany with the people. Every man looks after his friends, and any man who doesn't isn't likely to be popular. 🐾

BATH HOUSE JOHN AND HINKY DINK KENNA

"Bath House John" Coughlin and "Hinky Dink" Kenna were the joint bosses of Chicago's First Ward.

"The Bath" and "Hinky Dink" ruled politically in the vice-saturated First Ward for approximately the half century from 1890 to 1940. They were legendary characters. The Bath was the bumbling and none too bright extrovert, while Hinky Dink was the shrewd and laconic introvert. They indeed resembled characters in the old Laurel and Hardy movies. The Bath, with his gaily colored waistcoat, his inability to speak a coherent sentence, his penchant for owning racehorses which couldn't or wouldn't run, and his sponsorship of absurd songs such as "They Buried Her by the Side of the Drainage Canal" and "Dear Midnight of Love," is, in a sense, as irresistibly funny as the Keystone Cops.

But not so was his partner, Hinky Dink. "The Hink" knew the price of everything and, his opponents alleged, the value of nothing. It was charged that every saloon, every gambler, every prostitute had to come across at rates which were presumably fixed according to their ability to pay. Mike, with his aides, saw to it that this was done and that the vote was delivered on primary and election days.

I have always thought that Hinky Dink had the makings of a great idiomatic Latin scholar, for in his saloon across the longest bar in the world he had blazoned in bold letters, *In Vino Veritas*. When asked what that meant, he replied, "It means that when a man's drunk he gives his right name." I have never heard any of my professorial colleagues do better than that.

—*Justice Paul Douglas*

▲

John J. (Bath House John) Coughlin.

◄

Michael (Hinky Dink) Kenna.

WALT KELLY

Walt Kelly came from the generalized comedy of human beings trying to be important, and his natural target was politicians. He had this unique view of human politics and how it worked—the buffoonery of people trying to look solemn and important who were actually out doing evil things.

He would look about when he came to Washington in the rain, notice the sea of limousines—and realize that people in government never get wet! Kelly knew what it was to get wet, and he'd look at the pomposity of those people and capture them brilliantly. He had the magnificent formal swamp (Okefenokee), and he could always drag them down there and make them more evil than any character in that swamp ever was—dirtier and uglier.

In an odd way, he had a real attachment for the great villains of our time—Joe McCarthy or Agnew or Mitchell. It was great! Kelly would be doing the strip and then McCarthy would go out and do something crazy, and that would give us another two or three weeks of comic strips. It was marvelous. When McCarthy died, Kelly cried as though he'd lost a friend. Nixon came but couldn't quite fill the bill; in a funny way, Agnew came closest.

His was a completely original mind, with those ideas of his coming fast and furious, shooting over the rim of his glass at the bar (we spent a lot of time in bars) or over his shoulder as he stomped out. It was dazzling to see that mind at work. Not that he was so consistently gentle, so predictably pleasant, when he was around. He was like Irish weather. In places in that country there is a light rain which changes into a warm sunbath which dissolves into a fierce Atlantic storm all within the hour ... Kelly was that piece of Irish sky.

Kelly probably made a lot of money over the years, but he didn't care about money, he just gave it away. He took care of everybody but himself—that wouldn't do. He always told me that it did not matter how long you lived; the important thing was how far you got. Well, he got far enough; the pity is that he did not live very long. In this he was very thoughtless, because original minds arrive in our midst only every quarter of a century or so, and if they leave us too soon, as Kelly did, we are in trouble.

—*Jimmy Breslin*

Tip O'Neill, the
Life of the Party.

THE LIFE OF
THE PARTY

By Jack Beatty

Political leaders on the order of Tip O'Neill and James Farley were the bridge between old ward bosses, such as George Washington Plunkitt and Bath House John and Hinky Dink Kenna, and the modern generation of smooth, reform-minded, liberal Irish-American politicians. In retrospect, there seems to have been far too much corruption in the world of George Washington Plunkitt, and yet there is far too little charm in the world of today's yuppie technocrat. The proper balance was struck by the great bridge-builders. Irish-American politics was at its best, it now seems, in the age of James Farley and Tip O'Neill.

He's a bigger man than he looks. The very bulk of him tends to hide this; as Jimmy Breslin once said, it is hard to believe anyone this fat could have anything to do with history. For a sophisticated public as obsessed with style as it is indifferent to character, there is something ludicrous about this flagrant Irishman, this guy with a nose like a busted plum who doesn't know that the boats have already left for the suburbs and now it's every man for himself. Conscience owes it to taste not to show up in a coat that looks like a tent flap, or to own a mug with the map of Ireland spread over it from jowl to sagging jowl. We'd like the boys at Virtue Central to send a sleaker emissary, but Tip's what we got. In truth, he is a lot better than we deserve.

"All politics is local." You run no risk of being called a statesman by saying things like that. Nevertheless, that is Tip's philosophy, and it is not without profundity. To understand what it means, you have to understand something about the Eighth Congressional District of Massachusetts, and to understand the Eighth,

276

you have to walk it—end to end, it would take you only a day—you have to walk through Brighton, Charlestown, the North End, Somerville, and Cambridge, and you have to know what manner of people live there. The first thing you have to know is that Tip is not the Congressman from Harvard; that venerable college occupies only a sliver of the district. Harvard would no doubt prefer a representative with more polish, someone who didn't represent sweaty interest groups, like the unions. (Tip's father, then a bricklayer, was on strike against Harvard the day Tip was born.) But Cambridge is not Harvard; it is a blue-collar town made up of Irish and Italian and black neighborhoods, and that is about the composition of the rest of the district.

The Eighth has a scattering of industry—steel, chemical, candy manufacturers—but Boston is a commercial, not an industrial, city, and for many of Tip's constituents you work for either the Prudential or the John Hancock, the telephone company or the Boston Edison, or you work for one of the governments up there, and you have the federal, state, city, and county to choose from. And what your representative does is get you a job "on," as the local phrase has it, one of those governments. Employment is his business. Thanks to the patronage of that great American, John W. McCormack, my father, for example, was "on the City of Boston"; and if I had not flunked the tests, I would have been "on the Edison" through those same good offices. So to a man like Tip O'Neill, who has represented these people for nearly fifty years, the public sector is not a despised abstraction. It is what generations in his district have risen through and relied on. It is what teaches the kids, those who don't go to the nuns, what patrols the streets, what puts out the fires. And this attachment to government employment by the Irish and Italians of Boston goes way back, back to the Depression, when State Rep. Tip O'Neill used to pass out "snow buttons" to constituents who had families to feed and weren't adverse to shoveling the municipal snow to accomplish this. So when you tell a man like Tip O'Neill that jobs programs don't work, he is properly incredulous. Jobs programs built the Boston subways; they catalogued the Boston Public Library;

they put the meat on Timmy Sullivan's bones so that, when the time came, he could do the necessary on Omaha Beach. Don't work? Why, a good many Boston Irish families survived the Depression thanks to the W.P.A., just as a saving remnant of the Irish race survived the Great Famine only by laboring on the public works of Ireland. You know a thing works when it saves you, or even if it gives your Uncle Dinny the cash to buy his teeth. It is one of the strong empirical tests.

When Tip O'Neill says that all politics is local, then, he is reflecting the folk wisdom of the Eighth: that government has a responsibility to maintain "work and wages" in a given locality and that, when numbers of people find themselves out of work, government should find work for them to do or train them for the work that exists. Let's call it the ethic of solidarity.

In his sixteen years in the Massachusetts legislature, in his thirty years in the U.S. House of Representatives, Thomas P. O'Neill has been an organic politician.

Beatty: Mr. O'Neill, is it true that you are an organic politician?

O'Neill: Do I look organic to you? [To aide.] Who the hell is this guy?

Sorry, Mr. Speaker. I just meant that you're rooted in your constituency. In this Tip O'Neill could not be more different from his predecessor in the Eighth, John F. Kennedy, who knew more about the Solomon Islands than he did about Charlestown when his daddy bought the Eighth for him in 1946, and in this he could not be more different from Ronald Reagan, who was projected onto California by the movies. Irked by the progressive income tax, Democrat Reagan discarded his principles and his party like a used costume. Such inconstancy would be unimaginable in O'Neill. He is a stay-the-course type. It is not that he is a better man than Reagan—although I would bet myself broke before heaven on that proposition—but that his constituency sustains such virtue as is in him.

What he is, of course, is a symbol. At least that is what he has been for many of us these past two years:

277

an inspiring symbol of the best tradition of the Democratic Party. When we look back on this low time, we will remember him denouncing tax breaks for the rich, decrying cuts in aid for the poor. Some of us will even remember Tip admitting that, yes, he once did vote federal funds for research into increasing the height of dwarfs and being proud of it; and some of us were proud of it too and also of him. Especially proud when he would quote a passage from Hubert Humphrey's last speech, which he has on a plaque in his office and reads to his visitors like Scripture. Heart-full proud

when, with budget cuts for the vulnerable rushing through congress in a blaze of carelessness, he would stand up and remind the house and the president and the people too of what they had forgotten: that "the moral test of a government is how it treats those who are in the dawn of life, the children; those who are in the twilight of life, the elderly; and those who are in the shadows of life, the sick, the needy, and the handicapped." These people had need of protection these last two years, and in Tip O'Neill they had a tireless champion. He is a big man, all right. ❧

BIG SEAMUS AND THE NEW DEAL

James Aloysius Farley was in the classic, old-fashioned Irish mold—he wed a girl of his childhood, Elizabeth Finnegan, and they were together until her death in 1955. That was one of two happy unions for Mr. Farley. His other marriage was to the Democratic Party.

Like many young Paddys of that era, Farley found a raison d'etre in Democratic politics. His party career would go from the joys of town clerk to a few laughs with presidents, popes, prime ministers and princes.

Farley's entree into that elite circle was F.D.R. The two first met in 1920, and an odd meeting it must have been—Farley, the working-class Irish lad from Grassy Point, New York, who had helped hold his family together by swamping in a saloon; and Franklin Delano Roosevelt, the child of the aristocracy, who always had about him the smell of mansions.

Roosevelt knew a political animal when he saw one, and in his "Seamus" —as he would not quite patronizingly call Jim—he knew he had caught a bear. An active link to New York state's huge Irish-American population, Farley was one of the key reasons Roosevelt became governor of New York—twice. The fact that many Irish-Americans to this day still think that Dan O'Connell, Jesus Christ and F.D.R. are the real members of the Holy Trinity has a good deal to do with the P.R. work of a certain Mr. Farley.

When F.D.R. went on to the White House, Jim of course went with him. He served the New Deal as chairman of the Democratic National Committe and later as postmaster general. The two men finally parted ways over the subject of F.D.R.'s third term. Farley was against it for reasons of U.S. Tradition and also because of Roosevelt's declining health.

Farley's popularity within the party continued to

Franklin Delano Roosevelt and James A. Farley.

grow, however: at the 1940 Democratic National Convention, he even received a nomination for the office of president—a nomination he of course declined.

James Farley died at the age of eighty-eight on June 9, 1976. His body was found dressed in tuxedo pants and a formal shirt. It was almost as if he had been sitting by the phone, waiting to be called out to address one last Democratic Party, rubber-chicken dinner banquet.

—J. P. O'Shea and Bob Callahan

JOHN FITZGERALD KENNEDY

By Jimmy Cannon

We will leave the last words to the great Jimmy Cannon. Historians will continue to argue about the true political legacy of the Kennedy brothers. The foreign policy, the position on civil rights, even details about their respective private lives. These are legitimate questions, and of course they should be raised. But how can the historians—even the best of them—begin to measure the depth of a people's pride? That was Jimmy Cannon's job, and he brought the story home rather brilliantly. This is the column Mr. Falstaff might have written—were he a journalist—on the death of his fair Prince Hal.

▶

Senator John Fitzgerald Kennedy and his wife, Jacqueline, campaigning in Boston.

The great men explain what John Fitzgerald Kennedy meant to the world. Their utterances are stated in the majestic language of the statesman. The condolences are told in sentences shaped for the stoneman's tools, as if they were spoken to be chiseled into the granite of monuments. Sincere though their expressions of sorrow may be, they don't move me. It is as if the big music of a military band were translated into literature.

The prestige of John Fitzgerald Kennedy's office demands a cold respect and a dignity untouched by sorrow. My bereavement is personal. I am my father's son and my feelings are only important to those who share my heritage. It would be impertinent for me to measure John Fitzgerald Kennedy on the sports pages. The historians will do that, and in other parts of the paper qualified reporters will describe him as a public man.

In this department, obsessed only with the toys of the nation John Fitzgerald Kennedy represented to the world, our small laments generally sound as if they are played on kazoos. Our dirges are concerned with the insignificant regret of athletes. But I am my father's son, and John Fitzgerald Kennedy's death seems a private matter of my family. Never did I meet him, but I felt close to him—he was never a stranger.

He was, in a stately way, what Gene Tunney became when I was a boy. I didn't know Tunney then, but he was from the old neighborhood. He was one of my own and his affluent fame was a prize we all shared. On those mean streets, there were few who won many trophies.

John Fitzgerald Kennedy would have been no alien on the tenement-sad streets of my childhood where my people still live and mourn today. He was rich by inheritance, an educated man, but his ancestors suffered as we did. He was the perfection of our breed, and my affection for him was not influenced by political reasons, although my old man was a Tammany captain in a ward where Republicans were regarded as rebellious cranks. I regret my father died before John Fitzgerald Kennedy was elected president because he had his heart broken when Alfred E. Smith was beaten.

My old man felt betrayed by his country and went to his grave believing no man who was an Irish Catholic could ever be president. It is as indecently improper to vote for a man because of his racial origin or his religion as it is to turn against him for the same motives. But my old man brought me up to be proud of what I am. He never forgave anyone who objected to Al Smith for being an Irish Catholic and he denounced them as vandals of patriotism. It would have reinstated my old man's faith in his countrymen to know they accepted John Fitzgerald Kennedy on his reputation as a congressman and a senator.

Sports concerned John Fitzgerald Kennedy, but mainly his interests were provoked by patriotism. The President's Committee for Physical Fitness was devised to improve the health of the nation. He was an enlightened sailor and he enjoyed golf and touch football. Baseball didn't excite him much, and he patronized the opening days of the Senators as a duty. He attended football games, but he wasn't a rabid buff. He was fond of Stan Musial and Bud Wilkinson, the Oklahoma football coach, and he appointed Whizzer White, the great Colorado halfback, to the Supreme Court.

It amused him when Floyd Patterson told him before anyone else he would fight Sonny Liston for the heavyweight championship. In the Washington ballpark at an All-Star Game, I remember him kidding with Casey Stengel. The pair of them laughed it up when the old man explained he couldn't keep the small talk going because he was only a coach that day on the National League team, and Freddy Hutchinson was his manager.

He was a fine swimmer and his skill got him a medal when his PT boat was sunk in the Pacific by a Japanese destroyer. He had the appearance of an athlete, being lithe and quick, and his step was light and rapid. He encouraged the doctoring of man's esteem for his body, and he practiced the evangelism of the healthy physique that was a soul mind's confederate.

Once I wrote a line that I despised Boston because all the men on the streets resembled me. He was Boston Irish and I was New York Irish and his grandfather was Honey Fitz, who was mayor of the town and sang "Sweet Adeline" in the ballparks. He was what every Irishman of my grandfather's generation wanted his sons to be.

He was the best of us and when he made it to the White House, we were no longer Micks. Of course, we had other big men, but what happened to Al Smith made their accomplishments diminish until John Fitzgerald Kennedy proved that we were true citizens of our country, and not just tolerated intruders. It may sound exaggerated, but I lived with this.

In Al Smith's years, politics was the art form of the poor. In this time, it has become a field for the wealthy, but it was difficult for me to think of John Fitzgerald Kennedy as a privileged man. He was, as we called Jimmy Walker, one of the neighbor's children. The sun-darkened young face, recently lined with the anxieties and stresses of his position, is familiar to anyone who grew up in an Irish neighborhood. It is the way our poets intended us to look, and we cherished him as typical, but he was unique.

Other reporters will describe how tall he stood against the horizon of history. I only know that Boston voice always seemed to be talking to me and mine. Every time I heard it, I felt there was a message in it for my dead father. And for all those who took Al Smith's disappointment as a family tragedy. They weep for John Fitzgerald Kennedy today, and for him their candles burn. ❦

R.F.K.

Robert Kennedy differed from his brother, it seems to me, in lots of temperamental ways. Jack Kennedy was a much more eighteenth-century character; he was cool; he was so self-disciplined; he certainly wasn't a cold man—people who thought that were wrong—but he was a man who mistrusted passion. Bob trusted passion more. My impression of Bob the last year was that he was getting wryer, which is a quality his older brother had so markedly; wryer, funnier . . . funnier about himself . . . and perhaps the beginnings of some of that detachment. Jack was always standing off looking at himself; Bob never used to do that, but was standing off looking at life with a more ironic tone in the last year or so than he ever had before.

He was terribly impatient with institutions. I'm sure part of his public response had to do with that impatience in him. He even had an accord with the northern blue-collar workers who afterwards turned to Wallace. The kind of frustration that turns people to Wallace is frustration based partly on fear of the black, but it's really fear of nobody being in control.

Bob, much more than Jack, had this drive to the direct approach. Jack was much more resigned to the restraints of institutional life. He was wry about it; that was what was eighteenth century about him . . . he had such a sense of the limitations of what human life was all about; I'm not sure Bob ever accepted that there were limitations; maybe he did in his last few years, but his notion was that every wrong . . . somehow . . . if you can't right it, you've got to bust in the attempt. It's extraordinary. I've never met anybody like him; I've never met anybody like either of them, but they were quite different.

—*Richard Neustadt*

281

THE SOURCE BOOK

COVER Photograph by Egmont Van Dyck, San Francisco.

1. THE HOOFER'S CLUB

OPENING IMAGE (10-11) James Cagney from *Yankee Doodle Dandy* courtesy Museum of Modern Art Film Stills Archive. THE LEADER OF OUR CLAN (12-14) by Bob Callahan first appeared in abridged form in *Irish America*, reprinted courtesy of the author. Caricature of Cohan in *Yankee Prince*, courtesy of the San Francisco Academy of Comic Art. George M. Cohan/Eugene O'Neill photograph by Edward Steichen reproduced courtesy of Joanna T. Steichen. IN THE TRADITION (15-16) by Jack Donahue. George M. Primrose/William H. West courtesy of The Billy Rose Theatre Collection. The New York Library at Lincoln Center, Astor, Lennox and Tilden Foundations. THE IRISH HOOFER'S HALL OF FAME (17) by Tapper Malloy is original, courtesy of the author. Accompanying minstrel etchings from an 1851 Dan Emmett songbook, courtesy of the San Francisco Academy of Comic Art. THE SHOWGIRL (18-19) by Bill Blackbeard is original, courtesy of the author. Comic strip by J. P. McEvoy and John H. Steibel, courtesy of the San Francisco Academy of Comic Art. Excerpt (20-22) from *Gene Kelly: An Autobiography* by Clive Hirschhorn, copyright © 1974, 1984 by Clive Hirschhorn, reprinted by permission of St. Martin's Press, Inc. Gene Kelly photograph from *Thousands Cheer* courtesy of Museum of Modern Art/Film Stills Archive. Gene Kelly photograph from *Gene Kelly in New York, New York,* courtesy Museum of Modern Art/Film Stills Archive. THE ORIGIN OF THE O'CONNOR (22) by Bob Callahan is original, courtesy of the author. Donald O'Connor *Something in the Wind* photograph courtesy of The Billy Rose Theatre Collection. The New York Library at Lincoln Center, Astor, Lennox and Tilden Foundations. Excerpt (23-24) from *Jazz Dance* by Marshall and Jean Stearns, copyright © 1968 by Jean Stearns. Copyright © 1964, 1966 by Jean Stearns and the Estate of Marshall Stearns, reprinted by permission of Schirmer Books, a Division of Macmillan, Inc. James Barton photograph courtesy of The Billy Rose Theatre Collection, The New York Library at Lincoln Center, Astor, Lennox and Tilden Foundations. Illustration courtesy of Dover Publications, Inc. Excerpt (25) from *Jazz Dance* by Marshall and Jean Stearns, copyright © 1968 by Jean Stearns. Copyright © 1964, 1966 by Jean Stearns and the Estate of Marshall Stearns, reprinted by permission of Schirmer Books, a Division of Macmillan, Inc. George Primrose photograph courtesy of Culver Pictures.

2. EASY STREET

OPENING IMAGE (26-27) Edward Sutherland as Diamond Jim Brady courtesy of Museum of Modern Art/Film Stills Archive. Excerpt (28-29) from *The Lawless Decade* by Paul Sann, copyright © 1957 by Crown Publishers, Inc., reprinted by permission of Crown Publishers, Inc. Tex Guinan/El Fey Club photograph courtesy of Wide World Photos. THE QUEEN OF THE QUIP (30) by Margaret Brennan is original, courtesy of the author. Mary Louise Guinan photograph courtesy of Culver Pictures. Excerpts (31-32) from *The Great Gatsby* by F. Scott Fitzgerald, copyright 1925 by Charles Scribner's Sons; copyright renewed 1953 by Frances Scott Fitzgerald Lanahan, reprinted by permission of Charles Scribner's Sons. Lourdes Livingston illustration is original, courtesy of the artist. Excerpt (32-33) from *The Golden Clan* by John Corry, copyright © 1977 by John Corry, reprinted by permission of Houghton Mifflin Company. BRINGING UP FATHER (34-35) by Bill Blackbeard is original, courtesy of the author. Comic strips by George McManus. TIN LIZZIE (37-40) from *U.S.A. Trilogy* by John Dos Passos, courtesy of Elizabeth Dos Passos. Paul Mica illustration is original, courtesy of the artist. Excerpts (41-42) from *The Big Spenders* by Lucius Beebe, copyright © 1965 by HMH

Publishing Company, copyright © 1966 by Lucius Beebe, reprinted by permission of Doubleday & Company. Diamond Jim photograph reproduced courtesy of the San Francisco Academy of Comic Art. THE TURKEY TROT (43) by Parker Morrell is from *Diamond Jim* by Parker Morrell. Matthew Foster illustration is original, courtesy of the artist.

3. THE LIAR'S CLUB

OPENING IMAGE (44-45) Spencer Tracy and Pat O'Brien from *The People against O'Hara,* courtesy of Museum of Modern Art/Film Stills Archive. THE GREAT MOUTHPIECE (46-48) by Gene Fowler from *The Great Mouthpiece: A Life Story of William J. Fallon,* copyright © 1932 by Gene Fowler; renewed 1958 by G. Fowler, reprinted by permission of the heirs of Gene Fowler. William Fallon photograph courtesy of the *New York Daily News.* FALLON'S BROADWAY (48) by Gene Fowler from *The Great Mouthpiece: A Life Story of William J. Fallon,* copyright © 1931 by Gene Fowler; renewed 1958 by G. Fowler, reprinted by permission of the heirs of Gene Fowler. THE FUNERAL OF JAMES MARTIN MacINNIS (49-51) by Warren Hinckle from the *San Francisco Chronicle,* courtesy of the author. James Martin MacInnis/Irene Mansfeldt photograph courtesy of the *San Francisco Chronicle.* MacINNIS IN COURT (51) by Harry Jupiter from the *San Francisco Examiner,* courtesy of the author. WILLIE SUTTON IN IRISHTOWN (52-53) by Willie Sutton, with Edward Linn, from *Where The Money Was,* copyright © 1976 by Royal Production Corporation. Willie Sutton photograph courtesy of Wide World Photos. Excerpt (54-56) from *The Lion in Court* by Vincent Hallinan, copyright © 1963, courtesy of Putnam Publishing Group, Inc. Vincent Hallinan photograph by Gary Fong courtesy of the *San Francisco Chronicle.* THE IRGUN CONNECTION (56) by Paul O'Dwyer from *Council for the Defense,* courtesy of the author. Paul O'Dwyer photograph by Donna de Cesare courtesy of the photographer. Excerpt (57-59) from *The American Irish* by William V. Shannon, copyright © 1967, 1964 by William V. Shannon, reprinted with permission of Macmillan Publishing Company. Frank Murphy photograph courtesy of The Bettmann Archive. JUSTICE BRENNAN (59) by J. P. O'Shea is original, courtesy of the author. Justice Brennan photograph courtesy of the Supreme Court Historical Society.

4. THE STAGE DOOR

OPENING IMAGE (60-61) John Barrymore, Lewis Stone and Lionel Barrymore from *The Grand Hotel,* courtesy of Museum of Modern Art/Film Stills Archive. JOHN BARRYMORE PLAYS HAMLET (62-64) by Gene Fowler from *Good Night, Sweet Prince (The Life and Times of John Barrymore),* copyright © 1943 and 1944 by Gene Fowler; renewed 1970 and 1971 by A. Fowler, G. Fowler, Jr., J. F. Morrison and W. Fowler, reprinted by permission of the heirs of Gene Fowler. John Barrymore's Hamlet photograph by Bruguiere courtesy of the Museum of the City of New York. THE RELUCTANT ROMANTICIST (64) by Gene Fowler is from *Good Night, Sweet Prince (The Life and Times of John Barrymore),* copyright © 1943 and 1944 by Gene Fowler; renewed 1970 and 1971 by A. Fowler, G. Fowler, Jr., J. F. Morison and W. Fowler, reprinted by permission of the heirs of Gene Fowler. Peter Ibbetson Barrymore photograph courtesy of the Museum of the City of New York. DION BOUCICAULT (65-66) by Albert Johnson first appeared in *Theater Arts.* Two Boucicault Stage Settings woodcuts courtesy of Dover Publications, Inc. Excerpt (67) from *Great Times, Good Times* by James Kotsilibas-Davis, copyright © 1977 by James Kotsilibas-Davis, reprinted by permission of the author. Boucicault and Maurice Barrymore photographs courtesy of the New York Historical Society, New York. THE BARRYMORE FAMILY IN HOL-

LYWOOD (68-69) courtesy of The Billy Rose Theatre Collection, The New York Library at Lincoln Center, Astor, Lennox and Tilden Foundations. Excerpt (70-72) by Allen Churchill from *The Great White Way* by Allen Churchill, copyright © 1962 by Allen Churchill. Reprinted by permission of E. P. Dutton, a division of NAL Penguin Inc. Victor Herbert photograph courtesy of the San Francisco Academy of Comic Art. Drawing by Archie Gunn courtesy of the San Francisco Academy of Comic Art. Excerpt (72) from *On Reflection* by Helen Hayes with Sandford Dody, copyright © 1968 by Helen Hayes and Sandford Dody, reprinted by permission of the publisher, M. Evans and Co., Inc. THE BLACK IRISHMAN (73-76) by Croswell Bowen first appeared in *PM*. Eugene O'Neill photograph courtesy of The Bettmann Archive. Excerpt (76-77) from *The American Irish* by William V. Shannon, copyright © 1967, 1964 by William V. Shannon, reprinted with permission of Macmillan Publishing Company. *Long Day's Journey Into Night* original cast photograph courtesy of The Billy Rose Theatre Collection, The New York Library at Lincoln Center, Astor, Lennox and Tilden Foundations.

5. THE CITY DESK

OPENING IMAGE (78-79) *The Front Page* photograph courtesy of Museum of Modern Art Film Stills Archive. MR. DOOLEY (80-82) by Franklin P. Adams. Mr. Dooley drawings courtesy of the San Francisco Academy of Comic Art. MR. DOOLEY GOES TO THE OLYMPICS (82) by Finley Peter Dunne. Frederic Opper "Dooley" illustrations courtesy of the San Francisco Academy of Comic Art. Excerpt (83-84) from *Ladies Of The Press: The Story of Women in Journalism* by Ishbel Ross, copyright 1936 by Ishbel Ross, reprinted by permission of Harper & Row, Publishers, Inc. Nellie Bly photograph courtesy of Culver Pictures. HER FATHER'S DAUGHTER: THE DOROTHY KILGALLEN STORY (84-85) by Bob Callahan is original, courtesy of the author. Rose O'Neill illustration courtesy of the San Francisco Academy of Comic Art. MICKEY DUGAN, THE YELLOW KID (86-87) by Bill Blackbeard is original, courtesy of the author. Comic strips by R. F. Outcault courtesy of the San Francisco Academy of Comic Art. Excerpts (88-89) from *Bat Masterson: The Man and The Legend* by Robert K. DeArment, copyright © 1979 the University of Oklahoma Press. Bat Masterson photograph courtesy of the San Francisco Academy of Comic Art. SAM MCCLURE INVENTS MUCKRAKING (90) by S. S. McClure with Willa Cather from *My Autobiography* by S. S. McClure with Willa Cather. McClure photograph by Arnold Genthe courtesy of the San Francisco Academy of Comic Art. John Sloan drawing courtesy of the San Francisco Academy of Comic Art. Excerpt (91-92) from *Wits and Sages* by Neil A. Grauer, copyright © 1984 by The Johns Hopkins University Press. THE JOURNALIST AND THE PRESIDENT (91) by Bob Callahan is original, courtesy of the author. Jimmy Breslin/William F. Buckley illustration by William A. Cone is original, courtesy of the artist. Walt Kelly "editorial" cartoon courtesy of Selba Kelly and the San Francisco Academy of Comic Art.

6. THE WILD WEST

OPENING IMAGE (94-95) *Stagecoach* photograph, courtesy of Museum of Modern Art/Film Stills Archive. JUDGMENT FOR JESSE (97-98), a firsthand account of the death of Jesse James, appeared in the *St. Joseph Western News*. James Brothers illustration by Dugald Stermer is original, courtesy of the artist. Jesse James etching courtesy of the San Francisco Academy of Comic Art. THE SAD DEMISE OF WILD BILL CODY (99-101) by Gene Fowler from *Timber Line*, copyright 1933 by Gene Fowler; renewed 1960 by A. Fowler, reprinted by permission of the heirs of Gene Fowler. Buffalo Bill Cody photograph courtesy of Culver Pictures. Special Buffalo Bill lettering courtesy of Dover Publications, Inc. *Buffalo Bill Stories* magazine cover courtesy of the San Francisco Academy of Comic Art. THE TRUE STORY OF BILLY THE KID (102-103) by Dan O'Neill is original, courtesy of the artist. THE BOLIVIAN CONNECTION (104-106) by Percy Seibert with James

D. Horan is from *The Authentic Wild West: The Outlaws* by James D. Horan copyright © 1977 by James D. Horan, reprinted by permission of Crown Publishers, Inc. Butch Cassidy photograph courtesy of the James D. Horan Library. Butch Cassidy/Sundance Kid Wanted Poster courtesy of the San Francisco Academy of Comic Art. Excerpt (107-110) from "John Wayne: A Love Song" appearing in *Slouching Towards Bethlehem* by Joan Didion, copyright © 1965, 1968 by Joan Didion, reprinted by permission of Farrar, Straus and Giroux, Inc. *War of the Wildcats* photograph courtesy of The Billy Rose Theatre Collection, The New York Library at Lincoln Center, Astor, Lennox and Tilden Foundations. John Wayne profile photograph courtesy of Museum of Modern Art/Film Stills Archive. *Sons of Katie Elder* photograph courtesy of Museum of Modern Art/Film Stills Archive. SHOOT-OUT AT THE LAMBS CLUB (111) by William S. Hart from *My Life East and West* by William S. Hart. William S. Hart photograph courtesy of Museum of Modern Art/Film Stills Archive.

7. THE STRIP ARTISTS

THE STRIP ARTISTS (112) by Bob Callahan is original, courtesy of the author. J. WISE ON THAT AWFUL TIRED FEELING (113) by T.A.D. (Thomas Aloysious Dorgan) courtesy of the San Francisco Academy of Comic Art. MR. J. WISE'S DISSERTATION ON THE RUBBERNECK (114) by T.A.D. courtesy of the San Francisco Academy of Comic Art. THE KEWPIES & THEIR FAIRY AUNT (115) by Rose O'Neill courtesy of the San Francisco Academy of Comic Art. THE YELLOW KID IN IRELAND (116-117) by R. F. Outcault courtesy of the San Francisco Academy of Comic Art. THE TEENIE WEENIES (118) by Wm. Donahey courtesy of the San Francisco Academy of Comic Art. HAPPY HOOLIGAN DROPPED INTO THE HOUSE OF LORDS (119) by Frederic Opper courtesy of the San Francisco Academy of Comic Art. OUR BOARDING HOUSE (120) by Gene Ahern courtesy of the San Francisco Academy of Comic Art and reprinted with special permission of King Syndicate, Inc. BRINGING UP FATHER (121) by George McManus courtesy of the San Francisco Academy of Comic Art and reprinted with special permission of King Features Syndicate, Inc. DICK TRACY (122) by Chester Gould courtesy of the San Francisco Academy of Comic Art and reprinted with special permission of Tribune Media Service (T.M.S.). PLASTIC MAN (123) by Jack Cole courtesy of DC Publications. CAPTAIN EASY (124) by Roy Crane courtesy of the San Francisco Academy of Comic Art and the Newspaper Enterprise Association (N.E.A.). TERRY AND THE PIRATES (125) courtesy of the San Francisco Academy of Comic Art and T.M.S. THE FENIAN INVASION (126-127) by Dan O'Neill is original courtesy of the artist. POGO (128) by Walt Kelly courtesy of the San Francisco Academy of Comic Art and reprinted with special permission of Selba Kelly.

8. BLUE COLLAR TALES

OPENING IMAGE (130-131) *The Molly Maguires* photograph courtesy of Museum of Modern Art/Film Stills Archive. FARRELL (132-134) by Pete Hamill is original, courtesy of the author. Farrell photograph courtesy of The Bettmann Archive. Book cover courtesy of Penguin Books. MY SISTER EILEEN (134-135) by Bob Callahan is original, courtesy of the author. THOSE MULES WON'T SCAB TODAY (135-137) by Mother Jones from *The Autobiography of Mother Jones*. Mother Jones/Terence Powderly/John White photograph courtesy of The Catholic University of America. Excerpt from "The Irish and the American Labor Movement," an essay by David Montgomery appearing in *America and Ireland, 1776-1976, The American Identity and the Irish Connection*, edited by David Noel Doyle and Owen Dudley Edwards, copyright © 1980 by Cumann Merriman, reprinted by permission of Greenwood Press. THE MOLLY MAGUIRES (138-139) by Dan O'Neill is original, courtesy of the artist. Excerpt (140-141) from *Rebel Girl: An Autobiography (1906-1926)* by Elizabeth Gurley Brown, copyright © 1973 by Hyman Lumer, reprinted by permission of International Publishers. James Connolly photograph courtesy of the Transport Workers Union Collection, Robert F. Wagner Labor Archives, New York University. Excerpt (141-142) from *Rebel Girl: An Autobiography (1906-1926)* by Elizabeth Gurley Brown, copyright © 1973 by Hyman Lumer, reprinted by permission of International Publishers. **MIKE QUILL** (142-145) by Jimmy Breslin from *The World of Jimmy Breslin,* courtesy of the author. Michael J. Quill photograph courtesy of Culver Pictures. **THE IRISH UNDERGROUND RAILWAY** (144-145) by Gerald O'Reilly first appeared in *The Irish Echo,* courtesy of the author. Subway illustration by Matthew Foster is original, courtesy of the artist.

9. VAUDEVILLE DAYS

OPENING IMAGE (146-147) *The Daughters of Rosie O'Grady* photograph courtesy of Museum of Modern Art/Film Stills Archive. **THE HUMAN MOP** (148-149) by Buster Keaton with Charles Samuels from *My Wonderful World of Slapstick,* copyright © 1960 by Buster Keaton and Charles Samuels, reprinted by permission of Sterling Lord Literistic, Inc. Three Keatons photograph courtesy of The Billy Rose Theatre Collection, The New York Library at Lincoln Center, Astor, Lennox and Tilden Foundations. Excerpt (150) from "Comedy's Greatest Era" appearing in *Agee on Film, Volume II* by James Agee, copyright © 1958 by The James Agee Trust, copyright renewed © 1986 by Teresa, Andrea and John Agee, reprinted by permission of Grosset and Dunlap. Keaton/Paddy Wagon photograph courtesy of The Billy Rose Theatre Collection, The New York Library at Lincoln Center, Astor, Lennox and Tilden Foundations. Excerpt (151-153) from "What Musicals and Comedies Owe to Harrigan and Hart" by Samuel G. Freedman, copyright © 1985 by The New York Times Company, reprinted by permission of The New York Times Company. Mulligan Guards photograph courtesy of Culver Pictures. St. Patrick's Day sheet music courtesy of the New-York Historical Society, New York. **IS THAT MR. RILEY?** (153) by Douglas Gilbert from *American Vaudville* by Douglas Gilbert. Pat Rooney 1st photograph courtesy of the Museum of the City of New York. **GALLAGHER AND SHEAN** (154-155) by Bill Blackbeard is original, courtesy of the author. Comic strips courtesy of the San Francisco Academy of Comic Art. Excerpt (156-157) from *Saturday Night: A Backstage History of "Saturday Night Live"* by Doug Hill and Jeff Weingrad, copyright © by Doug Hill and Jeff Weingrad, reprinted by permission of the Jonathan Dolger Agency. Bill Murray/Chevy Chase photograph courtesy of the National Broadcasting System, Inc. **WHAT KELLY WON'T DO NEXT** (158) by Jay Robert Nash from *Zanies* by Jay Robert Nash, copyright © 1982 by Jay Robert Nash, reprinted by permission of the author. Shipwreck Kelly photograph courtesy of the San Francisco Academy of Comic Art. Excerpt (159-160) from *Much Ado About Me* by Fred Allen, copyright © 1956, 1984 by Portland Hoffa Allen, reprinted by permission of the William Morris Agency, Inc., on behalf of The Estate of Fred Allen. Fred Allen photograph courtesy of The Billy Rose Theatre Collection, The New York Library at Lincoln Center, Astor, Lennox and Tilden Foundations. **DUMMIES** (161) by Dan O'Neill is original, courtesy of the artist.

10. PARISH LIFE

OPENING IMAGE (162-163) *Going My Way* photograph courtesy of Museum of Modern Art/Film Stills Archive. **REQUIEM FOR AN ANARCHIST** (164-166) by Michael True courtesy of *Commonweal Magazine.* Ammon Hennacy photograph by Vivian Cherry courtesy of The Catholic Worker Collection, Marquette University. **THE TAX PROBLEM** (166) by Dorothy Day from *Loaves and Fishes,* courtesy of Harper and Row. Excerpts (167-168) from *Memories of A Catholic Girlhood* by Mary McCarthy, copyright © 1957, 1985 by Mary McCarthy, reprinted by permission of Harcourt Brace Jovanovich, Inc. Lourdes Livingston illustration is original, courtesy of the artist. **CHRISTMAS IN CORNING** (169) by Margaret Sanger from *Margaret Sanger: An Autobiography,* copyright © 1971, reprinted by permission

of Dr. Grant Sanger. Margaret Sanger photograph courtesy of the San Francisco Academy of Comic Art. **FATHER COUGHLIN'S FATAL CAMPAIGN** (170-171) by Sheldon Marcus from *Father Coughlin: The Tumultuous Life of the Priest of the Little Flower* by Sheldon Marcus, copyright © 1973 by Sheldon Marcus, reprinted by permission of Little, Brown & Company. Father Coughlin photograph courtesy of Culver Pictures. **CHRISTMAS IN BROOKLYN** (172-173) by Pete Hamill from *Irrational Ravings,* courtesy of the author. Tim Bower illustration is original, courtesy of the artist. Excerpt (174-175) from "The Waterfront Revisited" by Budd Schulberg, copyright © 1963 by The Curtis Publishing Co., reprinted by permission of *The Saturday Evening Post. On The Waterfront* photograph courtesy of Museum of Modern Art/Film Stills Archive. **CAN'T SLIP ANY DRUGS TO SISTERS ON FIFTH AVENUE** (176-177) by John McNulty is from *The World of John McNulty,* (Doubleday), copyright © 1947, 1975 by John McNulty. Originally appeared in *The New Yorker,* reprinted by permission of Faith McNulty. Norman Quebedeau illustration courtesy of the artist. **CHRISTMAS IN CALIFORNIA** (178) by Jim Carroll is from *Forced Entries: The Downtown Diaries, 1971-1973,* copyright © 1987 by Jim Carroll, reprinted by permission of Viking Penguin Inc. Debbie Drechsler illustration is original, courtesy of the artist. Excerpts (179-181) from *The American Pope: The Life and Times of Cardinal Francis Spellman* by John Cooney, copyright © 1984 by John Cooney, reprinted by permission of Times Books, a division of Random House, Inc. Spellman photograph courtesy Wide World Photos. Excerpt (181) from *The Golden Clan* by John Corry, copyright © 1977 by John Corry, reprinted by permission of Houghton Mifflin Company.

11. WAR HEROES

OPENING IMAGE (182-183) *The Fighting Sullivans* photograph courtesy of Museum of Modern Art/Film Stills Archive. **MR. DE VALERA AND MR. HEARST** (184-186) by Bob Callahan is original, courtesy of the author. Roger Casement illustration by Winsor McCay courtesy of the San Francisco Academy of Comic Art. De Valera in San Francisco photograph courtesy of Bob Callahan. **MEAGHER OF THE SWORD** (187-188) by Tom Clark is original, courtesy of the author. Meagher engraving courtesy of Culver Pictures. **JUST PLAIN HUMAN** (189) by Tom Clark is original, courtesy of the author. *The Fighting 69th* photograph courtesy of the Museum of Modern Art/Film Stills Archive. **THE SPEECH** (190-199) by Rick Marshall, courtesy of the author. Terry and the Pirates art by Milton Caniff courtesy of King Syndicate. **ONE SUMMER IN SPAIN** (192-193) by William "Bill" Bailey is original, courtesy of the author. Bill Bailey photograph by Clem Albers courtesy of the *San Francisco Chronicle.* **AN HONORABLE MAN** (194) by Warren Hinckle first appeared in the *San Francisco Examiner,* reprinted courtesy of the author. Excerpt (195-197) from "Not a Drum Was Heard" appearing in *More Interesting People* by Robert J. Casey, copyright 1947 by Robert J. Casey, reprinted by permission of Macmillan Publishing Company. War Story illustration reproduced courtesy of the San Francisco Academy of Comic Art.

12. THE SPORTING ARENA

OPENING IMAGE (198-199) *Knute Rockne: All American* photograph courtesy of Museum of Modern Art/Film Stills Archive. **RINGSIDE SEAT** (200-202) by Ring Lardner, copyright © 1929; renewed 1957 by Ellis A. Lardner, reprinted by permission of Ring Lardner, Jr. Gentleman Jim photograph courtesy of the San Francisco Academy of Comic Art. Boxing gloves engraving courtesy of the San Francisco Academy of Comic Art. **THE SULLIVAN-CORBETT FIGHT** (202) by Bob Callahan is original, courtesy of the author. Corbett illustration by T.A.D. courtesy of the San Francisco Academy of Comic Art. Excerpt (203-204) from "Notre Dame" appearing in *Nobody Asked Me, But . . . The World of Jimmy Cannon,* edited by Jack Cannon and Tom Cannon, copyright © 1978 by The Estate of Jimmy Cannon, reprinted by permission of Henry Holt and Company, Inc. O'Brien/

Rockne photograph courtesy of Museum of Modern Art/Film Stills Archive. **MR. LEAHY** (204-205) by Jimmy Cannon is from *Nobody Asked Me, But . . . The World of Jimmy Cannon* by Jimmy Cannon, edited by Jack Cannon and Tom Cannon, copyright © 1978 by The Estate of Jimmy Cannon, reprinted by permission of Henry Holt and Company, Inc. Leahy/Clatt photograph courtesy of Wide World Photos. **T.A.D.** (206-207) by Damon Runyon. T.A.D. illustrations courtesy of the San Francisco Academy of Comic Art. **JOHN MCGRAW'S GREATEST FIGHTS** (208-210) by Tom Clark is original, courtesy of the author. John McGraw illustration by William Cone is original, courtesy of the artist. **MR. MACK** (210) by Tom Clark is original, courtesy of the author. Connie Mack photograph courtesy of The National Baseball Hall of Fame and Museum, Inc. **HAIL AND FAREWELL, JACK, A CHAMPION LIKE NO OTHER** (211-213) by Jim Murray, copyright © 1953 by Los Angeles Times Syndicate, reprinted by permission of the Los Angeles Times Syndicate. Jack Dempsey ring photograph courtesy of Culver Pictures. Jack Dempsey in Hollywood photograph courtesy of Wide World Photos. **THE REAL MCCOY** (213) by Tom Clark is original, courtesy of the author. Kid McCoy photograph courtesy of Culver Pictures. Excerpt (214-215) from "Who Do You Think You Are—Dempsey?" appearing in *Farewell to Sport* by Paul Gallico, copyright 1938 by Paul Gallico, copyright renewed 1966 by Paul Gallico, reprinted by permission of Alfred A. Knopf, Inc. Son of Mars photograph courtesy of Culver Pictures. Boxing silhouettes courtesy of Dover Publications, Inc.

13. A LIFE OF CRIME

OPENING IMAGE (216-217) James Cagney in *The Public Enemy* courtesy of Museum of Modern Art/Film Stills Archive. **JACK'S ALIVE** (218-220) from *Legs* by William Kennedy, copyright © 1975 by William Kennedy, reprinted by permission of Viking Penguin Inc. Legs illustration by Gary Epting is original, courtesy of the artist. Excerpt (220) from *The Lawless Decade* by Paul Sann, copyright © 1957 by Crown Publishers, Inc., reprinted by permission of Crown Publishers, Inc. Owney Madden photograph courtesy of the *New York Daily News*. **DEATH FOR SOME LAUGHS** (221-222) by Damon Runyon from *Short Takes,* copyright 1931-1946 by King Features Syndicate, Inc., reprinted with special permission of King Features Syndicate, Inc. Death for Some Laughs illustration by Gary Epting is original, courtesy of the artist. **THE MOLASSES GANG** (223) by Dan O'Neill is original, courtesy of the artist. Excerpt (224-225) from "Joy Ride" appearing in *The Baby in the Icebox and Other Short Fiction* by James M. Cain, edited by Roy Hoopes, copyright © 1981 by Alice M. Piper, reprinted by permission of Henry Holt and Company, Inc. The Robbery illustration by Gary Epting is original, courtesy of the artist. **FAT THOMAS' FRIENDS AND DALE CARNEGIE** (226-228) by Jimmy Breslin from *The World of Jimmy Breslin,* courtesy of the author. Fat Thomas illustration by Gary Epting is original, courtesy of the artist. Excerpt (226-227) from *The Gangs of New York: An Informal History of the Underworld* by Herbert Asbury. Copyright 1928 by Alfred A. Knopf, Inc. Copyright renewed 1956 by Herbert Asbury. Reprinted by permission of Alfred A. Knopf, Inc. Excerpt (228-230) from *The Lawless Decade* by Paul Sann, copyright © 1957 by Crown Publishers, Inc., reprinted by permission of Crown Publishers, Inc. Dion and Viola O'Banion photograph courtesy of the *Chicago Tribune*. **THE LUCK OF THE IRISH** (231) by J. P. O'Shea is original, courtesy of the author. Bugs Moran photograph courtesy of the *Chicago Tribune*.

14. THE SILVER SCREEN

OPENING IMAGE (232-233) *Sullivan's Travels* photograph courtesy of Museum of Modern Art/Film Stills Archive. **IT'S ALL IN THE SCHEME** (234-237) by James Cagney and Studs Terkel from an interview by Studs Terkel, copyright © 1981 by Studs Terkel, reprinted by permission of Studs Terkel. James Cagney photographs courtesy of Museum of Modern Art/Film Stills Archive. **THE ICE PRINCESS** (238) by

Bob Callahan is original, courtesy of the author. Grace Kelly photograph courtesy of Museum of Modern Art/Film Stills Archive. Introduction to interview with Preston Sturges (239-241) by Andrew Sarris from *Interviews with Film Directors,* edited by Andrew Sarris, copyright © 1967 by Andrew Sarris, reprinted by permission of MacMillan Publishing Company. Preston Sturges photograph courtesy of Museum of Modern Art/Film Stills Archive. *Lady Eve* photograph courtesy of Museum of Modern Art/Film Stills Archive. Excerpt (241) from "Tinsel" appearing in *Quintana & Friends* by John Gregory Dunne, copyright © 1961, 1965-1971, 1973, 1974, 1976-1978 by John Gregory Dunne, reprinted by permission of E.P. Dutton a division of NAL Penguin. **THE HIBERNIAN HALL OF FAME** by Ron Chan courtesy of the artist. Excerpt (244-246) from *Special Effects* by Christopher Finch, copyright © 1984 by Cross River Press, Ltd., reprinted by permission of Abbeville Press. Willis O'Brien/Fay Wray/King Kong photograph courtesy of The Imagi-Movie Archives of Forrest J. Ackerman. **KING KONG AMONG THE LILLIPUTIANS** (246) by Jean Boullet. Pierre Bailly illustration courtesy of the San Francisco Academy of Comic Art. **THE TALL SOLDIER: MEMORIES OF JOHN FORD** (246-248) by James Cagney and Peter Bogdanovich is from *Cagney on Cagney* by James Cagney, copyright © 1976 by Bantam Doubleday Dell Publishing Company, by permission, and from *John Ford* by Peter Bogdanovich, courtesy of the author. John Ford photographs courtesy of the Museum of Modern Art/Film Stills Archive. **KING REBEL** (249) by J. P. O'Shea is original, courtesy of the author. John Huston photograph courtesy of The Billy Rose Theatre Collection, The New York Library at Lincoln Center, Astor, Lennox and Tilden Foundations.

15. THE MUSIC HALL

OPENING IMAGE (250-251) *Swanee River* photograph from Museum of Modern Art/Film Stills Archive. **OLD FOLKS AT HOME** (252-254) by Charles Hamm from *Yesterdays, Popular Songs in America* copyright © 1979 by W.W. Norton & Company, Inc., reprinted by permission of W.W. Norton & Company, Inc. **BEAUTIFUL DREAMER** by Stephen Foster. Stephen Foster photograph courtesy of the San Francisco Academy of Comic Art. **FOSTER'S CHILD** (254) by Bob Callahan is original, courtesy of the author. Tom Levy photograph of Van Morrison in Berkeley courtesy of the *San Francisco Chronicle*. **THE INCOMPARABLE BING** (255-256) by Gilbert Seldes is from *The Public Arts,* copyright © 1957 by Gilbert Seldes; renewed 1984 by Timothy Seldes and Marion Seldes, reprinted by permission of Simon & Schuster, Inc. Bing Crosby 1934 photograph courtesy of The Bettmann Archive. **FIFTH AVENUE DAYS** (257) by Bob Callahan is original, courtesy of the author. Bunny Berigan photograph courtesy of The Bettmann Archive. **PAL JOEY** (258-259) by John O'Hara from *Collected Stories of John O'Hara,* copyright 1952 by John O'Hara, reprinted by permission of Random House, Inc. Pal Joey illustration by Lourdes Livingston is original, courtesy of the artist. **EDDIE COCHRAN** (260-261) by John Tobler is from *Guitar Heroes,* copyright © 1978 by John Tobler, reprinted with permission of St. Martin's Press, Inc. Eddie Cochran photograph courtesy of the San Francisco Academy of Comic Art. **THE BIRTH OF ROCK AND ROLL** (262) by Jim Carroll is from *The Basketball Diaries,* copyright © 1963 through 1978 by Jim Carroll, published by Viking Penguin Inc. Illustration by Debbie Drechsler is original, courtesy of the artist. **THE POLICEMAN AND THE PIPER** (263-265) by Peter O'Neill and Eddie Stack is original, courtesy of the authors. Captain O'Neill and Chicago Uillean Pipers photographs courtesy of Captain Peter O'Neill. **THE MINSTREL LAD FROM ATHLONE** (265) by William Flynn. John McCormack photograph courtesy of Culver Pictures.

16. CLUB HOUSE GANGS

OPENING IMAGE (266-267) *The Last Hurrah* photograph courtesy of Museum of Modern Art/Film Stills Archive. **THE POL** (268-269) by

**Father Flanagan
and the Boys'
Town Choir.**